what's for dinner? second helpings

Romilla Arber

To my children Joseph, Emil, Emanuel and Yolanda, who will always know what's for dinner!

First published in hardback in Great Britain in 2012 by Park Family Publishing

1 2 3 4 5 6 7 8 9

A CIP catalogue record for this book is available from the British Library.

ISBN: 978-0-9570935-0-8

Photography by Dan Jones
Design and art direction by Smith & Gilmour
Food styling by Bianca Nice and Sue Henderson
Prop styling by Morag Farquhar
Edited by Jinny Johnson
Proofread by Mary-Jane Wilkins
Index by Elizabeth Wiggans
Printed in the UK by Butler, Tanner & Dennis

Park Family Publishing
Registered office: North Sydmonton House,
North Sydmonton, Newbury, Berkshire. RG20 4UL

www.foodeducationtrust.com

NOTES

Most recipes are for a family of six – two adults and four children. If you are feeding six adults, you might want to increase the quantities.

Cooking times are as accurate as possible, but all ovens differ so do check your food as it cooks. Temperatures given are for normal ovens so if you have a fan oven, adjust accordingly.

All onions and garlic should be peeled unless otherwise specified.

Always bring meat to room temperature before cooking as this affects the cooking time.

Use unsalted butter and free-range eggs if possible.

Salt quantities are for sea salt. If you are using fine salt it's best to use a little less.

I use metric measurements throughout this book, but there are metric/imperial conversion charts on page 767 if you need. Never mix metric and imperial measurements in a recipe. Stick to one or the other.

What's for Dinner? Second Helpings is the cookbook I've always needed – a book to help me cope with the challenge of getting a good home-cooked meal on the table, day after day. It's big and beautiful, with wonderful pictures, but it's still a book for the home cook, not Michelin-starred chefs. The recipes are for dishes that families like to eat and my own family can vouch for them being delicious! Most are simple to prepare and don't need lots of unusual ingredients, just good fresh produce.

I've put this book together as I've cooked my way through the year, just like my previous book: *What's for Dinner?* In a way, it's a food journal, as I cooked what was seasonal and available and what we felt like eating at different times of the year. I do believe that our bodies tell us what we should be eating during the seasons, which is why we have a taste for thick soups and stews in the winter, and salads and lighter food in the summer.

Everyday cooking is often a challenge because it's about more than the act of preparing food. It's about budgeting, balancing your diet, getting to the supermarket and knowing what you are going to cook. When it comes down to making a meal, most of us have limited time. We need to plan ahead, follow recipes and know that the food we put on the table is going to be eaten and enjoyed by children and adults alike.

What's for Dinner? Second Helpings will help you plan and prepare great home-cooked meals every day. The weekly menus are put together with a balanced diet in mind – plenty of fresh vegetables, no more than four meat dishes a week, and a regular amount of fish, pulses and cereals. Of course, everyone likes a treat once in a while, so there are lots of ideas for puddings, cakes and biscuits as well. Fortunately, home-made sweet treats are so much tastier and healthier than shop-bought.

My hope is that *What's for Dinner? Second Helpings* will inspire you to cook and enjoy your food more than ever. If you have children, perhaps it might help plant the seed in their minds that cooking everyday at home is a normal part of life and one of its great pleasures. There are plenty of dishes children can help with and some they might like to make for themselves. It's never too early to start learning the joys of cooking and good food.

The Food Education Trust

I established the Food Education Trust in 2008 to promote the benefits of a home-cooked, balanced diet, through the teaching of cooking skills to children and adults. It is currently funded by the profits from my previous book, *What's for Dinner?* and hopefully in the future from this new book.

The demands of modern living have placed home cooking and the quality of what we eat and how we eat it way down the list of our priorities. Food really should have far greater importance in our lives, given that it is the fuel that powers our bodies. Our health and general wellbeing are dependent on what we eat.

With a little bit of knowledge and confidence, everyone can eat home-cooked food on a regular basis, without resorting to ready meals and processed foods.

The Food Education Trust welcomes applications from all sectors of the community and society. It seeks to work collaboratively with organisations and institutions to further its aim of promoting the benefits of home-cooked food, whether by way of financial assistance, investment of time and expertise, or assistance in an advisory capacity.

Current projects include work with The Albany Centre. This centre provides education to students who have been excluded from mainstream education due to social, emotional or behavioural difficulties.

The majority of the children coming to the centre do not regularly eat breakfast before coming to school and have not been in an environment where they have received regular school lunches. Instead, they choose to use their lunch money to purchase cigarettes, fizzy drinks and snacks.

The Centre is seeking to change the lives of its students, partly through their diet. Research and common sense tells us that badly nourished children concentrate less, demonstrate low-energy levels and underachieve at school. In addition poor diet has an obvious affect on the long-term health and wellbeing of students.

The Food Education Trust has helped the centre refurbish its kitchen so that all students can take part in cooking lessons and provide their own lunches and thereby start to appreciate the benefits and enjoyment derived from a healthy, balanced diet.

The Trust has also been working with the Welford and Wickham Primary School in Berkshire. The school wanted to educate its pupils about good food and home cooking and the Trust enabled them to build and equip a kitchen for the children's use. This is what the head teacher had to say about the project:

'The Food Education Trust has made a tremendous impact on cookery in our school. We had no cooking facilities in school until we were able to install a kitchen for the children to use. Now we have weekly cookery classes when members of the community come into school to cook with the children, we have a cookery club after school, and many children are also able to cook during curriculum time. Our new kitchen has also meant we can run a breakfast club for children before school. We are so grateful to Romilla for her support of the school and the cooking that she came in to do with the children. We have really benefited from the generous grant and would like to thank the Food Education Trust for the support they have given us and the difference it has made to our children.'

Other projects currently underway are: the funding of a cookery club at Kirkbride Primary School in Cumbria; purchasing a cooker, fridge and other equipment for a cookery club at Moortown Primary School, Leeds; purchasing of induction hobs and other equipment for cookery classes at the Norman Street Primary School, Cumbria; purchasing replacement cookery equipment for the Clere Secondary School, Berkshire; funding a cookery club at the Ridgeway Primary School, South Shields; purchasing cookery equipment for St. Mary's Primary School, Burnham-on-Crouch.

We hope that many more projects will follow.

January is usually our coldest month, but there is still plenty to enjoy in the kitchen. The cold weather is a good excuse for making warming stews, roasts and curries, and there's nothing like coming home from a frosty walk and tucking into a home-made cake. Baking is an ideal activity for a January afternoon and the smell of a cake in the oven brings comfort on the bleakest day. Try some new recipes and make use of venison and game birds, which are plentiful at this time of year and so cheaper than usual. You may feel like some lighter dishes too, such as salad, winter coleslaw and fish, and there are lots of lovely tropical fruits that you can enjoy without too many pangs of guilt, as there are not really any home-grown varieties around. Seville oranges are in season so it's the perfect time to make a big batch of marmalade – something I always like doing. If you have a garden, there is not much to be done as yet, but you could plan a vegetable patch if you have room, and order your seeds from catalogues. During the long dark evenings, curl up in a warm corner with some cookbooks and magazines and find inspiration for the months to come. Think of January as a time to reflect on the year just passed and to plan the year ahead.

SEVILLE ORANGE
MARMALADE
2 lbs. Seville Oranges approx.
1 Lemon
4 pints Water
4 lbs. Preserving Sugar
Wash and shred the fruit, put
it in a basin with the water
and leave overnight. Put it
into a pan, bring slowly to the
boil and simmer till the peel
is soft and the contents of the
pan reduced by almost half -
about 1½ hours.
Add sugar, stir till dissolved,
and boil rapidly till a set is
obtained; cool a little, then
pot and cover as usual.

January

Cream cheese pithiviers

These have a small amount of pancetta in them, but otherwise this is a meat-free meal. You might think the puff pastry is a bit of a faff to prepare, but this is the real deal and makes these pastries very special.

MAKES 4

Puff pastry
250g plain flour, plus extra for dusting the work surface
¼ tsp paprika
1 tsp salt
½ tsp baking powder
225g cold butter, cut into 1cm cubes
175ml cold milk

Filling
2 tbsp olive oil
1 leek, finely sliced
1 small onion, finely chopped
70g pancetta, chopped
200g frozen peas, cooked
150g carrots, peeled, cut in 1cm chunks and cooked until tender
1 small bunch of chives, finely snipped
280g cream cheese
80g Gruyère cheese, grated
1 egg, beaten
sea salt
freshly ground black pepper

1 Mix the flour, paprika, salt, baking powder and butter in a bowl. Stir in the milk and combine into a squishy, lumpy dough.
2 Sprinkle the work surface with flour and roll the dough into a rectangle measuring about 16 x 30cm. Fold the top third of the pastry down towards you and the lower third away from you, as you would fold a letter. Rotate the dough by 90 degrees and do the same again.
3 Wrap the dough in clingfilm and chill in the fridge for 30 minutes. Then roll out the pastry again and fold twice as before. Rewrap it in clingfilm and chill for another 30 minutes. Repeat the rolling and folding, then chill again, while you prepare the filling.
4 Heat the olive oil in a sauté pan. Add the leek, onion and pancetta and cook over a medium heat for 10 minutes. Spoon this into a bowl and add the peas and carrots. Add the chives, cream cheese and Gruyère, then check the seasoning. Preheat the oven to 200°C/Gas 6.
5 Take the chilled pastry and roll it out as thinly as you can before it tears. Cut 4 x 15cm circles and 4 x 16cm circles. You'll find that you will have to re-roll the pastry twice, but you should be able to get 8 circles with a tiny snippet left over.
6 Place the 15cm circles on a baking sheet. Spoon 2 tablespoons of the filling mixture on to each, leaving a margin of 1.5cm around the edge. Using a pastry brush paint the margins with beaten egg, then lay the bigger circles on top.
7 Brush the pithiviers with the rest of the egg and bake in the oven for 20 minutes. Serve with a green salad.

Tomato, red pepper and coriander soup with stuffed flatbreads

This is a typical flatbread recipe as it contains no yeast. These flatbreads are not heavy and, stuffed with the Italian cheese and basil, they make a great side dish to serve with the soup.

SERVES 6

2 tbsp olive oil
1 red pepper, cored and roughly chopped
5 medium tomatoes, roughly chopped
1 red onion, chopped
40g coriander leaves, roughly chopped
2 tsp ground coriander
2 tbsp flour
1.5 litres chicken stock
1 x 400g can of tomatoes
sea salt
freshly ground black pepper

Stuffed flatbreads
500g strong white flour
1 tsp salt
2 tsp white wine vinegar
300ml water
150g softened butter
250g mascarpone cheese
3 tbsp chopped basil leaves
100g Parmesan, grated

1 Heat the olive oil in a large saucepan. Add the pepper, fresh tomatoes, onion and fresh coriander and cook for 10 minutes on a low heat, with the saucepan covered.
2 Sprinkle on the ground coriander and flour and stir. Pour on the stock and canned tomatoes, cover the pan, then simmer gently for 30 minutes. Blend the soup in a liquidiser and pass it through a sieve. Season well and serve with the flatbreads, cut into quarters.

To make the stuffed flatbreads
3 Put the flour, salt, vinegar and water in a mixing bowl. Bring everything together into a ball of dough and leave to rest for 30 minutes.
4 Take the dough and incorporate the soft butter, kneading the dough so that the butter becomes evenly distributed. Mix the mascarpone, basil and Parmesan together in a small bowl.
5 Preheat the oven to 180°C/Gas 4. Divide the dough into 6 equal pieces and roll each one out into a circle. Heat a frying pan and cook each dough circle until golden brown on each side. Wrap it in some foil or a clean tea towel to keep warm while you cook the remaining circles.
6 Now spread 3 of the circles with the mascarpone mixture and place the remaining circles on top. Place the stuffed breads on a baking sheet and warm them through in the oven until you can see the cheese beginning to seep out at the edges.

Breaded pollack fillets with potato and beans

Pollack is becoming increasingly available from fish counters, as it is seen as a more sustainable alternative to cod. Pollack was used to make the crab sticks that were popular in the 1980s and it is still often used for fish fingers. These breaded pollack fillets are a far cry from both of them.

1 Place the breadcrumbs on a plate and season them with the paprika and some salt and pepper. Beat the eggs in a bowl. Place the flour on another plate.
2 Dip each pollack fillet into the flour first, then the eggs and finally into the breadcrumbs.
3 Heat the oil in a frying pan and add 2 fillets to the pan. Cook the fillets for 1 minute on each side, by which time the breadcrumbs should be golden and the fish cooked. Place them on a warm plate while you cook the rest. Serve the fish on top of the beans and potatoes.

To prepare the potatoes and beans
4 Heat the olive oil in a large saucepan or sauté pan. Add the potato cubes and garlic and cook for 3 minutes, stirring so that the potatoes don't stick.
5 Add the cannellini and borlotti beans and cook for 1 minute. Pour on the stock and bring to a simmer. Cook, uncovered, for 15 minutes, until the potatoes are soft.
6 Sprinkle on the parsley and stir in the crème fraiche. Season to taste and simmer for a couple more minutes before serving.

SERVES 6

200g white breadcrumbs
2 tsp paprika
2 eggs
100g flour
6 pollack fillets, skinned
olive oil, for frying
sea salt
freshly ground black pepper

Potatoes and beans
2 tbsp olive oil
400g potatoes, peeled and cut into 2cm cubes
2 garlic cloves, crushed
280g cannellini beans from a can, drained and rinsed
140g borlotti beans from a can, drained and rinsed
250ml chicken stock
2 tbsp finely chopped flat-leaf parsley
1 heaped tbsp crème fraiche
sea salt
freshly ground black pepper

Venison and fennel stew

Venison is in plentiful supply at this time of year and it is one of the most organic meats you can get. It is low in fat and if you can source it from a local supplier, it should also be quite reasonable in price. I think it has a lovely livery flavour and it's a welcome change from the beef generally used for winter stews.

SERVES 6

1.5kg venison shoulder, cut into cubes
seasoned flour
olive oil
300ml red wine
1 onion, finely chopped
2 celery stalks, finely chopped
1 fennel bulb, sliced
1 tbsp tomato purée
1 sprig of fresh thyme
500ml beef stock (a stock cube will do)
sea salt
freshly ground black pepper

Mashed potatoes
1kg potatoes, peeled and cut into quarters
40g butter
200ml warm milk
sea salt
freshly ground black pepper

1 Toss the venison cubes in the seasoned flour.
2 Heat 2 tablespoons of olive oil in a casserole-type saucepan and brown the venison in the oil. Do this in small batches so that you don't overcrowd the pan. Transfer each batch of venison to a bowl while you brown the next.
3 Once all the venison has been browned, keep the empty pan on the heat. Add the wine and let it simmer away for 2 minutes, stirring and scraping up any bits stuck on the bottom of the saucepan. Pour the wine into the bowl over the venison. Preheat the oven to 160°C/Gas 3.
4 Heat a tablespoon of oil in the pan and add the onion, celery and fennel, stirring them on a reasonably high heat for 5 minutes or so. Return the venison and the wine to the pan, and add the tomato purée, thyme, stock and seasoning. Bring to a simmer, cover and place in the oven for 2 hours. Serve with mashed potatoes.

To make the mashed potatoes
5 Boil the potatoes in salted water until tender.
6 Pass the potatoes through a potato ricer or use your preferred method to mash them. Return them to the pan and place over a low heat. Mix in the butter and milk and season to taste.

Fried gurnard fillets with sautéed potatoes and broccoli

Gurnard, simply fried, needs no adornment other than some salt, pepper and a squeeze of lemon juice. If you can't get gurnard, use sea bass but it is more expensive. Make sure you remove all the little bones from the fillets, as children can be put off fish for a long time if they encounter a bone.

SERVES 6

1 tbsp olive oil
6 gurnard fillets
fresh lemon juice
sea salt
freshly ground black pepper

Sautéed potatoes
1kg potatoes, peeled and cut into quarters
2 tbsp olive oil or 1 tbsp goose fat
sea salt
freshly ground black pepper

Broccoli
300g broccoli
a squeeze of lemon juice
sea salt
freshly ground black pepper

1 Heat the olive oil in a frying pan on a medium heat. When the oil is hot, add 3 of the gurnard fillets, skin-side down, and fry them for 3 minutes. Turn them over and fry for 2 minutes more. Place them on a warm plate, covered, while you cook the rest.
2 Squeeze over some lemon juice and generously season with salt and pepper. Serve with the sautéed potatoes and broccoli.

To prepare the sautéed potatoes
3 Put the potatoes in a saucepan of salted water, bring to the boil and cook them until tender. Drain the potatoes and when they are cool enough to handle, slice them into 1cm slices.
4 Heat the olive oil or goose fat in a large sauté pan and add the potatoes. Stir the potatoes around as they cook ensure that they brown evenly. Season with salt and black pepper.

To prepare the broccoli
5 Divide the broccoli into florets, but don't cut the florets into single-stemmed pieces or they will get soggy when they cook. Instead, trim the stalks with a sharp knife so that most of the stalks are of a similar thickness.
6 Bring a pan of salted water to the boil and cook the broccoli at a gentle simmer for 3 minutes. Season with black pepper and a squeeze of lemon juice.

Sirloin steak sandwiches with winter coleslaw

You can buy bread, but I like making these rolls with the bread flour I buy from Shipton Mill (www.Shipton-mill.com). They sell a wide variety of flours.

SERVES 6

6 sirloin steaks
a little olive oil

Brown bread rolls
100g seed flour (5-seed flour from Shipton Mill), plus extra for dusting the work surface
200g malted brown flour
400g strong white bread flour
1 x 7g sachet of dried yeast
425ml hand-hot water
25g melted butter
1 tsp sugar
2 tsp salt

Winter coleslaw
1 tbsp Dijon mustard
2 egg yolks
150ml light olive oil
150ml groundnut oil
½ white cabbage, finely sliced
½ red cabbage, finely sliced
2 shallots, finely sliced
¼ celeriac, peeled and grated
1 large carrot, grated
sea salt
freshly ground black pepper

1 Brush the steaks with olive oil. Heat a griddle or frying pan and cook the steaks for 2 minutes or so on each side, depending on the thickness and how you like your meat. Serve the steaks in the rolls with the coleslaw.

To make the brown bread rolls
2 Put the flours in a mixing bowl and warm them in a microwave for 40 seconds. Mix the yeast with a little of the water and leave for 5 minutes.
3 Add the butter, sugar, salt, the rest of the water and the yeasted water to the flour. Mix with a wooden spoon until you have a loose dough.
4 Turn the dough out on to a floured surface and knead for 5 minutes. If the dough is too wet, add a little more flour, but don't add too much – a wetter dough makes a better loaf of bread.
5 Return the dough to the bowl. Cover with a clean tea towel and leave the dough to rise in a draught-free place.
6 Shape the dough into a sausage about 60cm long, then cut it into 6 equal pieces. Flatten each piece with the palm of your hand and place them on a baking sheet. Cover with a tea towel and leave for 20 minutes.
7 Preheat the oven to 220°C/Gas 7. Bake the rolls for 20–25 minutes.

To make the winter coleslaw
8 Mix the mustard with the egg yolks in a bowl. Mix the oils and start adding them to the eggs a drop or 2 at a time, stirring constantly with a whisk or wooden spoon.
9 Once you have added half the oil you can start adding it a little more quickly, but be patient – if you're too speedy the mayonnaise will curdle. Season with salt and pepper.
10 Put all the coleslaw vegetables in a serving bowl. You can mix in the mayonnaise or serve it separately.

Duck legs with pearl barley stew

Pearl barley really adds something special to a dish. It has great nutritional qualities and thickens a stew without making it feel too heavy.

SERVES 6

2 tbsp olive oil
6 duck legs
4 tbsp goose fat
3 sprigs of fresh thyme
sea salt
freshly ground black pepper

Pearl barley stew
300g pearl barley
600ml vegetable stock (a stock cube will do)
2 tbsp olive oil
2 medium potatoes, peeled and cut into quarters
1 carrot, peeled and chopped into 2cm chunks
1 celery stalk, finely chopped
1 onion, finely chopped
1 garlic clove, finely chopped
1 celeriac, peeled and cut into 2cm chunks
1 parsnip, peeled and cut into 2cm chunks
400ml chicken stock
200g frozen peas
2 tbsp finely chopped flat-leaf parsley
20g butter
sea salt
freshly ground black pepper

1 Preheat the oven to 150°C/Gas 2 Heat the olive oil in a large saucepan. Add the duck legs, skin side down, and fry for 5 minutes. Turn the legs over, season them with salt and pepper and fry for another 5 minutes.
2 Place the duck legs in a roasting tin. Pour over the fat that escaped when they were frying and add the goose fat and the thyme sprigs. Place the roasting tin in the oven and cook the duck legs for 2 hours.
3 Remove from the oven and drain off the fat. Increase the oven temperature to 200°C/Gas 6 and put the duck legs back in the oven to roast for another 30 minutes. Season with salt and pepper and serve with the pearl barley stew.

To make the pearl barley stew
4 Place the pearl barley in a saucepan and cover with the vegetable stock. Bring to a simmer and cook for about 50 minutes until tender.
5 In the meantime, heat the olive oil in another saucepan. When it's hot, add the vegetables, stir them into the oil and cook for 10 minutes. Add the chicken stock and simmer for 20 minutes. Add the cooked pearl barley, peas and parsley, season with salt and pepper, then cook at a simmer for 5 minutes. Remove from the heat and stir in the butter.

Marmalade

I come from a household where eating anything other than home-made marmalade was just not on, so I've continued the tradition in my own home. Remember to sterilise your jam jars. To do this, first wash the jars in the dishwasher. Preheat your oven to 120°C/Gas ½, place the clean jars on a baking sheet and put them in the oven for 20 minutes or so.

MAKES ENOUGH TO FILL ABOUT 5 STANDARD JARS

2kg Seville oranges
1 lemon
2 litres water
1.5kg sugar

1 Put the oranges and lemon, whole and unpeeled, in a large saucepan with the water. Cook at a gentle simmer for 2 hours, uncovered, until the fruit is very soft.
2 Remove the fruit from the liquid, leaving the liquid in the pan. Let the oranges and lemons cool a little and then cut them in half, removing the pulp from each half and putting it into a sieve over the liquid in the pan. Mash the pulp with the back of a spoon, extracting as much additional liquid as you can.
3 Thinly slice the rind of the oranges and add it to the liquid. I use about half the rind in my marmalade, because I don't like it too rindy.
4 Return the pan to the heat. Bring to the boil and add the sugar. Stir while the sugar dissolves, then simmer, uncovered, for about 1½ hours.
5 To test if the marmalade is ready, place a saucer in the fridge for a few minutes, then spoon a little of the marmalade on to the saucer and return it to the fridge for 2 minutes. Take it out and tip the saucer gently or push the marmalade with your finger – if the surface wrinkles slightly the marmalade should set to the right consistency.
6 Spoon the hot marmalade into jars, sterilised as above. Place a circle of waxed paper or baking parchment on top, then seal the jars as tightly as you can.

Steamed syrup pudding

This is a big pudding – partly in terms of its size and partly in terms of the lovely satisfied feeling it will leave you with once you have finished eating. It's the perfect Sunday lunch pudding and any leftovers heat up well in a microwave.

SERVES 6

3 tbsp golden syrup
juice and finely grated zest of ½ lemon
300g self-raising flour, plus extra for flouring the basin
175g butter, plus extra for greasing
175g caster sugar
a pinch of salt
2 eggs, mixed with enough milk to make 375ml of liquid

1 Grease a 1-litre pudding basin and dust the inside with flour. Spoon in the golden syrup and the lemon juice and zest. Place to one side.
2 Place the flour and butter in a food processor and blend until the butter is incorporated into the flour and the mixture resembles breadcrumbs. Add the sugar and salt and mix again briefly.
3 Add the egg and milk and mix until you have a smooth sponge batter. Spoon this into the pudding basin.
4 Cover the top of the pudding with a circle of baking parchment and then cover the basin with some more parchment overlapping the sides. Tie the parchment securely with string, then wrap the whole basin in foil. Fold another piece of foil into a thick square or circle, place it in the bottom of the saucepan to act as a little stand and put the basin on top. Add hot water to a depth of about 3cm.
5 Cover the saucepan and simmer the pudding for 2 hours. Keep an eye on the water level and top it up with boiling water when necessary.
6 Carefully take the basin out of the saucepan and remove the foil and parchment. Run a knife around the edge of the sponge and turn the pudding out on to a plate. Cut into large wedges and serve with cream.

Cider cake

A lovely light fruit cake that's very easy to make.

MAKES 1 X 21CM CAKE

200g self-raising flour
100g butter
100g caster sugar
100g sultanas
100g raisins
50g pecan nuts, roughly chopped
1 tsp mixed spice
½ tsp ground cinnamon
¼ tsp grated nutmeg
3 eggs
200ml cider

1 Grease a 21cm cake tin and line the base with baking parchment. Preheat the oven to 180°C/Gas 4.
2 Place the flour and butter in a food processor and blitz until the mixture resembles breadcrumbs, then tip into a mixing bowl.
3 Add all the remaining dry ingredients and then the liquid ingredients. Stir well, then spoon the mixture into the cake tin. Bake in the oven for 55 minutes.
4 Remove the cake from the oven and allow it to cool completely before turning out on to a plate.

Stuffed cabbage leaves with rice and broth

This dish is much easier to prepare than it sounds. I bake the stuffed leaves, instead of boiling them, so there is little risk of the stuffing escaping.

SERVES 6

2 savoy cabbages
300g sausage meat
2 tbsp pistachio nuts, finely chopped
1 onion, finely chopped
a grating of nutmeg
½ tsp fresh thyme leaves
100g white breadcrumbs
2 tbsp olive oil
250g basmati rice
100g salami, chopped into 1cm pieces
100g carrots, diced
1 litre beef stock
3 tbsp soy sauce
3 tbsp Marsala wine
sea salt
freshly ground black pepper

1 Preheat the oven to 200°C/Gas 6. Remove the tough outer leaves of the cabbage. Take 6 leaves from each cabbage, leaving the smaller inner leaves for soup another day.

2 Bring a large saucepan of water to the boil. Place the cabbage leaves in the boiling water and push them down with a wooden spoon to immerse them in the water. Leave the cabbage leaves in the water for 1 minute, then drain and place them to one side.

3 Put the sausage meat, nuts, onion, nutmeg, thyme leaves, breadcrumbs, black pepper and olive oil in a bowl. Mix gently to combine.

4 Take a large roasting tin or gratin dish. Sprinkle the rice on the bottom of the dish, then add the salami and carrots. Place to one side.

5 Lay the cabbage leaves on a work surface and divide the sausage mixture between them. Wrap each cabbage leaf around its portion of stuffing, then lay all the stuffed cabbage leaves on top of the rice and salami. Place them folded side down, so that no stuffing escapes during the cooking time.

6 Mix the beef stock with the soy sauce and Marsala wine and pour this liquid into the dish, over the stuffed cabbage leaves and rice. Season with some black pepper and a little salt. Pop the dish in the oven and bake for 1 hour. Serve piping hot.

Chunky shepherd's pie

Shepherd's pie is often made with minced lamb or beef, but traditionally leftover meat cut into chunks was used, as in this recipe.

1 Heat the olive oil in a large saucepan. Add the onion, celery, carrot and cook over a low heat for 10 minutes.
2 Add the meat, all in one go, and stir until it loses its pinkness. Season with the salt and some black pepper, then sprinkle on the flour and stir it in. Add the tomato purée, parsley and stock and simmer uncovered, on a low heat for 1 hour. Leave to cool slightly.
3 Spoon the meat sauce into a gratin dish and dollop the mashed potato on top. Dot with a little butter and then place under a hot grill to brown the potato slightly. Serve with green peas.

SERVES 6

2 tbsp olive oil
1 onion, finely chopped
1 celery stalk, finely chopped
1 carrot, finely chopped
1kg boneless lamb shoulder, cut into 1cm pieces
1 tsp sea salt
2 tbsp plain flour
1 tbsp tomato purée
2 tbsp finely chopped flat-leaf parsley
300ml vegetable stock
1.2kg potatoes, peeled, cut into quarters and cooked until tender and then mashed
a knob of butter
freshly ground black pepper

Deluxe macaroni cheese with grilled tomatoes

A good rich, flavoursome macaroni cheese is a simple but welcome treat on a winter's evening.

SERVES 6

1 tbsp olive oil
25g butter
1 onion, finely chopped
140g pancetta, chopped
1 tbsp flour
200ml milk
3 tbsp crème fraiche
200ml double cream
50g Gruyère, grated
50g Emmenthal, grated
600g macaroni

Grilled tomatoes
5 tomatoes, cut into 5mm slices
½ tsp dried oregano
1 tbsp olive oil
sea salt
freshly ground black pepper

1 Heat the olive oil and butter in a saucepan. Add the onion and pancetta and cook over a medium heat for 10 minutes. Sprinkle on the flour and stir to combine.
2 Add the milk and stir over a low heat until you have a smooth sauce. Spoon in the crème fraiche and cream and simmer gently, uncovered, for 10 minutes. Remove from the heat and stir in both cheeses.
3 Cook the macaroni according to the packet instructions. Drain, then lay the macaroni in a gratin dish. Spoon the sauce over the macaroni and put the dish under a hot grill for a few minutes until golden and bubbling. Serve with the grilled tomatoes.

To prepare the grilled tomatoes
4 Lay the sliced tomatoes in a gratin dish. Sprinkle with the oregano and olive oil, season with salt and pepper, then place under the grill for 10 minutes.

Curried lamb shanks

A few years ago, lamb shanks became popular with trendy super-chefs, but they are very easy to prepare at home. The important thing is to cook them for a long time in a flavoursome sauce. The shanks will then become a meltingly rich meat dish that is worthy of both the everyday table and the dinner party.

SERVES 6

1 tbsp coriander seeds
½ tbsp cumin seeds
½ tbsp fennel seeds
¼ tsp fenugreek seeds
6 curry leaves
½ tsp dried chilli flakes
1 tbsp olive oil
3 lamb shanks
1 onion, finely chopped
2 garlic cloves, finely chopped
1 tsp grated fresh root ginger
400g peeled raw potatoes, cut into 4cm chunks
1 x 400g can of cannellini beans, drained and rinsed
1 x 400g can of chopped tomatoes
1 x 400ml can of coconut milk
1 x 2cm piece of cinnamon stick
a handful of fresh mint leaves, torn
sea salt
freshly ground black pepper

Boiled rice
500g basmati rice
½ tsp salt
750ml water

1 Place the coriander, cumin, fennel, fenugreek, curry leaves and dried chilli flakes in a small frying pan. Dry fry them until they just start to smoke and you can smell their aroma. Grind them to a fine powder in a pestle and mortar. Preheat the oven to 160°C/Gas 3.
2 Heat the oil in a large ovenproof saucepan. Brown the lamb shanks, 1 at a time, in the oil, then remove and set aside.
3 Keep the pan on the heat and add the onion, garlic and ginger. Cook for 10 minutes on a medium heat. Add the ground spices and stir for a few seconds. Add the potatoes, beans, tomatoes, coconut milk, cinnamon stick and mint leaves, then stir and simmer for 5 minutes.
4 Return the lamb shanks to the saucepan and cook in the oven for 2 ½ hours. Serve with plain boiled rice.

To prepare the boiled rice
5 Place the rice, salt and water in a large saucepan and bring to a lively boil. Reduce the heat to very low, cover the pan and cook the rice for 15 minutes. Stir once during the cooking time.
6 Remove the pan from the heat. Keep the rice covered and leave it undisturbed for 10 minutes more.

Salmon stew with mashed potatoes

This meal is quick to prepare and there's very little washing up.

SERVES 6

- 2 tbsp olive oil
- 25g butter
- 1 large onion, finely chopped
- 2 garlic cloves, finely chopped
- 1 celery stalk, finely chopped
- 1 large carrot, chopped into bite-sized chunks
- 2 tbsp finely chopped flat-leaf parsley
- 4 sage leaves, finely chopped
- 1 tbsp tomato purée
- 1 x 400g can of chopped tomatoes
- 1 tbsp rinsed capers
- 250g frozen peas
- 200ml water
- 600g salmon fillets, skinless and cut into 4cm chunks
- sea salt
- freshly ground black pepper

Mashed potatoes

- 1kg potatoes, peeled and cut into quarters
- 40g butter
- 200ml warm milk
- sea salt
- freshly ground black pepper

1 Heat the olive oil and butter in a large saucepan. When they are foaming, add the onion, garlic, celery, carrot, parsley and sage and cook on a gentle heat, stirring occasionally, for 10 minutes.
2 Add the tomato purée, chopped tomatoes, capers, peas and water. Season with salt and pepper and cook at a simmer, covered, for 20 minutes. Add the fish. Check the seasoning and cook for 4 minutes more. Serve with mashed potatoes.

To make the mashed potatoes
3 Boil the potatoes in salted water until tender.
4 Pass the potatoes through a potato ricer or use your preferred method to mash them. Return them to the pan and place over a low heat. Mix in the butter and milk and season to taste.

Chicken and mushroom tarts with tops

These pies are a good way of using up any leftover cooked chicken, but if you don't have enough chicken, bulk it out with some chopped ham. You can use bought pastry or make your own puff pastry (see page 12) if you prefer. If you're feeding hungry teenagers, as I usually am, serve the tarts with mashed potatoes and cabbage. You need some individual tart tins.

SERVES 6

2 x 230g packs of ready-made puff pastry
flour, for dusting the work surface
1 tbsp olive oil
15g butter
1 onion, finely chopped
250g chestnut mushrooms, thickly sliced
1 tbsp plain flour
300ml chicken stock (fresh or made with a stock cube)
½ tsp chopped fresh tarragon
500g cooked chicken meat, cut into bite-sized chunks
2 tbsp crème fraiche
sea salt
freshly ground black pepper

1 Preheat the oven to 200°C/Gas 6. Roll out the puff pastry on a floured work surface and cut circles the size of your tart tins. Use these to line the tart tins, place them on a baking sheet and bake in the oven for 10 minutes.
2 Take a sharp knife and cut off the puffed-up top of each tart to create a lid and a little pie base. Reduce the oven temperature to 170°C/Gas 3 ½ and put the tarts to one side while you prepare the filling.
3 Heat the olive oil and butter in a saucepan. Add the onion and mushrooms and cook over a medium to high heat, stirring frequently, for 10 minutes, until the mushrooms have lost all their liquid and are beginning to turn a rich brown. Sprinkle on the flour and stir.
4 Remove from the heat and add the chicken stock a little at a time, stirring as you do so. Return the pan to the heat and add the tarragon. Simmer gently for 5 minutes, then stir in the chicken and crème fraiche.
5 Spoon this mixture into the little tart bases. Put the lids on top and place the tarts on a baking sheet in the oven for 10 minutes to warm through.

Gammon with orange cider sauce and potato and celeriac gratin

My mother used to serve us gammon in an orange sauce when we were growing up. The two make a lovely combination. I think the cider is a good addition, although I am pretty sure that she used a little sherry instead. Some purple sprouting broccoli makes a perfect accompaniment.

SERVES 6

1.5kg unsmoked gammon joint
1.5 litres cider
20g butter
20g flour
400ml stock from the cooked ham
finely grated zest of 1 orange
1 tsp soft brown sugar
1 tbsp finely chopped flat-leaf parsley
sea salt
freshly ground black pepper

Potato and celeriac gratin
500g potatoes, peeled and cut into 3mm slices
1 celeriac, peeled and cut into 3mm slices
350ml single cream
2 garlic cloves, crushed
20g butter
sea salt
freshly ground black pepper

1 Place the gammon joint in a large pan and cover it with the cider. Simmer the joint gently for 1 hour and 20 minutes. Remove the joint and cover it with foil to keep it warm. Set the cooking liquid to one side.
2 To make the sauce, melt the butter in a small saucepan. Add the flour, stir to combine and cook over a low heat for 1 minute. Remove the pan from the heat and gradually add the stock, stirring constantly.
3 Stir in the orange zest, sugar and parsley and simmer over a low heat for 10 minutes. Season with salt and pepper, then serve with slices of gammon and the gratin.

To make the gratin
4 Preheat the oven to 200°C/Gas 6. Place the potatoes and celeriac in a gratin dish. Pour on the cream, add the garlic and dot with butter. Season with salt and pepper and mix the whole lot together with your hands. Bake in the oven for 1 hour, by which time the vegetables will be perfectly tender.

Chocolate pudding with chocolate sauce

Chocolate and orange are perfect partners and once you've roasted and ground the hazelnuts this sublimely delicious pudding is simple to make. Grind the hazelnuts in a liquidiser.

SERVES 6

160g butter, plus extra for greasing
200g dark chocolate, broken into pieces
4 eggs, separated into yolks and whites
140g hazelnuts, toasted and finely ground
90g icing sugar
zest of 1 orange
1 tbsp Cointreau

Chocolate sauce
175g dark chocolate, broken into pieces
100ml double cream
2 tbsp Cointreau

1 Preheat the oven to 180°C/Gas 4. Grease a 23cm pie or soufflé dish. Put the butter and chocolate in a glass bowl and place over a saucepan of gently simmering water, taking care that the bottom of the bowl doesn't touch the water. Once the chocolate has melted, remove the bowl from the pan and let the chocolate cool for 5 minutes.
2 Meanwhile, beat the egg yolks in a bowl using an electric hand-whisk. Add the yolks to the melted chocolate, then add the hazelnuts, icing sugar, orange zest and Cointreau, incorporating them gently but thoroughly.
3 Whisk the egg whites in a clean bowl, using a clean whisk, until the whites form small peaks when the whisk is removed. Fold the whites into the chocolate mixture, using a metal spoon.
4 Spoon the mixture into the pie dish and bake for 20 minutes. When you touch the middle of the pudding with your fingertips it should feel spongy, with a slight give. Serve with the chocolate sauce.

To make the chocolate sauce
5 To make the chocolate sauce, melt the dark chocolate in a bowl over a pan of simmering water as above. Remove from the heat, then stir in the cream and Cointreau.

Plum and raspberry cobbler

A cobbler might not look very glamorous, but it never disappoints the taste buds. As the plums and raspberries cook, they give off just the right amount of juice to soak into the scone topping, making this a glorious pudding.

SERVES 6

800g plums, cut in half and stones removed
200g raspberries
2 tbsp brown sugar
25g butter

Cobbler topping
100g cold butter, cut into cubes
225g plain flour, plus extra for dusting the work surface
2 tbsp soft brown sugar
1 tsp baking powder
200ml buttermilk
1 tbsp caster sugar

1 Preheat the oven to 200°C/Gas 6. Place the fruit in a gratin dish and sprinkle on the brown sugar. Break up the butter with your fingertips, dropping little bits on top of the fruit.
2 To make the topping, place the butter and flour in a food processor. Blend until the mixture has the texture of breadcrumbs, then stir in the brown sugar and baking powder. Add the buttermilk, whizz briefly and turn the dough out on to a floured work surface.
3 Form the dough into 6 scones and place these at regular intervals on top of the fruit. Sprinkle the caster sugar over the top of the scones and bake in the oven for 35 minutes. Serve with cream.

Cheese and onion flan

This is called a flan, but the base is really more like a thick pizza base than a pastry base. It makes a lovely supper dish.

SERVES 6

2 tbsp olive oil
1 large onion, finely chopped
200g grated hard cheese, any tasty leftovers will do
300g crème fraiche
3 eggs
2 tbsp fresh thyme leaves
sea salt
freshly ground black pepper

Base
500g strong bread flour
2 tsp salt
2 tsp sugar
1 x 7g sachet of dried yeast
2 eggs
50g softened butter, plus extra for greasing
200ml warm milk

1 To make the base, place all the ingredients in a mixing bowl and combine with a wooden spoon. Cover the bowl and leave the dough to rise for 1 hour.
2 Preheat the oven to 220°C/Gas 7 and start to prepare the topping.
3 Heat the oil in a frying pan. Add the onion and cook over a low heat for 10 minutes, stirring occasionally. Spoon into a mixing bowl and combine with the cheese, crème fraiche and eggs, making sure the mixture is smooth. Season with salt and pepper.
4 Take the dough and press it into a greased baking tin, measuring about 25 x 40cm.
5 Spoon the cheese mixture on top, sprinkle with the thyme leaves and bake in the oven for 40 minutes, until the mixture is golden brown.

Meatball stew

There's something about meatballs! Serve these with boiled rice (see page 30), pasta or mashed potatoes.

1 Place the minced meat, sausage meat, onion, soy sauce, fennel seeds, paprika and a good grinding of salt and pepper in a large mixing bowl. Get your hands into the bowl and gradually and gently mix everything together. Roll the mixture into individual balls.
2 Heat the olive oil in a frying pan and brown the meatballs. Do this in batches so that you don't overcrowd the pan, putting each batch to one side while you brown the next.
3 Heat the butter in a large saucepan until gently foaming. Add the vegetables and stir until they are coated with butter, then cook them for 5 minutes over a gentle heat.
4 Sprinkle on the flour and mix until combined, then pour in the stock. Add the black-eyed beans, crème fraiche, season with salt and pepper and add the sprig of sage. Spoon the meatballs carefully into the pan, cover and simmer gently for 1 hour.
5 Serve with some carbs for a hearty supper.

SERVES 6

250g minced pork
250g minced beef
250g sausage meat
1 onion, finely chopped
1 tbsp dark soy sauce
½ tsp fennel seeds
1 tsp ground paprika
3 tbsp olive oil
20g butter
2 medium potatoes, peeled and cut into 2cm chunks
1 celeriac, peeled and cut into 2cm chunks
2 leeks, washed and sliced into 1cm pieces
1 tbsp flour
500ml chicken stock
1 x 400g can of black-eyed beans, drained and rinsed
1 tbsp crème fraiche
1 sprig of fresh sage
sea salt
freshly ground black pepper

Smoked haddock omelettes

I try to use seasonal ingredients as far as possible when cooking, but it's hard to find a better accompaniment to omelettes than a green salad, so green salad it has to be.

SERVES 6

250ml milk
500g smoked haddock fillets
25g butter
1 tbsp flour
4 tbsp double cream
100g Gruyère cheese, grated
2 tbsp chopped flat-leaf parsley
50g Parmesan cheese, grated
12 eggs
a couple of knobs of butter
for cooking the eggs
sea salt
freshly ground black pepper

1 First cook the haddock. Pour the milk into a wide pan and bring it to a simmer on top of the stove. Place the fish fillets in the pan with the milk and continue to simmer for 1 minute. Turn the fillets and cook for a further minute. Remove the fish from the milk and set the milk aside.
2 Skin the fish, remove any stray bones and flake the flesh into a bowl. Place it to one side.
3 Put a small saucepan on the stove and add the butter. Once it is bubbling, add the flour and stir well. Remove the saucepan from the heat and gradually stir in the milk you set aside earlier.
4 Return the saucepan to the heat and bring to the boil, then turn the heat to low and cook for 5 minutes. Stir in the cream and a little salt. Remove from the heat and stir in the flaked fish, Gruyère and parsley.
5 Whisk the eggs briefly and season with pepper. You'll need to cook the eggs in 2 lots.
6 Preheat the grill to hot. Heat the butter in a frying pan and when it is sizzling add half the egg mixture. Move the eggs around with a fork, drawing the edges into the centre of the pan and tilting it so that the uncooked egg flows to the sides.
7 Once the underneath of the egg is firm, remove the pan from the heat. Spoon half the fish mixture on to the eggs and sprinkle over half the Parmesan cheese. Place the pan under the hot grill until the top of the omelette is golden brown and bubbling. Repeat with the rest of the eggs and fish mixture. Cut each omelette into 3 and serve with a green salad.

Lamb pie

Diced lamb is a great meat to cook with when you're short of time as, unlike beef, it does not have to stew for a long time to be tender. Cabbage goes well with this.

SERVES 6

2 tbsp olive oil
15g butter
1kg lamb neck fillet, cut into 2cm chunks
1 onion, finely chopped
1 celery stalk, finely chopped
1 carrot, diced into 1cm cubes
1 celeriac, peeled and chopped into small chunks
300ml red wine
1 tbsp flour
300ml chicken or vegetable stock
2 sprigs of fresh thyme
sea salt
freshly ground black pepper

Potato topping
1kg potatoes, peeled and cut into quarters
40g butter
200ml milk
sea salt
freshly ground black pepper

1 Heat the olive oil and butter in a large saucepan. Brown the lamb chunks in the fat in small batches, setting each batch to one side once it has browned.
2 Keep the pan on the heat, adding a little more olive oil if necessary. Gently cook the onion and celery for 5 minutes, remove them from the pan and set aside with the lamb. Keep the pan on the heat and add the remaining vegetables, then stir and cook for 5 minutes. Remove the vegetables from the pan and place them with the lamb, onion and celery.
3 Pour the wine into the saucepan and simmer for 2 minutes, stirring occasionally, then tip all the meat and vegetables back into the pan. Sprinkle on the flour and stir.
4 Add the stock and thyme and season with salt and pepper, then simmer on a gentle heat, uncovered, for 30 minutes. Spoon everything into a pie dish and leave to cool slightly before covering with the potato topping.

To make the potato topping
5 Boil the potatoes in salted water until tender.
6 Pass the potatoes through a potato ricer or use your preferred method to mash them. Return them to the pan and place over a low heat. Add the butter and milk and mix gently. Adjust the seasoning to taste. Preheat the grill.
7 Pile the mash on top of the pie, then place it under a hot grill to brown for a few minutes.

Cajun-style fish broth

This fish soup is simple to prepare and it's bursting with great flavours.

1 First prepare the mussels. Scrub them well, remove the hairy beards and throw out any that are open and don't close when tapped.
2 Pour the wine into a large saucepan. Place the saucepan over a high heat and when the wine starts to simmer, add the mussels. Cover the saucepan and cook the mussels for 3 minutes, by which time all the mussel shells should have opened. Discard any that remain closed. Pour the mussels and the liquor into a heatproof bowl.
3 Place the saucepan back on the heat and add the olive oil. When it is warm, add the pepper, onion, celery and garlic. Cook on a low heat for 5 minutes, stirring occasionally. Sprinkle on the paprika and the thyme leaves and stir for a few seconds.
4 Stir in the flour, then gradually start to add the fish stock a little at a time, stirring constantly to avoid lumps. Pour on the vegetable stock and passata. Taste for seasoning and add a little salt and pepper if necessary.
5 Add the fish to the pan and cook at a slight simmer for 1 minute. Next add the mussels and liquor and simmer for 1 minute more. Ladle into bowls, sprinkle with Gruyère cheese and serve with plenty of bread.

SERVES 6

200ml white wine
500g fresh mussels
2 tbsp olive oil
1 red pepper, cored and finely chopped
1 onion, finely chopped
1 celery stalk, finely chopped
2 garlic cloves, crushed
2 tsp paprika
1 tsp fresh thyme leaves
2 tbsp flour
500ml fish stock
500ml vegetable stock
500ml tomato passata
500g white fish fillets (tilapia or pollack) cut into bite-sized chunks
grated Gruyère cheese, for serving
sea salt
freshly ground black pepper

Chicken and noodles

It's difficult to find good quality Thai ingredients if you don't live in a city, so little jars of ready-chopped lemon grass and galangal are welcome aids when you want to create a dish with a Thai flavour.

SERVES 6

- 3 nests of fine egg noodles
- 3 boneless chicken breasts, thinly sliced
- 1 tsp brown sugar
- 4 tbsp mirin
- 2 garlic cloves, crushed
- 1 tbsp light soy sauce
- 2cm piece of fresh root ginger, grated
- 300ml chicken stock
- 1 tsp sea salt
- 1 kaffir lime leaf
- 1 tsp prechopped lemon grass (from a jar)
- 1 tsp prechopped galangal (from a jar)
- 1 tbsp dried shitake mushrooms
- 25g creamed coconut
- ¼ savoy cabbage, shredded
- 2 tbsp dark soy sauce
- 3 spring onions, finely chopped
- fresh coriander
- 1 tsp sesame oil

1 Cook the noodles according to the packet instructions, then drain them and place to one side.
2 Put the chicken in a bowl with the sugar, mirin, garlic, soy sauce and ginger to marinate. Place to one side.
3 Heat the stock in a large saucepan. Add 1 teaspoon of salt, the lime leaf, lemon grass, galangal and shitake mushrooms. Simmer on a gentle heat for 10 minutes.
4 Add the creamed coconut, cabbage and soy sauce, then check the seasoning – you may need more salt. Simmer for 2 minutes, then add the noodles, coriander and spring onions. Remove from the heat. You can reheat this if you are not going to eat immediately.
5 Cook the chicken just before serving. Heat the sesame oil in a small frying pan, then fry the chicken, in small batches, for 2 minutes over a high heat. Serve the noodles with a couple of spoonfuls of chicken on top of each serving.

Roast pheasant with Brussels sprouts

Pheasant might not be as succulent as chicken, but it has a great flavour and makes a good Sunday lunch at this time of year.

SERVES 6

2 onions, cut in half
3 whole pheasants
50g butter, softened
3 sprigs of thyme, leaves stripped from the stems
70g pancetta slices
sea salt
freshly ground black pepper

Gravy
1 tbsp flour
500ml chicken stock (a stock cube will do)
sea salt
freshly ground black pepper

Shredded Brussels sprouts
200g Brussels sprouts, tailed and trimmed
15g butter
½ tsp caraway seeds
100ml Marsala wine
sea salt
freshly ground black pepper

1 Preheat the oven to 190°C/Gas 5. Insert half an onion into the neck cavity of each pheasant.
2 Smear the pheasants with the butter, then season and scatter the thyme leaves liberally over each bird. Lay the slices of pancetta on the breasts of the pheasants. Place the pheasants in a roasting tin and place them in the oven for 1 hour. Remove the pancetta and roast the birds for 10 minutes more to brown the breasts. Leave them to rest while you make the gravy.
3 Carve the pheasants as you would a chicken and serve with the sprouts and gravy. Roast potatoes (see page 94) and bread sauce (see page 699) would also be good accompaniments.

To make the gravy
4 Place the roasting tin on the top of the stove on a medium heat. Stir in the flour with a wooden spoon and once it's been absorbed by the fat and juices pour on the chicken stock. Simmer gently for 15 minutes, while the pheasants are resting and season to taste.

To prepare the sprouts
5 Shred the sprouts thinly using a sharp knife – if you cut them in half first this is not as tedious as it sounds. Place the butter in a saucepan with the caraway seeds and heat through. Add the sprouts and cook, stirring frequently, for 3 minutes. Pour on the wine and cook for 1 minute more. Season with salt and pepper.

White chocolate and brown breadcrumb mousse

This is a rich, sweet dessert that I've based on the brown breadcrumb ice cream idea. It makes a delicious alternative to ice cream.

SERVES 6

250g white chocolate, broken into pieces
4 tbsp brown breadcrumbs
1 tbsp caster sugar
1 egg white
250ml double cream

1 Bring a pan of water to a simmer. Put the chocolate in a glass bowl and place it over the pan of simmering water, taking care that the bottom of the bowl does not touch the water.
2 Stir occasionally with a spatula and remove the bowl from the heat when all the chocolate has melted.
3 Heat the grill and place the breadcrumbs and sugar on a baking sheet. Brown the breadcrumbs under the grill, keeping a careful eye on them as they will burn very easily. As soon as they have browned and have a crispness to them, remove them from the grill and leave to cool.
4 Pour the egg white and double cream into a mixing bowl and whisk until the cream has thickened but is not stiff. Once the chocolate is cool, fold it into the cream and then fold in the breadcrumbs.
5 You can spoon the mixture into individual dishes and chill in the fridge for an hour before serving or pour the mixture into a plastic container and freeze it, as you would for ice cream.

Home-made yoghurt

Yoghurt is so easy to make and it's surprising that more people don't do it. It is such a natural product and far removed from the sweet, flavour-enhanced yoghurts sold in supermarkets. You don't need a fancy yoghurt maker either, which would just take up vital space in your kitchen. All you need is a few jars to put the yoghurt in to set. Add fruit for a pudding or enjoy your home-made yoghurt for breakfast.

MAKES 3 LARGE POTS

1 litre whole or semi-skimmed milk
75ml full-fat natural yoghurt

1 Bring the milk to the boil in a saucepan. Remove from the heat and allow to cool for 45 minutes.
2 Add the natural yoghurt to the milk and stir it in. Pour the mixture into clean, sterilised jars and keep them in a warm place overnight. I usually put mine in the airing cupboard, wrapped in a tea towel. Chill in the fridge before serving.

Chocolate muffins

The key to making good muffins is not to over-mix the batter. Just mix it until everything is combined and don't get carried away with that wooden spoon.

MAKES 9

200g dark chocolate
120g butter
100g ground almonds
100g self-raising flour
4 eggs
50g white chocolate, roughly chopped
50g milk chocolate, roughly chopped

1 Preheat the oven to 180°C/Gas 4. Place 9 paper muffin cases into a muffin tray. Bring a pan of water to a simmer.
2 Put the dark chocolate in a glass bowl with the butter, then place the bowl over the pan of simmering water, taking care that the bottom of the bowl doesn't touch the water. Stir the chocolate and butter occasionally until they have melted.
3 Carefully remove the bowl from the pan and leave the chocolate and butter to cool for 5 minutes before mixing in the ground almonds. Next stir in the eggs and then fold in the flour and roughly chopped white and milk chocolate.
4 Divide the mixture evenly between the muffin cases and bake in the oven for 20 minutes. The cakes should still look a little moist in their centres when they come out of the oven.
5 Leave the cakes to cool for a few minutes in the tray and then pop them on to a cooling rack to cool completely. These cakes are fine eaten warm or cold.

Sausage and vegetable pie

When I was at university and sharing a house with friends, we used to have a weekly menu that we devised to save money. As I recall, the menu didn't really change for the entire length of our time there. One of the items was a sausage pie, which in those days consisted of a large amount of cheap sausage meat wrapped in puff pastry. Our cooking then was much more about ballast than flavour and nutrition! This pie has its origins in my university kitchen but is a far superior offering.

SERVES 6

200g potatoes, peeled and cut into quarters
200g celeriac, peeled and cut into 2cm chunks
100g turnips, peeled and cut into 2cm chunks
2 tbsp olive oil
2 onions, finely chopped
2 celery stalks, finely chopped
400g sausage meat
a sprig of fresh thyme, leaves stripped
2 x 230g sheets of ready-rolled puff pastry
2 eggs, hard-boiled, peeled and cut in half
1 egg, beaten, for glazing
sea salt
freshly ground black pepper

1 Preheat the oven to 200°C/Gas 6. Place a baking sheet in the oven to heat up – this is to place the pie on so that the heat gets to the base straight away.
2 Cook the potatoes, celeriac and turnips in salted water until tender, then drain and place them in a mixing bowl.
3 Heat the olive oil in a small frying pan. When the oil is hot, add the onion and celery and fry over a low heat for 5 minutes until nice and soft. Add the onion and celery to the other vegetables, then add the sausage meat and thyme leaves to the bowl and and mix well. Add salt and pepper as necessary, but go easy on the salt as sausage meat is often quite salty. To check the seasoning, fry a teaspoon of the mixture and taste it.
4 Take the 2 sheets of puff pastry and use 1 to line the bottom and sides of a 23cm pie or cake tin. Pile in the sausage meat and vegetable mixture and place the egg halves, yolks facing upwards, on top. Cover with the other sheet of puff pastry, trimming the edges as necessary.
5 Glaze the pastry with the beaten egg. Place the pie on the baking sheet in the oven and bake for 40 minutes. Serve with some dressed watercress.

Chicken and mushroom risotto

A good-sized pan makes cooking a risotto a much easier task. Prepare all the ingredients before you start and then be prepared to stand by the pan and daydream while you stir. If you do have to leave the stove, remove the pan from the heat,as the rice sticks all too easily, which spoils the end result.

SERVES 6

20g butter
1 tbsp olive oil
2 shallots, finely chopped
200g chestnut mushrooms, sliced
100g pancetta, chopped
500g Arborio risotto rice
200ml Marsala wine
1.5 litres hot chicken stock
150g cooked chicken, chopped into bite-sized pieces
2 tbsp double cream
3 tbsp grated Parmesan cheese
sea salt
freshly ground black pepper

1 Heat the butter and olive oil in a large pan. Add the shallots, mushrooms and pancetta and cook over a reasonably high heat for 5 minutes, until the pancetta and mushrooms become tinged with a golden brown colour.
2 Add the rice and cook, stirring all the time for 2 minutes. Pour on the Marsala and stir for a few seconds until the liquid has all but disappeared.
3 Now start to add the hot chicken stock, a couple of ladlefuls at a time. Once the liquid has nearly disappeared, add another 2 ladlefuls. Keep cooking the rice like this until it is done to your liking. This should take between 20 and 25 minutes.
4 Throw in the cooked chicken. Remove from the heat and stir in the cream and cheese. Season to taste and serve.

Thyme, leek and cheese tart

At this time of year, a flavoursome tart is perfect for refreshing a jaded palette and is a welcome relief from rich meaty food.

SERVES 6

50g butter
200g onions, thinly sliced
300g leeks, washed, trimmed and thinly sliced
2 eggs
2 egg yolks
400ml crème fraiche
3 tsp Dijon mustard
1 tsp thyme leaves
100g Gruyère cheese, freshly grated
sea salt
freshly grated black pepper

Pastry
200g plain flour, plus extra for dusting the work surface
120g cold butter, cut into cubes, plus extra for greasing
a pinch of salt
3 tbsp ice-cold water

To make the pasty
1 Place the flour and butter in a food processor and mix until the mixture resembles breadcrumbs. Add the salt and water and mix very briefly. Turn the pastry out on to a floured surface and bring together gently to form a ball. Wrap in clingfilm and chill in the fridge for about 30 minutes.

To make the filling
2 Place the butter in a sauté pan and cook the onions and leeks on a very low heat for 30 minutes until both are soft, limp and tinged with the faintest golden brown colour, then place to one side.
3 Mix the whole eggs, yolks, crème fraiche, mustard and thyme in a bowl and season well with salt and pepper.

To assemble the tart
4 Preheat the oven to 190°C/Gas 5. Grease a 25cm tart tin. Roll out the pastry on a floured surface and place it in the tin. Cover the pastry with a sheet of baking parchment and sprinkle on some baking beans. Cook in the oven for 15 minutes.
5 Remove the parchment and baking beans and return the tart case to the oven for 10 minutes. Remove from the oven.
6 Pour the egg mixture into the tart case. Spoon on the leeks and onions and spread them out evenly. Lastly sprinkle on the cheese. Bake the tart in the oven for 40 minutes until golden brown. Serve with a green salad.

Penne pasta with rosemary, pancetta and chestnuts

This is a pasta sauce with Tuscan flavours. In Tuscany it seems that nothing edible is wasted, whether it comes from the sea or the land. This includes chestnuts which are gathered and roasted or used to make chestnut flour.

SERVES 6

- 500g penne pasta
- 2 tbsp olive oil
- 150g pancetta, chopped
- 1 garlic clove, finely chopped
- a sprig of rosemary, leaves stripped and finely chopped
- 200g cooked chestnuts, roughly chopped
- 250ml double cream
- 3 tbsp finely grated Parmesan cheese
- sea salt
- freshly grated black pepper

1 Bring a large pan of salted water to the boil and cook the pasta according to the packet instructions.
2 Meanwhile, heat the olive oil in a large frying pan. Add the pancetta and garlic and fry for 2 minutes, until the pancetta starts to turn golden brown. Add the rosemary and chestnuts and cook for 1 minute, stirring constantly. Pour on the cream and simmer gently for 2 minutes.
3 When the pasta is ready, drain and pour the sauce over it. Season with black pepper. Stir in the cheese and serve immediately.

Fried tilapia with rapeseed mayonnaise and potato and quinoa salad

I had not tried using quinoa until I made this recipe but everyone enjoyed it.

SERVES 6

olive oil, for frying
6 tilapia fillets
flour, for dusting
1 lemon
sea salt
freshly ground black pepper

Rapeseed mayonnaise
2 egg yolks
1 tsp white wine vinegar
1 tsp Dijon mustard
a pinch of salt
250ml rapeseed oil
2 tbsp basil leaves, finely chopped

Potato and quinoa salad
100g quinoa
2 tbsp olive oil
500g potatoes, peeled and cut into 2cm cubes
1 x 400g can of borlotti beans, drained and rinsed
5 spring onions, finely sliced
100g cherry tomatoes, cut into quarters
150g rocket leaves
sea salt
freshly ground black pepper

Salad dressing
2 tbsp extra virgin olive oil
½ tsp balsamic vinegar
sea salt
freshly ground black pepper

1 Heat the olive oil in a frying pan. Dust each fillet with a little flour and fry the fillets, 2 at a time, until golden brown on each side. They will probably need about a minute on each side.
2 Season the fish with salt and pepper and a squeeze of lemon, then serve it with the mayonnaise and the salad.

To make the rapeseed mayonnaise
3 Mix the egg yolks, wine vinegar, mustard and salt in a small bowl. Slowly start to add the oil, beating constantly. Don't add the oil too quickly or the mayonnaise will curdle. Sprinkle in the basil and stir to mix evenly, then check the seasoning. Place in a serving bowl.

To make the potato and quinoa salad
4 Cook the quinoa according to the packet instructions. Then heat the olive oil in a frying pan and spoon in the potato cubes. Fry until the potatoes are golden brown and have softened. Season with salt and pepper.
5 Add the borlotti beans and mix to incorporate with the potatoes. Place the potatoes and beans in a serving dish and add the spring onions and quinoa. Add the remaining ingredients and mix. Combine the dressing ingredients in a small bowl and pour over the salad.

Cajun burgers with avocado salsa

These are really just spiced burgers, but I find that if I give dishes different names my children are more interested in the meal – not that they need much encouragement to eat burgers!

SERVES 6

1 tsp fennel seeds
1 tsp ground coriander
2 tsp ground paprika
1 tsp salt
500g minced turkey
300g minced pork
1 onion, finely chopped
2 tbsp finely chopped coriander leaves
1 tsp thyme leaves
1 egg, beaten
2 tbsp olive oil
6 bread rolls
freshly ground black pepper

Avocado salsa
2 avocados, stones and skin removed and flesh roughly chopped
juice of ½ lemon
6 spring onions, chopped
2 tbsp extra virgin olive oil
sea salt
freshly ground black pepper

1 Grind the fennel seeds to a powder with the coriander, paprika, salt and black pepper.
2 Put the turkey, pork and onion in a bowl and add the ground spices and herbs. Mix with the egg to bind and shape the mixture into 6 burgers. Place the burgers on a tray and pop them into the fridge for 30 minutes to chill.
3 Heat the olive oil in a frying pan and fry 3 burgers on each side until they are golden brown. Place to one side and cook the rest. Return all the burgers to the pan and cook on a low heat for 10 minutes until cooked through.
4 Split and toast the bread rolls. Slip a burger and a spoonful of salsa into each one.

To make the avocado salsa
5 Place all the ingredients in a small bowl and mix with a fork until everything is nicely combined.

Rack of lamb with mint sauce and roast vegetables

Roasting a rack of lamb can seem daunting, but follow the cooking times below and you should be fine. If you like your lamb well done, leave it for another 5 minutes at the lower temperature.

SERVES 6

2 or 3 racks of lamb
a little olive oil
sea salt
freshly ground black pepper

Mint sauce
a bunch of mint
1½ tbsp vinegar
2 tbsp olive oil
½ tsp sugar
1 tsp English mustard
3 tbsp natural yoghurt
sea salt
freshly ground black pepper

Roast vegetables
600g potatoes, peeled and cut into quarters
200g celeriac, peeled and cut into 2cm chunks
200g parsnips, peeled and cut into quarters
2 tbsp olive oil
sea salt
freshly ground black pepper

1 Preheat the oven to 220°C/Gas 7. Remove the thick outer skin from the racks. It should come away with a sharp knife. Rub olive oil into the fat and meat and season well with salt and pepper.
2 Put the racks in a roasting tin and cook for 15 minutes, then reduce the heat to 150°C/Gas 2 for another 10 minutes. Leave the meat to rest for 15 minutes before carving. Serve with the mint sauce and vegetables.

To make the mint sauce
3 Finely chop the mint and place it in a small serving bowl. Add the vinegar, olive oil, sugar and mustard and mix with a small whisk or fork until it thickens slightly. Stir in the yoghurt and season to taste.

To prepare the vegetables
4 Preheat the oven to 220°C/Gas 7. Bring the vegetables to the boil in a pan of salted water and let them cook at a slow simmer for 5 minutes.
5 Drain the vegetables and place them in a vegetable tray with the olive oil. Roast in the oven for 1 hour, turning them occasionally. Season with salt and pepper.

Toffee pudding

A typical nursery-style pudding. You will love it too, in very small quantities. Simple but delicious.

SERVES 6

- softened butter, for buttering the bread
- 12 slices of white bread
- 50g raisins
- 250ml milk
- 120g butter
- 120g demerara sugar
- 225g golden syrup

1 Preheat the oven to 180°C/Gas 4. Butter the slices of bread and lay half of them in an ovenproof dish, buttered side up. Sprinkle on the raisins and then lay the other slices on top, buttered side down, like a sandwich.
2 Bring the milk to the boil and pour it over the bread sandwiches. Leave to one side.
3 Put 120g butter, the sugar and syrup in a small pan, place on the stove and gently heat through. Once the mixture is simmering, let it bubble away for 4 minutes.
4 Pour this toffee sauce over the bread sandwiches and pop the dish in the oven for 15 minutes. Serve with cream.

Iced fruit buns

Everyone needs a few treats to keep the spirits up during the long, dark winter evenings. Iced fruit buns are perfect fare for this time of year.

MAKES 8 BUNS

350g strong white bread flour, plus extra for dusting the work surface
1 sachet of dried yeast
2 tsp sugar
½ tsp salt
½ tsp ground cinnamon
½ tsp mixed spice
grated zest of ½ lemon
1 egg
150ml warm milk
50g melted butter
100g chopped dates
50g sultanas
50g currants

Icing
250g icing sugar
2 tbsp warm water

1 Put all the ingredients for the buns in a bowl and mix with a wooden spoon. Turn the dough out on to a floured surface and knead for 5 minutes, then return it to the bowl. Cover the bowl with a tea towel and leave the dough to rise in a draught-free place for 1 hour.
2 Preheat the oven to 200°C/Gas 6. Divide the dough into 8 pieces and shape these into round buns. Place the buns on a baking tray, leaving space between them as they will spread. Cover and leave to rise again for 30 minutes.
3 Bake the buns in the oven for 15 minutes, then place them on a wire rack to cool.
4 To make the icing, sift the sugar into a mixing bowl. Using a wooden spoon, stir in the water until you have thick white icing. Ice the buns, using a knife or spatula.

Chocolate chip cookies

There was usually a jar of these in our kitchen when I was growing up, although with four children in the house they didn't last long. The smell of these baking really reminds me of childhood and further confirms my belief in the benefits of good home-cooked food. A banana milkshake goes down well with these.

MAKES 12

110g softened butter
60g soft brown sugar
140g self-raising flour
80g chocolate chips

1 Preheat the oven to 180°C/Gas 4. Cream the butter for 4 minutes using an electric hand whisk. Add the sugar and combine with the butter using the whisk – about 2 minutes should be enough.
2 Add the flour and chocolate chips and mix by hand until you have a ball of dough.
3 Grease a baking tray. Break off walnut-sized lumps of dough and shape them into smooth balls. Place them on the baking tray, leaving space between each one as they will expand. Press each ball of dough lightly with a wet fork to flatten it slightly – not too much.
4 Bake in the oven for 10–12 minutes. When the cookies are done, leave them on the tray for 5 minutes to cool slightly, then transfer to a cooling rack.

Banana milkshake

This is the shortest recipe in the book!

SERVES 6

900ml milk
300ml orange juice
3 tbsp natural yoghurt
6 ripe bananas

1 Place everything in a blender and blitz until smooth. Serve in glasses.

Cheese and red lentil croquettes

For me, one of the most challenging aspects of writing this book has been devising non-meat recipes that are inviting enough to tempt my children. But I do think it is never too early to learn that it is not right to consume a lot of meat, both in terms of world resources and from a health point of view.

SERVES 6

600ml water
200g red lentils
250g white breadcrumbs
200g Caerphilly cheese, grated
½ leek, finely chopped
2 tbsp finely chopped flat-leaf parsley
2 tsp English mustard
olive oil, for frying
sea salt
freshly ground black pepper

1 Pour the water into a saucepan and add the lentils. Bring to a simmer, partially cover the pan with a lid and cook the lentils for 45 minutes over a gentle heat. The water should all be absorbed by the lentils. Place the pan to one side.
2 Place 150g of the breadcrumbs in a mixing bowl and add the cheese, leek, parsley, mustard and cooked lentils. Season well with salt and pepper. Mix thoroughly and then form the mixture into 12 cigar or sausage shapes.
3 Roll each croquette in the remaining breadcrumbs until evenly coated and set them on a plate. If your kitchen is very warm, place them in the fridge to chill for 20 minutes.
4 Heat some olive oil in a frying pan and when the oil is hot brown a few of the croquettes in the oil, turning them as they brown until they are golden all over. Serve with a green salad.

Sausage and duck ragù with pappardelle

This is a simple recipe but gives a rewarding result. I find that a rich pasta sauce simmering on the stove is a most welcome sight at the end of a January day.

SERVES 6

1 tbsp olive oil
4 duck breasts, skin removed and meat chopped into 1cm pieces
70g pancetta, chopped
1 onion, finely chopped
2 garlic cloves, finely chopped
1 celery stalk, finely chopped
1 carrot, finely chopped
2 tbsp finely chopped flat-leaf parsley
250ml red wine
1 tbsp tomato purée
2 x 400g cans of chopped tomatoes
8 pork sausages, chopped into 1cm pieces
2 tbsp crème fraiche
500g pappardelle pasta
sea salt
freshly ground black pepper

1 Heat the olive oil in a large sauté pan and brown the pieces of duck. Remove them from the pan and place to one side.
2 Return the pan to the heat – there should be enough fat remaining. Add the pancetta, onion, garlic, celery and carrot and cook slowly for 10 minutes, stirring occasionally to ensure that all the ingredients get cooked evenly. Sprinkle on the parsley, then return the duck to the pan.
3 Add the wine and cook at a simmer for 5 minutes. Next add the tomato purée, the chopped tomatoes and the sausages. Check the seasoning. Cover the pan and cook at a slow simmer for 1 hour. Stir in the crème fraiche.
4 Serve with the pappardelle pasta, cooked according to the packet instructions.

Salmon hash on toast with poached eggs

This meal is very quick and easy. It won't win any awards for good looks, but it is really tasty.

SERVES 6

1 tbsp olive oil
a small knob of butter
1 onion, finely chopped
100g cooked potatoes, chopped into chunks
200g frozen peas, cooked
2 tsp plain flour
200ml milk
3 tbsp crème fraiche
500g fresh salmon fillets, skinned and sliced into bite-sized chunks
½ tsp chopped fresh dill
1 tsp white wine vinegar
6 eggs
6 pieces of bread
sea salt
freshly ground black pepper

1 Heat the olive oil and butter in a sauté pan. Add the onion and cook for 10 minutes until soft.
2 Add the potatoes and peas and stir to combine. Sprinkle on the flour and stir in the milk and crème fraiche, then simmer over a low heat for 5 minutes.
3 Add the salmon chunks and cook for 2 minutes. Throw in the dill and season well with salt and pepper.
4 To poach the eggs, pour water into a frying pan to a depth of 3cm. Add the vinegar and bring to a simmer. Break 3 of the eggs into the pan, being careful not to break the yolks. Simmer for 2 minutes, then remove and drain. Cook the rest of the eggs in the same way.
5 Toast the bread. Serve dollops of the hash on the toast along with the poached eggs.

Baked vanilla cheesecake

This is definitely my favourite cheesecake – it's rich and creamy and never fails to set in the cooking time. It also has just the right amount of cheesecake topping. I've found that with some recipes you end up with a thin, measly topping that's a bit of a disappointment.

SERVES 6

200g gingernut biscuits
75g butter, melted
500g mascarpone cheese
200g crème fraiche
3 whole eggs
3 egg yolks
juice of ½ lemon
150g caster sugar
1 tbsp vanilla extract

1 Blitz the biscuits in a food processor until they are fine crumbs, then stir in the melted butter.
2 Spoon the crumb base into the bottom of a 21cm spring-clip cake tin. Chill in the fridge for 20 minutes or so while you prepare the filling.
3 Use the food processor for mixing the filling, as this ensures that the mixture gets evenly combined without the addition of too much air. Place the mascarpone, crème fraiche, eggs and yolks, lemon juice, caster sugar and vanilla extract in the food processor and mix until combined. Pour the mixture on to the biscuit base. Preheat the oven to 180°C/Gas 4.
4 Bring a kettle of water to the boil, then pour the boiling water into a roasting tin. Place the cake tin inside a couple of layers of foil so that they come up above the height of the tin, rather like an outer skin or layer.
5 Place the tin in the roasting tin and put it in the oven for 1 hour. Turn off the oven, open the oven door and leave the cheesecake to sit in the oven for another 20 minutes. Remove, then place the cheesecake in the fridge to chill before serving.

There may be snowy days in February, but it is often predominantly wet. If you have a vegetable patch it will look bare and the garden will be hiding any signs of the stirrings that may be going on underground. Most of us will be looking forward to the spring and good times to come. I find I start to crave a change of food, reflecting the way our bodies are in harmony with nature and the seasons, and I begin to cook some lighter meals as well as winter fare. River fish, such as salmon and trout, are coming into season and allow you to vary your menus, and you can still enjoy rabbit and the delicious game that's around and good value for money. By this time of year, it is easy to become bored with eating seasonally and I sometimes find myself looking longingly at the strawberries, asparagus and green beans that have been flown in from thousands of miles away. I resist the temptation, knowing that the strawberries will taste all the sweeter in June and the asparagus all the more delicious in May.

February.

One-pot chicken curry

Chicken curry is a favourite in many households. This version is more Thai in flavour than Indian or Sri Lankan, as it contains fish sauce but no curry powder. Even though there are potatoes in the curry I like to serve it with some boiled rice to make it really satisfying.

SERVES 6

2 tbsp vegetable oil
1.5kg chicken thighs and drumsticks on the bone, skin removed
1 tsp chilli flakes
3 tsp paprika
1 onion, finely chopped
2cm piece of fresh root ginger, peeled and grated
2 garlic cloves, very finely chopped
¼ tsp turmeric
1 tbsp fish sauce
200ml chicken stock
200ml coconut milk
200g baby new potatoes
200g frozen peas
12 cherry tomatoes, cut in half
sea salt
freshly ground black pepper

Boiled rice
500g basmati rice
½ tsp salt
750ml water

1 Heat the vegetable oil in a large saucepan and brown the chicken pieces, a few at a time, all over. Place the browned chicken to one side. Keep the pan on the heat, add the chilli flakes and paprika, then cook gently for 30 seconds.
2 Add the onion, ginger and garlic to the pan and cook on a low heat for 10 minutes, stirring occasionally.
3 Sprinkle on the turmeric and cook for 30 seconds more. Return the chicken pieces to the pan and add the fish sauce, stock, coconut milk, potatoes, peas and tomatoes. Bring to a simmer and cook gently for 40 minutes.
4 Check the seasoning and serve with boiled rice.

To prepare the boiled rice
5 Place the rice, salt and water in a large saucepan and bring to a lively boil. Reduce the heat to very low, cover the pan and cook the rice for 15 minutes. Stir once during the cooking time.
6 Remove the pan from the heat. Keep the rice covered and leave it undisturbed for 10 minutes more.

Three cheese and walnut tart

This tart is made using a French-style pastry – the kind used for quiche in France – which adds a light touch. The flavours are subtle and particularly good at this time of year. Serve the tart with a green salad and some nice crusty bread.

SERVES 6

100g feta cheese
250g ricotta cheese
40g Parmesan cheese, grated
2 eggs
200ml double cream
2 tsp Dijon mustard
½ tsp ground cumin
2 tbsp chopped basil leaves
50g walnuts, finely chopped
sea salt
freshly ground black pepper

Pastry
225g plain flour, plus extra for dusting the work surface
125g cold butter, cut into cubes
50g cold lard, cut into cubes
½ tsp salt
a pinch of caster sugar
100ml cold water

1 To make the pastry, place the flour, butter and lard in a food processor. Whizz until the mixture has the consistency of breadcrumbs. Add the salt and sugar and whizz again briefly. Pour on the water and mix again for a few seconds.
2 Turn the mixture out on to a floured surface and bring it together to make a ball of dough. Wrap the dough in clingfilm and chill for 20 minutes or so.
3 Place the cheeses in a mixing bowl. Add the eggs and cream and mix with a wooden spoon. Stir in the mustard, cumin and basil, then season with salt and pepper. Preheat the oven to 200°C/Gas 6.
4 Roll out the pastry and use it to line a 26cm quiche tin. Lay a sheet of baking parchment on top of the pastry – it should be large enough to go up the sides of the tart as well as covering the base. Pour some baking beans on top of the parchment. Place the tin on a baking sheet and bake the pastry in the oven for 15 minutes. Remove the beans and paper and place the pastry case back in the oven for 5 minutes.
5 Remove the pastry case from the oven. Scatter the walnuts over the bottom of the tart, then pour on the cheese mixture. Bake in the oven for 40 minutes until the tart is flecked with small areas of golden brown, but the filling is still soft to the touch. Serve hot or warm.

Pot-roast pork

There is nothing quite as comforting as a pot roast.

1 Preheat the oven to 200°C/Gas 6. Heat the olive oil in a casserole dish that can be used on the hob and in the oven. When the oil is hot, place the pork in the pan and brown it all over. This will take about 10 minutes.
2 Add the fennel, celery, apple, sage and onion and season well with salt and pepper. Bring everything to a sizzle over a high heat, then pour in the cider. Keep simmering for a couple of minutes and then cover the pan and place in the oven for 2 hours.
3 When the meat is cooked, remove it from the pan and set it aside to rest. Remove the vegetables with a slotted spoon and set them aside, then place the pan on a high heat on the stove and boil the liquid in the pan until reduced by half. Whisk in the crème fraiche and mustard, then check the seasoning.
4 Serve the pork in slices with the vegetables, the sauce from the pan and mashed potatoes.

To make the mashed potatoes
5 Boil the potatoes in salted water until tender.
6 Pass the potatoes through a potato ricer or use your preferred method to mash them. Return them to the pan and place over a low heat. Mix in the butter and milk and season to taste.

SERVES 6

1 tbsp olive oil
1.8kg rolled, boned pork shoulder
1 fennel bulb, sliced
2 celery stalks, roughly chopped
1 apple, cored and sliced
5 sage leaves
1 onion, finely sliced
500ml dry cider
2 tbsp crème fraiche
1 dsrtsp Dijon mustard
sea salt
freshly ground black pepper

Mashed potatoes
1kg potatoes, peeled and cut into quarters
40g butter
200ml warm milk
sea salt
freshly ground black pepper

Salmon with coriander dressing and puy lentils

Salmon and puy lentils are a wonderful combination. The nuttiness of the lentils offsets the richness of the oily fish perfectly.

SERVES 6

6 salmon fillets, skin on
olive oil

Puy lentils
300g puy lentils
1.4 litres chicken stock
2 shallots, finely sliced
70g pancetta, chopped
100g carrots, peeled and cut into 1cm cubes
1 sprig of thyme
1 x 400 can of cannellini beans, drained and rinsed
½ tsp sea salt
freshly ground black pepper

Coriander dressing
4 tbsp finely chopped coriander
2 garlic cloves, crushed
200ml extra virgin olive oil
zest and juice of ½ lemon
1 plum tomato, cut into 1cm cubes
sea salt
freshly ground black pepper

To prepare the puy lentils

1 Put the lentils in a saucepan with the stock, shallots, pancetta, carrots and thyme and bring to the boil. Reduce the heat, cover the pan and simmer for 25 minutes, stirring occasionally, by which time the lentils should be tender. Stir in the cannellini beans, season with salt and pepper and place to one side. You can reheat the lentils when the salmon is ready.

To prepare the coriander dressing

2 Place all the ingredients in a small serving bowl and mix gently with a spoon until everything is well combined. Season with plenty of salt and pepper.

To prepare and serve the salmon

3 Put a frying pan on a high heat. Brush the skin side of the salmon with a little olive oil, then lay 3 of the fillets, in the pan, skin side down, and fry for 2 minutes. Flip them over and fry for 2 more minutes. If your pieces of salmon are particularly thick you'll need to cook them for a little longer. Place the fillets to one side to keep warm and cook the rest in the same way.

4 Serve the salmon fillets on top of the lentils with a spoonful of the coriander dressing.

Open-faced cheese and potato omelette

Serve this with a watercress salad and some bread for a quick and nourishing supper.

SERVES 6

2 tbsp olive oil
1 garlic clove, crushed with a rolling pin but kept in 1 piece
100g white bread, sliced into 1.5cm thick slices and then cut into cubes
12 eggs (2 per person)
30g butter
200g potatoes, cooked and cut into 2cm chunks
100g Gruyère cheese, grated
1 tbsp chopped chives
1 tbsp chopped flat-leaf parsley
sea salt
freshly ground black pepper

Watercress salad
300g watercress
2 tbsp olive oil
¼ tbsp balsamic vinegar
sea salt
freshly ground black pepper

1 First make the croutons. Heat the olive oil in a frying pan and add the clove of garlic. Let the garlic sizzle for a minute and then remove and discard it.
2 Add the bread chunks to the oil and fry until they are golden brown. Remove them from the pan and place to one side. Preheat the grill.
3 Whisk the eggs in a bowl with some salt and pepper, until they are frothy. Heat half the butter in the frying pan and when it is foaming, pour in half the egg mixture.
4 Stir the eggs with a fork for a few seconds until they are starting to set. Using the fork, draw the egg mixture away from the sides of the pan, tilting the pan as you do so and letting the uncooked egg run to the sides.
5 Sprinkle on half the potatoes and half the cheese, herbs and croutons and place the omelette under the hot grill for 1 minute. You want the omelette to be slightly runny, so don't leave it under the grill for too long.
6 Use the rest of the ingredients to make a second omelette in exactly the same way. Serve with the watercress salad.

To prepare the watercress salad
7 Place the watercress in a serving dish and dress it with the olive oil and balsamic vinegar. Season with salt and black pepper.

Fried chicken legs with sautéed potatoes and spinach

The French have so many different ways of cooking chicken – all pretty delicious. In this excellent recipe, the chicken legs are fried and then doused in crème fraiche and Comté cheese. If you can't find Comté cheese, use Gruyère which will work just as well.

SERVES 6

25g butter
1 tbsp olive oil
6 chicken legs
4 carrots, cut into 5mm thick slices
3 leeks, thinly sliced
2 celery stalks, thinly sliced
225g button mushrooms, halved
2 tbsp crème fraiche
150g Comté cheese, grated
sea salt
freshly ground black pepper

Sautéed potatoes and spinach
2 tbsp olive oil
800g potatoes, peeled and cut into 2cm cubes
200g young spinach leaves
sea salt
freshly ground black pepper

1 Heat the butter and olive oil in a casserole dish. When the butter is bubbling, place 3 of the chicken legs, skin side down, in the dish. Brown for 1 minute, then season and put them to one side while you brown the rest. Set all the chicken to one side.
2 Keep the dish on the heat and add the carrots, leeks and celery. Cook for 3 minutes, stirring occasionally. Remove the vegetables and place them with the chicken legs. Preheat the oven to 200°C/Gas 6.
3 With the dish still on the heat, brown the mushrooms lightly, adding a little more oil if necessary. Put the chicken and vegetables back in the dish, making sure that the chicken legs are skin side up, and season. Cover the dish with a lid and bake in the oven for 40 minutes.
4 Take the dish out of the oven, stir in the crème fraiche and check the seasoning. Sprinkle the chicken with cheese and place the dish under a hot grill until the cheese has melted. Serve with the potatoes and spinach.

To prepare the sautéed potatoes and spinach
5 Heat the olive oil in a large sauté pan. Add the potato cubes and fry, stirring occasionally, until the potatoes start to turn golden brown. Reduce the heat, add salt and pepper, then cover the pan and cook the potatoes for 10 minutes, stirring occasionally.
6 Remove the lid, increase the heat and fry to crispen up the potatoes a little. Turn the heat down again and scatter on the spinach. Cover and cook for 5 minutes, by which time the spinach will have wilted into the potatoes. Stir carefully and check the seasoning.

Braised guinea fowl with root vegetable gratin

The root vegetable gratin makes this meal really special and goes perfectly with the guinea fowl, which is also a treat. If you can't get guinea fowl, use small chickens.

SERVES 6

2 x 1kg guinea fowl
2 sprigs of rosemary
2 sprigs of sage
2 tbsp olive oil
1 onion, finely sliced
1 celery stalk, finely chopped
1 carrot, thinly sliced
a knob of butter
500ml pear cider
6 shallots, cut in half
2 garlic cloves, peeled but left whole
sea salt
freshly ground black pepper

Root vegetable gratin
250g celeriac, peeled and cut into 2mm slices
200g parsnip, peeled and cut on the slight diagonal to 2mm slices
200g sweet potato, peeled and cut into 2mm slices
350g potatoes, peeled and cut into 2mm slices
2 garlic cloves, crushed
300ml double cream, mixed with 200ml milk
50g Gruyère cheese, grated
sea salt
freshly ground black pepper

1 Preheat the oven to 200°C/Gas 6. Place a rosemary and sage sprig in the neck cavity of each guinea fowl
2 Heat the olive oil in a casserole dish and add the onion, celery and carrot. Sauté for 3 minutes, stirring frequently. Add the butter and when it is foaming, place the guinea fowl in the casserole, breasts down, and brown them. Turn the birds on their sides and brown for a few minutes.
3 Keeping the heat high, add the cider, then turn the heat down and simmer for 3 minutes. Add the shallots and garlic, then season well with salt and pepper. Cover the pan and place in the oven to cook for 1 hour.
4 Remove the guinea fowl from the casserole, cover them with foil and set aside to rest for 10 minutes before carving. Spoon some of the juices and shallots over the meat and serve with the gratin and a salad.

To make the vegetable gratin
5 Preheat the oven to 200°C/Gas 6. Lay the celeriac in the bottom of a gratin dish. Next, make a layer of sweet potato and parsnip and finish off with the potatoes. Season well with salt and pepper.
6 Mix the crushed garlic with the milk and cream and pour over the root vegetables. Cover the gratin dish with a sheet of foil and bake in the oven for 50 minutes. Remove the foil from the gratin dish, sprinkle the cheese on top and put the dish back in the oven for 20 minutes.

Chocolate peanut milkshakes

My children love these milkshakes. The peanut butter adds a great twist to the usual chocolate flavour.

SERVES 6

- 200g dark chocolate, broken into pieces
- 100g milk chocolate, broken into pieces
- 3 tbsp peanut butter
- 600ml milk
- 1 x 500ml tub of vanilla ice cream

1 Place the dark and milk chocolate in a glass bowl and set it over a pan of gently simmering water. Make sure the bottom of the bowl doesn't touch the water. When the chocolate has almost melted, give it a stir and then remove the bowl from the heat.
2 Spoon the chocolate into a blender and add the peanut butter and milk. Blend until smooth and creamy.
3 Add as much of the ice cream as you can fit into the blender and whizz again. Pour into glasses with a spoonful or two of the remaining ice cream.

Gingerbread cake

This is the simplest of recipes – one of those throw-it-all-in-and-mix cakes and just right for everyday baking.

MAKES 1 X 20CM CAKE

- 60g butter
- 110g treacle
- 30g ground almonds
- 60g caster sugar
- 110g plain flour
- 2 tsp ground ginger
- 1 tsp baking powder
- 1 tsp mixed spice
- 2 eggs

1 Preheat the oven to 180°C/Gas 4. Grease a 20cm cake tin and line the base with baking parchment.
2 Melt the butter and treacle in a saucepan over a gentle heat. Add the other ingredients and mix with a wooden spoon. Spoon into the cake tin and bake for 25 minutes.
3 Turn the cake out and leave it to cool on a wire rack before slicing and serving.

Pecan and cinnamon biscuits

Home-made biscuits are so much more delicious than the bought versions. They keep well, too, so it's worth making a large batch. These biscuits are a great way of getting children to eat pecan nuts which are highly nutritious.

MAKES ABOUT 22

225g butter, at room temperature, plus extra for greasing
110g caster sugar
225g self-raising flour
½ tsp ground cinnamon
50g chocolate, broken into pieces
50g pecans, roughly chopped

1 Preheat the oven to 180°C/Gas 4. Lightly grease a baking tray.
2 Place the butter and sugar in a mixing bowl and beat with an electric hand-whisk, until light and fluffy. Add the flour and mix again briefly until the mixture starts to come together. Stir in the cinnamon, chocolate and nuts.
3 Form the mixture into 3cm balls and place them on the baking tray. Flatten each biscuit very slightly with a fork and bake them in the oven for 15 minutes until brown.
4 Leave the biscuits to cool slightly, then transfer them to a wire rack to cool.

Scones

Scones are simple to make, which is exactly what everyday home cooking is about. There are lots of different theories as to how to make good scones, but here is my version. This only makes six scones, so double the ingredients if you want more.

MAKES 6 SCONES

- 225g plain flour, plus extra for dusting the work surface
- 50g cold butter, cut into cubes, plus extra for greasing
- 1 tbsp caster sugar
- 2 tsp baking powder
- 75ml milk
- 75ml double cream
- 2 tbsp of milk, for brushing the tops

1 Preheat the oven to 220°C/Gas 7. Lightly grease a baking sheet.
2 Place the flour and butter in a food processor and whizz until the mixture resembles breadcrumbs. Add the sugar and baking powder and mix. Add the 75ml of milk and the double cream and give the mixture the briefest stir.
3 Turn the mixture out on to a work surface and bring it together with your hands to make a soft ball of dough.
4 Lightly flour the work surface. Using a rolling pin, roll out the dough to a thickness of 2.5cm. Cut out the scones with a 6cm biscuit cutter and place them on the baking sheet. Brush the tops with milk.
5 Bake the scones for 12 minutes, then place them on a wire rack to cool until ready to serve.

Toffee bananas with pain perdu

Children love this pudding – and so do adults. It is very rich though, so be warned!

SERVES 6

25g butter
3 bananas, thickly sliced widthways
2 tbsp soft brown sugar
250ml double cream
vanilla ice cream, for serving

Pain perdu
6 slices of white bread (with a soft crust)
150ml double cream
2 eggs
1 egg yolk
2 tbsp caster sugar
a knob of butter, for frying

1 Make the toffee bananas first. Heat the butter in a medium saucepan, then add the bananas. Fry them over a low heat for 2 minutes, stirring gently from time to time.
2 Sprinkle on the sugar and pour the cream into the pan. Stir the cream in gently and continue cooking over a very low heat for 5 minutes. Keep the bananas warm while you get on with the rest of the pudding.
3 Now make the pain perdu. Cut the bread slices diagonally across to make 12 triangles.
4 Put the cream, whole eggs, egg yolk and sugar into a mixing bowl and mix well with a whisk. Dip 6 the triangles of bread into the mixture until they are completely sodden.
5 Heat the butter in a frying pan and when it is foaming, add the 6 bread triangles and fry for 1 minute before turning and frying on the other side. Be careful as the bread will burn very easily. Meanwhile, dunk the remaining 6 slices of bread into the mixture. Remove the first batch from the pan and keep them warm while you cook the rest.
6 Place 2 slices of pain perdu on each plate. Pile on the toffee bananas and add a scoop of vanilla ice cream.

Turkey steaks with bean and avocado salad and fried eggs

This recipe turns the humble turkey steak into something far more interesting. The light bean and avocado salad is the perfect accompaniment.

SERVES 6

6 turkey steaks
9 eggs
3 garlic cloves, crushed
4 tbsp finely chopped flat-leaf parsley
200g white breadcrumbs
olive oil, for frying
sea salt
freshly ground black pepper

Bean and avocado salad
1 x 400g can of borlotti beans, drained and rinsed
4 spring onions, chopped
80g rocket leaves
8 cherry tomatoes, cut in half
¼ cucumber, diced
1 avocado

Dressing
3 tbsp olive oil
1 tbsp balsamic vinegar
sea salt
freshly ground black pepper

1 Place the turkey steaks on a board and pound them with a meat hammer or a rolling pin until they are about 1cm thick. Season the steaks well with salt and pepper.
2 Beat the 3 of the eggs in a large bowl and add the garlic and 2 tablespoons of the parsley. Place the turkey steaks in the bowl and leave them to soak in the egg mixture for at least 30 minutes – the longer the better.
3 Spread the breadcrumbs on a large plate. Remove a steak from the egg mixture and press each side into the breadcrumbs. Press the coated steak between your hands to help the crumbs stick firmly. Coat all the steaks in the same way.
4 Heat the olive oil in a frying pan. Fry the steaks, a couple at a time, for 2 minutes on each side, by which time the breadcrumbs should be golden brown and the meat cooked through. Keep the steaks warm on a plate while you cook the others.
5 Fry the remaining 6 eggs and lay an egg on each turkey steak. Scatter with the rest of the parsley and serve with the bean and avocado salad.

To make the salad
6 Put the drained and rinsed beans in a bowl. Add the chopped spring onions, rocket leaves, tomatoes and cucumber. Peel the avocado, dice the flesh and add to the salad. Mix all the dressing ingredients together and toss with the salad.

Tomato bean soup and croque hot dogs

We had these hot dogs on the way back from France once and they were very popular with my hungry family. I recreated them at home to go with this warming winter soup.

SERVES 6

2 tbsp olive oil
1 celery stalk, finely chopped
1 onion, finely chopped
1 leek, trimmed and thinly sliced
250g new potatoes, peeled and cut into 1cm discs
1 x 440g can of cannellini beans, drained and rinsed
1kg tomato passata
1 litre chicken or vegetable stock
sea salt
freshly ground black pepper

Croque hot dogs
200g Gruyère cheese, grated
3 tbsp double cream
2 tsp Worcestershire sauce
2 tsp Dijon mustard
1 or 2 French sticks
6 frankfurter sausages
freshly ground black pepper

1 Heat the olive oil in a large saucepan. Add the celery, onion, leek and potatoes and cook for 5 minutes. Add the beans, passata and stock, then cover the pan and simmer gently for 45 minutes.
2 Season well with salt and pepper and serve with the croque hot dogs.

To make the croque hot dogs
3 Mix the cheese, cream, Worcestershire sauce and mustard in a bowl until combined. Season with black pepper.
4 Cut the French stick widthways into lengths to fit the frankfurters. Next cut the bread pieces lengthways part way through so that the bread is still in one piece. Spread the insides of the bread with a spoonful of the cheese mixture and then add a frankfurter – rather like a hot dog roll.
5 Place the filled bread pieces on a baking sheet and place under a hot grill for 5 minutes.

Thai-style fish cakes

This recipe shows that by opening a few cans and doing a little chopping you can end up with a great home-cooked meal. You can serve with some baked potatoes as well as salad if you would like more bulk.

SERVES 6

300g canned tuna, drained
200g canned white crab meat
200g smoked mackerel
12 spring onions, finely chopped
2 garlic cloves, very finely chopped
1 egg
125g ricotta cheese
2 tbsp sweet chilli sauce
1 red chilli, seeded and finely chopped
2 tbsp finely chopped chives
2 tbsp finely chopped coriander
2 tbsp finely chopped basil
2 tbsp finely chopped mint
2 tsp sesame oil
2 tbsp vegetable oil, for frying
sea salt
freshly ground black pepper

1 Place all the ingredients, except the oils, in a mixing bowl and mix thoroughly. Taste for seasoning and add more salt and pepper as you feel necessary.
2 Shape the mixture into 12 round cakes and leave them to chill in the fridge for 30 minutes.
3 Heat the oils in a frying pan and fry a couple of the fish cakes for about 2 minutes, then turn and cook for another 2 minutes. Once the fish cakes are cooked through and golden, set them aside to keep warm while you fry the rest.

Rosemary and tomato risotto

Many people today feel that they don't have time to cook meals from scratch, yet preparing good food is so vital for the health of our families. Risotto is a recipe that takes a while, and you do have to stand at the stove and stir, but the result is worth the effort.

SERVES 6

1.2 litres chicken stock
1 tbsp olive oil
25g butter
2 shallots, finely chopped
100g chopped pancetta
500g Arborio risotto rice
1 sprig of rosemary, leaves removed and finely chopped
1 x 400g can of chopped tomatoes
a knob of butter
2 tbsp grated Parmesan cheese
sea salt
freshly ground black pepper

1 Pour the chicken stock into a saucepan and bring it to a simmer. Taste the stock for seasoning and add some salt and pepper if necessary.
2 Heat the olive oil and butter in a large pan. Fry the shallots and pancetta for 2 minutes over a medium heat, then stir in the rice and rosemary and fry for 2 minutes. Pour in the tomatoes and stir until most of the liquid has been absorbed.
3 Start adding the hot stock, a couple of ladlefuls at a time, stirring frequently and adding more stock as the liquid is absorbed. Continue for about 25 minutes until the rice is cooked but still has a slight bite to it.
4 Remove the saucepan from the heat, then add the butter and cheese and stir until absorbed. Check the seasoning and add more salt and black pepper to taste.

Tagliatelle with venison and rosemary sauce

I use a lot of rosemary in my cooking, partly because it grows in a sheltered spot in my garden and so is available all year round. I think rosemary is worth its weight in gold as an ingredient. It does have a strong aroma and taste, but it still harmonises very well with all meats, most fish and many vegetables.

SERVES 6

1 large leg of venison
400ml red wine
2–3 tbsp olive oil
1 onion, finely chopped
1 sprig of rosemary, leaves removed and finely chopped
2 garlic cloves, finely chopped
1 tbsp flour
150ml water
1 tbsp tomato purée
600g tagliatelle
sea salt
freshly ground black pepper

1 Cut the meat off the bone in large pieces – don't chop it up at this stage. Place the meat in a bowl, pour over the wine and leave it to marinate for at least an hour.
2 Remove the meat from the wine and set the wine aside. Chop the meat into 1cm pieces.
3 Heat a tablespoon of olive oil in a large pan. Add the onion, rosemary and garlic and cook on a low heat for 5 minutes. Remove the onion, rosemary and garlic and place to one side.
4 Add another tablespoon of olive oil and start to brown the meat, a handful at a time. As the meat browns, remove it and place with the onions and garlic, while you do the next batch. Add more oil if the pan seems dry.
5 Once you have browned all the meat, keep the pan on the heat. Pour in the wine from the marinade and let it simmer for 2 minutes.
6 Put the meat, onion, garlic and rosemary back in the pan and stir in the flour. Add the water and tomato purée, then stir and season with salt and pepper. Simmer very gently, covered, for 1 hour.
7 Cook the pasta in salted boiling water according to the packet instructions. Drain and serve with the sauce.

Lemony lamb cutlets

Lamb cutlets are good at absorbing a flavoursome marinade. They are super-quick to fry and the sauce made with the marinade is delicious. Some roast potatoes are good with this.

SERVES 6

1kg lamb cutlets
2 tbsp olive oil
a sprig of rosemary, leaves removed and finely chopped
a knob of butter
1 tbsp finely chopped flat-leaf parsley

Marinade
100ml olive oil
grated zest and juice of 1 lemon
1 tbsp rinsed capers
3 garlic cloves, crushed
sea salt
freshly ground black pepper

Roast potatoes
1kg potatoes, peeled, quartered and rinsed in cold water
1 tbsp goose fat
sea salt

1 Place the lamb cutlets in a large bowl and cover them with the marinade ingredients. Season well with salt and pepper and leave in the fridge for 30 minutes or so.
2 Heat the 2 tablespoons of olive oil in a large sauté pan and add the rosemary leaves. Remove the cutlets from the marinade and set the marinade aside for later. Gently fry the cutlets in batches for about 2 minutes on each side until golden brown – you may need to cook them for a little longer if they are thick. Put the chops on a warm serving dish as they are cooked.
3 Keep the pan on the heat and pour in the marinade. Stir in the knob of butter, then add the parsley and stir. Pour this sauce over the cutlets and serve with spring greens and roast potatoes.

To prepare the roast potatoes
4 Preheat the oven to 220°C/Gas 7. Parboil the potatoes in salted water for 6 minutes. Drain them and then bash them around in the pan before you put them in the roasting tin.
5 Add the goose fat and then roast in the oven for 50–60 minutes until golden brown, turning them occasionally during this time.

Roast chicken Dijonnaise and green salad with warm pancetta

This is a heavenly roast chicken dish and great served with this tasty green salad.

SERVES 6

2 shallots, finely sliced
2 x 1.5kg chickens
2 tbsp Dijon mustard
4 tbsp crème fraiche
a few sprigs of thyme
50ml red wine
100ml chicken stock
(a stock cube will do)
sea salt
freshly ground black pepper

Green salad with warm pancetta
400g salad leaves
70g pancetta, chopped
2 tbsp olive oil
½ tbsp balsamic vinegar
sea salt
freshly ground black pepper

1 Preheat the oven to 200°C/Gas 6. Scatter the shallots in a roasting tin that can be placed on the hob and put the chickens on top. Spread each bird with mustard and season well with salt and pepper.
2 Dollop the crème fraiche on top of the chickens and wedge the thyme sprigs between the breasts and legs.
3 Pop the birds into the oven and roast for 1 ½ hours. After an hour, baste the chickens with the juices that should by now be accumulating in the roasting tin.
4 At the end of the cooking time, check that the juices are running clear from the chickens and remove them from the tin. Place them on a carving plate or board, cover with foil and leave them to rest for 20–30 minutes before carving.
5 Place the roasting tin on the stove on a medium heat and stir the juices as they start to sizzle. Add the wine, then scrape up any crusty bits from the bottom of the tin while continuing to stir. Add the stock and simmer very gently for 15 minutes or so.
6 Pour the gravy into a jug and serve with the carved chicken, green salad and roast potatoes.

To make the green salad with warm pancetta
7 Place the salad leaves in a serving bowl. Fry the chopped pancetta in a pan and add it to the salad just before serving. Mix the olive oil, vinegar and seasoning in a small bowl and pour the dressing over the salad.

Tiramisu ice cream cake

This is my adaptation of the traditional tiramisu, which features on restaurant menus thoroughout Italy.

SERVES 6

3 eggs
80g caster sugar
70g plain flour
a pinch of salt
120ml strong coffee
3 tbsp brandy

Topping
400ml double cream
3 egg whites
3 egg yolks
4 tbsp caster sugar
50g dark chocolate, finely grated

1 First make the cake. Grease and line a 23cm round cake tin. Preheat the oven to 180°C/Gas 4.
2 Whisk the eggs and sugar in a bowl with an electric beater for about 3 minutes, until thick and mousse-like. Using a metal spoon, fold in the flour and a pinch of salt.
3 Spoon the mixture into the cake tin and bake in the oven for 20 minutes, until a skewer inserted into the centre of the cake comes out clean. Remove the cake from the tin and place it on a wire rack to cool.
4 Take a square cake tin, measuring 17 x 17cm. Mix the coffee and brandy in a small bowl. Cut the sponge cake into sections to fit snugly into the bottom of the square tin. Dip the cake pieces into the coffee and brandy and then lay them in the bottom of the tin.
5 Whip the double cream in a bowl. Whisk the egg whites in another bowl. In a third bowl, beat the yolks with the sugar for 2 minutes until pale yellow and slightly thicker. Fold the egg yolk mixture into the cream, and then fold in the whites. Spoon the resulting mixture on to the cake. Sprinkle the chocolate over the top and pop the cake into the freezer for at least an hour before serving.
6 Cut the cake into squares from the tin to serve. Put the rest back into the freezer.

Pale ginger and pear cake

This pale ginger cake is different from the usual dark gingerbread, and the pears add a certain moistness.

MAKES 1 X 23CM CAKE

225g butter, softened, plus extra for greasing
225g caster sugar
4 eggs, beaten
280g self-raising flour
¼ tsp ground cinnamon
80g stem ginger, finely chopped
2 tbsp ginger syrup (from the stem ginger)
2 tbsp milk
2 pears, peeled and thinly sliced

1 Grease a 23cm cake tin and line the base with baking parchment. Preheat the oven to 180°C/Gas 4.
2 Using an electric beater or food mixer, cream the butter and sugar until pale in colour and fluffy. Add the eggs, 1 at a time, mixing after each addition, then fold in the flour and cinnamon. Add the ginger, syrup, milk and pears and gently mix to combine.
3 Spoon the cake batter into the cake tin and bake for 1 hour until firm to the touch of your fingertips. Leave to cool in the cake tin for 20 minutes before turning out on to a plate. Serve warm or cold.

Baked eggs with smoked salmon

There is something very comforting about baked eggs, and the addition of smoked salmon makes these particularly good.

SERVES 6

a knob of butter, for greasing
12 tbsp double cream
2–3 tbsp finely chopped dill
160g smoked salmon, roughly chopped
12 eggs
sea salt
freshly ground black pepper

1 Preheat the oven to 190°C/Gas 5. Butter the insides of 12 ramekins. Pour a tablespoon of cream into each ramekin and add a pinch of dill.
2 Place the ramekins in a roasting tin on top of the stove and pour in water to a depth of a couple of centimetres. Bring the water to a simmer and keep simmering until the cream has warmed through and you can see that the butter on the sides of the ramekins has melted.
3 Divide the salmon equally between the ramekins, then break an egg into each. Place the ramekins on a baking sheet and pop them into the oven for 8 minutes – the eggs should still have a slight wobble to them at the end of this cooking time. Serve with lots of warm toast.

Lamb neck fillets in red wine

This is great served with some swede cooked in butter and perhaps some roast potatoes (see page 94).

SERVES 6

3 lamb neck fillets, cut in half lengthways
flour, seasoned with salt and pepper
4 tbsp olive oil
1 onion, finely chopped
2 garlic cloves, finely chopped
2 carrots, finely sliced
1 celery stalk, finely chopped
300ml red wine
200ml lamb or beef stock
3 sprigs of rosemary
sea salt
freshly ground black pepper

Swede
1 swede, peeled and cut into 1 cm cubes
15g butter
sea salt
freshly ground black pepper

1 Preheat the oven to 180°C/Gas 4. Roll the pieces of neck fillet in enough seasoned flour to coat them lightly.
2 Heat 4 tablespoons of olive oil in a large casserole dish. Add the neck fillet pieces and brown them until the flour has formed a golden brown crust. Turn each one so that they brown all over. Remove the fillets from the pan, place them on a warm plate and set aside.
3 Return the casserole dish to the heat. Add the onion, garlic, carrots and celery and cook on a medium heat for 5 minutes. Pour on the wine and let it bubble away for another 5 minutes. Add the stock and stir.
4 Put the neck fillets back in the dish. Add the rosemary sprigs and season with salt and pepper. Cover the dish with a lid, place it in the oven and cook for about 2 hours, by which time the lamb will be as tender as can be.

To cook the swede
5 Place the swede in a small saucepan with the butter. Cook on a medium heat until you hear the butter fizzing. Reduce the temperature, cover the saucepan with a lid and cook gently for 12 minutes, stirring occasionally, until the swede is tender. Season with salt and pepper.

Rabbit and prune stew with mashed potatoes

This is a typically French way of eating rabbit. I use two rabbits for six people.

SERVES 6

2 rabbits, jointed
500ml red wine
2 carrots, peeled and roughly chopped
1 large onion, finely chopped
2 garlic cloves, finely chopped
1 sprig of rosemary
10 sage leaves
1 tbsp olive oil
20g butter
1 tbsp flour
1 tsp mustard powder
500ml chicken stock
100g soft pitted prunes, roughly chopped
1 swede, peeled and cut into 2cm pieces
2 tbsp finely chopped flat-leaf parsley
sea salt
freshly ground black pepper

Mashed potatoes
1kg potatoes, peeled and cut into quarters
40g butter
200ml warm milk
sea salt
freshly ground black pepper

1 Place the rabbit pieces in a bowl with the wine, carrots, onion, garlic, rosemary and sage. Season with salt and pepper. Leave to marinate for as long as you can – overnight is good, but if you only have 30 minutes, that's fine too.
2 Remove the rabbits, vegetables and herbs and set the marinade liquid aside for use later. Heat the olive oil and butter in a casserole-type pan, then brown the rabbit a few pieces at a time and set them aside.
3 Once all the rabbit pieces have been browned, keep the saucepan on the heat and add the onion, carrot and garlic from the marinade. Cook gently for 5 minutes, stirring occasionally. Sprinkle on the flour and mustard powder and stir to combine.
4 Return the rabbit to the pan and pour in the marinade liquid. Add the stock, the prunes and swede, season well and simmer for 30 minutes more. Sprinkle with the parsley and serve with plenty of mashed potato.

To make the mashed potatoes
5 Boil the potatoes in salted water until tender.
6 Pass the potatoes through a potato ricer or use your preferred method to mash them. Return them to the pan and place over a low heat. Mix in the butter and milk and season to taste.

Cheese, bean and onion pie

This simple meat-free pie makes a really sustaining mid-week supper.

SERVES 6

1 tbsp olive oil
1 small onion, finely chopped
6 spring onions, trimmed and thinly sliced
1 celery stalk, finely chopped
120g potatoes, peeled, cut into quarters and cooked until tender
200g canned borlotti beans, drained and rinsed
100g frozen petit pois
a handful of torn basil leaves
4 tbsp double cream
250g Cheddar cheese, grated
sea salt
freshly ground black pepper

Pastry
340g plain flour, plus extra for dusting work surface
170g cold butter, cut into cubes
a pinch of salt
1 egg yolk
3 tbsp cold water
1 egg, beaten, to glaze

1 Preheat the oven to 200°C/Gas 6. Place a baking tray in the oven to heat.
2 To make the pastry, place the flour, butter and salt in a food processor and whizz until the mixture resembles breadcrumbs. Add the egg yolk and water and mix again briefly. Turn the mixture out on to the work surface and bring together into a ball of dough. Wrap in clingfilm and chill in the fridge for 30 minutes.
3 For the filling, heat the olive oil in a frying pan and cook the onion, spring onions and celery for 5 minutes until soft. Spoon everything into a bowl and mix in the potatoes, beans, peas, basil, cream and cheese, then season well with salt and pepper.
4 Roll out half the pastry on a floured surface and use it to line a 24cm pie plate. Pile in the filling, then roll out the remaining pastry and cover the pie. Press the edges together to seal and trim them neatly.
5 Brush the pastry top with the beaten egg , then place the pie on the hot baking sheet and bake for 35 minutes. Serve with a green salad.

Pasta with prawns and pepper

This definitely qualifies as a '30-minute meal', with minimal washing up as well.

SERVES 6

1 tbsp olive oil
1 garlic clove, finely chopped
1 red pepper, cored, seeded and roughly chopped
400g raw prawns (shelled weight)
50ml water
squeeze of fresh lemon juice
1 tbsp roughly chopped basil leaves
1 tbsp double cream
600g spaghetti
sea salt
freshly ground black pepper

1 Heat the olive oil in a sauté pan, then add the garlic and red pepper. Cook for about 15 minutes over a gentle heat, stirring occasionally.
2 Turn up the heat and add the prawns, cooking them for 30 seconds or so until they turn pink. Add the water and lemon juice and stir, then throw in the basil and stir for a few seconds more.
3 Take out 3 tablespoons of the prawn and pepper mixture and liquidise until fairly smooth. Return the purée to the pan with the whole prawns and stir in the cream over a gentle heat. Season with salt and pepper.
4 Meanwhile, cook the spaghetti in boiling salted water according to the packet instructions. Drain the spaghetti, toss with the sauce and serve.

Pork tenderloin medallions with mustard sauce and red cabbage

Pork tenderloin is an economical cut of meat that is easy to prepare and cooks beautifully. Red cabbage is just right with this.

SERVES 6

2 eggs
100g white breadcrumbs
1 pork tenderloin, cut widthways into 1.5cm thick slices (medallions)
25g butter
1 tbsp olive oil
100ml white wine
100ml chicken stock (a stock cube will do)
1 tsp Dijon mustard
1 tbsp crème fraiche
sea salt
freshly ground black pepper

Red cabbage
1 tbsp olive oil
1 onion, finely diced
70g sliced pancetta, finely chopped
1 tbsp pistachio nuts
1 medium red cabbage, cored and thinly sliced
1 tbsp soft brown sugar
2 tbsp red wine vinegar
sea salt
freshly ground black pepper

1 Beat the eggs in a small bowl and set aside. Spread the breadcrumbs on a plate.
2 Dip the sliced pork pieces into the egg and then into breadcrumbs, patting each piece of pork to make sure that the crumbs stick and the slice is nicely coated.
3 Heat the butter and oil in a frying pan until the butter starts to sizzle. Add a few slices of the breaded pork and fry for 3 minutes, then turn and fry for another 3 minutes on the other side. By this time the breadcrumbs on both sides should be golden brown and the pork cooked through. Remove from the pan and keep the slices warm while you cook the rest.
4 Once all the pork is cooked, return the empty pan to the heat and pour in the wine. Let it simmer for a minute, then add the stock, mustard and the crème fraiche and simmer for 3 minutes on a low heat. Season to taste with salt and pepper.
5 Serve the pork with the sauce, but don't drench it. A spoonful with each serving is just right.

To cook the red cabbage
6 Heat the olive oil in a medium-sized saucepan and add the onion, pancetta and pistachio nuts. Cook over a medium heat for 10 minutes, stirring occasionally, or until the onion is nice and soft.
7 Add the cabbage, sugar and vinegar, then season well with salt and pepper. Cover the pan and cook the cabbage on a gentle heat for 30 minutes, giving it an occasional lazy stir. Serve with the pork and perhaps some mashed potatoes (see page 102).

Normandy chicken in cider

Plain roast chicken on a Sunday can get a bit tedious by this stage in the winter, so try this delicious variation.

SERVES 6

- 2 tbsp olive oil
- a knob of butter, plus extra for spreading on the chickens
- 1 onion, finely chopped
- 50g chicken livers, chopped
- 1 tsp dried tarragon
- 300g sausage meat
- 2 slices of stale white bread (100g in total), soaked in a little cold water
- 2 x 1.5kg chickens
- 12 shallots, peeled and halved
- 500ml cider
- sea salt
- freshly ground black pepper

1 Preheat the oven to 220°C/Gas 7.
2 Heat the olive oil and butter in a sauté pan. Add the onion, livers and tarragon and fry gently for 5 minutes. Add the sausage meat and fry for a few minutes until it has lost its pinkness. Turn the mixture out into a bowl.
3 Squeeze as much water as possible from the bread slices, then add the bread to the sausage meat. Mix well until everything is thoroughly combined. Season with salt and pepper.
4 Divide the mixture in half and use it to stuff the neck cavities of the chickens.
5 Smear both chickens with butter and season them well with salt and pepper. Put the birds in a large roasting tin and scatter the shallots around them. Place the tin in the oven for 15 minutes to brown the chickens.
6 Meanwhile, return the sauté pan to the stove on a medium heat and add the cider. Let it simmer for a few minutes.
7 Remove the chickens from the oven and turn the oven down to 190°C/Gas 5. Pour the cider into the roasting tin, cover the chickens with foil and put them back in the oven for 1 hour and 15 minutes. Let the birds rest for 30 minutes before carving. Scoop out the stuffing and serve with the chicken.

Sticky toffee pecan pudding with toffee sauce

A good sticky toffee pudding is hard to beat, especially if served with cream or vanilla ice cream when you're feeling extra indulgent.

SERVES 6

150g stoned dates, roughly chopped
100ml water
1 tsp bicarbonate of soda
50g butter, at room temperature, plus extra for greasing
150g caster sugar
2 eggs
225g plain flour
1 tsp baking powder
½ tsp mixed spice
50g pecan nuts, roughly chopped

Toffee sauce
300ml double cream
225g soft brown sugar
100g butter

1 Preheat the oven to 180°C/Gas 4. Grease a 20 x 25cm brownie tin.
2 Place the dates in a small saucepan with the water and bicarbonate of soda. Bring to a simmer, then remove the pan from the heat and set to one side.
3 Put the butter and sugar in a mixing bowl and beat until combined. Beat in the eggs, then the flour, baking powder and mixed spice. Add the dates and their liquid to the mixture, then the nuts and mix them in evenly.
4 Spoon the mixture into the brownie tray and bake for 30 minutes or until a skewer inserted into the middle of the pudding comes away cleanly. Serve cut into slices, with the toffee sauce poured on top.

To make the sauce
5 Place all the ingredients in a pan and warm through on a low heat until everything has melted and combined. Stir well.

Almond and lemon spice cake

This cake makes a lovely dessert or a snack and would be fine for breakfast as well, served with some fruit and plain yoghurt.

MAKES 1 LOAF

125g butter, at room temperature, plus extra for greasing
125g soft brown sugar
juice and grated zest of 1 lemon
175g ground almonds
2 tbsp crème fraiche
3 eggs, separated into yolks and whites
50g self-raising flour
¼ tsp mixed spice
¼ tsp ground cinnamon

1 Grease a 1-litre loaf tin and line it with baking parchment. Preheat the oven to 180°C/Gas 4.
2 Using an electric hand-whisk, cream the butter and sugar in a bowl until light and fluffy. Add the lemon juice, zest and ground almonds and mix until combined. Add the crème fraiche, egg yolks, flour and spices and mix again.
3 In a separate bowl, whisk the egg whites until they stand in stiff peaks. Using a metal spoon, fold them into the cake mixture.
4 Spoon the mixture into the loaf tin and bake for 55 minutes. To check whether the cake is done insert a skewer into the centre. It should come away clean but if not, put the cake back into the oven for 5 minutes.
5 Leave the cake to cool in the tin for 10 minutes, then turn it out on to a wire rack to cool completely.

Rabbit and leek pie

I find it hard not to remember 'The Tale of the Flopsy Bunnies' by Beatrix Potter when I think of rabbit pie, as I'm sure that this is where the bunnies would have ended up had they not escaped the clutches of Mr McGregor. Thoughts like these put people off cooking with rabbit, but I think it's time to put such ideas aside. If we want to keep eating meat in the quantities we are, then we do have to look at alternatives to the traditional beef, chicken, pork and lamb.

SERVES 6

2 rabbits, gutted and jointed
200ml white wine
1 bay leaf
2 sprigs of rosemary
2 tbsp olive oil
20g butter
1 onion, finely chopped
1 celery stalk, finely sliced
2 leeks, rinsed and sliced widthways into 1cm pieces
100ml dry sherry
20g flour
2 tsp Dijon mustard
2 tbsp crème fraiche
1 tbsp soy sauce
1 x 230g sheet of ready-rolled puff pastry
sea salt
freshly ground black pepper

1 Place the rabbit joints in a large saucepan with the wine, bay leaf and rosemary sprigs. Pour in enough water to just cover and season well with salt and pepper. Bring the pan to a simmer, cover with a lid and cook the rabbit for 1 hour and 15 minutes.
2 Remove the rabbit joints from the pan and reserve the cooking stock for later. When the rabbits are cool enough to handle, strip the meat from the bones, leaving it in large chunks. Preheat the oven to 200°C/Gas 6.
3 Heat the olive oil and butter in a large saucepan. Add the onion and celery and cook for 10 minutes until soft. Add the leeks and stir for a few seconds. Pour on the sherry and cook for 1 minute, then sprinkle on the flour and stir. Add the rabbit meat, 350ml of the rabbit stock, mustard, crème fraiche and soy sauce and stir well, then bring to a simmer.
4 Check the seasoning, then spoon the filling into a 24cm pie dish. Cover with the puff pastry and bake in the oven for 20 minutes until golden brown.

Potato and spinach rarebit cakes

This is a super meat-free meal.

SERVES 6

1kg potatoes, peeled and cut into quarters
800g young spinach leaves
2 shallots, finely chopped
¼ tsp grated nutmeg
plain flour, for dusting
olive oil, for frying
sea salt
freshly ground black pepper

Rarebit topping
75ml milk
200g Cheddar cheese, grated
2 tbsp mascarpone cheese
30g plain flour
40g white breadcrumbs
1 tbsp Dijon mustard
½ tbsp Worcestershire sauce
1 egg
1 egg yolk

1 Cook the potatoes in a large pan of salted water until tender. Remove the potatoes from the pan and keep the water boiling, then add the spinach leaves. Bring the water back to the boil for 1 minute and then drain the spinach leaves, pressing out as much water as you can.
2 Roughly chop the cooked spinach leaves and place them in a mixing bowl. Pass the potatoes through a potato ricer or use a potato masher and add the mash to the mixing bowl with the spinach. Add the shallots, nutmeg and plenty of seasoning.
3 Mix everything together and form into 6 large cakes. Dust each one with flour and place them in the fridge to chill while you prepare the rarebit topping.

To make the rarebit topping
4 Pour the milk into a saucepan, add the cheeses and place on a very gentle heat, until the cheddar has melted. Remove from the heat and stir in the flour, breadcrumbs and mustard. Put the pan back on a low heat and stir until the mixture has thickened. Remove from the heat and add the Worcestershire sauce. Leave to cool for 5 minutes and then stir in the egg and yolk and mix well.

To cook the potato and spinach cakes
5 Heat some olive oil in a frying pan and fry the potato cakes on both sides until golden brown. Heat the grill until hot. Spoon equal portions of the rarebit mixture on to the potato cakes and place them under the grill for 5 minutes or so until bubbling and brown. Serve with some dressed salad leaves.

Smoked cod and mussel chowder

If you can find some smoked pollack, then use it instead of cod, although this is a relatively new idea and you may not find it in supermarkets yet.

SERVES 6

500g fresh mussels
500ml water
700ml milk
1 bay leaf
500g smoked cod or pollack
4 tbsp olive oil
2 celery stalks, finely chopped
2 shallots, finely chopped
2 garlic cloves, finely chopped
100g pancetta, chopped
1 tbsp plain flour
200ml white wine
500g potatoes, peeled and cut into 2cm chunks
150ml double cream
2 tbsp finely chopped flat-leaf parsley
sea salt
freshly ground black pepper

Croutons
2 tbsp olive oil
3 slices of white bread, cut into cubes
6 slices of pancetta, chopped

1 De-beard the mussels and scrub them well, discarding any that are open and don't close when tapped. Rinse them well in cold water
2 Put the mussels in a pan with 200ml of the water. Bring to a simmer, cover and cook for 1 minute, by which time all the mussels should have opened – throw away any that don't. Strain, keeping the cooking liquor.
3 When the mussels are cool enough to handle, remove them from their shells and cut them in half. Place them to one side.
4 Pour the liquor back into the pan and add the milk, the remaining 300ml of water and the bay leaf. Bring to a simmer, add the fish and simmer for 2 minutes. Take the fish out of the pan and peel off the skin. Flake the fish, removing any bones, and set aside with the mussels.
5 Pour the milk and cooking liquor into a jug or bowl. Return the pan to the heat and add 2 tablespoons of the olive oil, the celery, shallots, garlic and chopped pancetta. Cook for 3 minutes, while stirring to stop the mixture sticking and burning.
6 Sprinkle on the flour and stir. Add the wine and simmer for 3 minutes, then pour in the milk mixture. Add the potatoes and simmer for 10–12 minutes until tender. Stir in the cream and check the seasoning.
7 Put the fish and mussels back into the pan and check the seasoning. Add the parsley and warm through.
8 To make the croutons, heat the olive oil in a frying pan and fry the bread and pancetta until crisp. Serve the chowder in bowls with the croutons sprinkled on top.

Potato and chickpea curry

This is a good vegetarian curry. I've suggested serving it with boiled rice, but you could also make some naan bread (see page 685) if you prefer.

SERVES 6

1 tbsp coriander seeds
2 tbsp cumin seeds
½ tsp fenugreek seeds
3 cloves
2 tbsp whole unsalted cashew nuts
2 tbsp olive oil
1 onion, finely chopped
2 garlic cloves, finely chopped
2cm piece of fresh root ginger, peeled and grated
1 x 400ml can of coconut milk
1 tbsp tomato purée
750g new potatoes, cut in half
1 x 400g can of chickpeas, drained and rinsed
3 hard-boiled eggs, sliced
1 red chilli, seeded and finely chopped (optional)
sea salt

1 First prepare your spices. Put the coriander, cumin, fenugreek and cloves in a small frying pan. Place the pan over a high heat and when the seeds start to smoke, stir them around in the pan. As soon as you can see that they are all darkening, remove them from the heat and grind them to a fine powder, using a pestle and mortar or a coffee grinder.
2 Place the cashew nuts in the same pan and toast them until they start to brown. Using the pestle and mortar, grind the nuts to as fine a powder as you can manage.
3 Heat the olive oil in a saucepan or deep sauté pan and fry the onion, garlic and ginger for 5 minutes on a low heat, stirring occasionally. Add the spices and ground cashew nuts and stir for a few seconds.
4 Add the coconut milk, then stir in the tomato purée and add the potatoes and chickpeas. Bring to a simmer, then cover and cook for 15 minutes until the potatoes are tender. Check the seasoning and add some salt to taste.
5 Gently stir in the eggs and the chilli if using, then remove from the heat and serve with boiled rice (see page 74).

Chicken thighs with root vegetables

Root vegetables might look unappealing when first pulled from the ground, but they can really enhance a recipe once cooked. Add them to a stew, as here, or use them as a base for a winter soup or for buttery mash to accompany a rich, roast meat joint.

SERVES 6

- 1 tbsp olive oil
- 20g butter
- 8 chicken thighs on the bone, skinned
- 3 shallots, finely sliced
- 200ml white wine
- 1kg mixed root vegetables (sweet potatoes, potatoes, swede, parsnips), peeled and cut into 1cm cubes
- 100ml chicken stock
- 1 sprig of thyme
- sea salt
- freshly ground black pepper

1 Heat the olive oil and butter in a saucepan. Add 2 of the chicken thighs and brown them all over. Set them aside in a bowl while you brown the rest.
2 Keep the pan on the heat, then add the shallots and cook them for 2 minutes. Pour on the wine and let it sizzle for 3 minutes.
3 Add the vegetables to the pan, lay the chicken thighs on top and pour on the stock. Season well with salt and pepper. Lay the thyme on top, cover the saucepan with a lid and simmer gently for 50 minutes.
4 Remove the chicken thighs and place them in a serving dish, then roughly crush the vegetables with a fork and serve them with the chicken.

Meatballs in a creamy pepper sauce

I love Saturday nights when dinner is already prepared and just needs to be heated through on the stove. It's a chance to settle down with the family in the early evening and take a breather before eating.

SERVES 6

500g minced pork
500g minced lamb
1 medium onion, very finely chopped
1 tsp paprika
½ tsp ground cumin
1 tbsp soy sauce
1 tsp salt
1 tbsp olive oil, for frying
600g spaghetti
freshly ground black pepper

Creamy pepper sauce
2 tbsp olive oil
1 medium onion, finely chopped
1 red pepper, cored and finely chopped
1 garlic clove, finely chopped
200ml chicken stock
2 tbsp crème fraiche
1 x 400g can of chopped tomatoes
2 tsp paprika
a large of pinch salt
½ tsp sugar
freshly ground black pepper

1 Mix all the ingredients for the meatballs, except the olive oil, in a bowl. It's probably easiest to do this with your hands. Shape the mixture into balls about 2cm in diameter.
2 Heat the olive oil in a frying pan, add a batch of meatballs and brown them all over – don't overcrowd the pan or the meatballs will steam and not brown. Place each batch to one side while you brown the next, then set them all aside.
3 Next make the pepper sauce. Heat the olive oil in a saucepan. Add the onion, pepper and garlic and cook on a medium heat, stirring occasionally, for 10 minutes.
4 Add the rest of the ingredients and simmer for about 5 minutes. Check and adjust the seasoning if necessary with more salt and pepper. Place the meatballs in the sauce, cover the pan and simmer gently for 1 hour.
5 Cook the spaghetti according to the packet instructions, then drain and serve with the meatballs and sauce.

Guinea fowl with root vegetables

A supreme, whether of chicken or guinea fowl, is the term used to describe a breast of a bird with the wing bone attached. Your butcher should be able to prepare these for you. They are a great way of preparing the breast as keeping the bone ensures that the meat does not become too dry during cooking.

SERVES 6

1 tbsp olive oil
a knob of butter
6 guinea fowl supremes
150ml Marsala wine
sea salt
freshly ground black pepper

Root vegetables
2 tbsp olive oil
250g celeriac, peeled and cut into 1cm cubes
250g parsnips, peeled and cut into 1cm cubes
250g swede, peeled and cut into 1cm cubes
250g carrots, peeled and cut into 1cm cubes
70g chopped pancetta
2 tbsp crème fraiche
sea salt
freshly ground black pepper

1 Preheat the oven to 200°C/Gas 6. Heat the olive oil and butter in a frying pan. Once the butter starts to foam, lay a guinea fowl supreme skin side down in the pan. Fry for 1 minute, by which time the skin should be golden brown. Lay the supreme in an ovenproof gratin dish and brown the remaining supremes in the same way before placing them in the gratin dish.
2 Return the frying pan to the heat and add the Marsala. It will spit but give it a stir. Simmer for 30 seconds and then pour it over the guinea fowl.
3 Season the meat with salt and pepper, then cover with a sheet of parchment paper and cook in the oven for 15 minutes. Serve with the root vegetables.

To prepare the root vegetables
4 Heat the olive oil in a large saucepan or sauté pan. Add all the vegetables and the pancetta and cook, stirring frequently, for 5 minutes. Cover and cook the vegetables very gently for 15 minutes, stirring occasionally. Stir in the crème fraiche and season well with salt and pepper.

Treacle and coconut squares

A treacly treat – I bake these in a flapjack-type tray, but a small tart tin would work just as well.

MAKES ABOUT 8 SQUARES

300g golden syrup
30g butter
40g desiccated coconut
100g walnuts, roughly chopped
50g raisins
3 tbsp double cream
2 eggs

Pastry
180g plain flour, plus extra for dusting the work surface
120g cold butter, cut into cubes
a pinch of salt
1 egg yolk
2 tbsp cold water

1 Preheat the oven to 200°C/Gas 6. Place a baking tray in the oven to heat through while the oven warms up.
2 To make the pastry, put the flour and butter in a food processor and process until the mixture resembles breadcrumbs. Add the salt and mix again, then add the egg and cold water and mix again briefly. Turn the dough out on to a floured surface and shape it into a ball. Wrap the dough in clingfilm and place it in the fridge for 30 minutes.
3 You need a rectangular baking tin that measures about 17 x 30cm. Roll out the pastry to this size and use it to line the tin.
4 Pour the golden syrup into a small saucepan, add the butter and heat until the butter has melted. Stir in the coconut, walnuts, raisins, cream and eggs, then pour this mixture on to the pastry.
5 Place the tin in the oven on top of the hot baking tray and bake in the oven for 20 minutes. Allow to cool slightly, then cut into squares and serve.

Apple, mincemeat, marzipan pie

It's a long time until next Christmas but I love mincemeat and I look for any excuse to enjoy it during the year.

SERVES 6

250g marzipan
icing sugar, for rolling the marzipan
1 x 400g jar of mincemeat
3 eating apples, peeled, cored and quartered and then thinly sliced
2 tbsp brandy
1 tbsp brown sugar

Pastry
400g plain flour
200g cold butter, cut into cubes, plus extra for greasing the tin
2 tbsp caster sugar
2 egg yolks
2 tbsp cold water
1 egg, beaten, for glazing

1 To make the pastry, place the flour and butter in a food processor and blend until it resembles breadcrumbs.
2 Add the sugar and mix again, then add the egg yolks and water and process briefly. Turn the dough out on to a cold surface and shape the pastry into a ball. Cut the ball into 2 equal pieces, wrap in clingfilm and chill in the fridge for 30 minutes.
3 Preheat the oven to 200°C/Gas 6 and lightly grease a Swiss roll tin. Roll out 1 piece of the pastry and lay it in the tray. The piece should be rolled to fit just inside the base of the tin.
4 Roll out the marzipan, using a little icing sugar if it sticks to the work surface or the rolling pin. Roll the marzipan to about the same size as the pastry and lay it on top of the pastry base.
5 Spoon the mincemeat on to the marzipan and spread it out. Lay the apple slices on top and then sprinkle on the brandy and the sugar.
6 Roll out the second piece of pastry and place it on top, sealing the edges of the pie as best you can. Brush the top with beaten egg and place the pie in the oven for 25 minutes until brown. Delicious served with some clotted cream.

We may glimpse some sunshine and milder temperatures during March, although it is a notoriously unpredictable month. The days become longer and the garden has an air of expectation – you may even see some green shoots. There should be enough good weather to allow you to fork over your beds and you may be able to get out with the lawnmower at some stage. If you are lucky enough to have a vegetable patch, you can plant your first seeds of the season, putting in early potatoes and onion sets. Although there is not much to harvest in Britain at this time of year, you can enjoy vegetables such as purple-sprouting broccoli, spring greens and watercress. A watercress salad can perk up almost any meal and its fresh, peppery-tasting greenery is just the remedy for a palate jaded by rich winter food. Enjoy the first of the rhubarb that grows so easily in this country and generally let the natural desire for slightly lighter cooking be reflected in your menus.

March

Spring greens and noodle soup with crispy spring rolls

Once you have mastered the method for making these crispy spring rolls you'll want to make them all the time. They are delicious and they can be reheated in a low oven if you want to prepare them earlier.

SERVES 6 (MAKES ABOUT 17 SPRING ROLLS)

2 tbsp olive oil
2 garlic cloves, finely chopped
1 tsp grated fresh root ginger
2 shallots, finely sliced
100g carrots, cut into thin discs
6 spring onions
1.5 litres chicken or vegetable stock
3 tbsp dark soy sauce
½ tsp sugar
1 tbsp fish sauce
250g spring greens, shredded
200g medium egg noodles
sea salt
freshly ground black pepper

Crispy spring rolls
40g fine egg noodles
250g cooked prawns
2 shallots, finely chopped
2 tsp fish sauce
1 garlic clove, finely chopped
80g bean sprouts, roughly chopped
1 egg white
2 tbsp grated carrot
250g pack of filo pastry (8–10 sheets)
olive oil
sea salt
freshly ground black pepper

1 Heat the olive oil in a large saucepan. Fry the garlic, ginger, shallots, carrots and spring onions for 2 minutes over a fairly low heat. Add the stock, soy sauce, sugar and fish sauce, then simmer very gently for 5 minutes. Add the spring greens and stir, then remove the pan from the heat until you are ready to serve.
2 Cook the noodles according to the packet instructions and drain. Reheat the soup if necessary and check the seasoning. Put a pile of noodles in each bowl, then pour the hot soup on top. Serve with the spring rolls.

To make the crispy spring rolls
3 Cook the noodles according to the packet instructions and drain. Roughly chop the noodles and place them in a mixing bowl.
4 Chop the prawns as finely as you can and add these to the bowl. Next add the shallots, fish sauce, garlic, bean sprouts, egg white, carrot and seasoning, then mix well.
5 Lay a sheet of filo pastry on a work surface and cut it lengthways down the middle so that you have a rectangle measuring 18 x 32cm. With a short side closest to you, fold over about 4cm. Take a dessertspoon of the filling and place it just above the 4cm fold in the centre of the pastry. Leave 3cm margins on each side and fold in each of these sides over the filling and then roll up the pastry, not too tightly. When you get to the end, brush a little olive oil on the end to seal the roll. Set to one side while you make the rest of the rolls.
6 Heat a couple of centimetres of olive oil in a frying pan and fry the spring rolls, 2 at a time, turning them as they brown. Place them on a piece of kitchen paper to soak up any excess oil, then put them on a baking tray in a low oven to keep warm while you cook the rest.

Ling fillets with shallot and mustard sauce

When I first wrote this recipe I thought it was acceptable to eat ling, from a sustainability point of view. I've since been told that it is best to avoid it or at least to buy only line-caught ling. This is the only ling recipe in the book and I don't suppose one meal of ling a year will have much of an impact on the population, but if you prefer to avoid it, use pollack or pouting.

SERVES 6

6 ling fillets
2 tbsp olive oil
6 slices of pancetta
a knob of butter
2 shallots, finely sliced
1 sprig of thyme, leaves removed and chopped
150ml dry white wine
250ml vegetable stock
2 tsp caster sugar
1 tsp soy sauce
1 tsp Dijon mustard
1 tbsp crème fraiche
sea salt
freshly ground black pepper

1 Preheat the oven to 200°C/Gas 6. Place the ling fillets in an ovenproof dish, drizzle them with a tablespoon of the olive oil and season with salt and pepper.
2 Heat a frying pan and fry the pancetta slices until golden and slightly crispy. Lay these on top of the ling fillets and set aside while you prepare the sauce.
3 Heat the remaining oil and the butter in a small frying pan and add the shallots and thyme leaves. Fry for 2 minutes, then add the wine and cook for 2 minutes. Next add the stock, sugar, soy sauce and mustard and simmer for 2 minutes more. Stir in the crème fraiche, season with salt and pepper and simmer gently for 1 minute more.
4 Pour the sauce over the fish and bake in the oven for 12–15 minutes, depending on the thickness of the fish. Serve with mashed potatoes (see page 16) and leeks.

Lamb and vegetable pie with baked beetroot

Lamb can be cooked in so many delicious ways. In this recipe, I use cubed neck fillet in a pie with some vegetables, which is very tasty indeed.

SERVES 6

- 3 tbsp olive oil
- 1kg lamb neck fillet, cut into 2cm chunks
- 3 tbsp flour seasoned with salt and pepper
- 200ml red wine
- 1 onion, finely chopped
- 1 parsnip, peeled and cut into 2cm chunks
- 1 carrot, peeled and cut into 2cm chunks
- 1 leek, rinsed and sliced into 1cm rounds
- 1 potato, peeled and cut into 2cm chunks
- 1 tbsp tomato purée
- 1 x 400g can of chopped tomatoes
- 1 sprig of fresh thyme
- 150ml water
- 1 x 230g sheet of ready-rolled all-butter puff pastry
- sea salt
- freshly ground black pepper

Baked beetroot

- 6–8 whole beetroots, scrubbed
- 2 tbsp olive oil
- 1 tbsp balsamic vinegar
- 2 garlic cloves, bashed
- 150g goat's cheese, roughly crumbled
- fresh thyme leaves
- sea salt
- freshly ground black pepper

1 Heat 2 tablespoons of the olive oil in a saucepan. Toss the lamb chunks in the seasoned flour, then brown them, a batch at a time, in the oil. Put the browned meat in a bowl.

2 Keep the pan on the heat and pour in the wine, stirring and scraping to remove any sticky bits from the bottom of the pan. Pour the wine into the bowl with the lamb.

3 Add the rest of the olive oil to the saucepan, throw in the onion and cook for 5 minutes until soft. Add the other vegetables and stir for 30 seconds or so to coat them in the olive oil. Add the tomato purée and chopped tomatoes and stir to combine.

4 Return the lamb and wine to the saucepan. Add the thyme and season with salt and pepper, then pour in the water and bring to a simmer. Cover the pan and cook the lamb and vegetables gently for 1 hour. Check the seasoning and then set aside to cool.

5 Preheat the oven to 200°C/Gas 6. Pile the cooled lamb and vegetable filling into a 23–24cm pie dish. Roll out the puff pastry and use it to cover the pie, then cook for 20 minutes until the pastry is golden brown and has risen. Serve with the beetroot.

To prepare the baked beetroot

6 Preheat the oven to 200°C/Gas 6. Take a large square of foil and lay it in a small baking tray. Place the beetroots in the foil, with the olive oil, vinegar, garlic and a good grinding of salt and pepper. Seal the foil over the beetroots, so that no steam can escape during cooking.

7 Bake in the oven for 1 hour. When the beetroots are cool enough to handle, peel them and cut them into quarters. Place them in a serving dish, with their cooking juices, the goat's cheese and some thyme leaves.

Cheese and potato omelette

This is an open-faced omelette, so you don't have the challenge of having to flip over the edges as you do to make the perfect French omelette.

SERVES 6

100g white bread, cut into 1.5cm thick slices
2 tbsp olive oil
1 garlic clove, peeled, hit with a rolling pin but in 1 piece
12 eggs (2 per person)
30g butter
200g potatoes, cooked and cut into 2cm chunks
100g Gruyère cheese, grated
1 tbsp chopped chives
1 tbsp chopped flat-leaf parsley
sea salt
freshly ground black pepper

1 Cut the bread into cubes. Heat the olive oil in a frying pan and add the garlic. Let it sizzle for 1 minute, then remove and discard it. Add the bread cubes to the oil and fry them until golden brown, then remove from the pan and place to one side. Preheat the grill.
2 Whisk the eggs in a bowl with some salt and pepper, until they are frothy. Heat half the butter in the frying pan and when it is foaming, pour in half the egg mixture.
3 Stir the eggs with a fork for a few seconds until they start to set. Using the fork, pull the egg away from the edge of pan, tilting the pan as you do so, so that the uncooked egg can spread to the edges.
4 Sprinkle on half the potatoes, cheese, herbs and croutons and place the omelette under the hot grill for 1 minute. You want to keep it slightly runny, so don't leave it under the grill for too long.
5 Use the other half of the ingredients to make another omelette in exactly the same way. Cut each one into 3 pieces and serve with some watercress salad and bread.

Garlic and lemon chicken legs with Persian rice

My mother was inspired to cook by writers such as Elizabeth David, Jane Grigson and Katie Stewart, so my brothers and I enjoyed plenty of good food, although on a limited budget, and we inherited a passion for cooking. I still have my mother's original copy of 'French Country Cooking' by Elizabeth David. It was her description of cooking grilled chicken that made me realise that cooking was one of life's greatest pleasures.

SERVES 6

6 chicken legs
3 tbsp olive oil
4 garlic cloves, bashed in their skins and kept whole
1 lemon, sliced into ½cm discs
olive oil, for frying
sea salt
freshly ground black pepper

Persian rice
3 tbsp olive oil
1 onion, finely chopped
2 garlic cloves, finely chopped
40g raisins
60g dates, roughly chopped
¼ tsp turmeric
¼ tsp ground cinnamon
5 cardamom pods
1 tsp ground cumin
a pinch of saffron threads
400g basmati rice
500ml water
1 tsp salt
3 tbsp finely chopped fresh coriander

1 Place the chicken legs in a bowl with the olive oil, garlic cloves and lemon slices. Season with salt and pepper. Leave them to marinate for 30 minutes to 4 hours.
2 Preheat the oven to 200°C/Gas 6. Heat 1 tablespoon of olive oil in a frying pan and brown the chicken legs, a couple at a time.
3 Place the browned legs in an ovenproof dish. Pour over any juices from the frying pan, the marinade juices, lemon slices and garlic and roast in the oven for 40 minutes. Serve with the rice and maybe a tomato salad.

To cook the Persian rice
4 Heat the olive oil in a large saucepan. Add the onion, garlic, raisins, dates and spices, including the saffron threads. Fry gently for 5 minutes.
5 Add the rice and stir. Pour on the water and the salt and bring to a good simmer. Reduce the heat to low, cover and cook for 15 minutes. Remove the pan from the heat completely and leave covered for 10 minutes. Stir the coriander into the rice before serving.

Seafood pasta

I cooked this in a few minutes one night, when we came home from our youngest son's parents' evening. This reinforces my belief that you don't need to turn to ready meals when you have only a small amount of time to devote to your evening meal, as long as you're organised with your shopping.

SERVES 6

500g live mussels
2 shallots, finely chopped
200ml white wine
500g linguine
1 tbsp olive oil
a knob of butter
3 garlic cloves, crushed
6 spring onions, finely sliced
100g monkfish tail, cut into 2cm chunks
150g raw prawns
2 tbsp double cream
1 red chilli, chopped (optional)
zest and juice of ½ lemon
3 tbsp finely chopped flat-leaf parsley
2 tbsp extra virgin olive oil, for serving
sea salt
freshly ground black pepper

1 Make sure the mussels are all well scrubbed and de-bearded. Discard any that are open and do not close when tapped.
2 Place the shallots and wine in a large saucepan over a medium heat. At the same time, bring a large saucepan of salted water to the boil for the pasta. Add the linguine and cook according to the packet instructions.
3 Once the wine is simmering, add the mussels in their shells. Cover the pan and cook the mussels for 4 minutes. Remove the mussels from the pan and pour the cooking juices into a bowl. Discard any mussels that haven't opened.
4 Return the pan to the heat and add the olive oil and butter. Add the garlic and cook over a low heat for 30 seconds, stirring constantly, as you don't want it to burn. Add the spring onions, monkfish and prawns and cook for 1 minute.
5 Add the cream, chilli, if using, lemon zest and juice, parsley and mussel liquor. Stir to combine and bring to a simmer. Tip the mussels back into the pan and stir to coat them in all the juices, then remove from the heat.
6 By this time the linguine should be ready, so drain it and combine everything in a large serving dish. Season with plenty of black pepper, a little salt and the extra virgin olive oil.

Crispy duck with haricot and flageolet beans

My children love crispy duck legs and even accept the beans as part of the duck deal. It's really good to get them eating pulses, as they are a great source of iron and potassium. If you rinse the beans you can get rid of any excess salt used in the canning process.

SERVES 6

6 duck legs
1 x 350g jar of duck or goose fat

Marinade
1 garlic clove
4 tbsp dark soy sauce
2 tbsp runny honey
1 tbsp soft brown sugar
1cm piece of fresh root ginger, grated
sea salt
freshly ground black pepper

Haricot and flageolet beans
15g butter
1 tbsp olive oil
1 shallot, finely chopped
2 carrots, peeled and sliced
2 x 400g cans of haricot beans, drained and rinsed
1 x 400g can of flageolet beans, drained and rinsed
350ml chicken stock (a stock cube will do)
2 tbsp chopped flat-leaf parsley
sea salt
freshly ground black pepper

1 Preheat the oven to 180°C/Gas 4. Place the duck legs in a roasting tin and cover them in duck or goose fat. Don't be alarmed by the amount of fat – you're not going to eat it, and once the duck is cooked, the fat can be poured back into the jar. Put the duck legs in the oven for 1½ hours and forget about them.
2 At the end of the cooking time, remove the duck legs from the roasting tin, set them to one side and pour the fat into a storage jar. Take care with the hot fat!
3 Place the marinade ingredients in a bowl and mix them together. Using a pastry brush, coat the duck legs with the marinade. Place them to one side for 10 minutes and then brush them with the marinade again.
4 Heat the grill to high and grill the legs for 5 minutes on each side. The skin will crisp up and turn golden brown. Serve with the haricot beans.

To prepare the haricot and flageolet beans
5 Warm the butter and olive oil in a small saucepan, add the shallot and carrots and cook for 5 minutes over a low heat. Add the beans, stock and parsley, then simmer gently for 30 minutes. Season with salt and pepper.

Baked rhubarb with custard

This is a simple, but much-loved pudding.

SERVES 6

750g forced rhubarb, cut into 2cm chunks
100g caster sugar
150ml water
1 tbsp chopped stem ginger
1 tbsp syrup from the stem ginger

Custard
200ml milk
300ml double cream
1 tsp vanilla extract
3 eggs
2 egg yolks
2 tbsp caster sugar

1 Preheat the oven to 200°C/Gas 6. Lay the rhubarb pieces in the bottom of an ovenproof dish. Place the sugar and water in a small saucepan, bring to a simmer and cook gently for 5 minutes. Stir in the ginger and syrup, then remove from the heat and pour this syrup over the rhubarb.
2 Cover the dish with a sheet of foil and bake the rhubarb for 30 minutes. Serve with the custard.

To make the custard
3 Pour the milk and cream into a saucepan and add the vanilla. Heat until the liquid comes to boiling point.
4 In the meantime, break the eggs into a glass bowl, add the yolks and whisk them with the sugar. Pour the hot liquid on to the eggs and sugar, whisking as you do so.
5 Place the glass bowl over a saucepan of simmering water. Try not to let the bottom of the bowl touch the water, as the custard could separate if it gets hot too quickly. Keep stirring the custard until it thickens slightly and coats the back of a spoon.

Orange cake

My spirits always lift when I see a recipe for a cake that simply requires all the ingredients to be thrown into a bowl and mixed together. I hope you feel the same.

1 Preheat the oven to 180°C/Gas 4. Grease a 900g loaf tin, measuring about 22 x 12cm, and line it with baking parchment, allowing the parchment to stick up over the top of the tin.
2 Put all the cake ingredients in a mixing bowl and whisk together thoroughly. Pour the mixture into the loaf tin and bake for 1 hour. Turn the cake out on to a wire rack to cool for 10 minutes before glazing.
3 To make the glaze, warm the marmalade and icing sugar in a small pan. Using a pastry brush, spread the glaze over the top and sides of the cake and leave to cool completely before serving.

MAKES 1 LOAF

4 eggs
250g caster sugar
100ml double cream
finely grated zest of 3 oranges
juice of ½ an orange
80g melted butter, plus extra for greasing
200g plain flour
½ tsp baking powder
a pinch of salt

Glaze
1 tbsp marmalade, warmed
3 tbsp icing sugar

Spicy turkey burgers with tomato and red pepper relish

There is nothing refined about burgers, but they are always tempting once fried and nestling between two pieces of bread.

SERVES 6

500g minced turkey
1 onion, finely chopped
1 tsp ground cumin
1 tsp Dijon mustard
1 x 400g can of kidney beans, drained and rinsed
1 tbsp Worcestershire sauce
2 tbsp finely chopped coriander
flour, for dusting the burgers
olive oil, for frying
6 bread rolls, for serving
sea salt
freshly ground black pepper

Tomato and red pepper relish
1 red pepper, halved and cored
2 plum tomatoes, peeled
2 tbsp olive oil
1 red chilli (optional), finely chopped
sea salt
freshly ground black pepper

Roasted potato chips
800g potatoes, peeled, rinsed in cold water and chopped lengthways into eighths
2 tbsp olive oil
salt

1 Place the turkey, onion, cumin, mustard, beans, Worcestershire sauce and coriander in a mixing bowl and mix everything together with your hands or a wooden spoon. Season well with salt and pepper, then form the mixture into 6 burgers. Place them in the fridge to chill for 20 minutes. Dust each burger with a little flour when you are ready to cook them.
2 Heat a couple of tablespoons of olive oil in a frying pan. Brown the burgers for 1 minute, then turn them and fry for another minute. Lower the heat and gently fry the burgers for 5 more minutes. Meanwhile, lightly toast the bread rolls.
3 Assemble the burgers with a dollop of the relish and serve them with salad and some roasted potato chips.

To make the tomato and red pepper relish
4 Heat the grill. Place the pepper halves on a baking tray, skin side up and grill until the skin blackens. Remove the peppers from the grill and when they are cool enough to handle, remove the skin.
5 Cut the tomatoes in half, discarding the pulp and seeds. Finely chop the tomatoes and the skinned peppers and place them in a small bowl with the olive oil and plenty of seasoning. Mix in the chilli if using.

To make the roasted potato chips
6 Preheat the oven to 220°C/Gas 7. Place the potatoes on a baking tray and pour over the olive oil. Roast them in the oven until crisp and golden, turning occasionally. Season with salt.

Egg mousse with watercress salad

This used to be a very popular dish in England at lunch parties and I enjoyed it recently at a friend's house. I think it's worthy of a culinary comeback. It's perfect for spring, when you start to want lighter food.

SERVES 6

15 eggs
200ml mayonnaise
2 tbsp finely chopped flat-leaf parsley
a pinch of paprika
2 tbsp grated horseradish
4 tbsp lightly whipped cream
sea salt
freshly ground black pepper

Watercress salad
1 bunch of watercress
1 green pepper, finely chopped
10 cherry tomatoes, finely chopped
3 tbsp extra virgin olive oil
1 tbsp balsamic vinegar
sea salt
freshly ground black pepper

1 Bring a large saucepan of water to the boil. Using a spoon, carefully place the eggs in the water, 1 at a time, taking care not to knock them against the side of the saucepan. Bring the water back to a gentle simmer and cook the eggs for 12 minutes. Pour off the hot water but keep the eggs in the pan. Bash them against the side of the saucepan so that the shells crack, then place the pan under cold running water. Leave the eggs in the cold water for 5 minutes or so and then drain. The shells should come away from the eggs easily.
2 Chop the eggs roughly and place them in a serving bowl. Add the mayonnaise, parsley, paprika and horseradish and mix everything together, then fold in the cream. Check the seasoning and serve with the watercress salad and some brown bread.
3 Lay the watercress on a large serving platter. Scatter the green pepper and tomatoes on top, then dress with the oil, vinegar, salt and pepper.

Seafood curry

This has the flavours of a typical Sri Lankan fish curry. A Sri Lankan probably wouldn't mix the different fish as I have done, but otherwise it is fairly authentic.

SERVES 6

1 tsp mustard seeds
¼ tsp fenugreek seeds
1 tsp cumin seeds
2 tsp whole coriander seeds
½ tsp fennel seeds
¼ tsp turmeric
7 curry leaves
1 tsp salt
1 tbsp vegetable oil
1 medium onion, finely chopped
1 garlic clove, finely chopped
6 cherry tomatoes, cut in half
1 x 400g can of chopped tomatoes
200ml coconut milk
1 tsp sugar
¼ tsp cayenne pepper
100g sea bass fillets, skinned and cut into 2cm chunks
250g monkfish tail, cut into 2cm chunks
250g raw shelled prawns
juice ½ lemon
sea salt

Vegetable curry
500g potatoes, peeled and cut in quarters
250g green beans, topped and tailed
1 tbsp vegetable oil
½ tsp mustard seeds
½ tsp cumin seeds
2cm piece of fresh root ginger, grated
1 shallot, finely chopped
1 garlic clove, finely chopped
sea salt

1 Toast the mustard, fenugreek, cumin, coriander and fennel seeds in a small frying pan, until they are slightly darkened and you can smell their toasting aroma. Put them in a pestle and mortar, with the turmeric, curry leaves and salt, and grind them to a fine powder.
2 Heat the vegetable oil in a medium sized saucepan. Add the onion and garlic and cook gently for 10 minutes, then add the cherry tomatoes and cook for another 3 minutes. Stir in the ground spices and mix to combine. Pour in the chopped tomatoes, coconut milk, sugar and cayenne pepper, then taste for seasoning. You may need to add more salt.
3 Simmer over a low heat for 20 minutes. Add the fish, prawns and lemon juice and cook for 5 minutes longer. Serve with rice and the vegetable curry.

To prepare the vegetable curry
4 Cook the potatoes in salted water until tender, then drain and set aside. Finely chop the green beans in a food processor.
5 Heat the vegetable oil in a pan and add the mustard and cumin seeds. When they start to pop, add the cooked potatoes and let them fry gently until they start to brown. Add the grated ginger, shallot and garlic and cook for 3 minutes, stirring occasionally. Next, stir the green beans into the potato mix and cook gently for 3 minutes. Season with salt.

Beef pot roast

This meal is a winner in so many ways, not least because it is all cooked in the same pot. It is also relatively easy to put together and is kind on the purse. As if that weren't enough, it smells delicious when cooking, filling anyone wandering through the kitchen with such anticipation that they will be praising your cooking skills for some time to come.

SERVES 6

- 1–2 tbsp olive oil
- 140g chopped pancetta
- 1 x 1.5–1.7kg beef brisket
- 2 onions, finely chopped
- 2 carrots, peeled and sliced into ½cm thick discs
- 4 garlic cloves, unpeeled and whole but bashed with a rolling pin
- 1 tbsp flour
- 800ml good red wine
- 1 x 400g can of chopped tomatoes
- 500ml beef stock
- 1 bay leaf
- 1 sprig of fresh thyme
- sea salt
- freshly ground black pepper

1 Preheat the oven to 180°C/Gas 4. Heat the olive oil in a casserole dish on top of the stove. Add the pancetta and fry for 1 or 2 minutes until it is just starting to look brown. Remove the pancetta and put to one side.
2 Increase the heat under the casserole dish and place the brisket joint in the hot fat. Brown it all over, turning it as necessary. Remove the joint and place to one side, leaving the dish on the heat.
3 Add a little more olive oil and put the onions, carrots and garlic in the pan. Brown them gently for 2 minutes, then sprinkle on the flour and stir until absorbed. Pour on the wine, stirring constantly, and simmer for 3 minutes. Pour on the tomatoes and stock and season well with salt and pepper. Add the bay leaf and thyme, then bring to a simmer again. Cover the casserole dish with a lid or some foil and place in the oven for 3 hours.
4 At the end of the cooking time, remove the beef from the pot and leave it to rest for 15 minutes. Serve, carved into slices, with boiled potatoes and spring greens.

Plaice goujons with tartare sauce

This is a classic way of serving plaice. This flatfish is so popular that it has been overfished, so assuage your guilt by buying Irish plaice if possible and avoiding purchasing in springtime when the fish are spawning. Goujons are really just little strips of fish – or sometimes chicken – nothing difficult.

SERVES 6

1kg plaice fillets
200g flour
3 eggs
3 tbsp milk
200g white breadcrumbs
2–3 tbsp vegetable oil, for frying

Tartare sauce
2 egg yolks
1 tsp Dijon mustard
1 tsp lemon juice
150ml groundnut oil
150ml light olive oil
1 tbsp cold water
1 shallot, finely chopped
1 tbsp finely chopped flat-leaf parsley
½ tbsp snipped chives
½ tbsp capers, rinsed and chopped
1 tbsp roughly chopped cornichons
sea salt
freshly ground black pepper

To make the tartare sauce

1 Put the egg yolks in a bowl with the mustard and lemon juice and whisk until combined.

2 Mix both the oils in a jug. Start to add the oil to the eggs, just a few drops at a time, whisking as you do so. Make sure that each addition has combined with the eggs before you add any more. Once you have added 50ml of the oil you can start pouring it on to the eggs in a steady trickle, but make sure you whisk continuously.

3 When all the oil has been mixed in, add the tablespoon of cold water to the sauce and stir. You can now throw in the other ingredients and season to taste.

To make the plaice goujons

4 Skin the plaice and cut the fillets into strips about 6cm long and 2cm wide.

5 Sift the flour on to a plate. Mix the eggs with the milk in a bowl and spread the breadcrumbs on a plate.

6 Coat the fish pieces in flour, shaking off any excess. Pop the strips of fish in the eggy liquid, again shaking off any excess, then coat each piece in breadcrumbs. Pat each one between your hands to ensure that the crumbs stick to the fish.

7 Heat the vegetable oil in a frying pan. Once the oil is hot, add the fish goujons a few at a time – don't crowd the pan. The fish cook quickly and the goujons are ready once the breadcrumbs have turned a rich golden colour. Serve with the tartare sauce and perhaps some baked potatoes and a green salad.

Fried chicken breasts with green, yellow and red lentils and peas

Fresh, home-grown vegetables are not that plentiful at this time of year, especially if spring is slow to get going. At such times, I find myself turning to store cupboard staples such as lentils, of which I am a huge fan.

SERVES 6

6 chicken breasts
4 tbsp olive oil
finely grated zest of 1 lemon
a knob of butter
sea salt
freshly ground black pepper

Lentils and peas
100g red lentils
100g green lentils
100g yellow lentils 1 tbsp olive oil
1 onion, finely chopped
2 garlic cloves, finely chopped
70g sliced pancetta, chopped
leaves from a large sprig of rosemary, finely chopped
200g frozen petit pois
300g potatoes, peeled and cut into quarters
1 litre beef or chicken stock
sea salt
freshly ground black pepper

1 Place the chicken breasts in a bowl with 3 tablespoons of the olive oil, the lemon zest and plenty of salt and pepper. Leave in the fridge for 20 minutes.
2 Preheat the oven to 180°C/Gas 4. Heat the knob of butter and a tablespoon of olive oil in a medium frying pan. When the oil and butter are hot, brown each chicken breast, skin side only, for a few seconds.
3 Place the breasts in a gratin dish, then cover with a sheet of baking parchment and pop them into the oven for 25 minutes. Serve with the lentils.

To cook the lentils
4 Put all the lentils in a sieve and rinse them well under the cold tap. Heat the olive oil in a medium saucepan. Add the onion, garlic, pancetta and rosemary and fry for 3 minutes until the onion is soft.
5 Add the lentils, peas, potatoes and stock and bring to a simmer. Partially cover the pan and simmer for 45 minutes until the lentils are tender. Add a little more water if they become too dry during cooking. Season well with salt and pepper before serving.

Roast beef sirloin with Yorkshire pudding

A joint of roast beef, with Yorkshire pudding, is a beautiful sight and hard to beat for Sunday lunch.

1 Preheat the oven to 220°C/Gas 7. Using your fingertips massage the olive oil into the fat of the joint, then season well with salt and pepper. Place the meat in a roasting tin and roast for 20 minutes.
2 Reduce the heat to 170°C/Gas 3½ and cook for another 35 minutes. These timings will give you well-done meat at the ends of the joint and rare meat in the middle of the joint, so something for everyone! If this is not to your liking, then adjust the cooking times accordingly. Remove the joint from the roasting tin and leave it to rest for 30 minutes before carving.
3 Place the roasting tin on the stove over a medium heat. Add the flour and stir it in with a wooden spoon, then pour on the stock and simmer the gravy gently until you are ready to serve.
4 Carve the beef and serve with the Yorkshire pudding, horseradish sauce and some roast potatoes (see page 94).

To make the Yorkshire pudding
5 Preheat the oven to 220°C/Gas 7. Place the flour in a mixing bowl with the salt and slowly start to add the whole eggs and yolks and then the milk and water. Mix to a smooth, creamy consistency. Place the batter to one side to rest for 30 minutes.
6 About 5 minutes before you are ready to cook the Yorkshire pudding, spoon the oil into a large roasting tin. Place it in the oven and once the oil starts to smoke remove the tin and pour in the pudding batter. Put the tin straight back into the oven and cook the pudding for about 20 minutes, until beautifully golden and risen. If you prefer, you can make individual puddings in Yorkshire pudding moulds.

SERVES 6

1 tbsp olive oil
1.5kg beef sirloin, boned
sea salt
freshly ground black pepper

Gravy
1 tbsp flour
500ml beef stock

Yorkshire pudding
250g plain flour
1 tsp salt
3 eggs
2 egg yolks
350ml milk
250ml water
2 tbsp olive oil

Rhubarb and white chocolate fool

Although a fruit fool is a simple dessert in terms of preparation there is something quite luxurious in its taste and appearance. It is a billowing mass of good things which welcomes your indulgence, rather like a large feather pillow at the end of a long day.

SERVES 6

- 400g rhubarb, cut into 1.5cm chunks
- 1 tbsp water
- 4 tbsp soft brown sugar
- 400ml double cream
- 120g white chocolate, broken into chunks
- 3 egg yolks
- 1 tsp cornflour

1 Place the rhubarb in a saucepan with the water and sugar. Bring to a simmer, then cover the pan and cook for 5 minutes. Do not stir, as you want the rhubarb to stay in chunks if possible.

2 Remove the pan from the heat and leave it covered and undisturbed for 10 minutes, by which time the rhubarb should be tender.

3 In the meantime, prepare the custard mixture. Pour the double cream into another pan and bring to boiling point. Add the white chocolate chunks, then remove the pan from the heat and stir until the chocolate has melted.

4 Place the egg yolks in a mixing bowl and whisk in the cornflour. Pour the cream and chocolate mixture on to the egg yolks and cornflour, whisking as you do so.

5 Pour this mixture back into the saucepan and cook over a very low heat, stirring constantly until thickened. You'll know when this is happening as the custard will start thickening at the bottom first.

6 Fold the rhubarb chunks into the custard, leaving some of the rhubarb juice behind. Chill in bowls or glasses for 40 minutes before serving.

Coconut and jam slices

This is rather an old-fashioned, but delicious, tea time treat and a good way of using up any leftover jam that may be sitting in your cupboard.

MAKES ABOUT 16

Coconut sponge
125g butter, softened
125g caster sugar
2 eggs
75g self-raising flour
75g desiccated coconut
½ tsp baking powder
2 tbsp milk
3 tbsp raspberry or strawberry jam

Pastry
225g plain flour
110g cold butter, cut into cubes
a pinch of salt
1 tbsp caster sugar
1 egg yolk, mixed with 2 tbsp cold water

To make the pastry

1 Place the flour, butter and salt in a food processor and whizz until the mixture resembles breadcrumbs. Add the sugar and whizz for a few more seconds.

2 Pour in the egg yolk and water mixture and whizz until absorbed. Turn the crumbs out on to a work surface and gently bring them together into a ball of dough. Wrap the dough in clingfilm and chill in the fridge for 30 minutes while you prepare the sponge.

To make the sponge

3 Preheat the oven to 180°C/Gas 4. Place a baking sheet in the oven to heat up.

4 Put the butter and sugar in a mixing bowl and, using an electric hand-whisk, beat until they are light and creamy looking. Add the eggs and a tablespoon of the flour and mix again, then fold in the rest of the flour, the coconut and the baking powder. Stir in the milk.

5 Take a rectangular Swiss roll tin measuring about 32 x 23cm and roll out the pastry to fit. Line the tin with the pastry, taking it just to the edges of the tin, not up the sides.

6 Spread the jam on the pastry evenly and then spoon the cake mixture on top and spread it evenly with a palette knife. Place the tin on the baking sheet and bake for 35 minutes until the cake is firm to the touch of your fingertips. Cut into rectangular slices and leave in the tray to cool before removing.

Chocolate orange steamed pudding with white chocolate sauce

This is a delightful mixture of chocolate and orange that will be sure to please.

SERVES 6

180g caster sugar
180g butter, plus extra for greasing
3 eggs
180g self-raising flour, plus extra for dusting the basin
100g dark chocolate
100ml double cream
1 tbsp Cointreau
finely grated zest of 1 orange

White chocolate sauce
200g white chocolate
100ml double cream
50ml milk

1 Put the sugar and butter in a bowl and beat with an electric hand-whisk until pale in colour and fluffy. Add 1 egg with 1 tablespoon of flour and beat until incorporated. Repeat with the remaining eggs, adding a tablespoon of flour each time. Fold in the rest of the flour.
2 Place the chocolate in a glass bowl over a pan of simmering water. Stir once or twice while the chocolate melts and then fold into the sponge mixture. Fold in the cream and then stir in the Cointreau and orange zest.
3 Grease a small pudding basin and dust it with flour. Spoon the sponge mixture into the basin. Lay a circle of greaseproof paper on top of the pudding, then cut a larger piece of paper and lay this over the basin, tying it in place with a piece of string.
4 Pour water into a large saucepan to a depth of a couple of centimetres. Put the basin into the saucepan, bring the water to a simmer, then cover the pan with a lid. Cook the pudding at a gentle simmer for 2 hours. Check the water level regularly and top up with boiling water as necessary.
5 Remove the pudding basin from the saucepan and take off the paper cover. Slip a knife around the edge of the pudding, invert the basin on a plate and the pudding should come out cleanly and easily. Serve in wedges with the white chocolate sauce.

To make the white chocolate sauce
6 Place the ingredients in a glass bowl over a saucepan of simmering water and stir occasionally until the chocolate melts. Pour into a jug to serve.

Vegetable curry wraps

These buckwheat pancakes are a bit like French galettes. They work well with the vegetable curry filling.

SERVES 6

Wraps
200g buckwheat flour
200g plain flour
1 tsp salt
400ml water
400ml milk
4 tbsp olive oil, plus extra for frying

Vegetable curry filling
1 tbsp vegetable oil
1 onion, finely chopped
1 garlic clove, peeled and finely chopped
1 tsp grated fresh ginger
1.2kg cooked vegetables, such as cauliflower, potato, carrots, frozen peas, parsnips
2 tbsp curry powder (see below)
1 tsp tomato purée
1 x 400ml can of coconut milk
sea salt
freshly ground black pepper

Garnish
2 plum tomatoes, diced
6 spring onions, finely sliced
Cheddar cheese, grated

Curry powder
1 tbsp coriander seeds
1 dsrtsp cumin seeds
1 tsp fennel seeds
½ tsp fenugreek seeds

To make the wraps

1 Mix together all the ingredients, except the extra olive oil for frying the wraps, in a small mixing bowl. Beat with a wooden spoon until smooth.

2 Place a frying pan on the heat and oil it well. When the pan is hot, add a large ladleful of mixture, smoothing it out with the back of a metal spoon until it won't spread any thinner. Flip over the pancake once one side is golden brown and cook the other side. Place on a plate while you cook the rest. The mixture makes about 12.

To prepare the curry filling

3 Heat the vegetable oil in a saucepan. Add the onion, garlic and ginger and fry over a medium heat for 10 minutes, until the onions are soft and transparent. Add the cooked vegetables and stir gently.

4 Sprinkle in the curry powder and cook for a few seconds. Add the tomato purée and the coconut milk, stir until everything is combined, then simmer over a low heat for 10 minutes. Season with salt and pepper.

5 Spoon a tablespoon of the vegetable curry on to 1 half of a wrap and sprinkle on some tomato, spring onion and grated cheese to garnish. Fold over the wrap, ready to serve. Prepare the rest in the same way.

To make the curry powder

6 Place the coriander seeds in a small, heavy-bottomed pan and heat them for 30 seconds. Add the other spices and toast until they start to smoke and you can smell their aroma. Transfer the spices to a coffee grinder or pestle and mortar and grind them to a fine powder. Store any leftover curry powder in a sealed jar.

Mackerel salad

Spring is here! Our palates welcome a fresher, less heavy meal than winter stews and roasts.

SERVES 6

600g new potatoes, skins on and cut in half lengthways
1 head of chicory
100g salad leaves
12 cherry tomatoes, cut in half
½ cucumber, diced
1 red onion, thinly sliced
5 tbsp olive oil
6 cornichons, cut in quarters
½ tbsp balsamic vinegar
6 mackerel fillets
1 tbsp roughly chopped walnuts
sea salt
freshly ground black pepper

Horseradish dressing
100ml whipping cream
2 tbsp olive oil
2 tsp creamed horseradish
1 tsp Dijon mustard
sea salt
freshly ground black pepper

1 Place the potatoes in a saucepan of salted water and bring them to the boil. Reduce the heat and simmer gently for 10–12 minutes, until the potatoes are tender. Drain the potatoes, then cut them in half again lengthways.
2 Assemble the salad in a serving bowl. First place the chicory and salad leaves in the bowl, then add the tomatoes, cucumber and red onion.
3 Heat 2 tablespoons of olive oil in a frying pan and fry the potato quarters until golden brown. Lay the potatoes on the salad leaves and scatter on the cornichons. Dress the salad with 3 tablespoons of olive oil and the balsamic vinegar, then season with salt and pepper.
4 Heat the grill, lay the mackerel fillets on the rack of the grill pan and cook for 2 minutes on each side. When the mackerel fillets are cool enough, tear each fillet into about 4 pieces and place them on the salad.

To make the horseradish dressing
5 Lightly whip the cream in a mixing bowl. Fold in the olive oil, horseradish and mustard. Season with salt and pepper. Spoon the dressing on to the salad and scatter with the walnuts.

Braised loin of pork and fennel with mustard sauce

To braise a joint means to cook it in a little liquid at a lower temperature than used for roasting. You need to remove the rind from the pork, as it would end up being rubbery, rather than crisp, and will look unappetizing when you come to serve.

SERVES 6

1kg rolled, boneless loin of pork
1 tbsp olive oil
1 medium onion, finely sliced
1 fennel bulb, trimmed and finely sliced
2 tbsp crème fraiche
2 tsp Dijon mustard
sea salt
freshly ground black pepper

Marinade
200ml white wine
2 or 3 sprigs of thyme
4 tbsp olive oil
sea salt
freshly ground black pepper

1 Remove the rind from the pork joint. Rub plenty of salt into the meat and season with some black pepper. Put all the marinade ingredients in a bowl, add the pork joint and leave it to sit in the marinade for an hour or so.
2 Preheat the oven to 180°C/Gas 4. Remove the joint from the marinade and set the marinade aside. Heat the olive oil in a casserole dish, add the pork and brown it all over in the oil – this will take about 10 minutes to do properly. Remove the joint from the casserole dish, leaving the dish on the heat.
3 Add the onion and fennel to the casserole dish and stir and cook for 3 minutes. Pour the marinade into the dish and let it bubble for a few minutes, then put the pork back in the dish and place it in the oven for 2 hours.
4 Remove the joint from the casserole dish and place the dish over a medium heat on the stove. Bring to a simmer and then add the crème fraiche and mustard and stir. Simmer for 2 minutes.
5 Cut the pork in slices and serve with the sauce poured over them, and some sautéed potatoes (see page 17) and broccoli on the side.

Spicy fish patties with Thai salad

Thai flavours are popular in Britain today, as we have become more adventurous in what we eat. I like this recipe because the fish can be formed into the fish cakes raw, which saves time and washing up.

SERVES 6

800g white fish fillets (pollack is ideal), roughly chopped
3 shallots, finely chopped
1 tsp ready-chopped and bottled lemon grass
2 garlic cloves, finely chopped
2cm piece of fresh root ginger, peeled and grated
3 tbsp chopped fresh coriander
1 tsp fish sauce
1 tbsp sesame oil
50g unsalted peanuts, roughly chopped
olive oil, for frying
sea salt
freshly ground black pepper

Thai salad
400g potatoes, peeled, cut into quarters and cooked until tender
2 tbsp olive oil
2 tbsp unsalted peanuts, roughly chopped
1 cos lettuce heart, shredded
2 plum tomatoes, diced
¼ cucumber, diced
4 spring onions, finely sliced
2 tbsp finely chopped fresh coriander

Dressing
1 tbsp olive oil
1 garlic clove, crushed
50ml coconut cream
1 tbsp soy sauce
sea salt
freshly ground black pepper

1 Place all the ingredients for the fish patties, except the olive oil for frying, in a food processor. Whizz until everything is combined and reasonably finely processed.
2 Form the mixture into 15–16 patties and place them on a baking sheet. Leave them in a cool place or in the fridge until you are ready to cook them.
3 Heat a tablespoon of olive oil in a frying pan and gently fry 4 or 5 patties at a time in the oil until golden brown. They will need about 2 minutes on each side. Serve with the salad.

To make the Thai salad
4 Place all the salad ingredients in a serving dish. Mix the dressing ingredients in a jug or bowl and pour over the salad when you are ready to serve.

Chicken breasts in tarragon sauce with red cabbage coleslaw

Chicken breasts are a favourite of the time-pressed cook because they cook so quickly. Watch that you don't overcook them and make them chewy, which can happen all too easily. I find that the method below guarantees a good texture.

SERVES 6

2 tbsp olive oil
6 chicken breasts, skinned
2 tbsp dry sherry
200ml chicken stock
100ml double cream
2 tsp chopped fresh tarragon
sea salt
freshly ground black pepper

Red cabbage coleslaw
½ red cabbage, finely shredded
2 carrots, grated
2 shallots, finely chopped
1 Little Gem lettuce, finely shredded
6 radishes, finely sliced
2 handfuls of roughly chopped basil leaves
100ml natural yoghurt
2 tbsp olive oil
1 tsp Dijon mustard
sea salt
freshly ground black pepper

1 Preheat the oven to 200°C/Gas 6. Heat the olive oil in a frying pan on the stove, then add 2 of the chicken breasts and brown them well. Two minutes on each side should be long enough, then place the breasts to one side while you brown the rest. Season the breasts with salt and pepper as they brown.
2 Put the browned chicken breasts in an ovenproof dish. Keep the frying pan on the heat, add the sherry and stir to scrape up all the sticky bits from the pan. Simmer for 30 seconds and then pour the liquid over the chicken breasts. Cover the breasts with a sheet of baking parchment and pop them into the oven for 20 minutes.
3 Remove the breasts from the dish and put them to one side. Place the ovenproof dish on the stove and heat the liquid through so that it starts to simmer gently. Add the chicken stock and simmer for another 5 minutes.
4 Add the cream and let it bubble for 30 seconds. Stir in the tarragon and season the sauce with salt and pepper. Pour the sauce over the breasts and serve with the coleslaw and baked potatoes.

To prepare the red cabbage coleslaw
5 Mix the cabbage, carrots, shallots, lettuce, radishes and basil in a bowl. Put the yoghurt in a small mixing bowl or jug and gradually add the olive oil, stirring constantly.
6 Stir in the mustard and season well with salt and pepper. Spoon the dressing over the coleslaw and combine so that the salad is evenly coated.

Sausage meat lasagne

This meal will be welcome on chilly evenings. Using sausage meat in lasagne, instead of minced beef, makes a nice change.

SERVES 6

1 x 375g packet of dried lasagne sheets

Meat filling
2 tbsp olive oil
1 onion, finely chopped
1 celery stalk, finely chopped
1 garlic clove, finely chopped
1 carrot, finely chopped
900g sausage meat
1 x 400g can of chopped tomatoes
3 tbsp chopped basil
sea salt
freshly ground black pepper

Cheese sauce
50g butter
50g flour
600ml milk
200g hard cheese (Parmesan or Gruyère), grated, plus extra for sprinkling on top
sea salt
freshly ground black pepper

To make the meat filling

1 Heat the olive oil in a large saucepan. Add the onion, celery, garlic and carrot and cook gently for 10 minutes over a low heat.

2 Add the sausage meat. Cook, stirring constantly, until the meat has lost its pinkness. Add the tomatoes and basil and cook for 30 minutes at a gentle simmer. Season with salt and pepper, then place to one side.

To make the cheese sauce

3 Heat the butter in a small saucepan. Add the flour and stir it over a low heat for 1 minute. Remove the pan from the heat and add the milk a little at a time, stirring constantly to avoid lumps. Return the sauce to the heat and simmer for 5 minutes over a low heat. Stir in the cheese, season with salt and pepper and place the sauce to one side.

To assemble the lasagne

4 Preheat the oven to 200°C/Gas 6. You need a lasagne dish or similar ovenproof dish. Spoon a little of the cheese sauce on to the bottom of the dish, followed by a layer of lasagne. Then spoon on a layer of the sausage meat sauce, followed by a layer of the cheese sauce, then more lasagne. Finish with a layer of cheese sauce and a sprinkling of grated Parmesan cheese. Cook for 1 hour until piping hot and bubbling.

Roast haunch of muntjac

A muntjac is a small deer so a normal venison haunch would do just as well. For both, follow the cooking times for perfect pink meat. Overcooked venison is not nice!

SERVES 6

1.5kg haunch of muntjac
olive oil
a sprig of fresh thyme
200ml red wine
1 tbsp flour
400ml beef stock
sea salt
freshly ground black pepper

Roast potatoes and parsnips
1kg potatoes, peeled, quartered and rinsed in cold water
400g parsnips, peeled and halved
1 tbsp goose fat
salt

Leeks
5 leeks
2 tbsp crème fraiche
sea salt
freshly ground black pepper

1 Preheat the oven to 220°C/Gas 7. Place the joint in a roasting tin and rub the meat with a tablespoon or 2 of olive oil. Season well with salt and pepper, then sprinkle the joint with the thyme leaves and pour 100ml of the red wine around the meat. Place the joint in the oven.
2 After 10 minutes, baste the joint with the red wine and any juices in the roasting tin. Reduce the oven temperature to 180°C/Gas 4 and cook the meat for a further 35 minutes. Remove the joint from the tin and place to one side to rest.
3 Place the meat tin on the top of the stove over a medium heat. Sprinkle on the flour and stir in. Pour in the stock and the rest of the wine and simmer for 15 minutes on a low heat. Carve the joint and serve with Yorkshire pudding (see page 145), roast potatoes and parsnips, and the leeks.

To prepare the roast potatoes and parsnips
4 Preheat the oven to 220°C/Gas 7. Put the potatoes and parsnips in a large pan of salted water, bring to the boil and cook for 6 minutes. Drain, then bash the potatoes and parsnips around in the pan to rough up the edges.
5 Tip the potatoes and parsnips into a roasting tin and add the goose fat. Roast the vegetables for 50–60 minutes until golden brown, turning them occasionally.

To prepare the leeks
6 Cut the leeks down the centre, almost to the end. Fan out under cold, running water to remove any grit, then slice the leeks widthways as finely as possible.
7 Place the leek slices in a pan and cook over a low heat for 5 minutes, stirring so they cook evenly. Stir in the crème fraiche and season with salt and pepper.

Coffee cake with mocha icing

This is a light coffee sponge which is made in the Genoese style, a change from the usual heavier sponge. The eggs and sugar are whisked over heat until thick and then the flour is added. There is no butter in the cake but there is a little in the mocha icing.

SERVES 6

butter, for greasing
4 eggs
115g caster sugar
1 tbsp instant coffee, dissolved in 1 tbsp hot water
115g plain flour
75g grated white chocolate

Filling and icing
75g soft butter
175g icing sugar
1 tbsp sifted cocoa powder
1 tbsp instant coffee, dissolved in 1 tbsp hot water
1 bar of white chocolate, to decorate

1 Preheat the oven to 180°C/Gas 4. Grease 2 x 18cm sandwich cake tins and line the bases with baking parchment.
2 Put the eggs, sugar and coffee in a mixing bowl and place the bowl over a saucepan of simmering water. Using an electric hand-whisk, whisk the mixture for 4 minutes until it has a thick, mousse-like texture. Remove from the heat.
3 Sift the flour into the mixture and fold it in gently with a metal spoon. Sprinkle on the grated chocolate and gently fold this in as well.
4 Divide the mixture evenly between the tins and bake the cakes for 20 minutes, until firm to the touch of your fingertips. Turn the cakes out on to a wire rack to cool completely.

To make the filling
5 Beat the butter and icing sugar together until soft and creamy. Mix in the cocoa powder and coffee.
6 Spread half the icing on top of 1 cake and put the other cake on top. Spread the top with the remaining icing.
7 To make the chocolate curls, place a slab of white chocolate on a work surface, smooth side up. Take a sharp knife and scrape it along the chocolate towards you, making as many curls as you want. Add these to the top of the cake.

Small chocolate puddings

These little puddings have the secret ingredient of a Belgian truffle so you are guaranteed a yummy moist centre. They are much easier to make than the fondant chocolate puddings you get in restaurants.

SERVES 6

- butter and flour, for preparing the pudding moulds
- 200g dark chocolate, broken into pieces
- 100g caster sugar
- 120g butter, cut into cubes
- 100g ground almonds
- 4 egg yolks
- 4 egg whites
- 6 Belgian truffles

1 Grease 6 small pudding moulds and dust each one with a little flour. This will ensure that the puddings do not stick to the moulds. Preheat the oven to 180°C/Gas 4.
2 Bring a pan of water to simmering point. Put the chocolate, sugar and butter in a glass bowl and place it over, but not touching, the water. Let the ingredients melt together, stirring them only occasionally.
3 Remove the bowl from the heat and stir in the almonds, then the egg yolks. Whisk the egg whites in a separate clean bowl until they form stiff peaks, then, using a metal spoon, fold them into the chocolate mixture.
4 Spoon a tablespoon of the mixture into each mould and place a truffle on top. Spoon the rest of the pudding mixture into the moulds, dividing it evenly between them. Place the moulds on a baking sheet and bake in the oven for 20 minutes until the tops of the puddings are slightly convex and feel firm to the touch.
5 Using a tea towel, take a mould and run a knife around the pudding to loosen it. Invert the mould on to a dessert plate so that the pudding comes free. Release the rest of the puddings in the same way and serve with cream.

Poached chicken in saffron rice

If you can't find a large chicken, two smaller ones will do just as well.

SERVES 6

- 1 tbsp olive oil
- 40g butter
- 1 x 2kg chicken
- 10 baby onions, peeled and cut in half
- 140g pancetta, chopped
- 2 garlic cloves, crushed
- 100ml dry sherry
- 1 large pinch of saffron strands
- 600g basmati rice
- 700ml water
- 1 tsp salt

1 Heat the oil and butter in a large casserole dish, add the chicken and brown it all over. It can be tricky to move the bird around in the pan to brown it evenly, but persevere as a beautiful golden poached chicken is so much more appealing than a pale anaemic-looking one. It should take about 10 minutes to brown the chicken properly.
2 Once the chicken is golden brown, remove it from the casserole dish and place to one side.
3 Keep the casserole dish on the stove and add the onions, pancetta and garlic. Stir them into the fat and cook for 3 minutes, until the pancetta cubes are golden brown.
4 Next pour on the sherry and let it sizzle away for a minute. Sprinkle on the saffron strands and stir for 30 seconds, then add the rice and stir with a wooden spoon to coat it in the fat and liquid. Preheat the oven to 160°C/Gas 3.
5 Put the chicken back in the pan on top of the rice, pour in the water and season with the salt. Bring to a simmer and then pop the casserole dish in the oven for 1 hour. Remove the casserole dish from the oven and give the rice a good stir, then return the pot to the oven for 40 minutes more.
6 Lift the chicken from the casserole and place on a board to rest for 15 minutes. Place a lid on the casserole to keep the rice warm. Carve the chicken and serve with the rice.

Spaghetti carbonara

This is an all-time favourite with my children. I included a recipe for carbonara in my last book, but the dish is so popular that the family insisted that another recipe should appear here.

SERVES 6

2 tbsp olive oil
2 garlic cloves, whole but bashed
200g sliced pancetta, finely chopped
150ml white wine
4 egg yolks
200ml double cream
100g Parmesan cheese, grated
600g spaghetti
sea salt
freshly ground black pepper

1 Heat the olive oil in a frying pan. Add the garlic cloves and fry them for 40 seconds or so to flavour the oil, then remove the garlic.
2 Add the pancetta and fry until golden brown. Pour on the wine and let it simmer for 45 seconds, then place the pan to one side.
3 Bring a large saucepan of salted water to the boil for cooking the spaghetti. In a small mixing bowl, mix the egg yolks, cream and Parmesan cheese, and season with salt and pepper.
4 Cook the spaghetti according to the packet instructions. Towards the end of the cooking time, reheat the pancetta mixture.
5 Drain the pasta and return it to the saucepan, then stir in the egg and cream mixture and the pancetta. Serve immediately with a green salad.

Vegetable biryani with cucumber raita

This is technically a pilaf rather than a biryani, as the vegetables are mixed in with the rice and then cooked. For a true biryani, the spiced vegetables or meat are cooked separately from the rice and then brought together in layers and served.

SERVES 6

2 tbsp olive oil
1 onion, finely chopped
2 garlic cloves, finely chopped
1 tsp grated fresh root ginger
500g basmati rice
1 tbsp curry powder
¼ tsp turmeric
50g carrots, finely diced
1 cauliflower, trimmed and cut into 2cm pieces
100g frozen peas
50g green beans, cut into 1cm pieces
3 tomatoes, finely chopped
1 green chilli, finely chopped (optional)
1 x 400ml can of coconut milk
750ml vegetable stock
1 tsp salt
2 tbsp finely chopped coriander leaves

Garnish
2 tbsp olive oil
1 small onion, finely chopped
50g cashew nuts

Cucumber raita
½ cucumber, diced
2 tbsp finely chopped fresh mint
300ml natural yoghurt
sea salt

1 Preheat the oven to 200°C/Gas 6. Heat the olive oil in a large saucepan that has a lid and can be put in the oven. Add the onion, garlic and ginger and cook for 3 minutes on a low heat. Add the rice, stir and cook for 1 minute, then add the curry powder and turmeric and stir again.
2 Next add the vegetables and tomatoes (including the chilli if you are using it) and stir. Pour on the coconut milk and stock and add the salt, then bring to a simmer.
3 Cover the rice with a sheet of baking parchment, put a lid on the pan and place in the oven for 40 minutes, by which time the rice and vegetables should be cooked. Stir in the coriander leaves.
4 Next prepare the garnish. Heat the olive oil in a small frying pan, add the onion and fry until golden brown. Add the cashew nuts and fry for 1 minute more. Sprinkle the garnish over the rice and serve with the raita.

To prepare the cucumber raita
5 Mix the ingredients together in a serving bowl and season with a little salt.

Fish cakes with ham and peas

I love fish cakes, but I don't like the palaver involved in making them: cooking the fish, cooking and mashing the potato, chopping all the other ingredients. This version is for those of you who love the simple life.

SERVES 6

700g pollack fillet, skinned
300g potatoes, peeled, cut into quarters, cooked until tender and mashed
7 tbsp single cream
½ tsp ground cumin
¼ tsp ground nutmeg
a small bunch of chives, finely snipped
2 tbsp olive oil, for frying
sea salt
freshly ground black pepper

Ham and peas
25g butter
4 shallots, peeled and cut into quarters
500g frozen petit pois
1 level tbsp flour
500ml chicken stock (a stock cube will do)
2–3 handfuls of green salad leaves
2 tbsp finely chopped flat-leaf parsley,
a pinch of sugar
200g piece of cooked ham, cut into small cubes
sea salt
freshly ground black pepper

1 Place the fish in a food processor and process until minced. Spoon the fish into a mixing bowl and add the mashed potato, cream, spices and chives. Season well with salt and pepper and mix so that all the ingredients are evenly combined.
2 Form the mixture into 12 evenly sized patties and place them in the fridge until you are ready to cook them.
3 To cook the fish cakes, heat the olive oil in a frying pan until quite hot and then add the fish cakes, a few at a time. They will take about 8 minutes, 4 minutes on each side, to cook through, as the fish is raw. Place each batch in a low oven to keep warm while you cook the rest. Serve with the ham and peas and some baked potatoes if you want a really hearty meal.

To prepare the ham and peas
4 Heat the butter in a medium-sized saucepan. Add the shallots and fry them for 2 minutes, stirring them occasionally. Add the peas and the flour, then stir gently with a wooden spoon.
5 Pour on the stock, add the salad leaves, parsley, sugar and ham, then simmer gently, uncovered, for about 25 minutes. Taste for seasoning and add some pepper and some salt if necessary.

Chicken Kiev

My children say they are served chicken Kiev at school and do not like it at all, mostly because of the way oil seeps out of the chicken on the plate. I hope my version changes their minds.

SERVES 6

75g softened butter
1 tsp finely chopped fresh tarragon
1 tsp finely chopped fresh parsley
6 skinless, boneless chicken breasts
3 eggs
2–3 tbsp flour
100g white breadcrumbs
2 tbsp olive oil, for frying
sea salt
freshly ground black pepper

1 Place the butter and herbs in a small bowl, season with salt and pepper and mix well. Shape the herb butter into a small roll, wrap it in clingfilm and place it in the fridge to chill.
2 Lay the chicken breasts on a board. Slice a thin fillet from the side of each breast and set them aside. Next, make a 6cm incision along the length of each breast. Slice the hard herb butter into 6 long strips and put a strip into the cut in each breast. Cover the butter strips with the 6 fillet pieces, pressing them in so that the cuts are closed and the butter sealed in.
3 Lightly beat the eggs in a bowl and spread the flour and breadcrumbs on separate plates. Dip each breast in some flour, then the egg and finally the breadcrumbs. Preheat the oven to 180°C/Gas 4.
4 Heat 2 tablespoons of olive oil in a frying pan and fry each breast for 1 minute on each side, then set aside on an oven tray. When all the breasts have been fried, place them in the oven for 10 minutes to finish cooking. Serve with baked potatoes and salad.

Lamb stew pie

This is a sort of hot pot pie and very delicious too.

SERVES 6

- 2 tbsp olive oil
- 1kg lamb leg meat, diced
- 1 onion, finely chopped
- 50ml white wine
- 1 heaped tsp flour
- 400g turnips, peeled and cut into 2cm chunks
- 100g carrots, peeled and cut into 2cm chunks
- 100g young spinach leaves
- leaves from 2 sprigs of rosemary, finely chopped
- 550ml beef or chicken stock
- 700g potatoes, peeled and cut into 3mm slices
- a knob of butter
- sea salt
- freshly ground black pepper

1 Heat the olive oil in a large saucepan. Brown the lamb in small batches, putting each batch aside once it has browned.

2 Once you have browned all the meat, cook the onion, adding a little more olive oil if necessary. Remove the onion, placing it with the meat. Keep the pan on the heat, add the wine and stir, scraping up any sticky bits from the bottom of the saucepan. Simmer for 1 minute.

3 Return the meat and onion to the pan, then sprinkle on the flour and stir. Add the turnips, carrots, spinach, rosemary and stock and season well with salt and pepper. Bring to a simmer, cover the pan and cook for 30 minutes.

4 Preheat the oven to 200°C/Gas 6. Spoon the lamb stew into a gratin dish and top with the potatoes, arranging them in an overlapping layer. Dot with a little butter and season with salt and pepper. Cook in the oven for 60 minutes until the potatoes are soft.

Roast loin of pork with baked apples and braised savoy cabbage

Loin of pork is ideal for Sunday lunch as you can cook it slowly, without worrying too much about exact cooking times. The fat protecting the meat makes this cut more forgiving for the relaxed cook, which is the sort of cook we all like to be occasionally.

SERVES 6

2kg piece of loin of pork, boned and with skin scored
1 tbsp olive oil
3 Granny Smith apples, halved horizontally and cored
salt

Gravy
1 tbsp flour
2 garlic cloves, smashed with a rolling pin
200ml dry cider
400ml chicken stock
sea salt
freshly ground black pepper

Braised savoy cabbage
1 savoy cabbage, cored and finely shredded
25g butter
1 tbsp water
1 tbsp Marsala wine
2 tbsp crème fraiche
1 tsp Dijon mustard
sea salt
freshly ground black pepper

1 Preheat the oven to 220°C/Gas 7. Place the joint in a roasting tin. Rub the olive oil into the rind of the pork and sprinkle over a good few pinches of salt. Place in the oven for 30 minutes.
2 Reduce the oven temperature to 160°C/Gas 3 and cook the pork for another 1½ hours.
3 Then place the apple halves around the pork and turn the oven back up to 220°C/Gas 7 for 30 minutes to crispen the crackling. The apples will collapse slightly but don't worry. Remove the roasting tin from the oven, place the meat on a plate or carving board and leave to rest for 30 minutes. Keep the apples warm.
4 To make the gravy, place the roasting tin over a high heat. Stir in the flour, mash in the garlic cloves and pour on the cider, then cook at a simmer for 5 minutes. Add the chicken stock and remove the garlic cloves, then simmer for 10 minutes. Season with salt and pepper. Carve the pork and serve with the apples, gravy, savoy cabbage and some roast potatoes (see page 94).

To prepare the braised savoy cabbage
5 Put the cabbage in a saucepan with the butter and water and place over a low heat. Cover the pan and gently cook the cabbage for 10–12 minutes until it has wilted and lost its crunch.
6 Increase the heat and add the Marsala wine, then cook, stirring constantly, for 1 minute. Reduce the heat again and add the crème fraiche and mustard. Stir to coat the cabbage and cook gently for 2 minutes. Season with salt and plenty of black pepper.

Cardamom shortbread

Cardamom is a very popular spice these days and adds a unique flavour to cakes and biscuits

MAKES ABOUT 16 FINGERS

250g softened butter
125g caster sugar
300g self-raising flour
60g plain flour
2 tbsp semolina flour
½ tsp ground cardamom seeds

1 Preheat the oven to 180°C/Gas 4. Beat the butter in a mixing bowl with the sugar, until pale and thoroughly combined. Add all the other ingredients and mix together to form a ball of dough.
2 Take a 32 x 23cm rectangular Swiss roll tin and cut out a piece of baking parchment slightly larger than the tin. Roll out the ball of dough on the paper so you can pick it up and place it in the Swiss roll tin. The shortbread dough needs to meet the edges of the tin.
3 Place the shortbread in the oven and bake for 25 minutes until the top is just turning golden brown. Cut into rectangular fingers while still in the tin.
4 When the shortbread has cooled slightly, lift it out with the parchment paper and leave to cool completely.

Baked pineapple, pear and plums with toffee sauce

There are no spring fruits in Britain, apart from rhubarb, so we have to rely on imported varieties in our cooking. This recipe is a delicious way of using fresh pineapple.

SERVES 6

300g fresh pineapple, peeled and cut into cubes
4 plums, cut in half
2 pears, cored and cut in quarters
2 tbsp maple syrup
2 tsp brown sugar

Toffee sauce
300ml double cream
225g soft brown sugar
100g butter

1 Preheat the oven to 180°C/Gas 4. Place the fruit in an ovenproof dish and bake for 15 minutes.
2 Place all the ingredients for the toffee sauce in a saucepan and warm through on a low heat until everything has melted and combined. Stir and serve with the baked fruit.

Lemon Knickerbocker Glory

This pudding needs no introduction or explanation.

SERVES 6

Meringues
3 egg whites
175g caster sugar
¼ tsp yellow food colouring

Lemon curd
50g butter
110g caster sugar
finely grated zest and juice of 2 lemons
2 eggs
1 egg yolk

Cream
70g mascarpone cheese
80g Greek yoghurt
100ml double cream
1 tbsp icing sugar
2 tsp vanilla extract

1 tub of vanilla ice cream, for serving

To make the meringues

1 Preheat the oven to 120°C/Gas ½. Cover a baking sheet with a sheet of baking parchment.

2 Place the egg whites in a mixing bowl and whisk until they form thick peaks. It is almost impossible to do this successfully by hand so use an electric hand-whisk or a food mixer. Add the sugar, a tablespoon at a time, whisking in each addition until all the sugar has been added. Add the food colouring and mix in.

3 Spoon separate tablespoons of the meringue on to the baking parchment and bake for 50 minutes.

To make the lemon curd

4 Melt the butter in a small saucepan on a low heat. Add the caster sugar, lemon zest and juice. Stir in the eggs and egg yolk and heat gently until the curd thickens enough to coat the back of the spoon. It will thicken more as it cools. If you find that the whites of the eggs have cooked separately from the yolks, just pass the curd through a sieve. Leave to one side to cool.

To prepare the cream

5 Gently mix all the ingredients in a bowl until well combined.

To serve

6 You can serve this dessert in tall glasses or in a large dish. If you are serving it in tall glasses, place a teaspoon of lemon curd in the bottom of each glass, followed by some broken meringues. Then spoon in some of the cream, some more meringue and then lemon curd. Finish off with a scoop of vanilla ice cream.

7 If you are using a large dish, serve the Glory rather like an Eton mess, with some broken meringues mixed into the cream. Spoon on the curd and top with ice cream.

Tuna and sweetcorn fritters with bean sprout salad

I try not to use canned tuna very often, as tuna is overfished in the Atlantic and the Mediterranean to the point of near extinction. I think one or two cans a year is acceptable, although there is an argument for not using it at all. If you prefer not to buy canned tuna, make these fritters with canned mackerel or some minced chicken. Add some fried eggs for a more filling meal.

SERVES 6

1 x 285g can of sweetcorn, drained
100g jar or can of tuna fish, drained
2 garlic cloves, finely chopped
3 shallots, finely chopped
2 tbsp fresh coriander
1 tsp sugar
1 tbsp fish sauce
100g plain flour
2 eggs
½ tsp salt
2 tbsp vegetable oil, for frying
sweet chilli oil, for serving
6 eggs, for frying (optional)
freshly ground black pepper

Bean sprout salad
3 tomatoes, cut into chunks
2 handfuls of bean sprouts
4cm piece of cucumber, sliced
5 spring onions, finely sliced
handful of torn basil leaves

Dressing
2 tbsp olive oil
½ tbsp dark soy sauce
sea salt
freshly ground black pepper

1 Place half the sweetcorn in a food processor with the tuna, garlic, shallot, coriander, sugar and fish sauce. Whizz to a paste, then spoon into a mixing bowl and fold in the rest of the sweetcorn, the flour and 2 eggs. The mixture should be quite wet.
2 Season with the salt and some black pepper. Heat the vegetable oil in a frying pan and cook tablespoons of the mixture until golden brown on each side. Place to one side to keep warm while you fry the eggs. Serve the fritters with the sweet chilli oil, fried eggs (if using) and salad.

To make the salad
3 Place the tomatoes, bean sprouts, cucumber, spring onions and basil in a serving bowl. Mix the olive oil, soy sauce and seasoning to make the dressing and set aside. Pour the dressing over the salad ingredients when ready to serve.

Gammon with lentil and vegetable stew

Gammon is mostly seen in the shops at Christmas and Easter, but I cook it much more often as it is so versatile. It's beautiful cold with salad and baked potatoes, it can be chopped up and added to a soup, or sliced and fried for a nice supper of ham and egg on toast. And what could be better than a ham sandwich with mustard?

SERVES 6

1kg unsmoked gammon joint

Ham glaze
2 tbsp honey, warmed
1 tbsp soy sauce
1 tbsp brown sugar
1 tbsp olive oil

Lentil and vegetable stew
2 tbsp olive oil
1 medium onion, finely chopped
1 carrot, cut into chunks
½ celeriac, cut into 2cm chunks
2 potatoes, peeled and cut into chunks
180g red lentils
½ tsp ground cumin
½ tsp ground coriander
550ml ham stock
1 tsp salt
1 tbsp chopped flat-leaf parsley
1 tbsp crème fraiche

1 Put all the ingredients for the glaze in a bowl and mix them well.
2 Place the gammon joint in a large saucepan and add enough cold water to cover the joint. Bring to a simmer and cook for 30 minutes. Preheat the oven to 200°C/Gas 6.
3 Take the gammon out of the water, reserving the cooking stock, and set it in a roasting tin tray. Trim off the top 4cm of rind and fat, leaving some fat below. Using a pastry brush or the back of a spoon, spread the glaze over both the fat and meat of the gammon. Place the gammon in the preheated oven and cook for 40 minutes. Carve the meat into slices and serve on top of the lentil and vegetable stew.

To make the lentil and vegetable stew
4 Heat the olive oil in a large saucepan and add the onion, carrot, celeriac and potatoes. Cook gently on a medium heat for 10 minutes.
5 Sprinkle on the lentils and spices, then pour on the ham stock (the cooking liquid from the gammon that you set aside). Cook at a low simmer for 40 minutes until the lentils and the vegetables are soft. You may need to add a little more ham stock as the vegetables cook.
6 Add the salt, parsley and crème fraiche, then check the seasoning, adding more salt if necessary.

Slow-cooked leg of lamb with vegetables

Lamb can be at its best at this time of year.

SERVES 6

2 tbsp olive oil
300g carrots, cut into 3cm chunks
200g parsnips, cut into 3cm chunks
300g butternut squash, cut into 3cm chunks
500g potatoes, peeled and cut in quarters
5 shallots, peeled and cut in half
4 garlic cloves, peeled and left whole
300ml white wine
2 tbsp pearl barley
2 sprigs of fresh thyme
1 x 2kg leg of lamb
sea salt
freshly ground black pepper

1 Preheat the oven to 220°C/Gas 7. Pour the olive oil into a large roasting tin and warm on the top of the stove. When the oil is hot, add the carrots, parsnips, squash, potatoes, shallots and garlic and brown for about 2 minutes. Turn the vegetables in the oil once or twice during this time.
2 Next pour on the wine and simmer for 2 minutes. Sprinkle in the pearl barley and stir to combine, then place the thyme in among the vegetables.
3 Place a wire rack over the roasting tin and put the leg of lamb on this. Season the lamb well with salt and pepper, place in the oven and cook for 30 minutes. Turn the oven down to 150°C/Gas 2 and cook for another 2 ½ hours, turning the vegetables occasionally during this time.
4 Remove the roasting tin from the oven and leave the meat to rest on the rack over the vegetables for 20 minutes, so that the juice from the lamb drips on to the vegetables. Carve the lamb and serve with the vegetables.

Honey and ginger apple tarte tatin

Apple tarte tatin is perfect just as it is. This version isn't better than the classic, just different, so give it a try.

SERVES 6

4 tbsp clear honey
2 tbsp maple syrup
2 tbsp caster sugar
500g Cox or Granny Smith apples, peeled, cored and cut into quarters
50g cold butter, cut into cubes
1 tsp ground ginger
1 tsp mixed spice
grated zest of 1 lemon
200g all-butter puff pastry
crème fraiche, for serving

1 Preheat the oven to 200°C/Gas 6. You will need a tarte tatin tin or a tart tin with a sealed base.
2 Place the honey, syrup and sugar in the tin and put the tin on top of the stove over a medium heat. Let the ingredients start to bubble and brown and then tip the tin away from you to distribute the sugar evenly around the pan. Don't be tempted to stir the caramel that starts to appear.
3 Once the caramel has darkened and thickened slightly, which should take about 5 minutes, add the apples and stir to coat them in the sugary syrup. Add the butter, spices and lemon zest and stir again. Once the apples start to sizzle, remove the pan from the heat.
4 Roll out the pastry until it is large enough to cover the apples and goes right to the edge of the tin. Lay the pastry on the apples and tuck in any uneven bits. Bake in the oven for 25 minutes. Cover the pastry with some foil if it is browning too quickly.
5 Turn the tart out on to a plate, once cool enough to handle, and serve with crème fraiche.

Easter often falls during this month and this is the time to enjoy the young lamb that is coming into the shops. The meat is tender and succulent and perfect for the change in the weather. Enjoy it roasted, rolled and stuffed or stewed – all are delicious. If you have not already done so, it is time to venture back into the garden. The weeds will be growing, even if the vegetables are a bit slow off the mark. This is a crucial time of year for vegetable gardeners, as too much sunshine early in the month can get plants growing quickly which may suffer if the weather in May is unkind. Make sure you take time to enjoy the sun on your back when it breaks through and be thankful for the showers that encourage the young plants to grow. This is a good time to sow broad beans, peas, beetroot and spinach, to name but a few. The amount of space you have will dictate how much you can grow. In the kitchen, take the chance to banish winter food for the next few months. Glorious mackerel reaches the fishmongers in April and the equally wonderful trout and shellfish really come into their own.

April

Green Thai curry

There are many recipes written for Thai green curry. My version is far from authentic as it contains no kaffir lime leaves, which are traditionally the source of the green colour and the reason for the dish's name. It is, though, full of flavour and fairly easy to put together.

SERVES 6

100g shallots
1 red chilli (optional)
3 garlic cloves
2 tsp Bart's lemon grass in sunflower oil
2 tsp Bart's galangal in sunflower oil
30g fresh coriander
50ml water
1 tsp salt
40g unsalted peanuts
1 tbsp coriander seeds
1 tsp cumin seeds
4 cloves
seeds from 4 cardamom pods
1 tbsp vegetable oil
1 kg chicken drumsticks and thighs on the bone, skin removed
1 medium red onion, finely sliced
1 x 400 ml can of coconut milk
1 tbsp fish sauce
1 tbsp soft brown sugar
250g baby new potatoes

Cucumber salad
1 cucumber, chopped into chunks
2 tbsp chopped fresh mint
1 tbsp chopped coriander
1 shallot, finely sliced
1 tsp sesame oil
1 tbsp olive oil
sea salt
freshly ground black pepper

1 Place the shallots, chilli (if using), garlic, lemon grass, galangal, fresh coriander and water in a liquidiser and blend to a smooth paste.
2 Place the salt, peanuts, coriander seeds, cumin seeds, cloves and cardamom seeds in a small frying pan and toast them until you can smell the aroma of the spices and the peanuts start to brown. Transfer to a pestle and mortar and grind to a fine powder.
3 Heat the vegetable oil in a saucepan and brown the chicken pieces a few at a time, placing them to one side as they are done.
4 Keep the pan on the heat. Add the red onion and fry for 3 minutes, then add the ground spice and peanut mixture and fry for a further minute. Return the browned chicken to the pan.
5 Pour on the coconut milk and fish sauce and add the sugar, shallot and coriander paste and potatoes. Cover the pan and simmer for 40 minutes, by which time the potatoes should be tender. Serve with boiled rice (see page 74) and cucumber salad.

To make the cucumber salad
6 Place the cucumber, mint, coriander and shallot in a serving dish. Mix the oils together and season with salt and pepper, then pour over the cucumber salad before serving.

Nasi goreng with coriander omelettes

This is fried rice Indonesian style.

SERVES 6

2 tbsp olive oil
1 onion, finely chopped
2 garlic cloves, crushed
200g fresh petit pois
2 carrots, thinly sliced
500g basmati rice
1 tbsp soy sauce
1 tsp paprika
1 tbsp tomato purée
400ml vegetable stock (a stock cube will do)
150g bean sprouts
sea salt

Coriander omelettes
12 eggs
2 tbsp finely chopped fresh coriander
olive oil
sea salt
freshly ground black pepper

1 First make the nasi goreng. Heat the olive oil in a large saucepan. Add the onion, garlic, peas, carrots and rice, then stir. Add the soy sauce, paprika and tomato purée and stir again, then season with a little salt and pour on the vegetable stock. Bring to a simmer, then reduce the heat, put a lid on the pan and cook very gently for about 15 minutes.

2 Remove the pan from the heat and leave it covered and undisturbed for 10 minutes. Stir in the bean sprouts and serve a good spoonful of the mixture on top of each omelette.

To make the coriander omelettes

3 Beat the eggs in a large mixing bowl, add the coriander, and season with salt and pepper.

4 Heat a little olive oil in a frying pan, then pour in a ladleful of egg mixture. Tilt the pan so that the egg forms a single, round layer on the bottom of the pan. Cook through, then tip the omelette out on to a plate. Make another 5 omelettes in the same way.

Tomato, noodles and fish

Children like anything with noodles and this is a brilliant way of getting them to enjoy mackerel.

SERVES 6

2 tbsp olive oil
1 onion, finely chopped
1 garlic clove, crushed
1 tsp Bart's lemon grass in sunflower oil
1 tsp Bart's galangal in sunflower oil
500ml tomato passata
165ml canned coconut cream
600ml vegetable stock
1 tsp sugar
1 tbsp dark soy sauce
200g shelled prawns
100g young spinach leaves, finely shredded
250g medium egg noodles
4 mackerel fillets
2 tbsp roughly chopped fresh coriander
sea salt
freshly ground black pepper

1 Heat the olive oil in a large saucepan. Add the onion and garlic and fry for 3 minutes, then add the lemon grass and galangal and cook for 2 minutes more.
2 Pour in the passata, coconut cream and stock, then add the sugar and soy sauce, cover the pan and simmer for 20 minutes. Check the seasoning and add some salt and pepper if necessary. Stir in the prawns and spinach and simmer for 1 minute.
3 In the meantime, cook the noodles according to the packet instructions, drain and leave to one side.
4 Heat a frying pan and brush it with a little oil. Lay the mackerel fillets skin side down in the hot pan for 1 minute on each side. Remove the skin and flake the fish into a bowl.
5 Take 6 bowls and place some noodles in each one. Pour on some of the tomato mixture and spoon some mackerel on top. Garnish with a sprinkling of chopped coriander leaves.

Sea bass fillets with braised fennel and cabbage, and saffron cream sauce

This meal is bursting with flavour. The saffron is superb with the sea bass and the fennel.

SERVES 6

6 x 140g sea bass fillets
plain flour, for dusting
1 tbsp olive oil
1 lemon
sea salt
freshly ground black pepper

Braised fennel and cabbage
25g butter
1 fennel bulb, finely sliced
1 small white cabbage, finely sliced
1 lemon
sea salt
freshly ground black pepper

Saffron cream sauce
15g butter
1 small onion, very finely chopped
a pinch of saffron threads, soaked in 1 tbsp warm water
1 garlic clove, finely chopped
1 tbsp brandy
3 tbsp crème fraiche
sea salt
freshly ground black pepper

1 Check that all the little bones have been removed from the sea bass fillets, then dust them lightly with flour.
2 Heat the olive oil in a frying pan and add a few of the sea bass fillets, skin side down. Cook for 1 minute, then turn them over and cook for another minute – thicker fillets will need a little longer. Remove from the pan and keep warm while you cook the rest. Season all the fillets with salt and pepper and a squeeze of fresh lemon juice.
3 To serve, place a couple of spoonfuls of fennel and cabbage on each plate, add a sea bass fillet and trickle over some of the saffron cream sauce.

To prepare the braised fennel and cabbage
4 Heat the butter in a large saucepan and add the fennel and cabbage. Cover and cook over a low heat, stirring occasionally, for 10 minutes. Season with salt and pepper and a squeeze of fresh lemon juice.

To prepare the saffron cream sauce
5 Heat the butter in a small saucepan until it is foaming, then add the onion and fry for 10 minutes on a low heat until soft.
6 Pour on the saffron threads and liquid. Add the garlic and the brandy and cook for 2 minutes on a low heat. Stir in the crème fraiche and simmer gently for 2 minutes. Season to taste.

Minced meat pie with a sweet potato crust

The sweet potato is a distant relative of the ordinary potato and is highly nutritious. Apparently, the Chinese grow most of the world's sweet potatoes and until recently ate most of the crop themselves. Now, with the rise in the standard of living there and the population demanding more meat, pork in particular, pigs are fed most of the crop. For this pie topping, I have mixed sweet potato with butternut squash and it makes a nice change from the usual mash.

SERVES 6

2 tbsp olive oil
1 onion, finely chopped
1 celery stalk, finely chopped
1kg minced beef
2 x 400g cans of chopped tomatoes
150ml chicken or beef stock
(½ a stock cube will do)
1 tbsp dark soy sauce

Topping
5 sweet potatoes
2 potatoes
1 butternut squash, peeled,
cored and cut into 2cm chunks
1 tbsp olive oil
25g butter
100g Gruyère cheese, grated
sea salt
freshly ground black pepper

1 Heat the olive oil in a large saucepan. Add the onion and celery and cook for 10 minutes over a medium heat, stirring occasionally. Add the mince, turn up the heat and brown the mince well.
2 Add the chopped tomatoes, stock and soy sauce, then simmer very gently, uncovered, for 1 hour. Check frequently and if the liquid starts to disappear, cover the pan for the rest of the cooking time.

To make the topping
3 Preheat the oven to 200°C/Gas 6 and bake all the potatoes, sweet and ordinary, in their skins for 1 hour.
4 Put the chunks of squash on a sheet of foil with a tablespoon of olive oil and some salt and pepper. Wrap them up into a parcel and place in the oven with the potatoes for 40 minutes.
5 Tip the cooked squash into a bowl. When the potatoes are cool enough to handle, scoop out the insides and add them to the squash. Stir in the butter and mix well.
6 Spoon the mince mixture into a gratin dish and cover with the potato and squash. Sprinkle with the cheese and brown under a hot grill for 10 minutes.

Spicy chicken and chorizo salad

This recipe started off as a chicken liver and pancetta salad but my children weren't keen on the chicken livers. They did try them but were unenthusiastic to say the least. I think it is important to stretch the children when it comes to food, but there is only so far you can go. I've turned the recipe into a chicken and chorizo salad.

SERVES 6

400g chicken breasts, chopped into bite-sized pieces
3 eggs
200g salad leaves
extra virgin olive oil
1 tsp balsamic vinegar
2 tbsp olive oil
800g potatoes, cooked until tender and then cut into chunks
15g butter
200g chorizo, cut into small discs
1 red onion, finely sliced
6 tbsp soured cream
sea salt
freshly ground black pepper

Spice mixture
1 tbsp coriander seeds
1 tbsp cumin seeds
½ tsp fennel seeds

1 First prepare the spice mixture. Place the spices in a frying pan over a medium heat and once they start to smoke, stir them around a little. When the seeds start to darken and you can smell their aroma, remove the pan from the heat. Grind the spices as finely as you can in a pestle and mortar.
2 Put the chicken pieces in a bowl and toss them with the spice mixture. Leave in a cool place or a fridge for 30 minutes or so.
3 Boil the eggs in simmering water for 4 minutes. Rinse them under cold water and set aside until you are ready to assemble the salad.
4 Place the salad leaves in a bowl and dress them with 1 tablespoon extra virgin olive oil and the balsamic vinegar. Season with salt and pepper. Arrange some salad leaves on each plate.
5 Heat the 2 tablespoons of olive oil in a frying pan and fry the potato chunks until golden brown. Place the potatoes to one side to keep warm.
6 Return the pan to the heat and add the butter. When it's warm, add the chicken pieces and fry for about 2 minutes, or until cooked, moving them gently around the pan. Place to one side. Add the chorizo sausage and fry until golden. Place to one side.
7 Place some potatoes on the salad leaves and then some chicken and chorizo. Sprinkle on some red onion. Shell the eggs, slice them in half and place a half on the top of each serving. Spoon on some soured cream and add a drizzle of extra virgin olive oil. Season to taste.

Lamb cutlets with new potatoes and puréed swede

We used to be given mashed swede at school and it was always a watery, dull, tasteless slop. It was an effort in later years to try it again, but I was pleasantly surprised. Cooked with more love and care, swede has a beautiful sweetness and it makes a good partner for lamb cutlets.

SERVES 6

1.2kg lamb cutlets, trimmed of the thin papery layer of fat
sea salt

New potatoes
700g new potatoes, unpeeled but cut in half
2 tbsp olive oil
1 onion, thinly sliced
leaves from 1 sprig of rosemary, finely chopped
sea salt

Puréed swede
1 swede, peeled and cut into 1cm cubes
300ml chicken stock (fresh or made with a stock cube)
grating of fresh nutmeg
sea salt
freshly ground black pepper

1 Heat a frying pan, then take 3 or 4 of the lamb cutlets and place them on their edges to brown the fat. Then turn the cutlets on their sides and fry them for 4 minutes. Flip them over and fry for 4 minutes on the other side.
2 As the cutlets are cooked, lay them on top of the potatoes and onion to serve. Serve with the swede.

To prepare the potatoes
3 Boil the potatoes in salted water until tender. Heat the olive oil in a large sauté pan, add the onion and rosemary and fry for 2 minutes. Add the potatoes and fry them with the onion until both are golden brown.

To prepare the swede
4 Put the swede in a saucepan and pour on the chicken stock. Bring to a simmer, cover the pan and cook for 15 minutes until the swede cubes are tender. Purée the swede in a liquidiser and then tip the purée back into the saucepan. Season well with salt, pepper and the nutmeg and heat through.

Brownies with white chocolate chunks

According to 'Larousse Gastronomique', the culinary reference book, chocolate brownies have been around since the 1890s in the United States, but in Britain they are a more recent passion. Despite their simplicity, there are a couple of rules that need to be followed. First, don't over mix the batter when all the ingredients have been added or you will end up with more of a cake. Second, don't overcook them. Remove the brownies from the oven when they still look slightly undercooked, as part of their appeal is their gooeyness.

MAKE 12

250g dark chocolate, broken into chunks
100g butter, plus extra for greasing
3 eggs
120g caster sugar
50g plain flour
100g white chocolate, cut roughly into chunks no bigger than 1cm

1 Grease a brownie tin, measuring about 20 x 25cm. Preheat the oven to 160°C/Gas 3.
2 Put the dark chocolate and butter into a glass bowl and place it over a saucepan of simmering water – don't let the bottom of the bowl touch the water. Stir the chocolate and butter until they have melted, then remove the bowl from the heat.
3 Place the eggs and sugar in a separate mixing bowl and beat with an electric hand-whisk until pale and creamy. Sift in the flour and stir in the chocolate and butter, being careful not to over mix. Gently fold in the white chocolate chunks.
4 Spoon the mixture into the tin and bake in the preheated oven for 15 minutes. The brownies will still look slightly undercooked, but don't worry. They will continue to cook in the tin.
5 Leave the brownies to cool completely before cutting into squares and removing from the tin. They can be stored in an airtight container and they are best eaten the day after baking.

Chocolate walnut buns

These are amazing for breakfast or for pudding. They look beautiful when they come out of the oven, as the individual buns join together as they cook. You can tear them apart while warm and spread them with butter for a real treat. Any that are left over can be turned into a great bread and butter pudding.

MAKES 12

450g strong white bread flour, plus extra for dusting work surface
½ tsp ground cinnamon
50g butter, chilled and cut into cubes, plus extra for greasing
50g caster sugar
1 egg yolk
1 x 7g sachet of easy-blend yeast
120ml water
60ml milk

Filling
50g butter, at room temperature
50g soft brown sugar
175g dark chocolate, roughly chopped
75g walnuts, roughly chopped

Glaze
1 egg, beaten
3 tbsp maple syrup

1 You need a 23cm loose-bottomed cake tin that's about 4cm deep. Grease the tin with butter and set it aside.
2 Mix the flour, cinnamon, butter, sugar, egg yolk, yeast, water and milk in a large bowl. Mix and knead the mixture to a ball of dough, then cover the bowl and leave the dough to rest for 15 minutes.
3 Roll out the dough on a floured surface to make a rectangle measuring 40 x 30cm.
4 Place the filling ingredients in a mixing bowl and mix until combined. Spread the filling evenly on to the rectangle of dough, going right up to the edges.
5 From one of the long sides, roll up the dough into a sausage shape. Cut into 12 equal pieces and place these, cut side up, in the cake tin, arranging them in a snug circle from the outside inwards.
6 Cover and leave to rise for 1 hour. Preheat the oven to 200°C/Gas 6. Brush the tops of the buns with beaten egg and bake in the oven for 35 minutes. Brush with the warmed maple syrup and pull apart to serve.

Rhubarb plate pie

It's easy to get carried away with complicated desserts and forget the deliciousness of a simple fruit pie. Here is one of the best.

SERVES 6

800g rhubarb, cut into 2cm chunks
2 tbsp soft brown sugar
finely grated zest of 1 orange
juice of ½ an orange

Pastry
200g plain flour, plus extra for dusting the work surface
85g butter
50g icing sugar
1 egg yolk, beaten with 1 tbsp cold water
1 tbsp caster sugar

1 To make the pastry, place the flour and butter in a food processor and whizz until the mixture resembles breadcrumbs. Add the rest of the ingredients and whizz again briefly. Turn the pastry crumbs out on to a kitchen surface and bring them together into a smooth ball of pastry dough. Wrap in clingfilm and chill in the fridge for 20–30 minutes.
2 Preheat the oven to 220°C/Gas 7. Divide the pastry into 2 and roll out both pieces on a floured surface. Use 1 piece to line a 23cm pie plate.
3 Place the rhubarb chunks on top of the pastry, then sprinkle on the sugar, zest and juice. Cover the fruit with the other piece of pastry and seal the edges together with your fingertips. For pretty edges, use the end of the handle of a teaspoon to make indentations. Sprinkle the pastry with the caster sugar.
4 Put the pie on a baking sheet and bake for 10 minutes. Lower the temperature to 200°C/Gas 6 and bake for a further 20 minutes, until the pastry crust is golden. Serve with whipped cream.

Tomato soup with mackerel empanadas

Empanadas are basically a Spanish pasty and they make a great meal with this fresh tomato soup.

SERVES 6

1 tbsp olive oil
25g butter
2 garlic cloves, finely chopped
2 shallots, peeled and finely chopped
1 celery stalk, sliced
3 leeks, sliced
1 red pepper, cored and chopped
4 plum tomatoes, roughly chopped
7 sundried tomatoes
6 curry leaves
1 tbsp flour
1 x 400g can of chopped tomatoes
1.75 litres chicken or vegetable stock
2 tsp curry powder
200ml coconut milk
2 tbsp finely chopped fresh coriander
sea salt
freshly ground black pepper

Empanada pastry
220g cold butter, cut into cubes
450g plain flour, plus extra for dusting work surface
a pinch of salt
1 egg, beaten
75ml cold water

Smoked mackerel filling
4 spring onions, finely sliced
2 tbsp finely chopped fresh coriander
300g smoked mackerel fillets, skinned and roughly chopped
1 x 185g can of tuna, drained
2 tsp curry powder
1 x 400g can of black beans, drained and rinsed
2 eggs, beaten
freshly ground black pepper

1 Heat the oil and butter in a large saucepan. Add the garlic, shallots and celery and cook for 3 minutes. Add the leeks, pepper, plum tomatoes, sundried tomatoes and curry leaves and cook for 5 minutes. Sprinkle on the flour and add the tinned tomatoes, stock and curry powder. Simmer for 20 minutes.
2 Blend the soup with a hand-held blender and pass it through a sieve. Return the soup to the heat and add the coconut milk and coriander. Bring to a simmer and season with salt and pepper. Serve with the empanadas.

To make the empanadas
3 To make the pastry, place the butter, flour and salt in a food processor and process slowly until the mixture resembles breadcrumbs. Add the egg and water and process until the liquid has been absorbed. Turn the dough out on to a floured surface and shape into a ball with your hands. Wrap the dough in clingfilm and place in the fridge for 30 minutes.

To prepare the filling
4 Place all the ingredients, except the eggs, in a mixing bowl and combine with a fork. Season with a little pepper. You won't need any salt.

To assemble the empanadas
5 Preheat the oven to 200°C/Gas 6. Roll out the pastry on a floured surface to a thickness of 2mm. Using a 10cm cutter, cut circles out of the pastry. Place a dessertspoon of the filling on half of a pastry circle.
6 Using a pastry brush or your fingertip, coat the edge of the pastry circle with some beaten egg and fold the pastry over to form a pasty shape. Make the rest of the empanadas in the same way, brush them with beaten egg and bake in the oven for 20 minutes.

Shepherd's bean pie

Beans have a reputation for causing wind, but believe me – the more often you eat them, the more your stomach gets used to dealing with them and the wind becomes less of an issue. If you want to eat less meat, it's good to embrace beans.

SERVES 6

2 tbsp olive oil
1 onion, finely chopped
1 celery stalk, finely chopped
1 x 400g can of cannellini beans, drained and rinsed
1 x 400g can of black beans, drained and rinsed
2 x 400g cans of chopped tomatoes
1 tbsp tomato purée
2 tbsp soy sauce
2 tbsp crème fraiche
3 tbsp finely chopped flat-leaf parsley
900g potatoes, peeled and quartered
30g butter
200ml milk
50g Cheddar cheese, grated
sea salt
freshly ground black pepper

1 Heat the olive oil in a saucepan. Add the onion and celery and cook over a low heat for 5 minutes.
2 Add the beans, tomatoes, tomato purée, soy sauce, crème fraiche and parsley, cover the pan and cook at a gentle simmer for 30 minutes. Season well with salt and pepper.
3 In the meantime, cook the potatoes in salted water until tender enough to mash with the butter and milk. Check the seasoning.
4 Place the bean mixture in a gratin dish. Layer the mashed potato on top, sprinkle with the grated cheese and place under a hot grill for 10 minutes until golden on top.

Grilled chicken wings with garlic mayonnaise

These chicken wings look so enticing that they are always gobbled up quickly. The only downside is that for a family of six you need so many of them.

SERVES 6

2 tbsp olive oil
3 garlic cloves, peeled and crushed
grated zest and juice of 1 lemon
1 tsp fennel seeds
1.5kg chicken wings
sea salt
freshly ground black pepper

Garlic mayonnaise
2 egg yolks
3 garlic cloves, peeled and crushed
1 tsp white wine vinegar
250ml light olive oil
1 tbsp cold water
sea salt
freshly ground black pepper

1 First make a marinade for the chicken wings by mixing the olive oil, garlic, lemon zest and juice, and fennel seeds in a bowl. Season well with salt and pepper. Put the wings into the bowl and mix well to coat them with the marinade, then set them aside for long as you can.
2 Preheat the grill to hot and place the wings on a wire tray. Cook for about 20 minutes until crisp and golden, turning them when necessary.

To make the garlic mayonnaise
3 Place the egg yolks in a mixing bowl with the garlic, white wine vinegar, a large pinch of salt and a good grinding of pepper.
4 Start adding the olive oil, a drop at a time, to the egg mixture, whisking constantly. Continue until you have added at least 50ml of the oil and then start adding it in a steady trickle, still whisking constantly. When all the oil has been added, pour in the water and stir to combine. Check the seasoning and serve with the chicken wings. and perhaps some baked potatoes and a salad.

Cheeseburgers with roasted new potato wedges

I find 100 per cent beef burgers a bit dry and lacking in taste, so I use a mixture of beef or lamb with some pork. This is always a popular meal in our house, as I am sure it will be in yours.

SERVES 6

500g minced lamb
250g minced pork
2 tbsp finely chopped flat-leaf parsley
2 shallots, grated
2 cloves of garlic, crushed
1 tbsp tomato purée
1 tbsp soy sauce
1 tsp salt
freshly ground black pepper

Garnish
1 onion, finely sliced
1 tbsp olive oil
6 slices of pancetta
6 burger buns
6 slices of Cheddar cheese

Roasted new potato wedges
750g new potatoes, skins on, quartered lengthways
2 tbsp olive oil
1 tsp paprika
1 tbsp fresh thyme leaves
1 tsp salt

1 Place the lamb, pork, parsley, shallots, garlic, tomato purée, soy sauce and seasoning in a mixing bowl and mix thoroughly with your hands. Form the mixture into 6 even-sized burgers.
2 Next prepare the garnish. Take a large frying pan and fry the onion in the olive oil on a high heat until golden brown. Remove and put to one side. Do the same with the pancetta.
3 In the same frying pan, reheat the oil and brown the burgers, 2 at a time, on both sides. When you have browned all the burgers, place them back in the pan over a low heat for 10 minutes to cook through.
4 Place a slice of cheese on top of each burger when the 10 minutes is nearly up. Return the onion and pancetta to the pan as well to warm through.
5 Slice the burger buns. Place a cheeseburger in each one, topped with onion and pancetta, and serve with the potato wedges.

Roasted new potato wedges
6 Preheat the oven to 220°C/Gas 7. Put the potatoes in a roasting tin with the olive oil, paprika, thyme and salt, making sure that the potatoes are well coated in the oil, herbs and seasonings. Roast in the oven for 50 minutes, until golden brown, moving them around in the tin once or twice during this time.

Chicken laksa

I've tried to make this soup as fuss-free as possible. Keep the stock light so its flavour doesn't dominate the soup too much and it tastes fresh and fragrant.

SERVES 6

4 shallots, peeled
4 garlic cloves, peeled
2cm piece of fresh root ginger, peeled
2 tsp ground coriander
2 tbsp olive oil
40g fresh coriander
2 tbsp vegetable oil
2 boneless chicken breasts, skinned and chopped into bite-sized pieces
150ml dry sherry
2 tsp curry powder
1 chicken stock cube dissolved in 1.5 litres of water (you want a light stock)
1 x 400ml can of coconut milk
125g fine egg noodles, cooked according to the packet instructions
sea salt
freshly ground black pepper

1 Place the shallots, garlic, ginger, coriander, olive oil and fresh coriander in a food processor and blend to a paste. Place to one side.
2 Heat a tablespoon of vegetable oil in a medium saucepan and brown the chicken pieces in small batches. Don't overcrowd the pan or the chicken will steam rather than fry. Put each batch to one side once browned while you do the next.
3 Once all the chicken has been browned, put it back in the pan and pour on the sherry, then sprinkle on the curry powder and season well with salt and pepper. Simmer for 2 minutes, then remove from the pan and set aside.
4 Add another tablespoon of vegetable oil to the pan, set it on a very low heat and cook the green paste for 10 minutes, stirring occasionally.
5 Add the chicken to the green paste, then pour in the stock and the coconut milk and simmer for 10 minutes. Taste to check if you need to add any salt – you may not need to.
6 Cook the noodles according to the packet instructions and add them to the soup. Serve in bowls with chunks of bread.

Shin of beef stew with braised carrots

This started off as a recipe for an oxtail stew. I was so underwhelmed by the oxtail, which seemed largely bone, that I decided to redo the stew using shin of beef. Beef skirt would work just as well.

SERVES 6

2 tbsp olive oil
2 parsnips, peeled and chopped into 2cm chunks
1 celery stalk, finely chopped
1 onion, finely chopped
70g sliced pancetta, roughly chopped
1.5kg shin of beef, trimmed
200ml red wine
1 sprig of thyme
1 bay leaf
750ml beef stock
1 tbsp tomato purée
2 x 400g cans of cannellini beans, drained and rinsed
sea salt
freshly ground black pepper

Braised carrots
400g carrots, peeled and thinly sliced
a knob of butter
1 tbsp water
sea salt
freshly ground black pepper

1 Heat 1 tablespoon of olive oil in a large casserole dish. Add the vegetables and pancetta and cook over a medium heat for 5 minutes until the vegetables have softened slightly. Remove the vegetables and pancetta from the pan and place to one side.
2 Return the pan to the heat. Add another tablespoon of olive oil and brown the beef, a few pieces at a time. Place the browned meat to one side while you brown the next batch. Preheat the oven to 170°C/Gas 3½.
3 Keep the empty pan on the heat and add the wine. Simmer for 3 minutes, then return the vegetables and meat to the saucepan. Add the herbs, beef stock, tomato purée and beans, and season well with salt and pepper. Bring the stew to a simmer.
4 Place a sheet of baking parchment over the top of the stew to keep the steam in and put the lid on the dish. Place in the preheated oven for 2 hours, by which time the beef should be very tender.

To prepare the braised carrots
5 Put the carrots in a small saucepan with the butter and place on a low heat. As soon as you hear the butter start to hiss, give the carrots a stir. Add the water, cover the pan and cook the carrots over a low heat for 10–15 minutes until tender. Season with salt and pepper.

Shoulder of lamb with onions and celeriac and potato purée

A meal that you can put in the oven and leave to cook is great for a Sunday lunch, giving you time to do things with the family or relax with the paper. A 2.3kg shoulder of lamb is plenty for a family of six.

SERVES 6

2.3kg shoulder of lamb
1 tbsp olive oil
4 shallots, peeled and cut in half
1 red onion, peeled and cut in quarters
1 white onion, peeled and cut in quarters
3 leeks, rinsed and cut widthways into 2cm chunks
3 garlic cloves, peeled and left whole
1 sprig of fresh rosemary
200ml white wine
sea salt
freshly ground black pepper

Celeriac and potato purée
1 celeriac, peeled and cut into 1cm cubes
milk
3 potatoes, peeled and cut into quarters
25g butter
sea salt
freshly ground black pepper

1 Preheat the oven to 220°C/Gas 7. Place the lamb joint in a roasting tin, rub it with olive oil and season well with salt and pepper. Place the lamb in the hot oven for 20 minutes to get it sizzling nicely.
2 Remove the roasting tin from the oven and take the joint out. Scatter the shallots, onions, leeks and garlic into the tin, add the rosemary and season with salt and pepper. Pour on the wine and put the lamb back in the tin. Cover the lamb with foil and return it to the oven for 3–4 hours, depending on how much time you have.
3 When the cooking time is up, place the lamb on a serving plate. The meat should just fall off the bone in chunks so you don't have to worry about carving.
4 Decant the juices and onions to a jug or bowl. You could reduce the juices slightly if you want but they should be fine just as they are – perhaps with a little extra seasoning to taste.

To make the celeriac and potato purée
5 Place the celeriac in a saucepan and pour in enough milk to cover. Season with a teaspoon of salt. Bring the pan to a simmer and cook the celeriac gently for 10 minutes. Spoon the celeriac into a liquidiser or food processor, leaving the milk in the pan. Blend the celeriac until smooth and place to one side.
6 Put the potatoes in the milk and simmer gently until tender enough to mash. Don't liquidise them as they will become like glue. Spoon the mashed potatoes into the celeriac, adding a little milk to loosen if necessary. Add the butter and season with salt and pepper to taste.

Rocky road

This never lasts long in our house!

SERVES 6

- 250g dark chocolate, broken into pieces
- 150g milk chocolate, broken into pieces
- 175g butter, at room temperature
- 4 tbsp golden syrup
- 200g digestive biscuits
- 150g mixed unsalted nuts (Brazil, cashew, macadamia), roughly chopped
- 100g raisins
- 100g white chocolate, roughly chopped

1 Put the dark and milk chocolate and the butter in a glass bowl and set it over a saucepan of simmering water. Don't allow the bottom of the bowl to touch the water. Remove from the heat when the chocolate and butter have melted, then stir in the syrup.
2 Crush the biscuits into pieces, some small and some a little larger. Add the biscuits, nuts, raisins and white chocolate to the melted chocolate mixture and mix everything together until evenly combined.
3 Tip the mixture into a brownie tray or a Swiss roll tin and chill in the fridge for 2 hours. Cut into squares and serve.

Chocolate eclairs

Choux pastry was one of the first things I remember baking when I was a child. It has a reputation for being difficult, but if you follow the recipe it should turn out perfectly. Choux pastry always seems like magic to me. You put one thing in the oven and something that looks completely different comes out.

SERVES 6

Choux pastry
70g plain flour
a pinch of salt
50g butter, plus extra for greasing
175ml water
2 eggs, beaten

Sweet vanilla cream
400ml double cream
1 dsp caster sugar
½ tsp vanilla extract

Chocolate sauce
150g dark chocolate
50g butter

1 Lightly grease a baking sheet and preheat the oven to 200°C/Gas 6. Sieve the flour on to a sheet of baking parchment and add the salt. (It's important that the flour is on a sheet of paper or parchment.)
2 Melt the 50g of butter with the water in a small saucepan and bring to the boil. Remove the pan from the heat and shoot the flour and salt into the butter and water in one go, then beat with a wooden spoon until combined. The mixture will form a lump in the bottom of the saucepan and as soon as this happens, stop beating. Let the mixture cool for 5 minutes.
3 Start to add the beaten eggs to the mixture a little at a time, incorporating each addition well before adding any more. Take a small plastic sandwich bag and snip off a small corner at the bottom or use an icing bag. Spoon the choux pastry mixture into the bag – don't worry if things get a bit messy.
4 Pipe fingers of the mix on to the baking sheet, making each one about the size of your middle finger. Leave space between them as they will expand, although at this stage the mixture looks flat and lifeless.
5 Pop the tray into the oven for 25 minutes, by which time the pastry will have transformed into beautiful golden puffed-up eclairs. Transfer these to a baking sheet and when they are cool enough to handle, cut a slash in the side of each eclair.
6 Place all the ingredients for the vanilla cream in a mixing bowl and whip with a whisk until nicely thick.
7 Next make the chocolate sauce. Put the chocolate and butter in a glass bowl and place over a saucepan of simmering water, stirring occasionally until melted.
8 Fill the eclairs with the sweet vanilla cream and dip the tops in the melted chocolate.

Apple and sultana cake

An apple cake with spices and dried fruit is about as sublime a baked treat as you can get. Lovely at any time of the day.

SERVES 6

3 eating apples, peeled and grated
125g melted butter
150g self-raising flour
120g caster sugar
2 tbsp soft brown sugar
50g sultanas
20g piece of fresh root ginger, peeled and finely grated
½ tsp ground cinnamon
3 eggs

1 Grease a 900g loaf tin, measuring about 22 x 12cm, and line the base with baking parchment. Preheat the oven to 180°C/Gas 4.
2 Put all the ingredients in a mixing bowl and beat with a wooden spoon to make a smooth batter.
3 Spoon the mixture into the prepared loaf tin and bake in the oven for 30–35 minutes or until a skewer inserted into the middle of the cake comes out clean. Remove the cake from the tin and leave it to cool on a wire rack. Serve in slices with crème fraiche if you like.

Pork with noodles, Thai style

I used leftover pork shoulder for this recipe and it worked beautifully. If you don't have any leftover pork, you can use pork shoulder steaks.

SERVES 6

2 tbsp olive oil
500g leftover pork shoulder
  or pork shoulder steaks,
  cut into 1cm thick slices
2 shallots, finely chopped
2 garlic cloves, finely chopped
1cm piece of fresh root ginger,
  peeled and grated
2 tbsp fish sauce
1 tbsp dark soy sauce
1 tsp soft brown sugar
100g fresh baby spinach leaves
1 x 400ml can of coconut milk
2 tbsp finely chopped fresh coriander
250g fine egg noodles
sea salt
freshly ground black pepper

1 Heat the oil in a large frying pan. Add the pork slices, fry them until brown and then place to one side.
2 Return the pan to the heat and add the shallot, garlic and ginger. Fry for 2 minutes, stirring. Return the pork to the pan, then add the fish sauce, soy sauce and brown sugar and combine with the pork and shallots.
3 Throw in the spinach leaves and let them wilt down for a few minutes. Add the coconut milk and coriander and stir, then simmer for 2 minutes. Season with salt and pepper.
4 Cook the noodles according to the packet instructions. Place some noodles in each dish or bowl and add some of the pork mixture on top.

Spicy lentil pasties with cucumber and mint salad

Cool and fresh-tasting, this cucumber and mint salad goes perfectly with the spicy pasties.

MAKES 8

Filling
1 tbsp olive oil
1 onion, finely chopped
1 tsp cumin seeds
½ tsp mustard seeds
4 curry leaves
¼ tsp turmeric
a pinch of chilli flakes
200g potatoes, cut into 2cm chunks
200g red lentils
600ml water
150g canned cannellini beans, drained and rinsed
sea salt

Pastry
500g strong white flour, plus extra for dusting the work surface
125g lard, chilled and cut into cubes
125g butter, chilled and cut into cubes
1 tsp ground coriander
good pinch of salt
100ml cold water
1 egg, beaten

Cucumber and mint salad
1 whole cucumber, thinly sliced
4 spring onions, finely sliced
1 small bunch of mint leaves, roughly chopped
2 tbsp olive oil
½ tbsp white wine vinegar
2 tbsp natural yoghurt
sea salt
freshly ground black pepper

To prepare the filling
1 Put the olive oil in a medium saucepan and when it's warm, add the onion, cumin seeds, mustard seeds, curry leaves, turmeric and chilli flakes. Fry gently, stirring occasionally, for 5 minutes, then add the potatoes, lentils and water.
2 Partly cover the pan and simmer for 45 minutes until everything is tender, stirring occasionally. Season well with salt and stir in the cannellini beans. Leave to cool.

To prepare the pastry
3 Place the flour, lard, butter, coriander and salt in a food processor and blend until the mixture resembles breadcrumbs. Add the water and mix again briefly. Turn the mixture out on to your work surface and bring it together into a smooth ball of pastry. Wrap in clingfilm and chill in the fridge for 30 minutes.
4 Preheat the oven to 200°C/Gas 6. Roll out the pastry on a floured surface and cut out 8 circles about 15cm in diameter – I cut round a cereal bowl. You can make smaller pasties if you prefer.
5 Place a tablespoon of the lentil mixture in the middle of each circle. Brush the rim of the circle with beaten egg and then bring up the edges and join them together, like a pasty. You can crimp the edges by pinching them between your finger and thumb if you like. Make the rest of the pasties and place them on a lightly greased baking tray. Brush the pasties with beaten egg and bake in the oven for 30 minutes. Serve with the salad.

To make the cucumber and mint salad
6 Place the cucumber, onions and mint in a dish. Dress with the olive oil, vinegar and salt and pepper, then top with the yoghurt and mix gently.

Mackerel rillettes and herbed soda bread

I have made this meal many times and it always goes down a treat. It makes a great supper and also works well as a starter for a more special meal. If you are having this for a main meal, I would serve it with a green salad on the side.

SERVES 6

250g fresh mackerel fillets
400g smoked mackerel fillets
2 shallots, finely chopped
100g butter, softened
juice and grated zest of 1 lemon
2 tsp green peppercorns
1 tbsp capers, rinsed
3 tbsp fresh coriander, finely chopped
10 fresh radishes, cut in half

Herbed soda bread (makes 2 loaves)
570g wholemeal flour
570g plain white flour
2 tsp salt
2 tsp bicarbonate of soda
1 tbsp finely chopped flat-leaf parsley
1 tbsp finely chopped fresh chives
850ml buttermilk
1 tbsp Dijon mustard

1 Check the fresh mackerel for bones, running your fingertips along the fillets. Remove any little bones with tweezers.
2 Heat a frying pan over a medium heat, add the fresh mackerel fillets, a few at a time, and cook for 30 seconds or so. Turn and cook for another 30 seconds on the other side. You won't need any fat. Continue until all the fresh mackerel fillets are cooked, then remove the skin from the fillets and flake the fish into a mixing bowl.
3 Remove the skin from the smoked mackerel fillets and flake the flesh from these into the mixing bowl as well. Add the shallots, butter, lemon juice and zest, green peppercorns, capers and coriander, then mix well with a wooden spoon until the texture has the texture of a coarse pâté.
4 Serve with the radishes, sprinkled with a little salt, and the soda bread.

To make the herbed soda bread
5 Heat the oven to 200°C/Gas 6. Place both flours in a large mixing bowl with the salt and bicarbonate of soda. Stir in the herbs, buttermilk and mustard and bring together in a dough. Don't overwork.
6 Cut the dough into 2 equal pieces and shape each piece into a round. Make a cross in the top of each loaf using a sharp knife, then bake in the oven for 35 minutes. Remove and cool on a wire rack.

Chicken kebabs with butternut squash dip

The butternut squash dip is just right with these chicken kebabs. The colours look great together as well and you'll hear murmurs of approval from your family or friends as they tuck in.

SERVES 6

6 chicken breasts, boned, skinned and cut into bite-sized pieces
olive oil
lemon juice, for serving
sea salt

Marinade
½ tsp turmeric
½ tsp ground cumin
½ tsp ground coriander
2 garlic cloves, crushed
½ tsp grated fresh root ginger
2 tbsp rapeseed oil
¼ tsp ground cinnamon
1 tsp sea salt
½ tsp paprika

Butternut squash dip
500g butternut squash, peeled and cut into 1cm cubes
2 tbsp olive oil
1 garlic clove, crushed
1 tbsp tahini
juice of 1 lemon
1 tbsp chopped flat-leaf parsley
sea salt
freshly ground black pepper

1 Place all the marinade ingredients in a bowl and add the chicken pieces. Cover with clingfilm and place in the fridge for 30 minutes to an hour. Thread the chicken pieces on to wooden skewers and place them to one side, in a cool place.
2 When you're ready to cook the chicken, drizzle some olive oil over the skewered chicken and heat a large frying pan. Cook the kebabs, a few at a time, turning them so that they turn golden on all sides and cook through. This will only take a couple of minutes. Sprinkle the kebabs with lemon juice and a little salt and serve with the dip and some flatbreads.

To make the butternut squash dip
3 Preheat the oven to 200°C/Gas 6. Place a large piece of foil on a baking tray. Add the cubes of butternut squash, spoon over the olive oil and season well with salt and pepper. Add the garlic clove and wrap the squash up in the foil, like a sealed parcel, then place in the oven for 20 minutes, by which time the squash will be tender.
4 Put the cooked squash into a food processor, with the tahini and lemon juice and blend until smooth. Season if necessary with salt and pepper and sprinkle on the parsley. Place in a bowl and serve warm.

Fried trout and new potato salad

A horseradish dressing goes perfectly with trout.

SERVES 6

4 beetroots, scrubbed and trimmed
4 tbsp olive oil
2 tsp balsamic vinegar
750g new potatoes, cut in half lengthways
1 tbsp grated horseradish
6 tbsp whipping cream, lightly whipped
6 trout fillets, skin on
200g salad leaves
5 spring onions, thinly sliced widthways
extra virgin olive oil, for serving
sea salt
freshly ground black pepper

1 Preheat the oven to 200°C/Gas 6. Place the beetroots on a large sheet of foil and add a tablespoon of olive oil and the balsamic vinegar. Season well with salt and pepper. Wrap the beetroots up in the foil to make a parcel, place them on a baking tray and bake in the oven for 1 hour. When the beetroots are cool enough to handle, peel them and cut into quarters.
2 Place the potatoes on a baking tray and drizzle them with 2 tablespoons of olive oil. Season with salt and pepper and roast for 45 minutes until golden brown.
3 Gently mix the horseradish with the cream in a small bowl and set aside.
4 When the potatoes are nearly ready, pour a tablespoon of olive oil into a frying pan and fry the trout fillets, skin side down, for 1 minute. Turn them over and fry for another minute.
5 To serve, place some salad leaves on each plate and dress with a little extra virgin olive oil. Add a few potatoes, some beetroot, slices of spring onion and a few more salad leaves, then top with the fried trout and a spoon of the creamy horseradish sauce. Drizzle over a little more extra virgin olive oil and season with salt and pepper.

Shoulder of lamb with Greek salad and roast potatoes

A light, fresh Greek salad is a welcome accompaniment to this slow-cooked lamb shoulder.

SERVES 6

1.8kg lamb shoulder, on the bone
2 garlic cloves, cut into slivers
1 tbsp olive oil
2 sprigs of fresh rosemary
sea salt
freshly ground black pepper

Roast potatoes
1kg potatoes, peeled, cut into quarters and rinsed in cold water
1 tbsp goose fat

Greek salad
5 beef tomatoes, thickly sliced
200g feta cheese, cut into cubes
½ cucumber cut into chunks
2 tbsp black olives
1 red onion, thinly sliced
a bunch of fresh mint, roughly chopped
2 tbsp olive oil
juice of ½ lemon
sea salt
freshly ground black pepper

1 Preheat the oven to 150°C/Gas 2. Place the lamb in a roasting tin. Make little slashes in the meat with the tip of a sharp knife and insert the slivers of garlic. Drizzle on the olive oil, then season with salt and pepper and lay the rosemary sprigs on top of the lamb.
2 Cover the lamb with foil and bake in the oven for 4 hours, by which time the meat should be falling off the bone. Serve with the potatoes and Greek salad.

Roast potatoes
3 Preheat the oven to 220°C/Gas 7. Put the potatoes in a saucepan of cold salted water, bring to the boil and cook for 6 minutes.
4 Drain the potatoes and then bash them around in the pan a little before putting them in a roasting tin. Add the goose fat and roast the potatoes for 50–60 minutes until golden brown, turning them occasionally.

Greek salad
5 Place the tomatoes on a serving dish. Sprinkle on the cheese, cucumber, olives, onion and mint. Pour on the olive oil and lemon juice and season well with salt and black pepper.

Roast chicken with mascarpone and herb stuffing and fennel gratin

The mascarpone cheese keeps the chicken breast nice and succulent during the roasting time. If you stuff the chickens carefully they look beautiful when they come out of the oven.

SERVES 6

2 x 1.5kg chickens
olive oil
sea salt
freshly ground black pepper

Mascarpone and herb stuffing
½ red onion, finely chopped
2 tbsp mascarpone cheese
1 tbsp finely chopped flat-leaf parsley
1 tbsp finely chopped basil
1 dsrtsp finely chopped tarragon
sea salt
freshly ground black pepper

Fennel gratin
1 tbsp olive oil
1 onion, finely sliced
2 bulbs of fennel, trimmed and sliced thinly across
150ml double cream
2 tbsp finely grated Parmesan cheese
sea salt
freshly ground black pepper

1 Preheat the oven to 190°C/Gas 5. Put all the ingredients for the stuffing in a mixing bowl and mix until well combined.
2 Put the chickens on the work surface. Gently lift the skin on the breast of 1 of the chickens and slide some stuffing underneath the skin with your fingers. Spread it over the breast as best you can, using about half of the stuffing mixture. Repeat with the other chicken.
3 Place both birds in a roasting tin. Drizzle them with olive oil and season well with salt and pepper, then roast in the oven for 1 ½ hours. Set aside to rest for 15 minutes before carving and serving with the fennel gratin.

To prepare the fennel gratin
4 Heat the olive oil in a sauté pan. Add the onion and fennel and cook over a low heat for 15 minutes, stirring occasionally. Season with salt and pepper.
5 Place the onion and fennel in a gratin dish, then pour on the cream and sprinkle the cheese on top. Place under a hot grill for 5 minutes or so until the top of the gratin is tinged with brown.

Chocolate gingerbread with chocolate icing

This gingerbread is extremely gooey but still light.

SERVES 6

150g butter, plus extra for greasing
125g dark brown sugar
200g golden syrup
200g treacle
1 tsp ground ginger
1 tsp ground cinnamon
100g dark chocolate, broken into pieces
200ml milk
1 tsp bicarbonate of soda, dissolved in 2 tbsp warm water
300g plain flour

Icing
200g dark chocolate, broken into pieces
100ml double cream

1 Preheat the oven to 180°C/Gas 4. Grease a roasting tin, measuring about 30 x 20cm and 5cm deep, and line it with baking parchment.
2 Put the butter, sugar, syrup, treacle and spices in a saucepan and heat gently until the butter has melted. Remove the pan from the heat, add the chocolate and stir until it has melted. Add the milk and bicarbonate of soda and stir.
3 Sift the flour into a mixing bowl. Slowly pour the melted butter and chocolate mixture on to the flour, stirring constantly, to make a smooth batter.
4 Pour the mixture into the prepared tin and bake in the oven for 35 minutes. The cake should feel springy when touched and a skewer inserted into the middle of the cake should come out clean. Let the gingerbread cool slightly in the tin, then turn it out on to a wire rack to cool completely before icing.

To ice the cake
5 Put the chocolate and cream in a glass bowl and set over a saucepan of simmering water, making sure the bottom of the bowl doesn't touch the water. Stir occasionally until the chocolate has melted.
6 Pour the icing on to the cake and smooth it over with a spatula. Don't cut the cake until the icing has cooled completely.

Doughnuts

My mother used to make these when we were children and shook them in a brown paper bag of sugar before handing them to us. I remember one evening she got the sugar muddled up with the salt and ruined the doughnuts. She was so upset and now, being a busy mother myself, I understand her distress. She would be pleased to see this recipe here and would agree with me that this is what doughnuts are supposed to taste like – no trans-fats in sight!

SERVES 6

260g plain flour, plus extra for dusting the work surface
a pinch of salt
175ml milk, warmed
1 egg
25g butter, melted
40g caster sugar
1 x 7g sachet of dried yeast
500ml vegetable oil, for deep-frying, plus extra for greasing
caster sugar, for serving

1 Put the flour and salt into a mixing bowl. In a measuring jug, combine the milk, egg, butter and sugar. Make sure the liquid is not too hot, then add the yeast and stir.
2 Tip the liquid into the flour and mix together gradually with a wooden spoon. Turn the mixture out on to a floured surface and knead for 5 minutes, using your fingertips only as the dough will be quite sticky. I find if I use my whole hand I end up in a terrible mess.
3 Oil a bowl with a teaspoon of oil, then rub the ball of dough all over with oil and place it in the bowl. Cover the bowl and leave the dough to rise in a draught-free place for 1 hour. Then knock back the dough with your knuckles and leave it to rise for another 30 minutes.
4 Roll out the dough on a lightly floured surface to a thickness of 1.5cm and cut the doughnuts into circles using an 8cm cutter. Take the end of an apple corer, or something similar, and make a hole in the middle of each one. Place the doughnuts on a baking sheet and leave for 15 minutes so that they rise a little more and become nice and light.
5 Heat the oil in a deep saucepan and when it's hot, carefully drop in 2 doughnuts. As soon as they are brown underneath, turn them over – try to avoid letting them become too brown too quickly. They take about 3 minutes to cook through.
6 Place the cooked doughnuts on a few sheets of kitchen paper to drain and then dip them in caster sugar. Continue until all the doughnuts are cooked.

Spanish rice

I'm not suggesting that this is an authentic paella, which is why I have called it Spanish rice. It is, though, a paella-style dish that is easy to prepare and makes a hearty meal.

SERVES 6

2 tbsp olive oil
1 onion, finely chopped
1 red pepper, cored, seeded and finely chopped
100g button mushrooms, sliced
4 pork sausages, skins removed and discarded and the sausage meat cut into chunks
500g basmati rice
200g frozen petit pois
100g cooked ham, cut into small pieces
100g raw prawns
2 boneless chicken breast fillets, chopped into 2cm chunks
1 tbsp pitted black olives
a pinch of saffron strands
850ml chicken stock
sea salt
freshly ground black pepper

1 Heat the olive oil in a large sauté pan or saucepan. Add the onion and red pepper and cook for 5 minutes, stirring occasionally.
2 Add the mushrooms and fry for 2 minutes, then add the sausage meat and fry for another 2 minutes. Pour on the rice and stir briefly to coat it in the oil.
3 Add the peas, ham, prawns, chicken and olives and stir.
4 Soak the saffron strands in a tablespoon of the stock for a few minutes, then pour this and the rest of the stock on to the rice. Bring to a good simmer, then reduce the heat, cover the pan and simmer for 20–25 minutes or until the rice is tender and the chicken is cooked through. Season to taste before serving.

Cod rarebit with spinach

This recipe really does glam up an ordinary piece of cod.

SERVES 6

2 tbsp olive oil
a small knob of butter
800g cod fillet, cut into 6 pieces
800g spinach leaves
sea salt
freshly ground black pepper

Rarebit topping
200g Cheddar cheese, grated
2 tbsp mascarpone cheese
75ml milk
30g plain flour
40g white breadcrumbs
1 tbsp Dijon mustard
½ tbsp Worcestershire sauce
1 egg
1 egg yolk

1 First cook the fish. Heat the olive oil and butter in a large sauté pan. When the butter is foaming, place 3 pieces of cod in the pan and fry for 1 minute. Turn them, then fry on the other side for 1 minute. Place to one side and cook the rest of the fillets in the same way.
2 Bring a large saucepan of water to the boil and add the spinach leaves. Bring the pan back to the boil, remove from the heat, then drain the spinach leaves. Once the spinach has cooled slightly, press out as much of the excess water as possible and roughly chop the spinach. Season with salt and pepper and place to one side.

To make the rarebit topping
3 Place the cheeses in a saucepan with the milk over a very gentle heat, until the Cheddar has melted. Remove from the heat and stir in the flour, breadcrumbs and mustard. Place the pan over a low heat and stir until the mixture has thickened. Remove from the heat and add the Worcestershire sauce. Leave to cool for 5 minutes and then stir in the egg and yolk and mix.

To assemble the dish
4 Heat the grill. Place the cod fillets on some foil on the grill rack. Spoon a portion of the rarebit topping on top of each piece of fish, spreading it as evenly as possible. Place under the grill until the topping is brown and bubbling. Serve the fish pieces on top of a pile of spinach with some sautéed potatoes (see page 17).

Ham in pea and bean stew

The weather is unpredictable at this time of year and just when you're looking forward to summer, the days can turn cold again. This hearty warming stew is perfect for a chilly April evening.

SERVES 6

- 1 tbsp olive oil
- 1 piece of unsmoked gammon (weighing about 800g)
- 1 onion, finely chopped
- 200ml white wine
- 1 sprig of fresh thyme
- 2 carrots, cut into chunks
- 2 parsnips, cut into chunks
- 1 x 400g can of flageolet beans, drained and rinsed
- 1 x 400g can of butter beans, drained and rinsed
- 4 medium potatoes, peeled and cut in half
- 200g frozen petit pois
- 400ml water
- sea salt
- freshly ground black pepper

1 Heat the olive oil in a large saucepan. Add the gammon joint and brown it on the meaty sides, which will take about 10 minutes. Remove the gammon from the pan.
2 Keep the pan on the heat, add the onion and cook it for 5 minutes until soft. Return the gammon to the pan, then pour over the wine and let it sizzle for 1 minute.
3 Add the thyme, carrots, parsnips, canned beans, potatoes and peas. Pour on the water and season with a little salt and pepper. Cover the pan and simmer for 1 hour.
4 Remove the gammon from the pot. Take off the fatty rind and discard it, then cut the meat into small cubes. Put these back into the stew, warm through and serve with crusty bread.

Baked whiting fillets with mustard sauce, sautéed potatoes and purple sprouting broccoli

Whiting is a white fish that is available most of the year. Apparently, it contains hardly any fat and so is easy to digest. I prefer to bake the fish rather than fry it, as whiting does have a tendency to fall apart.

SERVES 6

6 whiting fillets
2 tbsp olive oil
1 lemon
sea salt
freshly ground black pepper

Mustard sauce
6 tbsp crème fraiche
1 tbsp Dijon mustard
1 tbsp grain mustard
grated zest of ½ lemon
1 tbsp finely chopped flat-leaf parsley
sea salt
freshly ground black pepper

Sautéed potatoes
1kg potatoes, peeled and cut into quarters
1 tbsp duck or goose fat
sea salt

Purple sprouting broccoli
250g purple sprouting broccoli
a little butter, for serving
sea salt
freshly ground black pepper

1 Preheat the oven to 200°C/Gas 6. Place the whiting fillets in an ovenproof dish. Drizzle with the olive oil and season with salt and pepper, then pop them into the oven for 10 minutes. Squeeze with fresh lemon juice and serve with the sauce and the potatoes and broccoli.

To make the sauce
2 Heat the crème fraiche in a small saucepan. Once it starts to simmer, add the mustards, lemon zest and parsley. Season well with salt and pepper and simmer gently for 10 minutes.

To cook the potatoes and broccoli
3 Cook the potatoes in salted water until tender. Drain and when they are cool enough to handle, slice the potatoes into 1cm pieces.
4 Heat the duck or goose fat in a large sauté pan. Add the potatoes to the hot fat and move them around so that they all have chance to turn golden brown. Sprinkle with salt.
5 Boil a saucepan of water. Add the broccoli and simmer for 3 minutes. Drain and season with salt and pepper and a little butter.

Chicken thighs in beer

The cauliflower is a beautiful vegetable, with its undulating creamy florets set against the green of the leaves. In the kitchen, it does not always receive the respect it deserves and is often smothered in a cheese sauce. The key to enjoying cauliflower is to ensure that it maintains its shape and flavour and it makes a great addition to recipes such as this one, and to stews and curries, if not over cooked.

SERVES 6

8 chicken thighs, on the bone
2 tbsp flour
2 tbsp olive oil
25g butter
12 pork chipolata sausages
2 shallots, finely sliced
200g button mushrooms
400ml beer (such as London Pride or Boddingtons)
1 medium cauliflower, trimmed and cut into florets
1 sprig of fresh thyme
2 tbsp crème fraiche
2 tbsp finely chopped flat-leaf parsley
sea salt
freshly ground black pepper

1 Sprinkle the chicken thighs with the flour and some salt and pepper. Heat the olive oil and butter in a large saucepan, then add the thighs, 2 at a time, browning them well on each side. Set each batch aside while you brown the rest. Add the sausages to the pan to brown them as well and then place to one side with the chicken.
2 Add the shallots and brown for 2 minutes. Throw in the mushrooms and return the chicken and chipolatas to the pan. Pour on the beer. Add the cauliflower and thyme, season with salt and pepper and simmer slowly for 40 minutes.
3 Spoon the chicken, sausages and cauliflower into a serving bowl. Put the pan, with everything else, back on the heat, stir in the crème fraiche and parsley and simmer for 2 minutes. Pour the sauce over the chicken, cauliflower and sausages and serve.

Seafood curry with brown basmati rice

This sweet fish curry has a Thai flavour. The dates add an unusual sweetness that goes beautifully with the fish.

SERVES 6

1 tbsp vegetable oil
1 green pepper, finely chopped
1 green chilli, seeded and finely chopped
2 tbsp curry powder (see below)
400ml coconut milk
1 tbsp fish sauce
100g baby plum or cherry tomatoes, halved
100ml water
6 dates, stoned and roughly chopped
400g raw medium prawns
300g monkfish tail, cut into chunks
200g whiting fillet
fresh coriander, roughly chopped
sea salt

Curry powder
1 tbsp coriander seeds
1 dsrtsp cumin seeds
1 tsp fennel seeds
½ tsp fenugreek

Brown basmati rice
500g brown basmati rice
a pinch of sea salt
750ml water

1 First make the curry powder. Place the coriander seeds in a small, heavy-bottomed pan and heat for 30 seconds. Add the other ingredients and toast them until you smell the aroma of the spices. Put the spices in a coffee grinder or a pestle and mortar and grind them to a fine powder.
2 Heat the oil in a large frying pan. Gently fry the green pepper and chilli for 4 minutes. Add 2 tablespoons of the curry powder and fry for a further 60 seconds.
3 Add the coconut milk, fish sauce, tomatoes, water and dates and simmer gently for 10 minutes. Next add the prawns and fish and simmer for 4 minutes. Season well with salt. Sprinkle on the fresh coriander and serve with the rice.

To cook the rice
4 Place the rice and salt in a large saucepan with the water and bring to the boil. Reduce the heat to very low, cover the pan and leave the rice to cook undisturbed for 20 minutes. Check whether all the water has been absorbed, and if the rice is still a little hard, cook for a bit longer. Remove the pan from the heat, keep the lid on and leave for 10 minutes before serving.

Baked pork spare ribs with onions au gratin

My children love these ribs. The sauce is thick and sticky and the meat comes away from the bones easily.

SERVES 6

1 x 400g can of chopped tomatoes
4 tbsp dark soy sauce
2 tsp dry sherry
2 tbsp soft brown sugar
2 garlic cloves, crushed
2 tbsp hoisin sauce
2 tbsp olive oil
2kg spare ribs
sea salt
freshly ground black pepper

Onions au gratin
40g butter
1 tbsp flour
275ml milk
3 tbsp double cream
a pinch of nutmeg
500g onions
75g white breadcrumbs
70g chopped pancetta
2 tbsp grated Parmesan cheese
sea salt
freshly ground black pepper

1 Place the tomatoes, soy sauce, sherry, sugar, garlic, hoisin sauce and olive oil in a bowl and mix well until combined. Season with salt and pepper. Place the ribs in the mixture and leave in a cool place or a fridge to marinate for 1 hour.
2 Preheat the oven to 220°C/Gas 7. Transfer the ribs and marinade to a roasting tin and cook for 30 minutes. Serve with the onions au gratin and perhaps some baked potatoes.

Onions au gratin
3 To make a white sauce, melt 25g of the butter in a small saucepan, add the flour and cook on a very low heat for 2 minutes. Remove from the heat and gradually stir in the milk. Return the pan to the heat and simmer for 10 minutes.
4 Add the cream and nutmeg, then season with salt and pepper and remove the pan from the heat.
5 Slice the onions quite thickly and place them in a frying pan with the rest of the butter. Cook over a low heat for 30 minutes.
6 Remove the onions from the pan, place them in a gratin dish and cover with the white sauce.
7 Put the frying pan back on the heat and add the pancetta and the breadcrumbs. Cook for 5 minutes until they are golden brown, then spoon them on to the onions. Sprinkle with the Parmesan and place the dish under a hot grill until bubbling.

White chocolate and rhubarb Swiss roll

Swiss rolls may look difficult, but they are actually quite simple to make and the sponge rolls easily, with no cracking. This particular Swiss roll has so much glorious filling that it looks fit to burst, but it's all the better for that, I think.

SERVES 6

Swiss roll
2 eggs
110g caster sugar, plus extra for sprinkling
2 tbsp water
½ tsp vanilla extract
½ tsp baking powder
55g plain flour
icing sugar, for dusting

Filling
juice and zest of 1 orange
2 tbsp caster sugar
6 stalks pink rhubarb, chopped into 1.5 cm chunks
200g white chocolate, broken into chunks
¼ tsp ground ginger
200ml double cream

1 Preheat the oven to 190°C/Gas 5. Grease a Swiss roll tin and line the base with greaseproof paper.
2 Using an electric hand-whisk, beat the eggs until they have thickened to the consistency of double cream. Add the sugar, a little at a time, beating constantly until all the sugar has been added and you have a pale creamy mixture. Add the water, vanilla, baking powder and flour to the mixture all at once and mix briefly until combined.
3 Turn the mixture into the Swiss roll tin and bake for 12 minutes until golden brown and springy to the touch. Sprinkle a clean tea towel with caster sugar and immediately turn out the Swiss roll out on to the tea towel so that the base is facing upwards. Remove the greaseproof paper, roll up the Swiss roll in the tea towel and leave until completely cool.
4 To make the filling, put the orange juice and zest in a small saucepan with the sugar and bring to the boil. Add the rhubarb, cover and remove from the heat. Leave for 10 minutes by which time the rhubarb will be tender. Place to one side to cool completely. If you can't get pink rhubarb use the normal type, but you may need to simmer it for 5 minutes before you remove it from the heat.
5 Place the chocolate in a glass bowl over a saucepan of simmering water. Stir the chocolate occasionally as it melts, then leave to cool completely. Whip the double cream and fold in the white chocolate mixture.
6 Unroll the Swiss roll. Spread on a generous amount of the chocolate cream and 4 tablespoons of rhubarb, but leave the juice behind as this would make the Swiss roll soggy. Roll up the Swiss roll and dust with icing sugar. Serve in thick slices with the rest of the white chocolate cream and leftover rhubarb.

Nutty apple crumble

Some cooks disapprove of any adaptation of traditional crumble, but I say that there is room for both. Here's a crumble with a nutty topping.

SERVES 6

25g butter
6 eating apples, peeled, cored and cut into quarters
1 tbsp dark brown sugar
½ tsp ground cinnamon
100ml double cream

Topping
120g plain flour
75g butter
75g caster sugar
1 tbsp pistachio nuts
1 tbsp pecan nuts
1 tbsp cashew nuts
1 tbsp demerara sugar

1 Preheat the oven to 200°C/Gas 6. Heat the butter in a small pan and when it's bubbling add the apples. Sauté them for 3 minutes, stirring occasionally.
2 Sprinkle on the sugar and cinnamon and stir again. Pour on the cream and simmer for 3 minutes. Remove the pan from the heat and spoon the contents into a medium-sized pie dish.

To prepare the topping
3 Place the flour and butter in a food processor and whizz until the mixture resembles breadcrumbs. Add the caster sugar and whizz briefly.
4 On a chopping board, roughly chop the nuts and add them to the crumble mix in the food processor, then blend for a few seconds.
5 Spoon the topping over the apples and then sprinkle on the demerara sugar. Bake for 30 minutes until bubbling and golden and serve with cream.

Mocha ice cream cake

The only downside with this recipe is that the finished cake needs to put in the freezer for an hour before serving. The upside is that it is so delicious you may well finish it in one sitting and it won't have to go back into the freezer.

SERVES 6

100g plain chocolate, broken into pieces
1 tbsp instant coffee granules
2 tbsp water
3 eggs
75g caster sugar
400ml double cream, whipped

Base
175g digestive biscuits
75g butter, melted

To make the base

1 Blitz the biscuits to crumbs in a food processor or bash them in a plastic bag with a rolling pin. Tip the crumbs into a bowl and mix them with the melted butter.

2 Spoon the biscuit mix into a 25cm spring-clip tin or flan dish. Press the mixture down firmly with a wooden or metal spoon and place to one side while you prepare the filling.

To make the filling

3 Place the chocolate, coffee and water in a glass bowl. Place the glass bowl over a saucepan of simmering water, taking care that the bowl doesn't touch the water. Stir occasionally until the chocolate has melted, then remove from the heat.

4 Separate the eggs, putting the whites into a scrupulously clean bowl and the yolks into another clean bowl with the caster sugar. Beat the egg yolks and caster sugar until light and creamy. Using a clean whisk, beat the egg whites until stiff peaks form.

5 Stir the yolk and sugar mixture into the warm melted chocolate. Fold in the whites and then fold in the double cream. Gently pour the mixture on to the biscuit base, cover the cake with clingfilm and place it in the freezer for 1 hour.

6 Remove the cake from the freezer and leave it in the fridge 45 minutes before serving to make it easier to slice. Run a knife round the edge of the tin before releasing the spring-clip, but leave the base of the tin on the bottom of the cake to serve.

Asparagus with fried duck eggs and pancetta

Simple yet beautiful!

SERVES 6

24 asparagus stems
olive oil
6 duck eggs
6–12 slices of pancetta
6–12 slices of country bread, for toasting
extra virgin olive oil
sea salt
freshly ground black pepper

1 To trim the asparagus, hold the base of a stem between the finger and thumb of your left hand. Use the finger and thumb of your right hand to bend the piece of asparagus downwards, then discard the end that breaks off. Repeat to trim all the stems.
2 Bring a saucepan of water to the boil and cook the asparagus for 3 minutes. Drain and set aside.
3 Fry the pancetta and set aside to keep warm. Add a little olive oil to a frying pan and fry the duck eggs in the same pan. Toast the bread.
4 Put 1 or 2 pieces of toast on each plate with a drizzle of extra virgin olive oil. Lay an egg on top and place the asparagus by the side, drizzled with a little extra virgin olive oil and a grinding of salt and pepper. Garnish each plate with pancetta.

Spicy spatchcocked poussins with pilaf rice

Spatchcocking means removing the backbone of a bird so that you can flatten it. You could ask your butcher to do this for you, but it's not difficult to do yourself once you get the knack.

SERVES 6

3 poussins
1 tsp salt
1 tsp ground cinnamon
½ tsp ground turmeric
1 tsp ground cumin
1 tsp ground coriander
1 tsp fennel seeds
3 tbsp rapeseed or olive oil
2 shallots, finely sliced
3 eggs, hard-boiled, to serve

Pilaf rice
olive oil
1 shallot, finely chopped
1 garlic clove, crushed
400g basmati rice
2 tbsp blanched almonds
2 tbsp raisins
5 strands saffron, soaked
1 tbsp warm water
600ml chicken stock
10 cherry tomatoes

1 Turn the birds over so that they are resting on their breasts. Using a very sharp knife, jointing scissors or normal scissors, cut up from the neck all the way to the other end, then cut up the other side of the backbone to remove it. Turn the poussin over and press the centre with your palm to flatten it. Repeat with the other birds.
2 Place the poussins in a large roasting tin and add the salt, spices, fennel seeds, oil and shallots, mixing everything with your hands so that the birds are nicely coated. Ideally, leave them in a cool place for an hour, but 30 minutes will do if you're short of time.
3 Preheat the oven to 220°C/Gas 7. Place the roasting tin in the oven and roast the birds for 40 minutes. The skin should be nicely crisp and golden. Cut the birds in half and serve with the hard-boiled eggs and pilaf rice.

To prepare the pilaf rice
4 Heat a tablespoon of olive oil in a large saucepan that has a lid. Add the shallot and garlic and cook for 2 minutes. Add the rice, almonds and raisins and stir, then cook for 2 minutes. Add the saffron and chicken stock and bring to the boil, then cover the saucepan and leave the rice to simmer gently for 15 minutes.
5 Place the cherry tomatoes on top of the rice and add a glug of olive oil. Put the lid back on, remove the saucepan from the heat, and leave untouched for 10 minutes.

Simnel cake

This is a traditional Easter cake and very easy to make. For me, there's nothing better than the smell of a fruit cake baking in the oven – it makes everyone feel warm and comfortable the minute they enter the kitchen.

SERVES 6

180g butter, at room temperature, plus extra for greasing
180g soft brown sugar
4 eggs
225g self-raising flour
200g sultanas
200g raisins
200g currants
1 tsp mixed spice
grated zest of 1 lemon
2 tbsp brandy
1 eating apple, grated
1 tbsp apricot jam, warmed
500g block of marzipan
11 chocolate mini eggs

1 Preheat the oven to 170°C/Gas 3 ½. Grease a 23cm round cake tin and line it with baking parchment. You also need to wrap a piece of greaseproof paper or newspaper round the outside to come 3cm up the side of the tin, but you can do this once the cake mixture is in the tin and then tie it in place with string.
2 Cream the butter and sugar using an electric hand-whisk, until light and fluffy. This should take about 5 minutes. Add 1 of the eggs to the creamed mixture along with a tablespoon of flour and mix in thoroughly. Repeat with the remaining eggs, adding a spoonful of flour each time.
3 Next, add the rest of the flour, the dried fruit, mixed spice, lemon zest, apple and brandy and fold them in with a large metal spoon. Spoon the mixture into the cake tin and then wrap the collar of greaseproof paper or newspaper around the outside of the tin and tie it in place. Bake the cake for 1 hour and 45 minutes or until a skewer inserted into the centre of the cake comes out clean.
4 Let the cake cool in the tin for a short while, then remove it and leave to cool completely on a wire rack.
5 To decorate, brush the top of the cake with the apricot jam. Roll out a 23cm circle of marzipan and place this on top of the cake. Place the 11 mini eggs at intervals around the edge of the cake. You can tie a ribbon around the side of the cake to make it look prettier if you wish.

By the end of this month spring comes to an end and summer begins, so you may be able to spend more time in the garden and perhaps have the occasional barbecue. You may have some home-grown lettuces ready to harvest in the kitchen garden, as well as radishes and spinach. If you are a dedicated vegetable gardener you will have asparagus beds and be relishing the first few shoots that come through. Cooking from the garden in May requires some skill, as nothing comes through in huge amounts and making use of what's available can be a bit of a balancing act. In the shops, there are plenty of good things to tempt you, including new potatoes, peas, spinach, early broad beans and beetroot. Take the opportunity to eat asparagus this month; if you don't grow your own you may be able to buy it from farm shops, or even pick your own. Asparagus is exquisite when simply boiled and served with a little melted butter or a splash of olive oil and a grinding of salt and pepper.

May

Quick chicken stew

Chicken thighs and drumsticks on the bone are great for stews and curries. They have a better flavour than breasts and don't get overcooked so easily.

SERVES 6

2 tbsp olive oil
1.5kg chicken thighs and drumsticks, skinned but left on the bone
1 onion, finely chopped
1 carrot, sliced into 5mm discs
1 celery stalk, chopped
2 garlic cloves, finely chopped
100g Italian salami, chopped
2 tbsp finely chopped flat-leaf parsley
200ml white wine
1 x 400g can of chopped tomatoes
a large pinch of dried chilli flakes
sea salt
freshly ground black pepper

1 Heat the olive oil in a large saucepan. Brown the pieces of chicken, 2 or 3 at a time, placing each batch to one side as it browns. Season the chicken as you go.
2 Keep the pan on the heat and add the onion, carrot, celery, garlic, salami and parsley. Cook over a low heat for 3 minutes. Return the chicken to the pan and pour in the wine, then simmer over a medium heat for 10 minutes.
3 Add the tomatoes and chilli and stir to combine. Season well, then cover the pan and leave the stew to simmer for 20 minutes. Serve with chunks of crusty French bread.

Parmigiana di melanzane

This dish looks particularly inviting when it comes out of the oven, with the sauce oozing and bubbling away. The smells that waft around the kitchen are pretty enticing too.

SERVES 6

4 aubergines, sliced into 5mm discs
olive oil
1 onion, finely chopped
1 garlic clove, finely chopped
800g tomato passata
25g butter
25g flour
400ml milk
1 egg
250g buffalo mozzarella cheese, drained and torn into chunks
100g Parmesan cheese, finely grated
1 handful of basil leaves, roughly torn
sea salt
freshly ground black pepper

1 Place the aubergine slices in a colander, sprinkle them with salt and leave for 30 minutes or so to disgorge their bitter juices.
2 Heat 2 tablespoons of olive oil in a saucepan. Add the onion and garlic and fry over a low heat for 5 minutes then add the passata and simmer gently for 30 minutes.
3 Rinse the aubergines and dry them with some kitchen paper. Heat 2 tablespoons olive oil in a frying pan and place enough aubergine slices in the pan to cover the base. Fry them until golden brown, then turn and brown them on the other side. Place the fried slices on some kitchen paper to drain while you fry the rest.
4 Melt the butter in a small saucepan, then stir in the flour. Take the pan off the heat and gradually add the milk to the butter and flour, stirring as you do so. Return the pan to the heat and simmer the sauce gently for 10 minutes. Remove the sauce from the heat, stir in the egg and season with salt and pepper. Preheat the oven to 200°C/Gas 6.
5 Take a gratin dish measuring about 22 x 30cm. Spoon a layer of tomato sauce on to the base of the dish. Place half the aubergines on top, then add half the mozzarella. Scatter with some Parmesan and torn basil leaves, then season with salt and pepper. Spoon in another layer of tomato sauce and top with the remaining aubergines and the rest of the mozzarella, then sprinkle with Parmesan and basil leaves. Season with salt and pepper. Finish with some tomato sauce, then spoon on the white sauce and top with more Parmesan and seasoning.
6 Bake in the oven for 40 minutes. Serve with some bread and a green salad.

Stuffed peppers and tomatoes

The idea of stuffing a tomato or a pepper always seemed more trouble than it was worth to me, but I was pleasantly surprised when I tried these. The dish has a lovely fresh taste that's very welcome after long months of winter comfort food, and it's not as much work as I thought.

SERVES 6

2 tbsp olive oil
1 onion, finely chopped
3 sage leaves, finely chopped
leaves from 1 sprig of rosemary, finely chopped
500g minced pork
250g sausage meat
1 tsp sugar
1 tbsp soy sauce
1 tbsp tomato purée
1 x 400g can of chopped tomatoes
3 peppers
6 large tomatoes
150g feta cheese, crumbled
sea salt
freshly ground black pepper

1 Heat the olive oil in a large frying pan. Add the onion, sage and rosemary and fry gently for 5 minutes. Increase the heat and then add the minced pork and sausage meat and brown all over.

2 Add the sugar, soy sauce, tomato purée and canned tomatoes. Bring everything to a simmer and cook, uncovered, for 45 minutes. Season well with salt and black pepper.

3 In the meantime, preheat the oven to 200°C/Gas 6. Slice the peppers in half lengthways through the stalk and take out the white cores and seeds. Cut off the tops of the tomatoes and carefully remove the insides with a teaspoon. Place the pepper halves and the tomatoes on a baking tray.

4 Fill the peppers and tomatoes with the pork mixture and sprinkle some feta cheese on top of each one. Cover with a large sheet of foil and bake in the oven for 20 minutes. Remove the foil and cook for a further 10 minutes to brown the tops. Serve with a green salad.

Bean and pasta broth

This hearty broth is full of flavour and is perfect for this time of year.

SERVES 6

1 tbsp olive oil
1 onion, finely chopped
1 sprig of rosemary, leaves removed and finely chopped
2 garlic cloves, finely chopped
1 x 400g can of borlotti beans, drained and rinsed
1 x 400g can of cannellini beans, drained and rinsed
750ml vegetable stock
450g macaroni
Parmesan cheese, grated, for serving
sea salt
freshly ground black pepper

1 Heat the olive oil in a large saucepan. Add the onion and rosemary and cook over a low heat for 5 minutes, then add the garlic and cook for a few seconds longer. Add the beans and the stock and simmer slowly for 20 minutes.
2 Cook the macaroni according to the packet instructions and drain. Add the cooked macaroni to the broth and season with salt and pepper. Serve the broth in bowls with grated Parmesan and some bread if you like.

Chorizo potato cakes with fried sea bass

When writing recipes, I try to come up with interesting dishes that everyone would like to eat and that are easy to cook, without getting into difficulties. I think this recipe works well on both counts.

SERVES 6

700g small new potatoes, peeled and cut in half
200g sweet potatoes, peeled and cut in quarters
olive oil
200g good-quality chorizo sausage, chopped into 1cm chunks
8 spring onions, trimmed and finely sliced
6 sea bass fillets
balsamic vinegar, for drizzling
sea salt
freshly ground black pepper

1 Put all the potatoes in a large pan of salted water, bring to the boil and cook until tender. Drain the potatoes, then put them in a bowl and break them up roughly with a knife.
2 Heat a tablespoon of the olive oil in a sauté pan and fry the chorizo and spring onions for about 3 minutes until golden. Add the chorizo and spring onions to the potatoes, season to taste and place to one side until cool enough to handle.
3 Once the mixture has cooled slightly, shape it into 6 cakes with your hands. You will have to press the mixture together quite firmly.
4 Heat 2 tablespoons of olive oil in the frying pan and fry the potato cakes for 3 minutes on each side.
5 At the same time, heat a tablespoon of olive oil in another frying pan and fry the sea bass fillets for 1 minute on each side.
6 Serve the fish with the potato cakes and drizzle a little balsamic vinegar over the top. Serve with a green salad.

Pork and black bean curry with yellow rice

This is an authentic Sri Lankan curry until you add the black beans, but I think that most recipes can take some fiddling and changes.

SERVES 6

2 tbsp vegetable oil
½ tsp cumin seeds
¼ tsp fennel seeds
1 onion, finely chopped
5 curry leaves
2cm piece of fresh root ginger, grated
2cm stick of cinnamon
¼ tsp turmeric
1 kg diced pork shoulder
1 tsp salt
1 tbsp tomato purée
1 x 400ml can of coconut milk
200ml water
1 x 400g can of black beans, drained and rinsed

Yellow rice
1 tbsp vegetable oil
1 onion, finely chopped
5 curry leaves
500g basmati rice
750ml water
½ tbsp saffron threads placed in 1 tbsp warm water
2 tbsp raisins
½ tsp salt

Curry powder
4 tbsp coriander seeds
2 tbsp cumin seeds
2 tbsp fennel seeds
2cm stick of cinnamon
5 cloves
10 curry leaves

1 Heat the vegetable oil in a large saucepan. Add the cumin and fennel seeds, onion, curry leaves, ginger, cinnamon, turmeric and 2 tablespoons of the curry powder (see below) and cook over a low heat for 5 minutes.
2 Add the pork and stir to coat in the spices, then add the salt, tomato purée, coconut milk, water and black beans and bring to a simmer. Cover and cook for 1 hour and serve with the yellow rice.

To cook the yellow rice
3 Heat the vegetable oil in a large saucepan and fry the onion and curry leaves for 5 minutes. Add the rice, giving it a good stir. Pour in the water and add the saffron and raisins, then sprinkle in the salt. Bring to the boil and then reduce the heat to very low. Cover the saucepan and cook for 15 minutes.
4 Remove the pan from the heat and leave to stand for 10 minutes with the lid on the pan. At the end of this time the rice will be cooked.

To make the curry powder
5 This makes more than you need for this recipe, but it stores very well. Place all the ingredients in a small frying pan on a high heat. As soon as you smell the aroma and see the spices starting to smoke, stir them around with a wooden spoon. Once they look evenly toasted, grind them to a fine powder using a mortar and pestle or a coffee grinder. Store the curry powder in a clean dry jar.

Shoulder of lamb with vegetables and puy lentils

Both leg and shoulder of lamb make great Sunday dinners, but a shoulder is cheaper and I think more flavoursome. There's more fat on a shoulder, which keeps the joint beautifully succulent while it roasts.

SERVES 6

- 1.5kg shoulder of lamb
- 1 sprig of rosemary
- olive oil
- 500g new potatoes, cut into 2cm chunks
- 200g carrots, cut into 2cm chunks
- 200ml white wine
- 70g pancetta, chopped
- 1 tbsp finely chopped rosemary leaves
- 1 shallot, finely sliced
- 300g puy lentils
- 500ml chicken stock (a stock cube will do)
- sea salt
- freshly ground black pepper

1 Preheat the oven to 200°C/Gas 6. Place the lamb in a roasting tin with the rosemary sprig, then rub the skin of the lamb with olive oil and season well with salt and pepper.
2 Place the lamb in the preheated oven and cook for 20 minutes. Then turn the oven down to 150°C/Gas 2 and cook the lamb for another 40 minutes.
3 Take the roasting tin out of the oven and scatter the potatoes and carrots around the lamb. Pour on the white wine, season the vegetables and return to the oven for another hour. Turn the vegetables occasionally during the cooking time.
4 Meanwhile, place a saucepan on the stove and heat a tablespoon of olive oil. Add the pancetta, chopped rosemary and shallot and cook for 3 minutes, then add the puy lentils and the stock. Bring to a simmer and cook gently, uncovered, for 25 minutes.
5 Add the puy lentils to the roasting tin with the lamb and vegetables and cover with foil. Cook for another hour – that's 3 hours in all – until the lamb is falling off the bone. Serve the meat on top of the lentils and vegetables. I like to serve a green salad with this to temper the richness a little.

Dried fig and almond tart

Figs taste so great in Italy and Greece, where you can pick them from the tree, still warm from the sun. It's hard to find good figs in Britain, but I like dried soft figs. They're not a substitute for fresh figs but they are a great ingredient in their own right.

SERVES 6

100g butter, at room temperature
100g caster sugar
2 eggs
80g ground almonds
40g desiccated coconut
4 dried soft figs, soaked for 1 hour or so in enough brandy to cover, then drained and roughly chopped

Pastry
125g butter, at room temperature
90g caster sugar
½ tsp vanilla bean paste
1 large egg
250g plain flour, plus extra for dusting the work surface
a pinch of salt

1 First make the pastry. Using an electric mixer or a food processor, beat the butter and sugar together until smooth and combined. Add the vanilla bean paste and egg and mix again.
2 With the mixer on a slow speed setting, start to add the flour, a tablespoon at a time. Once all the flour has been added, turn the mixture on to a floured surface and shape it into a smooth ball with your hands. Wrap the pastry in clingfilm and chill in the fridge for 30 minutes.
3 Grease a 21cm tart tin and preheat the oven to 190°C/Gas 5.
4 Roll out the pastry on a floured surface and use it to line a tart tin. Put the tart tin on a baking sheet. Place a sheet of baking parchment over the pastry and pour on some baking beans, then bake the tart case in the oven for 10 minutes. Remove the beans and baking parchment and return the tart case to the oven for another 10 minutes.
5 Meanwhile, prepare the filling. Cream the butter and sugar with an electric hand-whisk for 3 minutes, then add the eggs and mix until combined. Fold in the ground almonds and coconut.
6 Spoon the sponge mixture into the pastry case and gently spread it out so that it covers the base of the tart tin evenly. Sprinkle the chopped figs on top, pressing them in slightly with your fingertips. Bake in the oven for 30 minutes. Serve with cream.

Olive oil cake

This is a beautifully light and flavoursome cake which is also very easy to make.

SERVES 12

4 eggs
200g caster sugar
grated zest of 2 lemons
250ml good olive oil
275g self-raising flour

Icing
juice of 2 lemons
200g icing sugar, sifted

1 Preheat the oven to 190°C/Gas 5. Grease a 23cm cake tin and line it with baking parchment.
2 Put the eggs, sugar and lemon zest in a food processor and blend for 1 minute. With the processor on, pour the oil through the funnel in a steady stream.
3 Place the flour in a mixing bowl, then pour the egg and oil mixture on to the flour, mixing all the while. Do not over mix.
4 Pour the cake batter into the cake tin and bake in the preheated oven for 45 minutes. Test the cake by inserting a skewer into the centre – if it comes out clean the cake is done.
5 Take the cake out of the oven and leave it to cool in the tin for 10 minutes. Then turn the cake out on to a wire rack to finish cooling.

To make the icing
6 Mix the lemon juice with the icing sugar. Spread this icing over the cake.

H.SAMUEL
SHEFFIELD

Lamb kebabs with yoghurt dressing and haloumi and pepper salad

These kebabs can be put together in a flash and make the perfect light meal for a mild May evening – perhaps with some warm pitta breads. You will need some wooden skewers for cooking the kebabs.

SERVES 6

1kg minced lamb
1 red onion, finely chopped
1 tsp sea salt
1 tsp ground cumin
1 tsp ground coriander
1 tbsp finely chopped fresh oregano
2 tbsp olive oil

Yoghurt dressing
200ml natural yoghurt
2 tbsp crème fraiche
1 tbsp finely chopped fresh mint
a pinch of salt

Haloumi and pepper salad
2 tbsp olive oil
200g haloumi, cut into 1cm cubes
2 red peppers, cored and chopped into 1cm cubes
15 cherry tomatoes, cut in half
2 tbsp chopped fresh basil
1 tbsp extra virgin olive oil for serving
freshly ground black pepper

1 Preheat the oven to 220°C/Gas 7. Place the lamb, onion, salt, spices and oregano in a bowl and mix them well with your hands.
2 Take about 50–60g of the mixture, form it into a sausage shape and put it on to a wooden skewer. Repeat until you have used up all the kebab mixture.
3 Cover a couple of baking trays with foil and lay the kebabs on top. Sprinkle the kebabs with olive oil and cook them in the oven for 30 minutes, then put them under a hot grill for 5 minutes to brown. Serve with the yoghurt dressing and the salad.

To make the yoghurt dressing
4 Simply mix all the ingredients together and serve.

To make the haloumi and pepper salad
5 Heat the olive oil in a frying pan. Add the haloumi and pepper cubes and fry for 3 minutes on a high heat, until the haloumi is golden brown and the peppers have softened.
6 Remove the pan from the heat and add the tomatoes, basil and a good grinding of pepper. Drizzle on the extra virgin olive oil.

Roast beef and potato salad

There is more to salad than lettuce and tomatoes and this dish makes a summery, yet robust meal.

SERVES 6

800g beef fillet (in 1 piece)
2 tbsp olive oil, plus extra for drizzling
1 red pepper, cored, seeded and sliced into 1cm strips
200g rocket leaves
100g feta cheese, cubed or crumbled
sea salt
freshly ground black pepper

Potatoes
1 tbsp goose fat
600g new potatoes, cooked until tender
sea salt
freshly ground black pepper

Dressing
1 tbsp crème fraiche
1 tbsp natural yoghurt
1 tbsp creamed horseradish sauce
2 tsp Dijon mustard
100ml olive oil
1 tbsp finely chopped flat-leaf parsley
sea salt
freshly ground black pepper

1 Preheat the oven to 220°C/Gas 7. Rub the beef fillet with olive oil and season it with salt and pepper. Place the beef in a roasting tin with the red pepper and pop it into the oven for 10 minutes. Reduce the oven temperature to 170°C/Gas 3 ½ and cook for a further 15 minutes.
2 Leave the beef to rest for 10 minutes, then carve it into reasonably thin slices. Spread the rocket leaves on a serving plate and arrange the beef fillet and pepper slices on top. Crumble on the feta cheese, drizzle with olive oil and sprinkle with salt and pepper. Serve with the potatoes and the dressing on the side.

To prepare the potatoes
3 Heat the goose fat in a sauté pan and fry the cooked potatoes until golden brown. Season with salt and pepper.

To make the dressing
4 Spoon the crème fraiche, yoghurt, horseradish sauce and mustard into a bowl and mix them together. Gradually pour on the olive oil, a little at a time, stirring constantly. Sprinkle on the parsley and season with salt and pepper.

Fried trout with watercress sauce and minted new potatoes

This is one of my favourite recipes. The trout is perfect with the watercress sauce, not only because of the taste, but also because of the colour combination – the gentle pink of the trout with the vibrant green of the sauce. Trout is definitely the fish to eat at this time of year.

SERVES 6

6 trout fillets, skin on and pin bones removed
a little olive oil
sea salt
freshly ground black pepper

Watercress sauce
25g butter
1 shallot, finely chopped
2 x 150g bags fresh watercress
150ml chicken stock
2 tsp creamed horseradish
1 tsp Dijon mustard
3 tbsp whipping cream, lightly whipped
sea salt
freshly ground black pepper

Minted new potatoes
800g new potatoes
a small handful of fresh mint leaves, finely chopped
2 tbsp olive oil
sea salt
freshly ground black pepper

To make the watercress sauce

1 Heat the butter in a medium saucepan. Add the shallot and cook for a couple of minutes, then add the watercress, stalks and all. Cover and cook over a low heat for 3 minutes. Add the stock, cover the pan again and simmer for 2 minutes.

2 Tip the contents of the saucepan into a blender and blitz until smooth. Stir in the horseradish and mustard and season well. Spoon into a bowl and fold in the cream just before serving.

To cook the new potatoes

3 Boil the potatoes in plenty of salted water until tender. Drain, tip them back into the pan and return to a low heat with the olive oil and mint leaves. Stir for a few seconds so that the potatoes become coated in the oil. Remove from the heat and season with salt and pepper.

To cook the fish

4 Brush the fillets on each side with a little olive oil. Heat a frying pan and fry a couple of the fillets for about 1 minute on each side. Season with salt and pepper. Keep warm while you cook the rest of the fillets. Serve with the sauce and the potatoes.

Black and white bean quesadillas with guacamole

My children love these. A quesadilla is a corn or wheat flour tortilla filled with cheese and other good things. The tortilla is then folded over and grilled or fried. Children like food that they can pick up and eat with their hands – it's more fun somehow.

SERVES 6

- 1 x 400g can of black beans, drained and rinsed
- 1 x 400g can of butter beans, drained and rinsed
- 150g Cheddar cheese, grated
- 3 shallots, finely chopped
- a handful of fresh basil leaves roughly chopped
- 12 flour tortillas
- olive oil
- sea salt
- freshly ground black pepper

Guacamole

- 1 ripe avocado, peeled and stoned
- 2 ripe tomatoes
- 1 red onion, finely chopped
- juice of 1 lemon
- a handful of fresh coriander, roughly chopped
- sea salt
- freshly ground black pepper

1 Place the beans, cheese, shallots and basil in a mixing bowl and stir gently. Taste and then season with salt and pepper as required.
2 Lay the 12 tortillas out and divide the mixture evenly between them, spooning it on to half of each tortilla. Fold the other half over so you have a half-moon shape.
3 Heat a little olive oil in a frying pan and gently fry the tortillas, a couple at a time, on both sides. Be careful as they turn golden very quickly. The bean mixture will spill out a little, but scoop it up with a spoon and pop it back in. Cut the quesadillas in half and serve with the guacamole.

To make the guacamole
4 Place the avocado in a bowl and mash it roughly with a fork.
5 Place the tomatoes in a glass bowl and pour some boiling water over them. Pierce the skins of the tomatoes with the tip of a sharp knife, leave for 1 minute, then remove them from the water. The skins should come away easily.
6 Roughly chop the tomatoes and add them to the avocado, then add the onion, lemon juice, coriander and seasoning and mix well.

Duck in a pot with vegetables

There can still be some chilly days in May when it's good to cheer everyone up with hearty meals, one of which has to be a duck stew.

SERVES 6

- 1 tbsp vegetable oil
- 6 duck legs
- 1 tbsp flour
- 500ml chicken stock
- 3 parsnips, peeled and cut into chunks
- 3 carrots, peeled and cut into chunks
- 500g baby new potatoes, left whole
- 1 celeriac, peeled and cut into chunks
- 3 leeks, rinsed and sliced into 2cm pieces
- 1 sprig of rosemary
- bay leaf
- sea salt
- freshly ground black pepper

1 Heat the vegetable oil in a large casserole dish. Place the duck legs in the pan, skin side down, and brown them over a medium heat for 10 minutes. Sprinkle the legs with salt and pepper while they cook, but don't move them around.
2 Remove the legs from the fat and drain the oil from the pan into a jam jar or bowl. You can use the fat for roast potatoes another time.
3 Return the duck legs to the casserole dish, this time skin side up. Sprinkle with salt and pepper again and cook for 10 minutes without moving. Remove the legs, then add the flour to the fat in the casserole dish, stirring constantly.
4 Stir in the chicken stock. Put the duck back in the pan with the vegetables and herbs and a good seasoning of salt and pepper. Preheat the oven to 150°C/Gas 2.
5 Pop the dish into the oven and cook for 1½ hours. Serve with chunks of bread.

Sausage and beans

Even though the days are longer and slightly warmer now, I still crave meaty, warming food and there are some evenings when only a good English pork sausage will do. This is a simple but satisfying dinner.

SERVES 6

- 1 tbsp olive oil
- 6 baby onions, peeled and left whole
- 12 pork sausages
- 1 red pepper, cored and finely diced
- 1 x 400g can of black beans, drained and rinsed
- 1 x 400g can of cannellini beans, drained and rinsed
- 1 x 400g can of chickpeas, drained and rinsed
- 1 x 400g can of chopped tomatoes
- 1 tbsp dark soy sauce
- 1 tsp soft brown sugar
- 1 tsp paprika
- 100g baby spinach, washed
- sea salt
- freshly ground black pepper

1 Heat the olive oil in a large saucepan. Add the onions and sausages and cook until they are brown all over, turning the sausages frequently. Throw in the red pepper and cook for 5 minutes.
2 Add the beans, chickpeas, tomatoes, soy sauce, sugar and paprika, then season with salt and pepper. Cover and simmer for 40 minutes.
3 Just before serving, add the spinach and stir it into the stew until it wilts.

Chicken and mushroom casserole

When I was growing up in the 1970s, chicken and mushroom casserole was very popular. We may have gone on eating it, but the word 'casserole' has gone out of fashion and been replaced by 'stew'. Whatever the name, this is a good dish.

SERVES 6

1 tbsp olive oil
2 tbsp butter
6 boneless, skinless chicken breasts, cut in half
300g mixed fresh mushrooms, roughly chopped
2 garlic cloves, crushed
150ml white wine
4 shallots, roughly chopped
2 tbsp crème fraiche
200ml chicken stock
2 tbsp finely chopped flat-leaf parsley
sea salt
freshly ground black pepper

1 Heat the olive oil and 1 tablespoon of butter in a heatproof casserole. When it's fizzing, add 4 or 5 pieces of chicken and brown them on both sides. Remove from the pan, set aside and brown the rest of the chicken in small batches.
2 Once all the chicken is browned, keep the empty pan on the stove and add another tablespoon of butter. Throw in the mushrooms and the garlic and cook over a high heat for 5 minutes, until all the moisture has left the mushrooms and they are beginning to turn golden brown. Remove them from the pan and set aside with the chicken.
3 Return the pan to the heat. Add the wine and shallots, then simmer uncovered for 3 minutes. Stir in the crème fraiche and add the stock.
4 Return the chicken and mushrooms to the pan and bring to a simmer, then taste for seasoning and add the parsley. Cover the pan and cook for 15 minutes. Serve with a rocket salad and baked potatoes.

Pineapple tarte tatin

I don't cook with pineapple often but I really like this variation on a classic tarte tatin.

1 First make the pastry. Place the flour, salt and butter in a food processor and pulse until the mixture resembles breadcrumbs. Add the egg yolk and water and pulse again for a few seconds. Turn the mixture out on to a floured work surface and bring together into a ball of dough. Wrap in clingfilm and chill in the fridge while you prepare the pineapple.
2 Trim and peel the pineapple, then cut the flesh into slices 2cm thick. Remove the centres of the pineapple slices with an apple corer or a knife, then cut the circles in half to make semi-circles. Leave to one side.
3 Place a tarte tatin pan or a heavy ovenproof frying pan on a medium heat, add the brown sugar and leave it to dissolve. Don't stir the sugar – just tilt the pan to move the caramelising sugar around so that it becomes evenly dark brown and is bubbling.
4 Once the sugar is dark brown, remove the pan from the heat and dot the butter into the pan. Stand the pineapple slices up in the pan, so the curves of the semi-circles point up. Arrange them as prettily as you can, making sure the pan is full and tilting the slices slightly to fill any gaps. Return the pan to the heat, let the butter bubble for 1 minute, then remove the pan again. Preheat the oven to 200°C/Gas 6.
5 Roll out the pastry and lay it over the pineapple, tucking it in at the sides. Make a couple of slashes in the pastry to allow the cooking steam to escape, then bake in the oven for 30 minutes. Remove and leave for 5 minutes. Invert the tart on to a large serving plate, taking care not to lose any of the juices when you turn the pan over. Serve with crème fraiche.

SERVES 6

1 large, sweet pineapple
80g soft brown sugar
40g cold butter, cut into cubes

Pastry
180g plain flour
a pinch of salt
85g cold butter, cut into cubes
1 egg yolk
2 tbsp cold water

Orange chocolate chip loaf

Oranges used to be a fruit for the wealthy, coveted by the kings of France, but these days we take them for granted. Their flavour goes superbly well with chocolate, as the sweet-toothed among us will already know, and this is a scrumptious cake. Serve it with some fresh orange segments.

MAKES 1 LOAF

225g plain flour
2 tsp baking powder
180g ground almonds
180g caster sugar
100g dark chocolate, roughly chopped
4 eggs, beaten
225g butter, melted, plus extra for greasing the tin
grated zest and juice of 1 orange

1 Preheat the oven to 180°C/Gas 4. Grease a 1-litre loaf tin and line it with baking parchment.

2 Place the flour, baking powder, ground almonds, sugar and chocolate pieces in a mixing bowl. Add the eggs, melted butter, zest and juice and mix everything together.

3 Spoon the mixture into the loaf tin and bake for 1 hour and 10 minutes. Turn the loaf out on to a wire rack and leave to cool before slicing.

Simple vanilla sponge with raspberry glacé icing

Life is complicated so allow yourself to enjoy simple pleasures, such as a vanilla sponge.

MAKES 1 X 24CM CAKE

200g butter, softened
200g caster sugar
3 eggs
200g self-raising flour
1 tsp vanilla extract
1 tsp baking powder
3 tbsp milk

Icing
100g icing sugar
1 tbsp warm water
2 tsp raspberry jam

1 Grease a 24cm sandwich tin and line it with baking parchment. Preheat the oven to 180°C/Gas 4.
2 Using an electric hand-whisk, beat the butter and sugar for 3 minutes, until pale and fluffy. Add 1 egg and a tablespoon of flour and beat to combine. Do the same with the remaining 2 eggs, adding a spoonful of flour after each. Add the vanilla, baking powder and milk and fold in with the remaining flour.
3 Spoon the mixture into the sandwich tin and bake for 35–40 minutes, until the top of the centre of the cake is firm to the touch of your fingertips. Leave the cake to cool in the tin for 5 minutes, then remove it from the tin and leave to cool on a wire rack.

To ice the cake
4 Sift the icing sugar into a mixing bowl, add the water and mix with a wooden spoon. Stir in the raspberry jam. When the cake is completely cool, spread the icing on top and smooth with a knife.

Baked meatballs and potatoes

The only drawback with meatballs is the hassle of having to fry them after you have rolled them into balls. This is messy and time consuming, so I've developed this recipe, in which the meatballs are baked, not fried.

SERVES 6

½ chicken stock cube
150ml boiling water
2 slices of white bread
1kg minced lamb
1 tbsp finely chopped fresh oregano
30g pistachio nuts, finely chopped
1 onion, finely chopped
1kg potatoes
2 tbsp olive oil
1 tbsp chopped oregano leaves
sea salt
freshly ground black pepper

1 Preheat the oven to 200°C/Gas 6. Dissolve the stock cube in a small bowl with the boiling water and add the bread to the bowl. When the bread is cool enough to handle, break it up with your hands and gently squeeze out some of the liquid.
2 Add the lamb, oregano, pistachio nuts and onion to the bread, season well and mix all the ingredients together well with your hands. Shape into balls about 6cm in diameter.
3 Peel the potatoes and cut them into slices about 1cm thick. Lay the sliced potatoes in a roasting tin and place the meatballs on top. Sprinkle with the olive oil and the oregano leaves, then season with salt and pepper. Place the dish in the oven and bake for 1 hour. Serve with a simple green salad.

Chilli beans with baked potatoes

There is never anything left over when I make this dish. If you are feeding teenagers, you might want to increase the quantities a little.

SERVES 6

- 6 baking potatoes
- 2 tbsp olive oil
- 1 onion, finely chopped
- 2 tsp ground coriander
- 2 tsp ground cumin
- 2 tsp paprika
- 1 x 400g can of aduki beans, drained and rinsed
- 1 x 400g can of haricot beans, drained and rinsed
- 1 x 400g can of black beans, drained and rinsed
- 1 x 400g can of chopped tomatoes
- 1 vegetable stock cube
- 150ml water
- 2 tbsp finely chopped coriander leaves
- 1 x 150-170ml carton soured cream, for serving
- 150g Cheddar cheese, grated, for serving
- sea salt
- freshly ground black pepper

1 Preheat the oven to 220°C/Gas 7. Place the potatoes in the oven and bake for 1–1 ½ hours.
2 Heat the olive oil in a large saucepan. Add the onion and fry gently for 5 minutes, then stir in the spices. Add the beans and tomatoes and bring everything to a simmer. Crumble on the vegetable stock cube, add the water, then stir and simmer, uncovered, for 40 minutes.
3 Check for seasoning and add salt and pepper as necessary. Scatter on the coriander leaves and serve the beans with the baked potatoes and some soured cream and grated cheese.

Chicken and cabbage curry

I think cabbage is an underused vegetable. Perhaps we have become so used to it being there that we tend to ignore it – or maybe we've been put off by the poor way it used to be cooked. It's available almost all year round and tastes good, so is worth cooking more often. It goes really well with curry, whether as a side dish or in the curry itself, as in this recipe.

SERVES 6

2 tbsp vegetable oil
1kg chicken pieces, skinned but left on the bone
1 onion, finely chopped
2 garlic cloves, finely chopped
250g white cabbage, finely shredded
¼ tsp turmeric
2 tbsp curry powder
seeds from 5 cardamom pods
5cm piece of cinnamon stick
½ tsp cayenne pepper
1 tsp tomato purée
1 x 400g can of coconut milk
100ml water
1 x 400g can of butter beans, drained and rinsed
sea salt

Boiled rice
500g basmati rice
½ tsp salt
750ml water

1 Heat the oil in a large saucepan. Brown the chicken pieces all over and place them to one side. Do this in batches so you don't overcrowd the pan.
2 Once all the chicken is browned, add the onion and garlic and fry for 5 minutes over a medium heat, stirring often so that the garlic does not burn. Add the cabbage and cook for 3 minutes.
3 Add the turmeric, curry powder, cardamom seeds, cinnamon stick, cayenne and a little salt, then fry for 1 minute. Next add the tomato purée, coconut milk, water and beans. Return the chicken to the pan, cover and simmer gently for 45 minutes. Serve with some boiled rice.

To prepare the boiled rice
4 Place the rice, salt and water in a large saucepan and bring to a lively boil. Reduce the heat to very low, cover the pan and cook the rice for 15 minutes. Stir once during the cooking time.
5 Remove the pan from the heat. Keep the rice covered and leave it undisturbed for 10 minutes more.

Salmon burgers

I love these salmon burgers, but they are quite delicate. Be gentle when frying and move them around as little as possible so they don't break up.

SERVES 6

700g salmon fillet, skinned
200g sweet potato, chopped and cooked until tender
2 shallots, chopped very finely
grated zest of 1 lemon
1 tsp chopped fresh dill
1 level tbsp wholegrain mustard
6 burger buns
2 tbsp olive oil
sea salt
freshly ground black pepper

Watercress and pancetta salad
300g watercress
100g chopped pancetta
1 tsp olive oil

Salad dressing
2 tbsp extra virgin olive oil
½ tbsp balsamic vinegar
sea salt
freshly ground black pepper

1 Finely chop the salmon fillet, removing any stray bones. Place the fish in a mixing bowl with the sweet potato, shallots, lemon zest, dill and mustard, then season well with salt and pepper.
2 Mix everything together and shape into 6 burgers. Place the burgers in the fridge to chill and firm up for at least 30 minutes.
3 Heat the olive oil in a frying pan and gently brown the burgers on both sides until golden brown. Then leave them to cook for 5 minutes on a low heat, without moving them, by which time the salmon should be cooked and have a nice pink tinge.
4 Place each burger inside a bun and serve with the watercress and pancetta salad.

To make the salad
5 Fry the pancetta in a small pan in the olive oil until golden brown. Place the watercress in a serving dish and sprinkle the pancetta on top. Toss with the dressing and serve.

Puy lentils and soft eggs on toast

I like cooking lentils, partly because they have so many health benefits, but also because they don't need soaking before use and they usually only need to be simmered for about 30 minutes. They absorb other flavours well so are a low maintenance ingredient in the kitchen, which is always good for time-pressed cooks.

SERVES 6

350g puy lentils
1 vegetable stock cube
6 eggs
5 tbsp olive oil
12 cherry tomatoes, cut into quarters
a large of bunch mint, finely chopped
10 salad onions, finely chopped
5–12 slices of sourdough bread
sea salt
freshly ground black pepper

1 Place the puy lentils in a saucepan with the stock cube and enough water to cover. Bring to a simmer and cook for 30 minutes, until tender.
2 In the meantime, bring a pan of water to the boil, add the eggs and cook for 4 minutes. Cool them under running water, then shell carefully and leave them whole until you are ready to serve.
3 Drain the lentils, put them in a bowl and dress with the olive oil. Stir in the tomatoes, mint and salad onions, then season with a little salt and some black pepper.
4 Toast the bread lightly on both sides and drizzle each slice with a little olive oil. Pile some lentils on top and then an egg, cut in half. Season again if necessary with some black pepper and serve.

Pork steaks with green sauce, roast potatoes and spring greens

A herby green sauce is a great accompaniment for plainly cooked meat, lifting it from the ordinary to something more special.

SERVES 6

6 pork steaks
2 tbsp olive oil
juice from 1 lemon
sea salt
freshly ground black pepper

Green sauce
200g mixed herbs (parsley, mint and basil)
2 shallots, peeled and chopped
2 garlic cloves
200ml olive oil
1 tbsp capers, rinsed
sea salt
freshly ground black pepper

Roast potatoes
1kg potatoes, peeled and quartered
salt
2 tbsp olive oil

Spring greens
500g spring greens, finely shredded
2 tbsp water
small knob of butter
squeeze of fresh lemon juice
sea salt
freshly ground black pepper

To make the green sauce
1 Place all the ingredients in a blender and mix until everything is combined and you have a smooth sauce. Taste and then season with salt and pepper.

To cook the potatoes
2 Preheat the oven to 220°C/Gas 7. Put the potatoes in a pan of salted water, bring to the boil and cook for 5 minutes. Drain the potatoes and place them in a roasting tin, then add the olive oil and toss well. Roast in the preheated oven for 45–50 minutes until golden.

To cook the pork steaks
3 Heat the olive oil in a frying pan. When it's hot, brown the pork steaks until golden on each side. Place the steaks in the oven on top of the roast potatoes for the last 10 minutes of the cooking time. Serve with the greens and the green sauce.

To cook the greens
4 Place the greens in a saucepan with the water and butter. Cook over a very gentle heat for 5 minutes, then remove and season with salt and pepper and a squeeze of lemon juice just before serving.

Lamb in a pot

This is a spicy lamb stew, but the lamb flavour still comes through. It's all too easy to add too much spice to dishes, drowning out other tastes and over-stimulating your palate so that you always want spicy foods.

SERVES 6

- 1kg lamb leg meat, cut into cubes
- 2 tbsp plain flour
- 1 tsp salt
- 3-4 tbsp olive oil
- 2 garlic cloves, finely chopped
- 1 onion, diced
- 1 tbsp tomato purée
- 1 tsp ground cumin
- 1 tsp ground coriander
- 1 tbsp fresh thyme leaves
- 3 medium tomatoes, roughly chopped
- 500ml beef stock
- 200g carrots, peeled and chopped into 2cm chunks
- 200g potatoes, peeled and cut into eighths
- freshly ground black pepper

1 Toss the lamb chunks in the flour, salt and a good grinding of pepper. Heat the olive oil in a large saucepan and brown the lamb in batches, placing each batch to one side while you do the next. Don't overcrowd the pan or the meat will steam rather than brown.

2 When all the lamb has been browned, put the empty pan back on the heat with a dash more olive oil. Fry the garlic and onion on a very low heat for 10 minutes.

3 Return the lamb to the saucepan and add the tomato purée, ground cumin, coriander and thyme leaves. Fry for 2 minutes. Next add the tomatoes, stock and vegetables and bring everything to a simmer. Cover the pan and cook gently for 45 minutes. Serve with some new potatoes.

Rhubarb crumble with ginger cream

The flavour of ginger goes beautifully with rhubarb, which makes one of the very best crumbles.

SERVES 6

700g rhubarb, trimmed and chopped into 1.5cm chunks
3 tbsp soft brown sugar

Crumble topping
50g butter
100g plain flour
50g caster sugar

Ginger cream
250ml double cream
1 tbsp syrup from a jar of stem ginger
1 tbsp stem ginger, chopped

1 Preheat the oven to 180°C/Gas 4. Put the rhubarb and sugar in a medium saucepan over a high heat. Once you hear the rhubarb starting to cook, reduce the heat, cover the pan and cook for 10 minutes. Stir the rhubarb occasionally so that it all cooks evenly. Place to one side to cool while you prepare the topping.
2 Place the flour and butter in the bowl of a food processor and blend until it has the texture of breadcrumbs, then stir in the sugar.
3 Tip the cooked rhubarb into an ovenproof dish. Sprinkle on the topping and cook for 30 minutes until the topping is brown and the filling is bubbling. Serve with the ginger cream.

To make the ginger cream
4 Whip the double cream in a mixing bowl until light and fluffy, then fold in the stem ginger syrup and the stem ginger pieces.

Coconut layer cake

This cake looks magnificent when it has been iced and it makes a great birthday cake.

MAKES 1 X 20CM CAKE

110g butter, at room temperature
250g caster sugar
2 eggs
175ml milk
210g plain flour
2 tsp baking powder
2 drops vanilla extract

Frosting
340g caster sugar
2 egg whites
3 tbsp water
¼ tsp cream of tartar
½ tsp vanilla extract
50g desiccated coconut, to decorate

1 Preheat the oven to 180°C/Gas 4. Grease 2 x 20cm sandwich tins and line them with baking parchment.
2 Place the butter and sugar in a mixing bowl and cream thoroughly with an electric hand-whisk until pale in colour and light and fluffy in texture. Add the eggs and milk and mix again, then gently stir in the flour, baking powder and vanilla extract.
3 Divide the cake mixture evenly between the tins and bake for 25 minutes, until the sponge is springy to the touch. Leave the cakes to cool in the tins for 5 minutes, then turn them out on to a wire rack.

To make the frosting
4 Put all the frosting ingredients (except the coconut) in a glass bowl and place the bowl over a pan of simmering water, making sure the bottom of the bowl doesn't touch the water. Gently stir the mixture until the sugar has dissolved and you can no longer see or feel any grittiness from the sugar.
5 Whisk the mixture for about 5 minutes until the icing stands in peaks. Remove the pan from the heat and continue to beat until the icing is thick and easy to spread.
6 When the cakes are completely cool, sandwich them together with some of the frosting. Using a knife, spread the rest of the frosting over the top and sides of the cake, then sprinkle the top with desiccated coconut.

Spinach and flageolet bean soup with Irish rarebit

Flageolet beans are particularly good in soups and stews as they cook to a dense, creamy texture. The Irish rarebits are a great accompaniment.

SERVES 6

2 tbsp olive oil
1 onion, finely chopped
knob of butter
200g spinach leaves
1 x 400g can of flageolet beans, drained and rinsed
200g peas (frozen will do)
1.5 litres vegetable stock
150ml single cream
sea salt
freshly ground black pepper

Irish rarebit
300g hard, full-flavoured cheese, grated
5 tbsp Guinness
2 tsp English mustard
6 thick slices of bread
butter
black pepper

1 Heat the olive oil in a saucepan and cook the onion gently for 10 minutes. Add the butter, spinach, beans and peas and continue to cook gently for 10 minutes over a low heat, covered. Pour on the stock, cover the pan and simmer for 40 minutes.
2 Allow the soup to cool slightly, then pour it into a blender and liquidise. Return the soup to the pan and season well with salt and pepper. Warm through to serve, then stir in the cream.

To make the rarebit
3 Mix the cheese, Guinness and mustard together in a small bowl, then season with black pepper. Heat the grill.
4 Lightly toast the bread on both sides. Spread 1 side of each slice with some of the cheese mixture and place under a hot grill until bubbling and golden.

Stuffed chard leaves

Stuffed leaves are a popular dish in France and Germany but are served less often here. These are a real treat and are quite simple to make, as chard leaves are easy to handle and not too delicate.

1 Bring a large saucepan of water to the boil. Place the chard leaves, 1 at a time, in the water for 30 seconds, remove, drain and place to one side. Then cook the chard stalks in the same boiling water for 3 minutes. Drain the stalks, chop them finely and set aside.
2 Split the skin of the sausages and squeeze the meat into a mixing bowl. Add the parsley, chard stalks, nutmeg and a good grinding of black pepper, then mix thoroughly.
3 Lay the chard leaves out on a chopping board and spoon 100g of the stuffing mixture on to each leaf. Roll up each leaf like a thick cigar, folding in any wide or uneven ends so that you have a neat parcel. Place the stuffed chard leaves in a gratin dish. Preheat the oven to 200°C/Gas 6.

To make the sauce
4 Melt the butter in a small saucepan. Add the flour and mix well with a wooden spoon. Remove from the heat and gradually stir in the milk and cream, stirring constantly to avoid lumps. Return the pan to a low heat and simmer the sauce very gently for 10 minutes. Season with salt and pepper and add the mustard.

Assembling the dish
5 Pour the sauce over the stuffed chard leaves and sprinkle the Parmesan cheese on top. Bake in the preheated oven for 30 minutes, then serve with a green salad.

SERVES 6

500g Swiss chard leaves
100g Swiss chard stalks
16 pork sausages
1 tbsp finely chopped flat-leaf parsley
¼ tsp grated nutmeg
freshly ground black pepper

White sauce
25g butter
25g flour
250ml milk
100ml double cream
2 tsp Dijon mustard
2 tbsp grated Parmesan cheese
sea salt
freshly ground black pepper

Eggs with prawns and asparagus

Gourmets may baulk at the idea of serving fresh asparagus with scrambled egg and prawns, preferring to eat it with hollandaise sauce or melted butter. But buying asparagus for a family of six is expensive. This recipe allows everyone a little taste of heaven without breaking the bank.

SERVES 6

12 eggs
2 tbsp double cream
a pinch of paprika
200g asparagus spears, trimmed
1 tbsp olive oil
a knob of butter, plus extra for spreading the toast
1 garlic clove, finely chopped
200g small cooked prawns
6 slices of bread for toasting
sea salt
freshly ground black pepper

1 Mix the eggs in a bowl with the cream and paprika, then season with salt and pepper. Leave to one side.
2 Cook the asparagus in boiling salted water for 5 minutes until tender. Drain the asparagus and cut it into 2cm pieces, then place to one side.
3 Heat the oil and knob of butter in a frying pan until sizzling, then add the garlic and cook for 30 seconds. Add the prawns and cook for another 30 seconds. Pour in the egg mixture and stir over a low heat to make creamy scrambled eggs.
4 Remove the pan from the stove while the eggs are still nice and runny, then gently mix in the asparagus and prawns.
5 Toast the bread and spread with butter. Serve the eggs piled on top of the warm buttered toast.

Pasta with tomato and pancetta sauce

This quick pasta sauce will keep the family happy.

SERVES 6

2 tbsp olive oil
1 onion, finely chopped
70g sliced pancetta, finely chopped
1 x 400g can of chopped tomatoes
2 tbsp roughly chopped basil
1 tsp sugar
500g spaghetti
Parmesan cheese, grated, for serving
sea salt
freshly ground black pepper

1 Heat the olive oil in a medium saucepan. When it's hot, add the onion and cook for 10 minutes until soft.
2 Add the pancetta and cook for 2 minutes until it starts to turn golden. Pour in the tomatoes and sprinkle on the basil. Season with salt and pepper and the sugar and simmer on the lowest heat for 40 minutes. Check the seasoning again before serving.
3 Cook the spaghetti in boiling salted water according to the packet instructions. Drain the pasta, mix with the sauce and serve with grated Parmesan cheese.

Tilapia stew

Based on a dish cooked by Spanish fishermen, this meal is a starchy but delicious treat. It takes only about 30 minutes to prepare, from start to finish.

SERVES 6

3 tbsp olive oil
2 onions, finely chopped
2 green peppers, cored and diced
a generous pinch of saffron threads
800g potatoes, peeled and cut into 2cm chunks
600ml water
250g linguine
800g tilapia fillets, cut into 2cm pieces
2 tbsp crème fraiche
2 tbsp finely chopped flat-leaf parsley
sea salt
freshly ground black pepper
olive oil and fresh lemon, for serving

1 You need a large sauté pan or saucepan with a lid. Heat the olive oil in the pan and add the onion, peppers, saffron and potatoes. Sauté for 5 minutes, stirring to stop the potatoes sticking and to make sure that the vegetables cook evenly.
2 Pour in the water and bring to a gentle simmer. Season generously with salt and pepper, then cover and cook for 10 minutes.
3 Break the linguine in half and add it to the pan, then add the fish and stir in the crème fraiche and parsley. Simmer, uncovered, for 4–6 minutes or until the pasta is tender.
4 Season again, then serve the stew in wide bowls with a drizzle of olive oil and a squeeze of fresh lemon.

Roast stuffed chicken legs

Chicken legs are really easy to stuff. The skin stretches, allowing you to wedge the stuffing underneath so it won't fall out. Ideally, roast the stuffed legs on a wire rack over the potatoes so the potatoes are enhanced by the lovely flavours of the chicken and the stuffing.

SERVES 6

100g ricotta cheese
1 shallot, finely chopped
20g flat-leaf parsley, finely chopped
50g sliced pancetta, finely chopped
40g pitted prunes, finely chopped
50g chestnut mushrooms, finely chopped
1 garlic clove, finely chopped
6 chicken legs
2 tbsp olive oil
a few sprigs of fresh thyme
sea salt
freshly ground black pepper

Roast potatoes
800g potatoes, peeled and cut into 8 pieces
1 tbsp olive oil
sea salt

1 Preheat the oven to 200°C/Gas 6. Place the ricotta, shallot, parsley, pancetta, prunes, mushrooms and garlic in a mixing bowl and stir well to combine. Season with salt and pepper.
2 Ease your fingertips under the skin of a chicken leg and push some stuffing underneath. Brush with the oil and season with salt and pepper, then repeat with the rest of the chicken legs and stuffing. Place the legs on a wire roasting rack, sprinkle with the thyme sprigs and set to one side.
3 Put the potatoes in a pan of salted water, bring to the boil and cook for 4 minutes. Drain the potatoes and place them in a roasting tin with the olive oil, then roast in the oven for 40 minutes.
4 Place the chicken legs on the wire rack over the potatoes and return the pan to the oven to roast for a further 40 minutes. This way the delicious chicken juices drip down on to the potatoes.
5 If you don't have a roasting rack, you can roast the potatoes and chicken separately. Serve with asparagus or a green salad.

Stuffed pork tenderloin

Lovely served with buttery mashed potato (see page 16) as well as spring greens.

SERVES 6

2 pork tenderloins (or pork fillets as they are sometimes called), about 450g each
100ml dry white wine
olive oil
sea salt
freshly ground black pepper

Stuffing
100g chestnuts, finely chopped
2 shallots, finely chopped
1 tsp finely chopped fresh rosemary
3 sausages, skins removed and discarded
2 tbsp white breadcrumbs
a large knob of butter
1 egg
sea salt
freshly ground black pepper

Sauce
2 tsp flour
200ml chicken stock
2 tsp Dijon mustard
100ml double cream
sea salt
freshly ground black pepper

Spring greens
500g spring greens, finely shredded
2 tbsp water
a small knob of butter
1 lemon
sea salt
freshly ground black pepper

1 First make the stuffing. Place the chestnuts, shallots, rosemary, sausage meat, breadcrumbs, butter and egg in a mixing bowl and mix well by hand. Season with a little salt and pepper.
2 Take each tenderloin and cut through it lengthways, as you would split a baguette to make a sandwich. You now have 4 pieces. Spread the stuffing along 2 of the pieces, then place the other 2 on top so you have 2 stuffed tenderloins. Using some kitchen string, tie each tenderloin at 4cm intervals so they hold together while cooking. Preheat the oven to 220°C/Gas 7.
3 Take a large piece of foil and lay it in a roasting tin that can be placed on top of the stove. The foil should be big enough to envelope the pork loosely, but not cover them completely. Place the pork tenderloins on top of the foil and pour in the wine. Rub each tenderloin with a little olive oil and season with salt and pepper.
4 Place the stuffed tenderloins in the hot oven and cook for 20 minutes. Then reduce the heat to 190°C/Gas 5 and cook for 30 minutes longer.
5 Remove the tenderloins from the tin and place them on a plate to keep warm. Tip the wine and juices out of the foil into the roasting tin and then place the tin on top of the stove and make the sauce.
6 Add the flour to the cooking juices and stir until well combined and bubbling nicely. Pour on the stock and stir, then simmer for 5 minutes. Add the mustard and cream and simmer for 2–3 minutes, then season to taste. Serve the pork with the sauce and spring greens.

To cook the spring greens
7 Place the greens in a saucepan with the water and butter, then cook on a very gentle heat for 5 minutes. Remove from the heat and season with salt and pepper and a squeeze of fresh lemon juice just before serving.

Cherry almond cake

Cherry and almond cake doesn't just sound delicious – it is delicious!

MAKES 1 X 20CM CAKE

175g butter, softened
175g caster sugar
3 eggs
175g self-raising flour
50g ground almonds
75g marzipan, grated
120g glace cherries, halved
2 tbsp milk

1 Grease a 20cm cake tin and line the base with baking parchment. Preheat the oven to 180°C/Gas 4.
2 Place the butter and sugar in a mixing bowl and using an electric hand-whisk, mix until pale and fluffy. Add the eggs and mix again, then fold in the flour, almonds, marzipan, cherries and milk until evenly combined.
3 Spoon the mixture into the prepared tin and bake the cake in the oven for 45 minutes. Let the cake cool slightly, then turn it out on to a wire rack to cool completely before serving.

Rhubarb pudding

Rhubarb and custard are perfect partners. The acidity of the rhubarb works superbly with the sweetness of the custard

SERVES 6

500g rhubarb, chopped into 2cm chunks
2 tbsp soft brown sugar
2 tbsp water
grated zest of 1 orange

Cake topping
250g butter, softened
200g soft brown sugar
4 eggs
250g self-raising flour
juice of 1 orange

Custard
4 egg yolks
50g caster sugar
300ml double cream
1 tsp cornflour

1 Place the rhubarb, sugar, water and orange zest in a saucepan, then bring to a simmer and cook gently for 5 minutes. Remove the saucepan from the heat, cover the pan and leave for 5 minutes. Preheat the oven to 180°C/Gas 4.
2 Meanwhile, make the cake topping. Put the butter and sugar in a bowl and beat with an electric hand-whisk for 3 minutes. Add 1 egg and a tablespoon of the flour and beat again until combined. Do exactly the same with the rest of the eggs, following each with a spoonful of flour. Fold in the remaining flour and gently mix in the orange juice.
3 Spoon the rhubarb into the base of a gratin or a pie dish and spread the cake mixture on top. Bake the pudding in the oven for 40 minutes, then serve with custard or cream.

To make the custard
4 Mix the yolks with the sugar and cornflour in a glass bowl. Heat the cream until it is just about to boil, then whisking constantly, pour the cream on to the eggs. Place the glass bowl over a saucepan of simmering water and stir until the custard has thickened slightly.

Eggs with onion curry sauce on toast

Serve this dish with a salad on the side to make it more substantial for people with large appetites – or serve two eggs each. It also makes a good starter for a dinner party, especially if you take some extra care with the presentation.

SERVES 6

6 eggs
40g butter
200g onions, finely chopped
1 celery stalk, finely chopped
1 tbsp flour
1 tbsp curry powder
250ml chicken stock
2 tbsp finely chopped fresh coriander
slices of bread for toasting
2 tbsp crème fraiche
a little olive oil
sea salt
freshly ground black pepper

1 Bring a large saucepan of water to the boil. Carefully place the eggs in the water, 1 at a time, taking care not to knock them against the side of the saucepan. Bring the water back to a gentle simmer and cook the eggs for 10 minutes.
2 Pour off the hot water but keep the eggs in the pan. Bash them against the side of the pan so that the shells crack and then place the pan under a tap of cold running water. Leave the eggs in the cold water for 5 minutes or so and then drain, by which time the shells should come away from the eggs easily. Cut the eggs in half, lengthways.
3 Heat the butter in a saucepan and fry the onion and celery for 15 minutes over a low heat until soft. Stir in the flour and curry powder.
4 Pour on the stock gradually and stir while the sauce thickens. Spoon in the crème fraiche and stir to combine, then add the coriander and season with salt and pepper.
5 Toast the bread and drizzle with a little olive oil. Place the egg halves on the toast and spoon some sauce over the top.

Breaded whiting fillets with broad bean and pea purée

This breaded white fish is served with an updated version of mushy peas. Whiting can be eaten guilt free, as it is reasonably priced and plentiful.

SERVES 6

flour for coating
200g white breadcrumbs
2 eggs, beaten
6 whiting fillets
salt and pepper
olive oil for frying

For the broad bean and pea puree
300g podded broad beans
200g green peas (frozen will do)
10 mint leaves, roughly chopped
200ml chicken stock
2 tablespoons double cream

1 Place a couple of tablespoons of flour on a plate, the eggs in a bowl and the breadcrumbs on another plate. Check the fillets for any undetected bones, then dust them with flour. Dip the fish in the egg and then coat with the breadcrumbs.
2 Heat 2 tablespoons of olive oil in a frying pan and fry the fillets, 1 at a time, for 2 minutes on each side. Season with salt and pepper and serve with lemon wedges, broad bean and pea purée and some sautéed potatoes (see page 572) if you like.

To prepare the broad bean and pea purée
3 Make a slit in the top or bottom of each bean with a sharp knife and place them in a pan of boiling unsalted water for 4 minutes. Drain, and when the beans are cool enough to handle, slip off their grey outer skins and place to one side.
4 Using the same saucepan, bring the stock to a simmer and cook the peas with the mint leaves until tender, uncovered. Pour the peas, mint leaves and remaining stock into a blender with the broad beans and pulse for a few seconds to make a rough purée. Season with salt and pepper and stir in the cream.

Asparagus and pancetta risotto

Risotto is a firm favourite in our household. Pancetta goes beautifully with asparagus, both in taste and colour.

SERVES 6

1.75 litres chicken stock
12 asparagus spears
1 tbsp olive oil
25g butter
1 onion, finely chopped
1 stick celery, finely chopped
70g pancetta, chopped
500g Arborio risotto rice
150ml white wine
2 tbsp grated Parmesan cheese
1 tbsp roughly chopped basil leaves
6 thin slices of pancetta
sea salt
freshly ground black pepper

1 Heat the stock in a saucepan and check the seasoning. Once it has come to a simmer, cook the asparagus spears in the stock for about 4 minutes, until tender. Remove the spears from the stock, chop them into 2cm pieces and place to one side.
2 Heat the oil and butter in a large pan until the butter starts to foam. Add the onion, celery and chopped pancetta and cook for 5 minutes. Then add the rice and cook for 1 minute, stirring. Pour in the wine and stir until it has nearly all evaporated.
3 Add a ladleful of stock to the rice, stirring all the while, then add another ladle of stock when the last has almost been absorbed. Keep adding stock until the rice is cooked, which should take about 20–25 minutes, depending on how you like your rice. Keep tasting it to check and adjust the seasoning at this stage.
4 Once the rice is cooked to your liking, remove from the heat and fold in the asparagus, cheese and basil. Fry the pancetta slices and place 1 on top of each serving of risotto.

Raspberry sponge drops

These take a few minutes to make and are lovely as a little treat for children. They also work well as an accompaniment to a fruit fool.

MAKES 24 CAKES

4 eggs
100g caster sugar
50g ground almonds
100g plain flour, plus extra for sprinkling the tins
100g butter, melted, plus extra for greasing the tins
170g raspberries
icing sugar, for dusting the cakes

1 Grease 2 x 12-hole fairy cake tins and sprinkle the insides of the holes with flour. Preheat the oven to 180°C/Gas 4.
2 Place the eggs and the caster sugar in a food mixer and whisk until the mixture becomes thick and pale yellow. Alternatively, you can do this with a hand-held whisk.
3 Fold in the almonds, flour and melted butter and keep folding until everything is combined. Put spoonfuls of the mixture into the fairy cake tins, then place a raspberry in the centre of each one.
4 Bake in the oven for 15 minutes. Carefully remove the cakes from the tins with a round-bladed knife and place them on a cooling rack. When the cakes are cool dust them with icing sugar.

Strawberries with rhubarb

Rhubarb and strawberries go surprisingly well together, the sweetness of the strawberries helping to combat the sourness of the rhubarb. Simple but good.

1 Place the rhubarb in a medium saucepan, add the water and sugar and bring to a simmer. Cover the pan and simmer the fruit for 2 minutes.
2 Take the pan off the heat, keep the lid on and leave it undisturbed for 10 minutes. Add the strawberries and stir them in gently. Cover the pan again and leave for 5 minutes before serving. Some cream is good with this.

SERVES 6

500g rhubarb, cut into 1.5cm chunks
2 tbsp water
2 tbsp brown sugar
400g strawberries, hulled

June heralds the first glory of the summer in the garden and the countryside. In a good year, temperatures rise and rainfall is moderate. Flowers start to bloom and the vegetable garden is generous in its bounty. Keep enjoying lettuces, spring onions, potatoes and radishes, and although the asparagus is passing you can look forward to other good things. Last year I found British-grown cherries in the supermarket and they were such a pleasure to eat compared to the American ones. Gooseberries are also in the shops, so put them in a fool or a crumble with plenty of custard. The first strawberries are coming through and there is no better way to eat them than with some fresh cream and a sprinkling of sugar. Indulge yourself in all the treasures of the season, such as salmon and sea trout, both excellent now. I like to serve salads every day at this time of year. You can vary the recipes and the dressings you make, but keep summer salads simple so the ingredients can speak for themselves.

June

Gnocchi with meat sauce

Home-made gnocchi bears little resemblance to the bought kind, which is heavy and stodgy. I used to wonder what the fuss was about until I made my own. They're really not that difficult and once you get used to the process you will be able to make them quite quickly. And trust me, when you put the gnocchi into the boiling water they won't all clump together in a horrible mess but will actually float to the surface of the water when they're ready, like magic!

SERVES 6

Meat sauce
2 tbsp olive oil
1 onion, finely chopped
1 garlic clove, finely chopped
1 celery stalk, finely chopped
700g beef skirt, chopped into 2cm dice
1 tbsp flour
200ml red wine
1 tbsp tomato purée
1 x 400g can of chopped tomatoes
a sprig of rosemary, leaves removed and finely chopped
sea salt
freshly ground black pepper

Gnocchi
900g potatoes, cooked and mashed (preferably with a potato ricer for fluffiness)
225g '00' flour, plus extra for dusting the work surface
2 small eggs
25g butter, softened
a good pinch of sea salt
Parmesan cheese, grated, for serving

To make the meat sauce

1 Preheat the oven to 150°C/Gas 2. Heat the olive oil in a large ovenproof saucepan or a casserole dish. Add the onion, garlic and celery and cook over a low heat for 10 minutes, stirring occasionally, until the vegetables have softened. Increase the heat, add the meat and stir to brown it all over. As soon as the meat starts to stew rather than fry, add the flour and stir, then add the wine.

2 Simmer for 2 minutes, then season the sauce generously with salt and pepper. Add the tomato purée, chopped tomatoes and the rosemary, then cover the pan and place in the oven for 2 hours.

To make the gnocchi

3 Mix the potatoes, flour, eggs, butter and a good pinch of salt in a bowl until combined. Sprinkle your work surface with flour.

4 Break off lumps of the dough and roll them into snake-like lengths, about 1.5cm thick. Cut the lengths into 2cm pieces. Press the tip of your finger into the top of each piece so that you have a slight indentation and place to one side.

5 When you're ready to serve, bring a large pan of salted water to the boil and drop in half the gnocchi. Cook them for 2 minutes, remove with a slotted spoon and place them in a serving bowl. Cook the rest of the gnocchi in the same way. Serve the gnocchi with the meat sauce and plenty of grated Parmesan cheese.

Grilled salmon on coconut rice

Adding some coconut flavour to rice makes a change and it goes nicely with the salmon.

SERVES 6

6 salmon fillets
1 tbsp olive oil
1 lemon
sea salt
freshly ground black pepper

Coconut rice
1 tbsp vegetable oil
1 red onion, finely chopped
1 garlic clove, finely chopped
¼ tsp cumin seeds
¼ tsp turmeric
500g basmati rice
3 tbsp fresh coriander, finely chopped
½ tsp salt
650ml water
100ml coconut cream
200g frozen petit pois

1 Preheat the grill. Place the salmon fillets on the grill pan, drizzle with a little olive oil and season with a good grinding of salt and pepper. Put the salmon under the grill and cook for 3 minutes on each side.
2 Squeeze some lemon juice over the fish and serve with the coconut rice.

To make the coconut rice
3 Heat the oil in a large saucepan. Add the onion, garlic, cumin and turmeric and fry for 5 minutes. Add the rice, coriander and salt and stir to coat the rice in the oil and spices.
4 Pour on the water and coconut cream, add the peas and bring to the boil. Reduce the heat to very low, cover the pan and cook for 15 minutes. Remove the pan from the heat, keeping it covered, and leave for 10 minutes.

A grand salad

This really is a 'grand' salad because it is full of lip-smackingly good ingredients. A salad can be made with almost anything these days, as long as it all goes together. To be something special, a salad must be dressed well and, of course, be appealing to the eye.

SERVES 6

3 eggs
1 cos lettuce heart, shredded
200g salad leaves
3 sausages, cooked and sliced
1 cooked chicken breast, roughly chopped
100g asparagus, cooked and chopped
½ celeriac, finely shredded
a handful of flat-leaf parsley, finely chopped
6 spring onions, sliced
3 tomatoes, cut into quarters
½ cucumber, cut into dice

Dressing
1 heaped tbsp crème fraiche
1 tsp Dijon mustard
½ tsp finely chopped fresh tarragon
sea salt
4 tbsp olive oil
freshly ground black pepper

1 Bring a large saucepan of water to the boil. Carefully place the eggs in the water, 1 at a time, taking care not to knock them against the side of the saucepan. Bring the water back to a gentle simmer and cook the eggs for 10 minutes.
2 Pour off the hot water but keep the eggs in the pan. Bash them against the side of the pan so that the shells crack and then place the pan under a tap of cold running water. Leave the eggs in the cold water for 5 minutes or so and then drain, by which time the shells should come away from the eggs easily. Cut the eggs into quarters lengthways.
3 Place all the salad ingredients in a large serving dish.
4 To make the dressing, put the crème fraiche, mustard and tarragon in a small bowl, then add the olive oil in a drizzle, stirring as you go. Season with salt and pepper to taste. Spoon over the salad and serve with bread.

Fresh pappardelle with tomato and basil sauce

Bought pasta is fine, but when I have time I do like to make my own and for this dish it really is worth it. You do need a pasta machine.

SERVES 6

Pasta
500g '00' flour
5 eggs

Tomato and basil sauce
600g cherry tomatoes, halved with seeds removed
2 garlic cloves, peeled and finely sliced
3 tbsp olive oil
3 tbsp chopped fresh basil
3 tbsp mascarpone cheese
Parmesan cheese, grated, for serving
sea salt
freshly ground black pepper

1 Pile the flour in a mound on a clean work surface, make a large well in the middle and break the eggs into it. Beat the eggs with a fork, pulling a little of the flour into them as you go. Gradually pull in more flour until you can work the dough with your hands without it sticking to your fingers. You probably won't need all the flour.
2 Knead the dough for 5 minutes, then wrap it in clingfilm and place it in the fridge for 30 minutes.
3 Set the pasta machine to its widest setting. Divide the pasta dough into 3 pieces and keep the other pieces covered while you work. Pass one piece of pasta through the machine. Fold it in 3 as you would fold a letter, turn it 90 degrees, then pass it through the machine again. Repeat the folding and turning and pass the pasta through the machine on the widest setting 3 or 4 times.
4 Keep passing the piece of pasta through the machine, reducing the size of the setting each time you do this, until you come to the penultimate setting, which is probably the best thickness for pappardelle. Cut this length of pasta into ribbons of about 2cm wide and 6cm long. Sprinkle these with a little flour and place to one side while you roll out the remaining pasta.
5 Bring a large saucepan of salted water to the boil. When the sauce is ready, put the pasta into the boiling water and cook for about 2 minutes.

To make the tomato and basil sauce
6 Preheat the oven to 200°C/Gas 6. Put the tomatoes in a roasting tin with the garlic, olive oil and chopped basil and roast for 20 minutes.
7 When the tomatoes are cooked, mash them with the back of a spoon, then add the mascarpone cheese and season well. Sprinkle with some more basil leaves and then toss with the cooked pasta. Serve with Parmesan.

Quiche Lorraine

There are lots of versions of quiche Lorraine, but I think you really do need to use cream or crème fraiche to get the authentic taste. The perfect accompaniment for a quiche Lorraine has to be a crisp green salad.

SERVES 6

140g pancetta, chopped
1 medium onion, finely chopped
2 eggs
1 egg yolk
300ml double cream
75g Cheddar cheese, grated
1 tbsp grated Parmesan cheese
50g Gruyère cheese, grated
1 tbsp finely chopped flat-leaf parsley
1 tbsp finely snipped chives
freshly ground black pepper

Pastry
225g plain flour
150g cold butter, cut into cubes
2 tbsp finely grated Parmesan cheese
1 egg yolk
2 tbsp cold water

1 First make the pastry. Place the flour and butter in a food processor and whizz until the mixture resembles breadcrumbs. Add the Parmesan and whizz again briefly. Add the egg yolk and water, then process for a few seconds until the mixture is starting to come together.
2 Turn the dough out on to a cool surface and gently shape into a ball with your hands. Wrap the dough in clingfilm and chill in the fridge for 30 minutes. Preheat the oven to 180°C/Gas 4.
3 Fry the pancetta and onion in a frying pan for about 10 minutes over a low heat until the onion is soft and the pancetta is golden in colour. Leave to one side to cool. Whisk the eggs and yolk together and add the cream, cheeses and herbs. Season with black pepper.
4 Roll out the pastry and use it to line a 24cm tart tin. Cover the pastry with a sheet of baking parchment and fill with baking beans. Bake in the oven for 15 minutes, then remove the baking parchment and beans and return the pastry case to the oven for a further 5 minutes. Remove the pastry and leave the oven on.
5 Spread the pastry with the pancetta and onion and pour on the egg mixture, then bake for 25 minutes. Leave the quiche to cool for 10 minutes, then serve it straight from the tin, which is what I do when I am in a hurry, or remove it on to a plate to take to the table.

Fish and mushy pea cakes with oven chips

These were a great success with my children and not too much trouble to make.

SERVES 6

600ml milk
700g fresh pollack fillets
1 tbsp olive oil
2 shallots, finely chopped
500g frozen petit pois
300ml chicken stock
250g potatoes, peeled and cut in quarters
2 eggs, beaten
flour
white breadcrumbs
olive oil for frying
sea salt
freshly ground black pepper

Home-made oven chips
6 baking potatoes, peeled and sliced into chip shapes
2 tbsp goose fat
sea salt
1 tsp paprika

1 Pour the milk into a roasting tin and bring to a simmer on top of the stove. Place the pollack fillets in the milk and simmer them gently for 4 minutes. Drain the fish and then place it in a bowl, removing any stray bones and skin. Flake the fish with a fork.
2 Heat the olive oil in a small saucepan and fry the shallots for 3 minutes, taking care not to burn them. Add the frozen petit pois to the pan and pour in the stock. Bring to a simmer, cover and cook for 10 minutes. Remove the saucepan from the heat and mash the peas with a fork or with a hand blender to make a rough purée with some texture. Place the pea purée in the bowl with the flaked pollack.
3 Put the potatoes in a saucepan of salted water, bring to the boil and cook until tender. Drain and mash the potatoes in with the fish and peas. Season well with salt and pepper and then place in the fridge to chill for 15–30 minutes.
4 Shape the mixture into neat cakes. You should have about 6. Beat the eggs in a shallow bowl and spread the breadcrumbs and flour on separate plates. Pat each cake in some flour, then dip them in the beaten egg and lastly in the breadcrumbs.
5 Heat some olive oil in a frying pan and fry the fish cakes for 3 minutes on each side until golden brown. Serve with the oven chips.

To make the oven chips
6 Preheat the oven to 220°C/Gas 7. Sprinkle the potatoes with salt and the paprika and then place them in a vegetable tray with the goose fat. Cook in the oven for 50–60 minutes.

Leg of lamb, minted new potatoes and creamed spinach

Anyone who isn't keen on spinach will be converted by this version, which goes well with the lamb.

SERVES 6

2 tbsp olive oil
1 x 2kg leg of lamb
12 baby onions, peeled and left whole
6 carrots, peeled and chopped into 2cm chunks
1 fennel bulb, trimmed and thinly sliced
100ml dry white wine
sea salt
freshly ground black pepper

Minted new potatoes
800g new potatoes
1 sprig of fresh mint
1 tbsp olive oil
10 mint leaves, finely chopped
sea salt
freshly ground black pepper

Creamed spinach
50g butter
25g plain flour
250ml milk
a grating of nutmeg
500g fresh spinach leaves, rinsed and drained
2 tbsp double cream
sea salt
freshly ground black pepper

1 Preheat the oven to 170°C/Gas 3½. Pour the olive oil into a large roasting tin and place on the hob to heat up. Brown the leg of lamb in the oil, turning it so that it browns on all sides. Remove the leg of lamb, then brown the baby onions, carrots and fennel.
2 Put the leg of lamb back in the roasting tin. Season well with salt and pepper, then add the wine. Cover the lamb with foil and roast in the oven for 2½ hours. Remove from the oven, release the foil so that the steam can escape and then leave to rest for 20 minutes. Serve with the potatoes and creamed spinach.

To prepare the potatoes
3 Put the potatoes and the sprig of mint in a saucepan of salted water, bring to the boil and cook until tender.
4 Drain the potatoes, then put them back in the pan over a low heat with the olive oil and a good seasoning of salt and pepper. Stir for 30 seconds, scatter on the mint leaves and serve.

To prepare the creamed spinach
5 Heat the butter in a pan until gently foaming. Sprinkle on the flour and stir for 1 minute. Remove the pan from the heat and gradually add the milk, stirring constantly until combined. Return the pan to the heat and simmer gently for 10 minutes, then season with salt, pepper and nutmeg.
6 Bring a large saucepan of salted water to the boil and add the spinach. Simmer for 1 minute, then drain. Press as much water as you can out of the spinach and then place it on a board and chop it with a knife.
7 Add the chopped spinach to the white sauce and stir gently. Add the double cream and check the seasoning.

White chocolate rice pudding with strawberry compote

The addition of white chocolate makes this the creamiest, smoothest rice pudding ever.

SERVES 6

100g white chocolate, broken into pieces
8 heaped tbsp of risotto rice
300ml milk
5 tbsp water
300ml double cream

Strawberry compote
200g strawberries
1 tbsp sugar
1 tbsp water

1 Put the chocolate in a glass bowl with the cream. Bring a saucepan of water to a simmer, then place the bowl over, but not touching, the simmering water. Let the chocolate melt, stirring occasionally.
2 Place the rice, milk and water in a saucepan. Add the melted chocolate and cream and then place the saucepan over a very low heat. Simmer gently for 30 minutes, stirring occasionally, until the rice is tender. You may need to add a little more milk if the pudding becomes too thick. Serve with the compote.

To make the strawberry compote
3 Place all the ingredients in a saucepan on a low heat. Bring to a simmer and cook, stirring occasionally for 20 minutes.

Panna cotta with strawberry sauce

Panna cotta has a reputation for being difficult to make, but in fact the only tricky bit can be unmoulding the puddings. As long as you don't hold the moulds in the warm water for too long they are usually all right. They do look lovely when they are unmoulded and sitting on plates; perfectly formed little towers of creaminess. You will need 6 dariole moulds.

SERVES 6

200g mascarpone cheese
100ml milk
150ml double cream
100g caster sugar
1 vanilla pod
4 sheets of gelatine

Strawberry sauce
200g strawberries
50g icing sugar

1 Place the mascarpone in a bowl and gradually whisk in the milk. Make sure the mixture is completely smooth.
2 Pour the double cream into a saucepan and add the sugar. Split the vanilla pod and, using a sharp knife, scrape the seeds into the double cream. Bring the cream to boiling point and as soon as you see small bubbles forming on the surface of the cream, remove the pan from the heat.
3 Place the gelatine leaves in a bowl of cold water until they are soft. This usually takes about 4 minutes. Drain the leaves and pat them dry with kitchen paper, then gently squeeze out any excess water
4 Add the softened gelatine to the double cream mixture and whisk until the gelatine has dissolved. Pour the cream on to the mascarpone and mix thoroughly. Decant the mixture into the dariole moulds and refrigerate for at least 4 hours.
5 When you're ready to serve, place each mould in some warm water before inverting it on to a plate. Give the mould a wiggle and the panna cotta should come free.

To make the strawberry sauce
6 Blend the strawberries and icing sugar together. Pass through a sieve and serve with the panna cotta.

Apple and jam muffins

There's often an alarming amount of sugar in some small cake recipes. The only sweetening in these muffins is a tiny bit of sugar in the topping and the jam in the centre, but my children still love them.

MAKES 10

250ml natural yoghurt or buttermilk
125ml vegetable oil
1 egg
200g dessert apples, grated
250g plain flour
1 tsp bicarbonate of soda
1 tsp ground cinnamon
10 tsp raspberry jam

Cream cheese topping
125g mascarpone cheese
100g fromage frais
½ tablespoon caster sugar
½ teaspoon ground cinnamon

1 Preheat the oven to 200°C/Gas 6. Line a muffin tin with 10 paper muffin cases.
2 Beat the yoghurt or buttermilk, oil, egg and grated apple in a bowl. Sift in the flour, bicarbonate soda and ground cinnamon and mix gently.
3 Spoon a dessertspoon of the batter into each muffin case and add a teaspoon of jam on top of the batter. Distribute the rest of the batter evenly between the muffin cases so that the jam is covered.
4 Bake the muffins in the oven for 20 minutes. Leave them to cool in the tin for 10 minutes, then turn out on to a wire rack to cool completely.
5 Mix together the ingredients for topping and spread it over the muffins before serving.

Mini steamed fruit puddings

You will need six mini pudding moulds for these little fruity delights.

SERVES 6

200g strawberries
200g blueberries
200g raspberries
1 tbsp elderflower cordial
2 tbsp caster sugar
grated zest of 1 lemon
1 tbsp crème fraiche
300g self-raising flour, plus extra for flouring the moulds
175g cold butter, cut into cubes, plus extra for greasing the moulds
a pinch of salt
175g caster sugar
2 eggs, whisked with enough milk to make 375ml of liquid

1 Grease 6 mini pudding moulds and dust the insides with flour. Preheat the oven to 180°C/Gas 4.
2 Put the fruit, elderflower cordial, sugar, lemon zest and crème fraiche in a bowl and mix everything together. Spoon a heaped teaspoon of this mixture into the bottom of each mould. Any leftover fruit can be served with the puddings.
3 Whizz the flour and butter in a food processor until the mixture resembles fine breadcrumbs. Add the salt and sugar and mix again briefly. Pour on the egg and milk mixture and blend until you have a smooth batter.
4 Divide the batter evenly between the pudding moulds, filling them to about 1cm below the top. Cover the top of each pudding with a small circle of baking parchment and then wrap each mould in foil.
5 Place the puddings in a roasting tin and pour in enough hot water to come just over half way up the sides of the moulds. Place the tin of puddings in the oven and cook for 55 minutes.
6 When you are ready to serve, uncover the puddings and run a round-bladed knife around the edge of each one, then turn out on to plates. Serve with cream and any leftover fruit.

Potato, sausage and cabbage gratin

One night, I had a pack of sausages and some spring greens in the fridge and came up with this recipe. Fortunately, the family loved it.

SERVES 6

200g spring greens, shredded
1 shallot, finely chopped
900g potatoes, peeled and cut into 5mm slices
8 pork sausages
400ml double cream
300ml milk
2 tsp Dijon mustard
sea salt
freshly ground black pepper

1 Preheat the oven to 200°C/Gas 6. Place the greens, shallot and potatoes in a large mixing bowl.
2 Split the skins of the sausages and remove the meat. Discard the skins and shape the sausage meat into small rough balls. Place these in the mixing bowl with the vegetables. Pour on the cream and milk, then add the mustard. Season with salt and pepper and stir to combine, then spoon the mixture into a gratin dish.
3 Pop the dish into the oven and cook for 30 minutes. Take the gratin dish out of the oven and stir the contents so that they are coated in the cream and milk. Return the dish to the oven for another 30 minutes. Serve with some crusty bread.

Vietnamese chicken wings with rice salad

Fish sauce is used a lot in Thai food. It can smell awful when you first add it to a dish, but don't be put off, as it adds an intense flavour and there is no hint of the smell once the dish has been cooked.

SERVES 6

2 tbsp olive oil
1kg chicken wings
1 onion, finely chopped
100ml dry sherry
4 tbsp caster sugar
4 tbsp fish sauce
1 tbsp finely grated fresh root ginger
2 tbsp roughly cut fresh basil leaves
freshly ground black pepper

Rice salad
750ml water
½ tsp sea salt
500g basmati rice
3 tbsp olive oil
2 tbsp dark soy sauce
70g pancetta, sliced
4 eggs, beaten
2 tbsp finely chopped flat-leaf parsley
100g frozen peas, cooked
sea salt
freshly ground black pepper

1 Heat the olive oil in a large sauté pan. Brown the chicken wings in 3 batches, putting each batch aside while you fry the next. Don't cook them too long – lightly golden brown on the edges is enough.
2 Keep the pan on the heat and fry the onion for 3 minutes, until soft, then add it to the chicken wings. Add the sherry to the pan and let it sizzle for 1 minute, then add the sugar and simmer for 1 minute. Add the fish sauce and stir.
3 Return the chicken and onions to the pan, add the ginger and stir to combine. Season with pepper, then cover and simmer gently for 30 minutes. Add the basil leaves just before serving with the rice salad.

To make the rice salad
4 Pour the water into a pan, add the salt and then the rice. Bring the rice to the boil, then reduce the heat, cover the pan and cook for 15 minutes. Remove the pan from the heat and leave to stand, covered, for 10 minutes.
5 Pour the olive oil and soy sauce on to the rice while it is still warm. Season well with salt and pepper and stir to combine. Fry the pancetta in a small pan until crisp. Remove, chop roughly and add to the rice.
6 Put the frying pan back on the heat and add the beaten eggs to make an omelette. Chop the omelette roughly and stir it into the rice with the peas and parsley. Check the seasoning before serving.

Puff pastry tartlets

These tartlets are a doddle to make. If you don't have tartlet tins, you can make one large tart.

MAKES 8 INDIVIDUAL TARTS OR 1 BIG TART

450g ready-rolled puff pastry
100g frozen petit pois
100g asparagus spears
70g pancetta, chopped
4 tbsp crème fraiche
1 egg, beaten
1 tbsp chopped fresh basil
1 tbsp grated Parmesan cheese
4–5 cherry tomatoes, sliced
sea salt
freshly ground black pepper

1 Preheat the oven to 200°C/Gas 6. Line the tartlet tins with puff pastry and set them aside in the fridge.
2 Cook the peas in boiling water and drain. Steam the asparagus spears until tender, then drain and cut them into 1cm pieces.
3 Fry the pancetta until golden brown, put it in a bowl and add the peas, asparagus, crème fraiche, egg, basil and Parmesan. Season with salt and pepper and mix everything together gently.
4 Spoon this mixture into the tart cases and garnish each one with the sliced tomatoes.
5 Place the tart cases on a baking sheet and bake in the oven for 15 minutes. If making one big tart, cook it for 30 minutes.
6 Let the tarts cool slightly before turning them out. Best served warm.

Mackerel salad

We really should sing the praises of this cheap and plentiful fish. Its only drawback, particularly for children, is that there are a lot of bones, but most can be removed with a pair of tweezers and some patience. I do think it's a good idea, though, to get children used to coping with the odd bone, rather than always serving easy-to-eat cod and haddock. It all helps to make them more adventurous and sophisticated eaters.

SERVES 6

500g Jersey Royal potatoes
3 eggs
6 mackerel fillets
250g watercress, washed
a handful of basil leaves
freshly ground black pepper

Dressing
2 egg yolks
1 garlic clove, crushed
1 tsp Dijon mustard
1 tsp white wine vinegar
100ml light olive oil
1 tsp finely chopped dill
sea salt
freshly ground black pepper

1 Scrub the potatoes well, put them in a pan of salted water and boil until tender. Drain and set aside.
2 Put the eggs in a pan of cold water, bring to the boil and cook for 7 minutes. Cool the eggs under running water, then peel off the shells, cut the eggs in half and set aside.
3 Preheat the grill to hot. Check the mackerel fillets for bones and remove any with a pair of tweezers. Put the mackerel fillets on the grill pan and season with black pepper. Place under the grill and cook for 4 minutes on each side. Remove and place to one side.

To make the dressing
4 Whisk the egg yolks in a bowl with the garlic, mustard and wine vinegar. Add the olive oil to the egg mixture in a very slow trickle, whisking constantly. Sprinkle on the dill and season as necessary.

To assemble the salad
5 Lay the watercress on a serving dish. Arrange the potatoes, eggs and mackerel on top. Sprinkle on the basil and spoon over the dressing. Serve with some brown bread or toast.

Spiced loin of lamb with pilaf rice and cucumber salad

These lamb fillets are easy and quick to cook. They take on the spicy flavours well without sacrificing their own flavour.

SERVES 6

½ tbsp coriander seeds
1 tbsp cumin seeds
1 tbsp hazelnuts
1 tbsp almonds
1 tsp salt
1 tbsp sesame seeds
1 tsp sugar
2 tbsp olive oil
2 whole lamb loin fillets

Pilaf rice
2 tbsp olive oil
1 onion, finely sliced
80g stoned dates, roughly chopped
1 tbsp pistachio nuts
100g young spinach leaves, finely shredded
500g basmati rice
750ml vegetable stock

Cucumber salad
1 cucumber, finely sliced
1 shallot, thinly sliced
2 tbsp natural yoghurt
sea salt
freshly ground black pepper

1 Preheat the oven to 200°C/Gas 6. Place the spices, nuts, salt and sesame seeds in a small sauté pan and toast for 2 minutes over a low heat, moving them around occasionally during that time. Sprinkle on the sugar and then grind everything to a powder, using a pestle and mortar or a coffee grinder.
2 Coat the lamb loins in the powder, then place them in a roasting tin and pour on the olive oil. Cook in the oven for 15 minutes, for pink meat. Slice the lamb and serve with the rice and cucumber salad.

To cook the pilaf rice
3 Heat the olive oil in a large saucepan. Add the onion slices and cook over a medium heat for 5 minutes, until they are soft and turning golden. Add the dates, nuts and spinach and stir for 30 seconds. Add the rice and stir into the other ingredients. Pour on the stock and bring to a good rolling boil.
4 Cover the saucepan, reduce the heat to very low and simmer for 15 minutes, stirring occasionally to prevent the rice from sticking. Remove the pan from the heat and keep it covered for 10 minutes before serving.

To prepare the cucumber salad
5 Place the cucumber slices in a serving bowl. Sprinkle on the shallot, then spoon on the yoghurt and mix. Season with salt and pepper.

Sole and prawn mornay

A lovely light fish supper for an early summer evening.

SERVES 6

6 lemon sole fillets
100ml white wine
2 lemon quarters
a small sprig of parsley
200g cooked prawns
sea salt
freshly ground black pepper

Sauce
250ml milk
1 bay leaf
25g butter
25g flour
50ml double cream
1 tsp Dijon mustard
50g Gruyère cheese, grated
sea salt
freshly ground black pepper

To make the sauce

1 Heat the milk in a small saucepan with the bay leaf, until it is just simmering. Place to one side for 5 minutes.

2 Meanwhile, melt the butter in another pan, then add the flour and stir to incorporate. Remove the saucepan from the heat and gradually stir in the warm milk. Return the pan to the heat and bring to a simmer for 5 minutes. Add the cream, mustard and cheese and stir. Check the seasoning, then remove from the heat.

To cook the sole

3 Preheat the oven to 180°C/Gas 4. Place the sole fillets in an ovenproof dish and pour on the wine. Place the lemon quarters and parsley sprig on top of the fish and season with salt and pepper. Cover the fish fillets with a piece of baking parchment and bake for 10 minutes. Heat the grill.

4 Remove the dish from the oven and add the prawns. Spoon the sauce over the top and place the dish under a hot grill for a few minutes just prior to serving.

Roast chicken with coleslaw and mashed potatoes

Roast chicken goes remarkably well with mashed potatoes and this home-made coleslaw.

SERVES 6

2 x 1.5kg roasting chickens
6 sprigs of fresh thyme
2 tbsp olive oil
sea salt
freshly ground black pepper

Coleslaw
¼ celeriac, peeled and grated
2 carrots, peeled and grated
1 small white cabbage, finely sliced
1 red onion, finely sliced
1 tbsp natural yoghurt
1 tbsp crème fraiche
200ml olive oil
1 tsp Dijon mustard
sea salt
freshly ground black pepper

Mashed potatoes
1kg potatoes, peeled and cut into quarters
40g butter
200ml warm milk
sea salt
freshly ground black pepper

1 Preheat the oven to 180°C/Gas 4. Place the chickens in a roasting tin. Remove the thyme leaves from the sprigs and sprinkle them over the chickens. Drizzle the chickens with the olive oil and season well with plenty of salt and pepper, then roast for 1 ½ hours. Set them aside to rest for 20 minutes, then carve and serve with the mash and coleslaw.

To make the coleslaw
2 Place the grated celeriac and carrots in a serving bowl and add the cabbage and onion. To make the dressing, place the yoghurt and crème fraiche in a small bowl and slowly add the olive oil, stirring as you do so. Stir in the mustard and then season with salt and pepper. Add the dressing to the vegetables and toss well before serving.

To make the mashed potatoes
3 Boil the potatoes in salted water until tender. Pass the potatoes through a potato ricer or use your preferred method to mash them. Return them to the pan and place them on a low heat. Add the butter and milk and gently combine. Check the seasoning and adjust as necessary.

Tangy citrus cake

This tasty dessert is a cross between a key lime pie and a lemon cheesecake.

MAKES 1 X 24CM CAKE

- 250g ginger nuts
- 75g butter
- 5 egg yolks
- 1 x 397g can of condensed milk
- 75ml fresh lime juice
- 75ml fresh lemon juice
- grated zest of 2 oranges
- 3 egg whites

1 Preheat the oven to 180°C/Gas 4. Blitz the ginger nuts in a food processor or put them in a plastic bag and bash them to fine crumbs with a rolling pin.
2 Melt the butter in a small saucepan. Take the pan off the heat, add the biscuit crumbs and mix them into the butter with a wooden spoon. Press the biscuit crumbs into the base of a 24cm spring-clip tin and then chill in the fridge.
3 Put the egg yolks in a mixing bowl and using an electric hand-whisk, beat the yolks until they thicken and become mousse-like. Add the condensed milk, juices and zest and mix again.
4 In a clean bowl, whisk the egg whites until they form stiff peaks. Fold the egg whites into the egg yolk mixture and then pour everything into the tin on top of the biscuit base.
5 Place the cake in the oven and bake for 25 minutes, by which time the filling should feel firm to the touch. Cool slightly, then chill before removing the cake from the tin and placing it on a serving plate.

Gooseberry fool

The gooseberry fell out of favour for a while but seems to be having a bit of a renaissance recently. In Europe, it is only really the British who appreciate the virtues of this fruit. Other countries, at this time of year, favour the soft red berries that are just starting to appear. This is definitely their loss.

SERVES 6

400g gooseberries, topped and tailed
25g butter
4 tbsp soft brown sugar
400ml double cream
3 egg yolks
1 tsp cornflour

1 Place the gooseberries, butter and sugar in a saucepan. Cook, uncovered, for 10 minutes over a gentle heat, until the gooseberries give way to slight pressure from a wooden spoon.
2 Pour the double cream into another pan and bring it to boiling point. Place the egg yolks in a glass bowl with the cornflour and whisk together. Pour the cream on to the egg yolks and cornflour, whisking as you go.
3 Pour this thin custard back into the saucepan and cook it over a very low heat, stirring constantly, until it has thickened.
4 Fold the gooseberries into the custard and pour the mixture into bowls. This is best eaten chilled, so put the bowls in the fridge for 40 minutes before serving.

Pasta with rich meat sauce

I find that skirt has much more flavour than stewing or braising steak but you can't stint on the cooking time. It's a great cut if you have plenty of time, and perfect for a slow-cooked sauce like this one.

SERVES 6

2 tbsp olive oil
1kg beef skirt, cut into 1cm cubes
1 large onion, finely chopped
200ml red wine
1 tbsp tomato purée
2 x 400g cans of chopped tomatoes
2 tsp paprika
500g pappardelle pasta
Parmesan cheese, grated, for serving
sea salt
freshly ground black pepper

1 You need a large saucepan with a lid that you can put in the oven or a casserole dish. Heat the olive oil in the pan, then start to brown the meat in batches, setting it aside once it has browned. You may need to add a little more olive oil.
2 When all the meat is browned, cook the onion in the oil for 10 minutes until soft. Place the onion with the meat. Keep the pan on the heat, pour in the red wine and let it bubble away for 3 minutes over a medium heat. Preheat the oven to 150°C/Gas 2.
3 Return the meat and onions to the pan and stir in the tomato purée, tomatoes and paprika. Season well with salt and pepper. Bring the sauce to a simmer on the stove and then cover the pan and place it in the oven for 2 hours.
4 Cook the pasta according to the packet instructions and serve with the sauce and grated Parmesan.

Grilled salmon with remoulade, and broad bean and courgette fricassée

A remoulade is a French mayonnaise-based sauce which is flavoured with herbs or vegetables to enhance a meat or fish dish. Celeriac remoulade is a particularly popular example. This version is really a glorified tartare sauce which adds depth of flavour to the fish.

SERVES 6

6 x 150g pieces of salmon fillet
a little olive oil
sea salt
freshly ground black pepper

Remoulade
2 egg yolks
1 dsrtsp white wine vinegar
225ml light olive oil
1 tbsp finely chopped flat-leaf parsley
1 tsp finely chopped fresh tarragon
2 tsp Dijon mustard
1 tbsp capers, rinsed and chopped
sea salt
freshly ground black pepper

Broad bean and courgette fricassée
200g broad beans (podded weight)
25g butter
8 baby courgettes, sliced into 5mm discs
1 plum tomato, diced
100ml white wine
sea salt
freshly ground black pepper

To make the remoulade

1 Place the egg yolks in a mixing bowl with the vinegar and some salt and pepper. Mix briefly to combine, then start to add the olive oil, a little at a time, whisking constantly to incorporate and make a thick sauce. Don't add the oil too fast or the sauce will curdle.

2 Add the herbs, mustard and capers and check the seasoning. Place to one side while you prepare the rest of the meal.

To make the broad bean and courgette fricassée

3 Make a slit in each broad bean with a sharp knife. Place the beans in a saucepan of unsalted boiling water for 5 minutes, by which time the beans will start to pop out of their outer skins. Skin those that haven't popped and leave them to one side.

4 Heat the butter in a sauté pan until sizzling. Add the courgettes and cook them for 10–15 minutes on a medium heat until golden brown all over. Add the broad beans, diced tomato and the wine and let everything sizzle for 1 minute. Season with salt and pepper.

To cook the fish and serve

5 Preheat the grill. Brush the salmon with a little olive oil and season with salt and pepper. Cook under the grill for 3 minutes, then turn the fillets and cook for another 3 minutes. Serve with the remoulade and the fricassée.

Lamb, bean and macaroni broth

This is an Italian-style broth that's packed with goodness. Serve with plenty of bread if you're feeding hungry teenagers.

1 Place the diced aubergine in a colander and sprinkle it with 2 teaspoons of salt. Cover with a clean tea towel or some kitchen paper and leave for 30 minutes, then pat dry.
2 Heat the olive oil in a large saucepan. Add the onion and aubergine and cook over a high heat for 5 minutes, stirring occasionally. Add the lamb and stir until it is browned all over.
3 Add the beans, tomatoes, rosemary and stock and simmer for 20 minutes. Season with salt and pepper. Add the macaroni, cover and simmer for 10 minutes until the macaroni is tender. Check the seasoning and serve in bowls.

SERVES 6

1 aubergine, diced
2 tsp salt
2 tbsp olive oil
1 onion, finely chopped
500g minced lamb
1 x 400g can of borlotti beans, rinsed and drained
1 x 400g can of chopped tomatoes
1 tsp finely chopped rosemary leaves
1 litre beef stock
300g macaroni
sea salt
freshly ground black pepper

Chicken thighs with carrots and tarragon

Chicken thighs are cheaper than breasts and a good cut for many dishes. It's hard to overcook thighs and, because you cook them for a little longer than breasts, they take on any accompanying flavours more readily.

SERVES 6

8 chicken thighs, skinned and boned
flour, for sprinkling
2 tbsp olive oil
2 tbsp white wine vinegar
2 tsp finely chopped fresh tarragon
1 tbsp dark soy sauce
250ml chicken stock
150g carrots, peeled and cut into 1cm discs
sea salt
freshly ground black pepper

1 Chop the chicken thighs in half, sprinkle them with a little flour and season them with salt and pepper.
2 Heat the olive oil in a large sauté pan and gradually brown the chicken thighs, a few at a time. Once you have browned all the thighs, set them to one side and return the pan to the heat.
3 Add the vinegar and the tarragon to the pan and stir for 30 seconds. Pour in the soy sauce and the stock and simmer gently for 2 minutes.
4 Return the chicken to the pan and scatter on the carrots. Cover and cook at a gentle simmer for 20 minutes. Serve with buttered new potatoes.

Fillet steaks in pastry with a vegetable medley

These are rather like mini beef wellingtons and can go straight from the oven to the plate.

SERVES 6

3 tbsp olive oil
300g chestnut mushrooms, chopped into small pieces
100g sliced pancetta, finely chopped
2 tbsp finely chopped flat-leaf parsley
1 onion, finely chopped
6 x 150–200g fillet steaks
750g ready-made puff pastry
1 egg, beaten, to glaze
sea salt
freshly ground black pepper

Gravy
1 tbsp flour
150ml Marsala wine
500ml beef stock
sea salt
freshly ground black pepper

Vegetable medley
2 tbsp olive oil
4 carrots, cut into 2cm chunks
500g potatoes, peeled and cut into 2cm chunks
200g celeriac, peeled and cut into 2cm chunks
2 tbsp water
2 tbsp crème fraiche
sea salt
freshly ground black pepper

1 Heat 2 tablespoons of the olive oil in a frying pan. Add the mushrooms, pancetta, parsley and onion and cook over a medium heat for 5–7 minutes until the mushrooms have lost their moisture and the pancetta is golden. Season with salt and pepper, then transfer to a plate or bowl to cool. Return the pan to the heat.
2 Add another tablespoon of olive oil and brown the steaks, a couple at a time, on each side for 30 seconds. Season, then place to one side to cool. Don't wash the pan as you will need it to prepare the gravy.
3 Roll out the pastry into 6 rectangles measuring 16 x 23cm. Lay 1 steak on each piece and put a tablespoon of the mushroom mixture on top. You will have a little mixture left over that you can use for the gravy. Preheat the oven to 220°C/Gas 7.
4 Fold the pastry up to encase the steak. To do this, pull up the 2 long sides, and fold them over the steak, then tuck the ends under to seal. Lay the parcels in a roasting tin and brush the pastry generously with beaten egg. Bake for 20–25 minutes, depending on how rare you like your steak. Serve with the gravy and vegetables.

To prepare the gravy
5 Place the frying pan on the heat and add any leftover mushroom mixture. Stir in the flour and pour on the Marsala wine and let it bubble away for 30 seconds. Pour on the stock and simmer for 10 minutes. Season with salt and pepper.

To prepare the vegetable medley
6 Heat the olive oil in a wide-bottomed saucepan. Add the vegetables and stir, then reduce the heat and cover the pan. Cook for 5 minutes, then stir again and add the 2 tablespoons of water. Stir, cover the pan and cook for 20 minutes until the vegetables are tender. Stir in the crème fraiche and season with salt and pepper.

Summer pasta

This is a popular pasta dish in Italy during the summer. It's light yet full of flavour – just right in hot weather.

SERVES 6

- 2 tbsp olive oil, plus extra for drizzling
- 1 onion, finely chopped
- 4 courgettes, trimmed and cut into 1cm dice
- 1 aubergine, trimmed and cut into 1cm dice
- 500g spaghetti
- 150g cherry tomatoes
- 1 red chilli
- 2 tbsp finely chopped flat-leaf parsley
- a large handful of fresh basil leaves
- 100g Parmesan cheese, grated
- sea salt
- freshly ground black pepper

1 Heat the olive oil in a frying pan. Add the onion and cook for 5 minutes on a gentle heat. Add the courgettes and aubergine, increase the heat slightly and cook for 5 minutes, stirring occasionally.

2 Bring a large pan of salted water to the boil and cook the pasta according to the packet instructions, then drain.

3 Meanwhile, add the tomatoes, chilli and parsley to the frying pan with the vegetables. Cook for 1 minute, then remove the pan from the heat and season with salt and pepper.

4 Toss the vegetables with the cooked pasta. Sprinkle on some basil leaves, a good drizzle of extra virgin olive oil and a scattering of Parmesan cheese.

Roast duck legs with radish, pea and new potato salad

Radishes are an under-valued vegetable in Britain, usually found languishing in a salad. They are much more prized in France, where they are savoured on their own with just a little salt. Apparently, we've been eating radishes for at least 1,000 years, so perhaps we should give them more respect. In this recipe they add texture and colour to a potato and pea salad.

SERVES 6

6 duck legs
2 red onions, finely sliced
4 sprigs of thyme
100ml white wine
1 orange, cut into 4 pieces with skin on
sea salt
freshly ground black pepper

Radish, pea and new potato salad
1kg new potatoes
10 radishes, thinly sliced
300g fresh peas, cooked
a handful of roughly torn fresh basil leaves
1 tbsp crème fraiche
2 tbsp extra virgin olive oil
½ tbsp balsamic vinegar
sea salt
freshly ground black pepper

1 Score the skin of the duck legs with a sharp knife, then place them in a large saucepan, skin side down. Cook over a medium heat for 10 minutes so that some of the fat runs out. Briefly place the legs to one side while you drain the fat into a jar – you can use it for roasting potatoes on another occasion. Preheat the oven to 180°C/Gas 4.
2 Return the legs to the pan, the other way up this time, and cook them over a medium heat for 5 minutes. Drain the fat again, then place the legs in a roasting tin, with the onions, sprigs of thyme, wine and orange pieces. Season with salt and pepper, then place in the oven for 45 minutes. Serve with the salad.

To prepare the potato, radish and pea salad
3 Peel the potatoes and cook them in a saucepan of salted water until tender. Cut them in half, then place in a serving dish with the radishes, peas and basil. Mix the crème fraiche with the olive oil and season with salt and pepper. Spoon this mixture over the potatoes, peas and radishes and then drizzle with the balsamic vinegar.

Apricot and raspberry cream tart

This is a lovely rich, indulgent tart, oozing summer colours and flavours.

MAKES 1 X 23CM TART

15g butter
10 fresh apricots, stoned and cut in half
2 tsp caster sugar
300ml double cream
3 tbsp mascarpone cheese
grated zest of 1 lemon
½ tsp vanilla extract
2 tbsp icing sugar, plus extra for dusting the top
200g fresh raspberries

Pastry
180g cold butter, cut into cubes
75g icing sugar
2 egg yolks
225g plain flour, plus extra for dusting the work surface

1 Put the butter, icing sugar, egg yolks and flour in a food processor and whizz until a dough starts to form. Turn the dough out on to a floured surface and shape the dough into a ball with your hands. Wrap the ball in clingfilm and chill in the fridge for 30 minutes.
2 Warm the butter in a sauté pan. When it's sizzling, place the apricot halves in the butter for 30 seconds. Turn them over and brown for another 30 seconds. Sprinkle on the caster sugar and leave in the pan to cool. Preheat the oven to 200°C/Gas 6.
3 Roll out the pastry and use it to line a 23cm tart tin. Place a sheet of baking parchment on the pastry and pour some baking beans on top. Place the tart tin on a baking sheet and bake in the oven for 10 minutes. Remove the beans and parchment and return the tart to the oven for a further 10 minutes. Remove and place to one side to cool completely.
4 Whip the double cream until light and fluffy. Fold in the mascarpone cheese, zest, vanilla and icing sugar.
5 Fill the cooled tart case with the cream and lay the apricots on top. Scatter on the raspberries and dust with icing sugar before serving.

Jam iced fairy cakes

You can use any flavour jam you like to ice these cakes – blackcurrant, apricot and lemon curd as well as raspberry, for example. It's nice to use different colours to make a pretty plateful.

MAKES 16 CAKES

170g softened butter
170g caster sugar
3 eggs
170g self-raising flour
1 tsp vanilla extract

Icing
300g sifted icing sugar
1 tbsp raspberry jam
2 tbsp water

1 Preheat the oven to 180°C/Gas 4. You'll need 2 fairy cake tins, lined with 16 paper fairy cake cases.
2 Put the butter and sugar in a bowl and cream with an electric hand-whisk until the mixture is pale and fluffy. Add an egg and a tablespoon of flour and beat again. Do the same with the remaining 2 eggs, following with a spoonful of flour each time, and then fold in any remaining flour. Add the vanilla extract.
3 Spoon a heaped dessertspoon of cake mixture into each case. Bake the cakes in the oven for 20–23 minutes until golden brown and firm to the touch. Remove the cakes from the tins and place them on a wire rack until they are completely cool.
4 Put the icing sugar, jam and water in a mixing bowl and stir until smooth and combined. Spread the icing over the cooled cakes with a round-bladed knife.

Fruit streusel cake

This looks rather like a fruit-topped pizza, with a scattering of crumble mixture on the top.

SERVES 6

340g strong bread flour
a large pinch of salt
2 tbsp caster sugar
grated zest of 1 lemon
1 sachet of dried yeast (or 10g fresh yeast)
75ml milk
2 eggs, beaten
110g butter, melted

Topping
180g blueberries
200g strawberries, halved
250g fresh raspberries
3 tbsp caster sugar
2 tbsp ground almonds
40g butter, cut into small cubes

1 Place the flour, salt, sugar and lemon zest together in a mixing bowl. Add the yeast, milk, eggs and butter and mix well, first with a wooden spoon and then with your hands, until you have a smooth dough.
2 Place the dough back in the bowl, cover and leave for 1 hour to rise. Gently roll out the dough so that it fits in a 23 x 30cm rectangular swiss roll tin. Cover and leave to rise for 30 minutes. Preheat the oven to 190°C/Gas 5.
3 Gently mix the topping ingredients until combined. Spoon the topping on top of the dough and bake in the oven for 30 minutes. Leave the cake cool in the tin for 10 minutes or so and then gently ease on to a board and slice to serve.

Tomato risotto

There was a tomato risotto in my last 'What's for Dinner?' cookbook, but I've added some cherry tomatoes and red wine to this one, giving it a slightly richer, rounder taste. Young children usually enjoy this as they love the colour of the rice.

SERVES 6

1.5 litres chicken stock
1 tbsp olive oil
25g butter
1 onion, finely chopped
500g risotto rice
1 x 400g can of peeled cherry tomatoes
300ml red wine
2 tbsp mascarpone cheese
100g Parmesan cheese, grated
2 tbsp roughly torn basil leaves
sea salt
freshly ground black pepper

1 Heat the chicken stock in a saucepan and leave it to simmer.
2 Heat the olive oil and butter in a separate saucepan, add the onion and fry for 5 minutes on a low heat.
3 Add the rice and fry for 1 minute, then pour in the tomatoes and wine and let the rice simmer for 1 minute. Once the liquid has almost been absorbed, start to add the hot stock a couple of ladlefuls at a time. Keep stirring and adding more stock as it is absorbed. Continue until the rice is cooked but still has a slight bite to it.
4 Remove from the heat and stir in the mascarpone cheese and the Parmesan. Scatter in the basil and check the seasoning, adding salt and pepper to taste.

Smoked trout and spinach tart

Apart from making fine pâté, smoked trout is also an excellent filling for a tart. In this recipe I have partnered it with spinach.

SERVES 6

200g spinach leaves
a knob of butter
250g smoked trout fillets, roughly flaked
1 tbsp wholegrain mustard
350ml double cream
2 egg yolks
75g Gruyère cheese, grated
freshly ground black pepper

Pastry
225g plain flour, plus extra for dusting the work surface
a pinch of salt
150g cold butter, cut into cubes
1 egg yolk
2 tbsp cold water

To make the pastry

1 Place the flour, salt and butter into a food processor and whizz until the mixture resembles breadcrumbs. Add the egg yolk and water and whizz again briefly.

2 Turn the dough out on to a floured surface and bring it together into a ball, then wrap it in clingfilm and chill for 30 minutes.

To prepare the filling

3 Rinse the spinach leaves in cold water, then place the wet leaves in a saucepan with a little salt and cook until they have all wilted. Tip the spinach into a colander and press out any excess water. Put the spinach back in the saucepan with a small knob of butter and cook for a few seconds so that the butter is incorporated into the spinach.

4 Put the spinach on a chopping board, chop it with a knife, then place it in a mixing bowl. Add the trout, mustard, cream, egg yolks and cheese and season with some pepper. Gently mix the ingredients until well combined.

To assemble the tart

5 Preheat the oven to 200°C/Gas 6. Roll out the pastry and use it to line a 30cm tart tin. Place a large sheet of baking parchment over the tart case and pour some baking beans on top. Place the tart case on a baking sheet and bake in the oven for 15 minutes. Remove the beans and parchment and return the pastry to the oven for 5 minutes. Spoon the filling into the case and bake in the oven for 30 minutes. Serve with a green salad.

Grilled chicken and green salad

Grilled chicken and simple salad leaves make a blissful supper. Forget about knives and forks – the best way to enjoy this meal is to eat it with your hands.

SERVES 6

2 x 1kg chickens
olive oil
sprigs of fresh oregano, thyme and parsley, finely chopped
400g salad leaves
½ tbsp balsamic vinegar
squeeze of lemon juice
sea salt
freshly ground black pepper

1 The only fiddly bit of this recipe is preparing the chickens, although you could ask your butcher to do this for you. Lay a bird down on its breast and, using a sharp knife or jointing scissors, cut along each side of the backbone and remove it. Turn the bird over and squash it down with the heel of your hand. Next, cut through the middle of the breast so that you end up with 4 pieces of chicken. Repeat with the other chicken. Heat the grill.
2 Place the chicken in a tin that will fit under the grill or ideally just place it on the grill pan – if it will fit. Drizzle the chicken with plenty of olive oil, season liberally with salt and pepper and scatter with the herbs. Place under the grill for 10 minutes. Turn the chicken joints over, drizzle with more olive oil and put under the grill for another 10 minutes.
3 Turn the chicken again. Lower the level of the grill and continue cooking the chicken for 15 minutes, by which time it should be done.
4 Place the salad leaves in a large serving dish and drizzle with the balsamic vinegar. Place the chicken on top and season with more salt and pepper and a good squeeze of lemon juice. Pour on a good spoonful or so of the chicken juices and serve.

Emergency scrambled eggs

There are always moments in our hectic lives when we need to make something that's quick and easy but still pleases the hungry hordes. This recipe is also the perfect way to use up any leftover cooked potatoes in the fridge.

SERVES 6

2 tbsp olive oil
300g cooked new potatoes, roughly chopped
6 spring onions, sliced
100g sliced pancetta, chopped
12–15 eggs (depending on appetites), beaten slightly
sea salt
freshly ground black pepper

1 Heat the olive oil in a large sauté pan or saucepan. Add the potatoes, spring onions and pancetta and cook over a medium heat for 5 minutes, stirring to ensure that everything browns evenly.
2 Remove the pan from the heat and let it cool for a couple of minutes. Add the eggs, return the pan to a low heat, then cook and stir until the eggs begin to come together and firm up. Season with salt and pepper and serve with slices of buttered toast.

Spaghetti with green sauce

Fussy eaters may well devour this not knowing that they are eating chard or spinach. The addition of the cheeses and the herbs makes it even tastier.

SERVES 6

300g chard leaves
(or beet or spinach leaves)
200g lettuce leaves
2 tbsp fresh basil leaves
2 tbsp fresh mint leaves
1 tbsp olive oil
1 shallot, finely chopped
200g mascarpone cheese
3 tbsp grated Parmesan cheese
600g spaghetti
sea salt
freshly ground black pepper

1 Bring a large saucepan of water to the boil and add the chard, lettuce, basil and mint. Bring the pan back to a simmer and cook for 1 minute. Drain the leaves and once they are cool enough to handle, press out any excess water. Chop the leaves as finely as you can and place to one side.

2 Heat the olive oil in the saucepan. Add the shallot and fry for 1 minute, then stir in the cooked leaves and cook for a few seconds. Season with salt and pepper, then spoon in the mascarpone and stir to combine. Add the Parmesan and check the seasoning.

3 Meanwhile, bring a large pan of salted water to the boil and cook the spaghetti. Drain the spaghetti, then toss with the sauce and serve.

Beef fillet in tomato sauce

Fillet is expensive so it's a good idea to bulk the meal out with vegetables. The cooking times below are for medium steaks so change according to your taste, bearing in mind that overcooked fillet has little charm.

SERVES 6

2 tbsp olive oil
600g beef fillet steak, sliced into 2cm thick pieces
4 tbsp Marsala wine
3 tsp green peppercorns
1 tbsp tomato purée
300ml beef stock
20g cold butter, cut into cubes
1 tbsp roughly chopped fresh basil leaves

1 Heat the olive oil in a sauté pan. When it's hot, cook the steaks for 3 minutes on each side for medium meat. Remove the steaks from the pan and leave to one side.
2 Return the pan to the heat, add the wine and cook for a few seconds at a rapid bubble. Add the peppercorns, stir in the tomato purée and then the beef stock. Simmer for 1 minute on a low heat. Using a fork, beat in the butter and then sprinkle in the basil.
3 Return the steaks to the pan to heat through briefly, then serve with the sauce.

Lamb steaks with caper and mint sauce

The British fondness for lamb and mint sauce goes back centuries, perhaps to a time when we ate the herbs that were in season at the same time as the meat. When lambs were slaughtered in spring, wild mint would also have been growing. People also believed that particular combinations of herbs and meats aided the digestion.

SERVES 6

1 tbsp olive oil
6 lamb steaks
20g butter
50g sliced pancetta, finely chopped
1 shallot, finely chopped
20g flour
150ml Marsala wine
500ml beef stock
1 tbsp capers, rinsed and chopped
2 tbsp finely chopped mint
sea salt
freshly ground black pepper

1 Heat the olive oil in a large sauté pan and brown the lamb steaks, a couple at a time, on both sides. Season them with some salt and pepper and place to one side. Keep the pan on the heat.
2 Add the butter, chopped pancetta and shallot to the pan and cook over a low heat for 5 minutes. Sprinkle on the flour and stir to combine. Pour on the wine and let it sizzle for 3 minutes, then gradually pour on the stock, stirring constantly. Let the sauce simmer gently for 5 minutes. Add the mint and capers, season with salt and pepper and continue to simmer, uncovered, for 15 minutes or so.
3 Just before serving, place the lamb steaks in the sauce and cook for 4 minutes by which time the steaks should be pink inside and ready to serve. Serve with roast potatoes and baby carrots.

Nectarine pies

When devising the recipe for these individual pies, I tried making them without the ramekins, just wrapping the nectarines in pastry and baking them, but the pastry collapsed. Then I tried placing the little pies in muffin tins, but they stuck. In the end I found the best method was to use buttered ramekins and serve them in these. You can make an incision in the top of each pie and pour in the cream before eating.

MAKES 6

6 tsp soft brown sugar
3 nectarines, cut in half and stones removed
ground cinnamon
double cream, for serving

Pastry
125g butter, softened to room temperature
90g caster sugar
½ tsp vanilla bean paste
1 large egg
250g plain flour, plus extra for dusting the work surface

1 To make the pastry, cream the butter and sugar in a food processor until smooth and well combined. Add the vanilla bean paste and egg and mix briefly. Gradually add the flour and mix as briefly as possible until combined. Turn the dough out on to a floured surface and form it into a ball, then wrap it in clingfilm and chill in the fridge for 30 minutes.
2 Lightly butter the 6 ramekins and preheat the oven to 200°C/Gas 6. Divide the pastry into 6 equal pieces.
3 Put a teaspoon of sugar into the hole left by the stone of each nectarine and add a pinch of cinnamon. Roll out the pieces of pastry so that they are large enough to wrap around the nectarine halves.
4 Put the nectarine halves, cut side up, on the work surface and then place a piece of pastry over the top of each one, tucking it under so that it is smooth on top but covers the nectarine completely. Pop the pies into the ramekins and slash the top of each one with a knife.
5 Place the ramekins on a baking sheet and bake for 30 minutes until the pastry is golden brown. Pour some double cream on to the top of each pie and serve.

Chocolate and toffee semi-freddo

Semi-freddo is a great alternative to ice cream if, like most people, you don't have an ice cream machine. This recipe is particularly yummy.

SERVES 6

55g caster sugar
4 egg yolks
500ml double cream
4 egg whites
50g white chocolate, roughly chopped
50g dark chocolate, roughly chopped

Toffee sauce
55g butter
80g soft brown sugar
55g caster sugar
140g golden syrup
100ml double cream

1 First, prepare the toffee sauce filling for the semi-freddo. Place the butter, sugars and syrup in a saucepan and melt over a low heat until combined. Remove from the heat, then stir in the cream. Put the pan back on a low heat and cook for 15 minutes. Place to one side to cool completely.
2 To make the semi-freddo, whisk the sugar and egg yolks together in a large bowl until pale yellow. In a separate bowl, whisk the cream until it forms soft peaks. Wash the whisk well and then, in a third bowl, whisk the egg whites until they form stiff peaks.
3 Gently fold the cream, egg whites, 3 tablespoons of the cold toffee sauce and the chopped chocolate into the egg yolks and spoon the mixture into a container to freeze for at least 2 hours. Remove from the freezer 10 minutes before serving with the remaining toffee sauce.

Grilled chicken thighs with white bean salad and garlic and lemon mayo

It may well be raining somewhere in the UK in June, but this meal will brighten up the day. Never underestimate the power of food to lift the spirits.

SERVES 6

2 tsp sesame seeds
2 tsp linseed
2 tsp ground cumin
2 tsp salt
1 tbsp thyme leaves
1 tbsp finely chopped oregano
¼ tsp turmeric
12 chicken thigh fillets
grated zest of 1 lemon
3 tbsp olive oil

White bean salad
4 tbsp olive oil
1 red onion, finely chopped
1 garlic clove, finely chopped
1 x 400g can of butter beans, drained and rinsed
1 x 400g can of cannellini beans, drained and rinsed
150ml vegetable stock
5 spring onions, finely sliced
2 tbsp finely chopped flat-leaf parsley
6 cherry tomatoes, quartered
5 radishes, sliced
sea salt
freshly ground black pepper

Garlic and lemon mayo
2 egg yolks
1 garlic clove, crushed
grated zest of ½ lemon
200ml light olive oil
sea salt

1 Place the seeds, cumin, salt, herbs and turmeric in a small frying pan and toast on a medium heat until the seeds start to pop. Tip everything into a bowl, add the chicken thighs, lemon zest and olive oil, then gently mix everything with your hands until the fillets are well coated. Set aside in a cool place until you are ready to grill the chicken.
2 Heat the grill until hot. Put the thighs on a rack and place under the grill. When the thighs are brown on both sides, turn the grill down and cook them for about 5 minutes more on each side to ensure that they are cooked through – about 20 minutes altogether. Serve the chicken with the white beans and the mayo.

To prepare the white bean salad
3 Heat 2 tablespoons of olive oil in a sauté pan and cook the red onion and garlic for 5 minutes until soft. Add the beans and the stock and simmer gently for 5 minutes.
4 Crush half of the beans with the back of a fork, leaving the rest whole. Spoon into a serving dish with the spring onions, parsley, tomatoes and radishes, then dress with 2 tablespoons of olive oil. Season well.

To make the garlic and lemon mayo
5 Beat the egg yolks in a mixing bowl. Add the garlic and lemon zest and mix to combine. Slowly start adding the oil, a trickle at a time, beating to make sure that the oil is absorbed into the egg. Keep doing this until you have used all the oil. Do not be tempted to add the oil too quickly or the mayonnaise will curdle. Season the mayonnaise with salt to taste.

Red pepper and tomato sauce with pasta

The only pasta sauces which take a while to cook are meat sauces. If your pasta water is coming to the boil while you are preparing the peppers and other ingredients, this meal should not take longer than 40 minutes to get to the table. The best kind of fast food!

SERVES 6

2 red peppers
2 tbsp olive oil
1 onion, finely chopped
500g cherry tomatoes, halved
2 tsp finely chopped fresh oregano
1 tbsp mascarpone cheese
600g spaghetti
sea salt
freshly ground black pepper

1 Slice the red peppers in half lengthways and remove the seeds and cores. Put the peppers on an ovenproof tray and place under a hot grill until the skins become patched with black. Remove the peppers from the grill and remove their skins with a sharp knife. Roughly chop the peppers and place to one side.
2 Heat the olive oil in a saucepan. Add the onion and fry over a low heat for 5 minutes. Add the peppers and the tomatoes and cook over a low heat, stirring occasionally for 30 minutes.
3 Stir in the oregano and mascarpone, then season well with salt and pepper and simmer gently for 5 minutes.
4 Cook the pasta according to the packet instructions. Drain, then toss with the sauce and serve.

Chocolate raspberry cake

This is a wonderfully moist cake. Dust with icing sugar and serve with plenty of cream.

MAKES 1 X 24CM CAKE

200g dark chocolate
4 egg yolks
175g caster sugar
4 egg whites
200g butter, melted
250g ground almonds
200g raspberries, plus extra for decorating the cake
icing sugar, for dusting

1 Preheat the oven to 180°C/Gas 4. Grease a 24cm cake tin that has a removable base and line it with baking parchment.
2 Whizz the chocolate in a food processor until it's chopped into pieces – but don't chop it too finely.
3 Beat the egg yolks in a large bowl with the sugar until you have a pale yellow mixture with a mousse-like consistency. Whisk the egg whites in another bowl until they form stiff peaks.
4 Add the chopped chocolate to the egg yolks and pour in the melted butter. Fold in the egg whites, ground almonds and raspberries and then spoon the mixture into the cake tin. Bake in the oven for 50 minutes until firm to the touch of your fingertips.
5 Leave the cake to cool for 20 minutes in the tin, then turn it out on to a serving plate. Dust with icing sugar and decorate with raspberries if you like. Delicious served warm or cold with cream.

In July the garden reaches its peak. Over the last few years July has been one of the wetter months, but keeping everything watered at this time can sometimes be a problem, as vegetables do not cope well in a drought. In July cooks have to cope with gluts of soft fruit and vegetables such as courgettes from the garden. It's worth preserving and bottling if you can, so nothing goes to waste, or give fruit and vegetables away to neighbours. In the shops you can choose from a wide selection of British produce, including lettuce, kohlrabi, carrots, peas and potatoes to name just a few, and you can be really creative in the kitchen. July also provides a welcome opportunity to do more cooking outdoors and as well as barbecuing, we can explore cooking over open fires, in pits and over white ashes. July is a time to be sociable and relax after work, to make the most of the long light evenings and relish the good weather our climate can bring. British cooking has truly developed over the last decade or so, particularly in terms of summer food. Dishes from many different countries have become part of the British way of cooking – treats such as grilled haloumi or sardines, Spanish tapas, Italian crostini and Moroccan and Greek salads.

July

Lamb sauce with pasta

You should be able to buy Italian Vin Santo in British supermarkets but if not, Marsala wine is a good substitute. I often use Marsala in cooking as it has a gentle sweetness to it that goes well with most meats.

SERVES 6

2 tbsp olive oil
1 onion, finely chopped
1 carrot, finely chopped
1 celery stalk, finely chopped
2 tsp finely chopped rosemary leaves
80g minced lamb
200ml Vin Santo or Marsala wine
1 x 400g can of chopped tomatoes
1 tbsp tomato purée
600g tagliatelle
grated Parmesan cheese, for serving
sea salt
freshly ground black pepper

1 Heat the olive oil in a medium saucepan. Add the onion, carrot, celery and rosemary and cook gently for 10 minutes, stirring occasionally.
2 Add the minced lamb, wine, canned tomatoes and tomato purée and bring everything to a simmer. Season well with salt and pepper, then leave to simmer for 1 hour, uncovered. Check the seasoning.
3 Cook the pasta according to the packet instructions, then drain and serve with the sauce and plenty of grated Parmesan cheese.

Saffron risotto with summer vegetables

Saffron is one of those ingredients that can transform a dish into something very special. I believe the Spanish introduced the spice to the rest of Europe and in particular to Italy, where it is used in the famous Milanese risotto.

SERVES 6

1.5 litres chicken or vegetable stock
200g carrots, diced
200g peas (frozen will do)
100g courgettes, diced
a good pinch of saffron threads
2 tbsp olive oil
a small knob of butter
1 onion finely chopped
500g Arborio risotto rice
2–3 tbsp grated Parmesan cheese
a handful or 2 of torn basil leaves
sea salt
freshly ground black pepper

1 Bring the stock to a simmer in a saucepan. Add the carrots and simmer for 1 minute. Add the peas and simmer for 1 minute and then add the courgettes and saffron threads. Keep at a very gentle simmer for 1 minute more.
2 Heat the olive oil and butter in a separate large saucepan. Add the onion and fry for 3 minutes, then stir in the rice and fry for another minute.
3 Start to add the stock and vegetables, a couple of ladlefuls at a time, stirring as you do so and adding more as the stock is absorbed by the rice. Make sure the heat isn't too high or the stock will be absorbed too quickly and the rice won't cook properly. Keep adding the stock until the rice is tender but has a slight bite to it; about 20–25 minutes.
4 Remove the pan from the heat and stir in the Parmesan cheese. Check the seasoning and adjust as necessary. Scatter on the basil leaves and serve.

Chicken with mushroom and mustard sauce

A dish that includes chicken, mushrooms and mustard will always be well received.

SERVES 6

olive oil
200g mushrooms, roughly chopped
1kg chicken thigh fillets, each cut into 3 or 4 pieces
150ml white wine
2 shallots, finely chopped
1 garlic clove, finely chopped
200ml chicken stock (a stock cube will do)
1 tbsp Dijon mustard
sea salt
freshly ground black pepper

Baby carrots
300g baby carrots
a little butter
a sprig of rosemary
sea salt
freshly ground black pepper

1 Heat a tablespoon of olive oil in a large pan. Add the mushrooms and cook them over a high heat for 5 minutes until they are golden brown and have stopped releasing liquid. Remove the mushrooms from the pan and place them in a bowl to one side.
2 Return the pan to the heat and add another tablespoon of olive oil. Brown the chicken pieces in small batches, putting each batch of chicken in the bowl with the mushrooms.
3 Put the empty pan back on the heat and add the wine, scraping up all the sticky bits of chicken on the bottom of the pan. Simmer the wine for 30 seconds and then pour this over the chicken and mushroom mixture.
4 Add another tablespoon of olive oil to the pan and fry the shallot and garlic for 1 minute. Tip the chicken and mushroom mixture back into the pan, pour on the stock and stir in the mustard. Bring everything to a simmer, cover the pan and cook gently for 30 minutes. Season with salt and pepper and serve with the baby carrots and perhaps some potatoes or rice.

To cook the baby carrots
5 Trim the carrots so that they are all about the same size. Put them in a saucepan with the butter and rosemary and place on a medium heat. Once you hear the butter fizzing, reduce the heat and cover the pan. Cook for 10 minutes until the carrots are tender, stirring frequently. Season with salt and pepper.

Prawn and egg curry with cucumber and potato curry

Prawns and egg are a great combination and go well with the cucumber and potato curry. Some home-made naan (see page 685) makes this a really special meal.

SERVES 6

Prawn and egg curry
2 tbsp vegetable oil
1 tsp black mustard seeds
1 onion, finely chopped
2 garlic cloves, cut into slivers
1 tsp grated fresh root ginger
450ml water
1 tbsp paprika
a pinch of cayenne pepper
2 tbsp curry powder (see below)
¼ tsp turmeric
1 green chilli, seeded and chopped finely
1 tbsp tamarind paste
400ml coconut milk
a large pinch of salt
250g cooked, shelled prawns
6 hard-boiled eggs, cut into quarters

Cucumber and potato curry
2 tbsp desiccated coconut
1 tsp ground coriander
½ tsp fennel seeds
1 large cucumber, peeled and cut into 2cm chunks
4 potatoes, peeled and cut into 2cm chunks
1 onion
5 curry leaves
2cm piece of cinnamon stick
¼ tsp turmeric
200ml coconut milk
1 green chilli, seeded and chopped
salt

Curry powder
2 tbsp coriander seeds
1 tsp black peppercorns
1 tsp cumin seeds
¼ tsp fenugreek seeds
10 dried curry leaves

To make the prawn and egg curry
1 Heat the oil in a saucepan. Add the mustard seeds and when they start to pop, turn the heat down.
2 Add the onion and fry for 10 minutes until soft. Add the garlic and ginger and cook for 30 seconds, then add the water, paprika, cayenne, curry powder, turmeric, green chilli and tamarind paste.
3 Pour in the coconut milk, bring to a simmer and cook for 5 minutes. Check for seasoning and add a little salt if necessary. Add the prawns and eggs and warm them through for a minute or two.

To make the cucumber and potato curry
4 Place the desiccated coconut, coriander and fennel seeds in a frying pan over a medium heat and cook briefly until the coconut turns brown.
5 Tip everything into a saucepan with the cucumber, potatoes and the rest of ingredients, except the salt, and simmer for 10 minutes until the potato is tender. Season with a little salt if necessary.
6 Spoon the curry into a serving dish and serve with the prawn and egg curry and naan breads (see page 685).

To make the curry powder
7 Place the coriander seeds and peppercorns in a small frying pan on a medium heat and dry fry them for 1 minute. Now add the cumin, fenugreek and curry leaves. Stir them around until the seeds darken in colour slightly and you can smell their aroma. The spices will also start to smoke.
8 Remove the spices and place them in a coffee grinder or a mortar and grind them to as fine a powder as you can manage. You can store any leftover curry powder in a glass jar for a few months.

Summer vegetable soup

Keeping meat off the menu at this time of year is not so much of a challenge as it is in winter because there's such a wide range of vegetables around. One of the key tricks with a simple vegetable dish like this is to take great care with the preparation. If you chop vegetables carefully and try not to stir them too often during cooking so they keep their shape, the dish will look more visually appealing.

SERVES 6

2 tbsp olive oil
1 onion, finely chopped
2 celery stalks, finely chopped
100g string or French beans, topped and tailed and cut into 2cm pieces
250g small courgettes, sliced into 1cm discs
300g new potatoes, cut into chunks
200g carrots, peeled and chopped into 1cm discs
12 cherry tomatoes
1.5 litres chicken stock
1 bunch flat-leaf parsley, finely chopped
sea salt
freshly ground black pepper

1 Heat the olive oil in a large saucepan. Add the onion and celery and cook over a low heat for 10 minutes, stirring occasionally.
2 Add the beans, courgettes, potatoes, carrots and tomatoes, then stir to coat everything in the oil. Pour on the stock and simmer for 30 minutes. Season the soup with salt and pepper, sprinkle with parsley and serve with plenty of bread.

Cubed veal with summer vegetables

Veal can be difficult to get in some areas of the UK, but hunt it out via the internet or small producers and you will be glad you made the effort.

SERVES 6

2–3 tbsp olive oil
1kg cubed veal or veal cutlets
seasoned flour, for dusting
1 onion, finely diced
300g carrots, peeled and cut in half
300g courgettes, sliced into 2cm discs
1 yellow pepper, cored and diced
250g fresh tomatoes, cut in quarters
500g new potatoes, cut in half
250ml beef stock
a handful of torn basil leaves
sea salt
freshly ground black pepper

1 Heat 2 tablespoons of olive oil in a large saucepan. Toss the veal cubes in the seasoned flour and then brown the meat in batches. Set aside each batch while you fry the next.
2 Add a little extra oil if you need, then fry the onion over a medium heat for 5 minutes. Add the carrots, courgettes, pepper, tomatoes and potatoes and fry for 2 minutes.
3 Return the veal to the pan. Pour on the stock and season well with salt and pepper, then cover the pan and simmer for 1 hour. Scatter on the basil leaves just before serving.

Beef fillet with chimichurri sauce, roasted new potatoes and green salad

This is an Argentinian dish and a very welcome discovery. Chimichurri is a thin spicy sauce that often accompanies grilled beef in that part of the world.

SERVES 6

2 tbsp olive oil
600g beef fillet, sliced into 2cm pieces
sea salt
freshly ground black pepper

Chimichurri sauce
1 tbsp flat-leaf parsley
2 garlic cloves, crushed
1 shallot, finely chopped
1 tbsp finely chopped basil
1 tbsp finely chopped oregano
1 green chilli, seeded and finely chopped
200ml olive oil
juice of 1 fresh lemon
grated zest of 1 lemon
sea salt
freshly ground black pepper

Roasted new potatoes
750g baby new potatoes, cut in half
1 tbsp olive oil
sea salt

Green salad with mozzarella
1 crispy lettuce
2 tbsp extra virgin olive oil
½ tbsp balsamic vinegar
1 x 125g tub of buffalo mozzarella
salt and pepper

1 Heat the olive oil in a sauté pan and cook the steaks, 2 or 3 at a time, for 3 minutes on each side. Place each batch to one side while you cook the rest.

To prepare the chimichurri sauce
2 Place the parsley, garlic, shallot, basil, oregano and green chilli in a bowl or jam jar. Pour on the olive oil and lemon juice, then add the zest and season with salt and pepper. Give this a good shake or stir and serve with the beef.

To make the roasted new potatoes
3 Preheat the oven to 220°C/Gas 7. Place the potatoes in a roasting tin, with the olive oil. Season with salt and roast in the oven for 45–50 minutes, turning them occasionally.

To prepare the salad
4 Roughly tear the lettuce leaves and place them in a serving bowl. Drizzle with most of the oil and then the vinegar. Chop the mozzarella and add it to the salad, then dress with a little more olive oil and season.

Carrot and courgette muffins

These are a fairly virtuous treat that can be made a bit more indulgent if you add the frosting.

MAKES 12

100g grated carrot
100g grated courgette
200g caster sugar
150g natural yoghurt
225g self-raising flour
3 eggs
1 tsp finely chopped rosemary
200ml olive oil
a pinch of salt

Cream cheese frosting (optional)
125g mascarpone cheese
100g fromage frais
½ tbsp caster sugar
½ tsp ground cinnamon

1 Preheat the oven to 200°C/Gas 6. Line a muffin tray with 12 paper muffin cases.
2 Place all the ingredients for the muffins in a mixing bowl and mix until just combined. Divide the mixture evenly between the 12 cases and bake for 30–35 minutes in the preheated oven. Remove and cool on a wire rack.
3 To make the frosting, place all the ingredients in a mixing bowl and mix until combined. When the muffins are cool, top them with frosting, if using.

Baked peaches and raspberries with lemon mascarpone

The flavours of peaches and rosemary go remarkably well together – a successful marriage of two star ingredients from the Mediterranean.

SERVES 6

6 ripe peaches
50g fresh raspberries
2 tbsp soft brown sugar
100ml white wine
1 sprig of fresh rosemary

Lemon mascarpone
grated zest of 1 lemon
200g mascarpone, loosened with 2 tbsp double cream

1 Preheat the oven to 200°C/Gas 6. Cut the peaches in half and carefully remove the stones.
2 Place the peaches in a gratin dish and put a few raspberries in the stone hollow of each peach half. Sprinkle on the sugar and pour over the wine, then scatter on some rosemary leaves. Bake in the oven for 40 minutes.
3 Stir the lemon zest into the mascarpone and cream and serve with the peaches.

Duck ragù with pasta

A rich meat sauce with pasta is one of my favourite meals.

SERVES 6

olive oil
4 duck legs
a few celery leaves
1 celery stalk, finely chopped
1 garlic clove, finely chopped
1 sprig of rosemary, leaves removed and finely chopped
1 onion, finely chopped
340g pork chipolatas, roughly chopped
70g pancetta, finely chopped
200ml red wine
1 tbsp tomato purée
1 x 400g can of chopped tomatoes
600g tagliatelle
sea salt
freshly ground black pepper

1 Heat a tablespoon of olive oil in a saucepan. Place the duck legs in the pan and fry them, skin side down, for 10 minutes. Turn the legs over and fry them on the other side for another 10 minutes. Drain off the fat into a bowl.
2 Return the duck legs to the pan with the celery leaves and pour in enough water to just cover them. Bring them to a simmer and continue to simmer, uncovered, for 30 minutes. Remove the legs from the pan and place them on a chopping board to cool slightly. Pour off the cooking liquor – you can use some of this later.
3 Return the pan to the heat and add 2 tablespoons of olive oil. Add the celery, garlic, rosemary and onion to the pan and cook gently for 3 minutes, until the onion is soft. Add the chipolatas and the pancetta and fry for 4 minutes until golden brown.
4 Remove the skin from the duck legs and roughly chop the meat, wasting as little as possible. Add the meat to the pan with the onions, sausage and pancetta, then pour on the red wine and simmer for 2 minutes. Add the tomato purée and canned tomatoes and 250ml of the cooking liquor you set aside earlier. Season with salt and pepper and simmer over the lowest heat, uncovered, for 30 minutes.
5 Cook the pasta in salted boiling water according to the packet instructions. Drain, toss with the sauce and serve.

Fish cakes with chive cream sauce

One of the good things about fish cakes is that you can prepare them in advance, pop them in the fridge, then fry them when you are ready to eat. This sauce can be prepared in advance too.

1 Put the potatoes in a mixing bowl and mash them with a fork until you have a rough purée. Add the prawns, cod, spring onions, garlic, ginger, coriander and soy sauce. Season well with salt and pepper and mix well.
2 Form the mixture into 8 fish cakes and place them in the fridge for 20 minutes or so to chill.
3 Spread some flour on a plate and the breadcrumbs on another plate. Dip each fish cake in the flour, then the egg, then the breadcrumbs.
4 Heat some olive oil in a frying pan and fry the fish cakes for 3 minutes on each side. Serve with the chive cream sauce and a mixed salad.

To make the chive cream sauce
5 Place the shallot and white wine in a small saucepan and simmer for 1 minute. Add the vegetable stock and simmer for 1 minute more, then add the cream and simmer gently for 2 minutes. Stir in the mustard and the chives and season with salt and pepper.

SERVES 6

350g sweet potatoes, cooked until tender
120g cooked, shelled prawns, finely chopped
370g smoked cod, finely chopped
40g chopped spring onions
2 garlic cloves, crushed
1 tsp finely grated fresh root ginger
3 tbsp finely chopped fresh coriander
1 tbsp dark soy sauce
flour
200g fresh white breadcrumbs
1 egg, beaten
olive oil, for frying
sea salt
freshly ground black pepper

Chive cream sauce
1 shallot, finely chopped
100ml white wine
200ml vegetable stock
150ml single cream
1 tsp Dijon mustard
2 tbsp finely chopped chives
sea salt
freshly ground black pepper

Omelettes on toast

I always feel that omelettes are a last-choice meal, when there's nothing else in the cupboard. Once I sit down to eat one, though, I realise how really delicious they are and worthy of being treated with more respect.

SERVES 6

12 eggs
2 tbsp olive oil
1 shallot, finely chopped
3 small courgettes, diced
a bunch of chives, snipped finely
100g cooked ham, chopped into 1cm squares
15g butter
2 tbsp grated Gruyère cheese
6-12 slices of bread for toasting
sea salt
freshly ground black pepper

1 Mix the eggs in a bowl. Season with salt and pepper and set to one side. Heat the olive oil in a sauté pan. Gently fry the shallot and courgettes together for 5 minutes, then add the chives and ham and cook for a further 3 minutes. Tip the contents of the sauté pan into a small bowl and season with salt and pepper.

2 Return the pan to the heat and add the butter. When it is sizzling, pour in half the beaten eggs. Tip the pan away from you, pulling back the cooked egg with a fork as you do so.

3 Spoon half the vegetable and herb mixture over half of the omelette. Sprinkle on half of the cheese and flip the uncovered half of the omelette over the filling. Continue to cook the omelette, but remove it from the heat while the interior is still nice and runny. Do exactly the same with the other half of the ingredients.

4 Toast the bread, cut each omelette into 3 and serve on pieces of toast.

Chicken, sausage and vegetable pie

This chicken pie is packed with seasonal vegetables.

SERVES 6

200g carrots, sliced into 1cm discs
2 tbsp olive oil
1 onion, finely chopped
2 courgettes, diced
4 chicken breasts, chopped into 2cm chunks
150ml dry white wine
200g sausage meat or 4 sausages
225g spinach, trimmed and shredded
1 x 230g sheet of ready-rolled puff pastry
milk, for brushing the pastry
sea salt
freshly ground black pepper

White sauce
25g butter
25g plain flour
300ml milk
2 tbsp crème fraiche
1 tsp Dijon mustard
sea salt
freshly ground black pepper

1 Start by making the white sauce. Melt the butter in a small saucepan, then add the flour and stir to incorporate. Remove the pan from the heat and gradually add the milk, stirring constantly to avoid lumps. Return the pan to the heat, bring the sauce to a simmer and cook slowly for 5 minutes. Stir in the crème fraiche and mustard, then check for seasoning and place to one side.

To make the filling
2 Preheat the oven to 200°/Gas 6. Cook the carrots in boiling salted water until tender, then drain them and place to one side.
3 Heat the olive oil in a saucepan or sauté pan. When it's hot, add the onion and cook for 5 minutes. Add the courgettes and cook for 3 minutes, then add the chicken and continue to cook for 5 minutes. Pour on the wine and cook for 2 minutes.
4 Split the sausages if using and roll the sausage meat into balls the size of small apricots. Add these to the mixture with the carrots and spinach and cook for 3 minutes. Pour on the white sauce and stir gently until all the ingredients are evenly combined.
5 Spoon the mixture into a pie dish and lay the sheet of puff pastry on top. Brush the pastry with a little milk and then bake in the oven for 30 minutes. Serve with some runner beans.

Pollack gratin

Fish is real fast food. If all the filleting and gutting has been done for you by your friendly fishmonger, you can have a meal ready in 30 minutes, with the minimum of washing up.

SERVES 6

300g spinach leaves
25g butter
25g flour
300ml milk
2 tsp Dijon mustard
100ml double cream
2 tbsp finely chopped flat-leaf parsley
1 tbsp finely cut chives
1kg pollack fillet, skin removed
2 tbsp grated Parmesan cheese
sea salt
freshly ground black pepper

1 Preheat the oven to 200°C/Gas 6. Bring a large saucepan of water to the boil, add the spinach leaves and simmer for 1 minute. Drain and squeeze the water from the leaves and then roughly chop the spinach and set it aside.
2 Heat the butter in a small saucepan, then stir in the flour. Remove the pan from the heat and gradually add the milk, stirring as you do so. Return the pan to the heat and simmer gently for 5 minutes, then stir in the mustard and cream. Add the spinach and herbs and stir to combine, then season with salt and pepper.
3 Lay the pollack fillet in a gratin dish and spoon on the sauce. Sprinkle the cheese on top and bake in the oven for 15 minutes until golden brown and bubbling. Serve with new potatoes.

Veal Milanese with green beans

Vicky and Matias, our Argentinian friends, gave me the details of this recipe. It's their favourite and completely delicious. You can also use thin-cut sirloin steak for a more economical version.

SERVES 6

1kg veal escalopes
5 eggs, beaten
3 garlic cloves, finely chopped
1 bunch flat-leaf parsley, finely chopped
200g white breadcrumbs
olive oil, for frying
sea salt
freshly ground black pepper

Green beans
2 tbsp olive oil
3 courgettes, sliced widthways into thin discs
200g green beans, cooked in salted water until tender
100g cherry tomatoes, cut in half
1 tbsp extra virgin olive oil
2 tsp balsamic vinegar
sea salt
freshly ground black pepper

1 Trim any fat from the meat. If the slices are thicker than about 5mm, give them a bash with a steak mallet or rolling pin to make them a little thinner. Season the escalopes with salt and pepper.

2 Beat the eggs in a large bowl and add the garlic and parsley. Place the veal in the egg, making sure that all the meat is covered. Leave to one side for at least 30 minutes, longer if you have time.

3 Put the oven on at 100°C/Gas ¼. Spread the breadcrumbs on a large plate. Remove a piece of veal from the egg mixture and lay it in the breadcrumbs, pressing it down firmly so that the crumbs stick to the meat. Turn the escalope over and do the same on the other side. Place to one side while you coat the rest of the escalopes in the same way.

4 Heat 2 tablespoons of olive oil in a frying pan. When the oil is hot, add an escalope and fry it on each side for 1–2 minutes, until the breadcrumbs are golden brown. Place it on a baking sheet in the low oven to keep warm while you cook the rest, adding more oil if necessary. Serve with the green beans, plenty of mustard and some mashed potatoes (see page 16).

To cook the green beans

5 Heat the olive oil in a large sauté pan and add the courgette slices. Fry them for 5 minutes, turning so that they are golden brown all over. Add the beans and tomatoes, stir and cook for 1 minute. Remove the pan from the heat.

6 Drizzle the vegetables with the extra virgin olive oil and balsamic vinegar, then season with salt and pepper.

Roast chicken, salted new potatoes and tomato salad

I first ate these salted new potatoes in Tenerife and thought they were very special. After some trial and error I've come up with my own version. You need to keep an eye on the potatoes while they're cooking, and judge when to add a little more water or increase the heat to boil off the water, but have a go and enjoy the results.

SERVES 6

2 x 1.5kg chickens
olive oil
sea salt
freshly ground black pepper

Salted new potatoes
1.5kg baby new potatoes
30g salt
a small bunch of mint, roughly chopped
1 litre water

Tomato salad
4-6 large tomatoes
a handful of roughly chopped fresh oregano or thyme leaves
2 tbsp olive oil
sea salt
freshly ground black pepper

1 Preheat the oven to 180°C/Gas 4. Place the chickens in a roasting tin and rub each one with couple of tablespoons of olive oil. Season well with salt and pepper.
2 Roast the chickens for 1 hour and 20 minutes, then remove them from the oven and place on a warm plate. Pour the juices from the pan over the chicken and leave to rest for 30 minutes before carving. Serve with the potatoes and salad.

To prepare the salted new potatoes
3 Place the potatoes in a wide pan in one layer. Sprinkle over the salt and mint and pour on the water. Bring to a lively simmer and cook until the water has disappeared and the potatoes are tender. You will need to move the potatoes around during the cooking time to ensure that they cook evenly.

To prepare the tomato salad
4 Slice the tomatoes and place them in a serving dish. Sprinkle on the oregano or thyme, drizzle over the oil and season.

Apricot pie

A mixture of dried and fresh apricots bring a good rich sweetness to this pie.

SERVES 6

250g dried apricots
6 fresh apricots, cut in half and stones removed

Pastry
250g plain flour
40g caster sugar, plus extra for dusting
½ tsp baking powder
175g cold butter, cut into cubes
1 egg
1 egg yolk
50ml milk

To make the pastry

1 Put the flour, sugar, baking powder and butter in a food processor and whizz until the mixture resembles breadcrumbs. Mix the egg, yolk and milk in a small bowl and pour this on to the flour mixture. Whizz briefly and then turn out on to a floured surface. Bring the mixture together with your hands and shape into a ball. Wrap the pastry in clingfilm and place it in the fridge to chill while you prepare the filling.

To prepare the filling

2 Place the dried apricots in a small saucepan, cover them with water and bring to a simmer. Cover the pan and cook the apricots for 30 minutes until soft. Drain, then whizz them in a food processor or liquidiser until puréed. Set aside to cool.

To assemble the pie

3 Preheat the oven to 200°C/Gas 6 and place a baking sheet in the oven.

4 Cut the pastry dough in half. Roll out 1 piece on a floured surface and use it to line a 24cm pie plate – don't worry about greasing the plate. Spoon the apricot purée over the pastry and place the halved apricots on top, cut- side down.

5 Roll out the other piece of pastry, cover the pie and seal the edges. Sprinkle the top of the pie with some caster sugar, then pop it into the oven on the baking sheet and bake for 40 minutes, until golden brown. Let the pie cool slightly and then serve in slices with cream.

Raspberry trifle

This is a light trifle, suitable for a summer dessert.

SERVES 6

Sponge
3 eggs
80g caster sugar
70g plain flour
½ tsp vanilla extract

Raspberry jam filling
500g fresh raspberries
juice of 1 lemon
300g preserving sugar

Custard
4 egg yolks
1 egg
75g caster sugar
300ml double cream
100ml milk

whipping cream, for topping

To make the sponge

1 Grease a 23cm round cake tin and line the base with baking parchment. Preheat the oven to 170°C/Gas 3½.

2 Using an electric hand-whisk, beat the eggs and sugar together in a bowl until thick and mousse-like. This will take about 3 minutes. Fold in the flour with a metal spoon and add the vanilla extract.

3 Spoon the mixture into the cake tin and bake for 20 minutes until the cake is firm to the touch and a skewer inserted into the middle comes out clean.

4 Remove the cake from the tin when it has cooled slightly and place it on a wire rack.

To make the raspberry jam filling

5 Place the raspberries and lemon juice in a saucepan over a medium heat and cook for 10 minutes, stirring occasionally. Reduce the heat to low and add the sugar. Let the sugar dissolve completely before you turn the heat up to bring the jam to a boil. Boil for 25 minutes and leave to one side to cool.

To make the custard

6 Whisk the egg yolks and whole egg in a glass bowl with the sugar. Measure out the cream and milk together and heat until just coming to boiling point.

7 Whisk the cream and milk into the egg and sugar mixture. Place the glass bowl over a pan of simmering water, making sure that the bowl does not touch the water. Stir the custard with a wooden spoon until it starts to thicken and coat the back of the wooden spoon.

To assemble the trifle

8 Break up the sponge into large pieces. Pour half the raspberry filling into the bottom of the serving dish and lay the sponge pieces on top. Pour on the custard, the rest of the filling and cover with whipped cream.

Carrot and tarragon soup with tomato bruschetta

Carrots make a much nicer soup than one would imagine – rich and creamy. Their flavour goes well with many different herbs.

SERVES 6

25g butter
600g carrots, roughly chopped
1 onion, roughly chopped
1 celery stalk, roughly chopped
2 medium potatoes, peeled and chopped
1.5 litres chicken or vegetable stock, warmed
1 tsp finely chopped tarragon
1 tbsp dark soy sauce
sea salt
freshly ground black pepper

Tomato bruschetta
6 tomatoes
2 tsp capers, drained and rinsed
2 anchovy fillets, finely chopped
a handful of roughly chopped basil
3 tbsp extra virgin olive oil
6–8 slices of sourdough or country bread
2 garlic cloves, cut in half
sea salt
freshly ground black pepper

1 Heat the butter in a large saucepan. Add the carrots, onion, celery and potatoes, cover the pan and cook gently for 10 minutes.
2 Pour on the stock, cover the pan and simmer gently for 40 minutes. Blend the soup in a liquidiser or using a hand-held blender.
3 Add the chopped tarragon and soy sauce, then season with salt and pepper.

To make the tomato bruschetta
4 Dice the tomatoes and place them in a bowl with the capers, anchovies and basil. Season with salt and pepper and a tablespoon of the olive oil.
5 Place the slices of bread on a grill pan and toast on one side. Drizzle the other side with olive oil and rub with the garlic halves, then place the bread back under the grill, olive oil side up, and toast until slightly brown.
6 Divide the tomato mixture between the slices of bread and serve with the soup.

Penne pasta with crab and chilli sauce

When cooked, crab produces a sweet liquor that goes brilliantly with pasta. Even the canned crab used here produces a good result, with the help of the white wine. I love this simple dish and it's really quick to make.

SERVES 6

2 tbsp olive oil
2 garlic cloves, crushed
1 red chilli, seeded and finely chopped
10 cherry tomatoes, cut into quarters
100g Kalamata olives, stones removed
100ml white wine
240g canned crab meat, drained
2 tbsp roughly torn basil leaves
600g penne pasta
extra virgin olive oil
sea salt
freshly ground black pepper

1 Heat the olive oil in a large sauté pan. Add the garlic and chilli and cook quickly for 30 seconds, stirring to avoid any burning. Add the tomatoes, olives and wine and simmer briskly for 1 minute.
2 Add the crab and break it up with wooden spoon. Season with salt and pepper and add the basil leaves.
3 Cook the penne according to the packet instructions and drain. Toss the pasta with the sauce and sprinkle with some extra virgin olive oil before serving.

Crispy pork sandwiches with apple sauce

In most markets in Italy you'll see pork-filled ciabatta rolls being sold from the hatches of white vans. They are utterly delicious and filling enough to be served up as a weekend dinner. If you don't have time to make the bread rolls, buy ciabatta rolls from the supermarket.

SERVES 6

1.2kg belly pork
olive oil
sea salt
freshly ground black pepper

Bread rolls
1 x 7g sachet dried yeast
1 tsp sugar
350ml mix of warm water and warm milk
500g strong bread flour, warmed briefly in a microwave
1½ tsp salt

Apple sauce
3 eating apples, peeled, cut into quarters and cored
1 dsrtsp brown sugar
2 tbsp water

1 Preheat the oven to 150°C/Gas 2. Dry the pork rind with a piece of kitchen paper, then massage the olive oil into the rind and sprinkle with salt.
2 Place the joint in a roasting tin and roast for 2 hours. For the last 30 minutes, turn the heat up to 200°C/Gas 6 to ensure nice crispy crackling. Remove the meat from the oven and place it on a board to rest for about 15 minutes before carving and serving in the rolls with some apple sauce.

To make the bread rolls
3 Mix the yeast and sugar with a little of the warm milk and water and leave for 5 minutes.
4 Measure the flour and salt into a mixing bowl. Add the yeasted milk and water and the rest of the liquid and mix to a dough. Turn out on to a work surface and knead for 10 minutes until smooth and pliable. Place back in the bowl, cover and leave in a draught-free place for 1 hour.
5 Preheat the oven to 200°C/Gas 6. Cut the dough into 6 equal pieces and shape each piece into a roll. Place the rolls on a greased baking sheet and brush them with a little milk, then cover with a tea towel and leave to rise for 30 minutes. Bake in the oven for 25 minutes, then remove and take them off the baking sheet as soon as they are cool enough to handle.

To make the apple sauce
6 Place the apples, sugar and water in a small saucepan. Place on a medium heat on the stove and bring to a simmer. Reduce the heat to low, cover and cook for about 15 minutes, until the apples are beginning to fall apart. Break them up with a fork.

Cod, salmon and prawn gratin

It is always comforting to open a cookbook and find recipes with short and succinct instructions. This is one such recipe.

SERVES 6

600g cod fillets
350g salmon fillets
250ml milk
150g cooked, shelled prawns
20g butter
2 shallots, finely chopped
100ml white wine
200ml double cream
2 tsp Dijon mustard
1 tbsp finely chopped chives
2 tbsp finely grated Parmesan cheese
sea salt
freshly ground black pepper

1 Place the cod and salmon in a gratin dish that can be put on top of the stove. Pour over the milk and place the dish on top of the stove. Bring the milk to a simmer and cook for 2 minutes, then turn the fish and cook for another 2 minutes. Discard the milk and remove any skin from the fish fillets. Put the fish fillets back into the gratin dish and add the prawns.

2 Heat the butter in a frying pan. Add the shallots and fry them for 1 minute, then pour on the wine and simmer for 1 minute. Add the cream, mustard and chives, then simmer for 30 seconds. Season with salt and pepper. Preheat the grill.

3 Pour the cream mixture over the fish. Sprinkle on the Parmesan cheese and place the dish under the grill – be careful, as it will be very hot. Serve with mashed potato (see page 16) and broad beans.

Lamb cutlets with mint hollandaise and sweet baby new potatoes

Serve a green vegetable with this meal – maybe some broccoli or cabbage. Prepare the hollandaise sauce first, then the potatoes and cook the lamb last.

SERVES 6

6-12 lamb cutlets, depending on size and appetites
olive oil

Mint hollandaise
2 egg yolks
1 tsp lemon juice
110g butter, melted
1 tbsp finely chopped fresh mint
sea salt
freshly ground black pepper

Sweet baby new potatoes
700g baby new potatoes
20g butter
1 tbsp soft brown sugar
sea salt

1 Trim the lamb cutlets, removing any tough fat. Heat a little olive oil in a frying pan and fry the cutlets for 1 or 2 minutes on each side, depending on their thickness. Cook a few at a time so you don't overcrowd the pan, placing each batch to one side to keep warm while you fry the rest. Serve with the hollandaise and the potatoes.

To make the mint hollandaise
2 Whisk the egg yolks in a small bowl with the lemon juice and some salt. Slowly start to add the melted butter a little at a time, whisking the sauce as you do so. Stir in the mint and season with some pepper and a little more salt if necessary.

To cook the sweet baby new potatoes
3 Boil the potatoes in salted water until tender, then drain them in a colander.
4 Add the butter to the saucepan and heat until foaming. Return the potatoes to the pan with the butter and sprinkle on the sugar. Cook over a reasonably high heat for a minute, constantly moving the potatoes around in the butter and sugar. Season with a little more salt before serving.

Braised chicken

My children will only eat broad beans if the outer greyish skins are removed, but you can leave them on if they don't worry you.

SERVES 6

1kg chicken pieces, on the bone
4 tbsp dark soy sauce
4 tbsp Japanese rice wine
1 tbsp caster sugar
1 tsp salt
200g broad beans (podded weight)
2 tbsp olive oil
100ml Marsala wine
2 shallots, finely chopped
1 tsp grated fresh root ginger
3 spring onions, sliced

1 Place the chicken pieces in a bowl with the soy sauce, rice wine, sugar and salt and leave for 30 minutes or so. Preheat the oven to 200°C/Gas 6.
2 Meanwhile, prepare the broad beans. Cut a slash in the outer skin along the top or bottom of each broad bean before boiling them and they will pop out of the skins easily. Put the beans in a pan of boiling unsalted water and cook for about 5 minutes. Drain, and when the beans are cool enough to handle, slip off the skins.
3 Heat the olive oil in a large casserole dish and brown the chicken, a couple of pieces at a time. Watch them carefully as they will brown quickly because of the sugar in the marinade. Set each batch aside while you fry the rest.
4 Once all the chicken is browned, keep the casserole dish on the heat, add the Marsala wine and let it sizzle for 30 seconds. Throw in the shallots and ginger and return the chicken to the pan. Put a lid on the casserole, place it in the oven and cook for 45 minutes.
5 Add the broad beans and spring onions to the casserole and serve with rice.

Sirloin steaks with Dolcelatte and a rocket and courgette salad

I usually avoid using blue cheese in cooking, as it tends to overpower and dominate dishes. Dolcelatte is a mild blue cheese, however, and the perfect partner for these sirloin steaks. When the steaks have been fried and adorned with the cheese, which lazily melts on top, then served with the rocket and courgette salad they look almost too good to eat.

SERVES 6

6 sirloin steaks
olive oil
180g Dolcelatte cheese, cut into 6 slices
sea salt
freshly ground black pepper

Rocket and courgette salad
2 tbsp olive oil
300g courgettes, sliced into 1cm discs
220g rocket leaves
sea salt
freshly ground black pepper

Dressing
3 tbsp olive oil
½ tbsp balsamic vinegar
sea salt
freshly ground black pepper

1 Massage the steaks with a little olive oil on both sides. Heat a frying pan and cook the steaks, a couple at a time, for 1 minute. Turn the steaks over, season them with salt and pepper and lay a slice of Dolcelatte cheese on top of each one. The cheese will start to melt as the steak cooks. Cook for another minute for medium-rare steak.
2 Cook the rest of the steaks in the same way. Pour any juices left in the pan over the steaks and serve with the salad.

To prepare the rocket and courgette salad
3 Heat the olive oil in a frying pan. Add the courgettes and fry them until golden brown and tender. Season with salt and pepper. Place the rocket leaves in a serving bowl and scatter the courgettes on top. Mix the dressing ingredients and drizzle on to the salad.

Rice pudding and summer fruit tart

I used to think that rice pudding was nice and comforting but not much more than that. I have since discovered that it makes a great basis for a trifle, it is utterly fantastic as an ice cream and it makes a more than satisfactory tart filling, as I hope you will agree.

SERVES 6

Rice pudding
- 8 heaped tbsp pudding rice
- 300ml milk
- 400ml double cream
- ½ tsp vanilla bean paste
- 4 tbsp caster sugar
- 200ml whipped cream

Pastry
- 125g butter, at room temperature
- 90g caster sugar
- 1 egg
- 250g plain flour, plus extra for dusting work surface

Fruit topping
- 2 nectarines, stones removed and cut into 8 pieces each
- 200g strawberries, cut in half
- 150g raspberries
- 1 tbsp icing sugar, sieved

To make the rice pudding

1 Place all the ingredients, except the whipped cream, in a saucepan and bring to a simmer. Cook gently, uncovered, for 30 minutes, stirring occasionally to ensure that all the rice is cooked evenly. Set to one side to cool. Once cool, fold in the whipped cream.

To make the pastry

2 Place the butter and sugar in a food processor and whizz until light and creamy, then add the egg and mix again. Add the flour a little at a time, blending between each addition. Once you have added all the flour, turn the pastry out on to a floured work surface and bring it together with your hands. Wrap it in clingfilm and chill for 30 minutes.

3 Preheat the oven to 200°C/Gas 6. Roll out the pastry on a floured work surface and use it to line a 23cm tart tin. Trim the edges neatly, then lay a sheet of baking parchment over the pastry and pile some baking beans on top. Bake the tart case in the oven for 15 minutes, then remove the paper and beans and return the pastry to the oven for 10 minutes more. Leave to cool slightly.

To assemble the tart

4 Spoon the rice pudding on to the tart case. Decorate the top of the tart with the fruit and sprinkle with some icing sugar.

Lemon custard tart with raspberry sauce

This tart is delicious and very straightforward to make. It's quite big, so there should be enough left over for another night.

SERVES 8-10

Filling
600ml double cream
juice and grated zest of 2 lemons
3 egg yolks
2 eggs
3 tbsp caster sugar

Pastry
2 egg yolks
75g icing sugar
225g plain flour, plus extra for dusting the work surface
180g cold butter, cut into cubes

Raspberry sauce
200g fresh raspberries
50g icing sugar

To make the pastry

1 Grease a 28cm tart tin. Place all the ingredients in a food processor and whizz until the mixture resembles fine breadcrumbs. Turn the dough out on to the work surface and bring it together with your hands. It may look as though it is not going to come together, but be gentle – it will! This is foolproof pastry. Shape the pastry into a ball, wrap it in clingfilm and chill for 30 minutes.

To make the filling

2 Place all the ingredients in a mixing bowl and combine with a whisk.

To prepare the tart

3 Preheat the oven to 200°C/Gas 6. Roll out the pastry on a floured surface and use it to line the tart tin. Trim around the edge of the pastry. If your kitchen is warm, chill the pastry case in the fridge again for 20 minutes. This will stop the pastry shrinking in the oven.

4 Cover the pastry with a sheet of greaseproof paper and place some baking beans on top. Pop the tart tin on to a baking sheet and bake in the oven for 10 minutes. Remove the greaseproof paper and the beans and return the case to the oven for 5 minutes more.

5 Reduce the oven temperature to 180°C/Gas 4. Pour the lemon filling into the pastry case and bake the tart for 30 minutes. Serve with a little crème fraiche and the raspberry sauce.

To make the raspberry sauce

6 Whizz the raspberries and sugar together in a blender, then pass through a sieve.

Chicken and sweetcorn soup with crispy vegetable spring rolls

There's something very appealing about the combination of chicken and sweetcorn and this meal is a favourite with my children. Making the crispy vegetable rolls might seem a bit of a rigmarole, but get stuck in – they are definitely worth the effort.

SERVES 6

1 tbsp olive oil
1 tsp sesame oil
2 shallots, finely sliced
1 garlic clove, finely chopped
2cm piece of fresh root ginger, peeled and finely chopped
400g chicken thigh fillets, chopped into small pieces
100ml dry sherry
2 x 326g cans of sweetcorn, drained
2 litres chicken stock
1 tbsp dark soy sauce
2 tbsp finely chopped fresh coriander

Crispy vegetable spring rolls
40g fine egg noodles, cooked according to packet instructions, drained and roughly chopped
1 red pepper, cored and finely chopped
2 shallots, finely chopped
2 tsp fish sauce
1 garlic clove, finely chopped
80g bean sprouts, roughly chopped
1 egg white
3 tbsp grated carrot
2 tbsp chopped fresh coriander
250g filo pastry
olive oil, for frying
sea salt
freshly ground black pepper

1 Heat the olive oil and sesame oil in a large saucepan. Cook the shallots, garlic and ginger over a gentle heat for 3 minutes, then add the chicken. Increase the heat and cook for 5 minutes.
2 Pour on the sherry and let it simmer for 2 minutes. Add the sweetcorn, stock and soy sauce, then bring the soup back to a simmer. Cover the pan and cook gently for 15 minutes. Serve with the spring rolls.

To make the crispy vegetable spring rolls
3 Place all the ingredients, except the filo pastry and olive oil, in a bowl and mix them gently. Season with salt and pepper, then set to one side.
4 Lay a sheet of the filo pastry on your work surface. Using a sharp knife, cut it in half down its length. Take 1 piece and lay it out in front of you, then fold the short end closest to you over 3cm. Spoon a dessertspoon of the filling ingredient on to the pastry just above the overlap. Fold the long sides over 3cm, then roll the pastry up, enveloping the filling. Don't roll up the spring rolls too tightly. When you get to the end of the pastry, brush the end with a little olive oil to seal. Repeat to make the rest of the spring rolls.
5 Pour olive oil into a frying pan to a depth of about 2cm. Fry the spring rolls, a couple at a time, until golden brown all over, then set aside on kitchen paper. You can reheat the rolls in the oven when you've finished frying them all, but don't leave them rolled up and uncooked for too long, as the moisture from the filling penetrates the filo pastry and makes holes in it.

Prawn, spinach and potato curry

This is a good curry for a July evening. It is quite light, but filling enough for the family.

SERVES 6

2 tbsp whole coriander seeds
¼ tsp fenugreek seeds
1 tsp black peppercorns
10 dried curry leaves
2 tbsp olive oil
1 tsp black mustard seeds
1 onion, finely diced
2 garlic cloves, crushed
2cm piece of fresh root ginger, grated
¼ tsp turmeric
1 tbsp tamarind paste
200ml water
1 tsp salt
1 x 400g can of coconut milk
400g new potatoes, peeled
150g spinach leaves
300g cooked, shelled prawns

Boiled rice
500g basmati rice
½ tsp salt
750ml water

1 Put the coriander and fenugreek seeds and the peppercorns in a small frying pan. Toast them over a medium heat for a few minutes until they are smoking and have darkened slightly.
2 Place the spices with the curry leaves in a coffee grinder or a pestle and mortar, then grind them all to a fine powder. Place to one side.
3 Heat the olive oil in a saucepan. Add the mustard seeds and when they start to pop, add the onion, garlic and ginger. Fry gently for 3 minutes, then add the ground spices, turmeric, tamarind paste, water, salt, coconut milk, potatoes and spinach. Cook at a gentle simmer for 20 minutes.
4 Add the prawns, warm them through and serve the curry with boiled rice.

To prepare the boiled rice
5 Place the rice, salt and water in a large saucepan and bring to a lively boil. Reduce the heat to very low, cover the pan and cook the rice for 15 minutes. Stir once during the cooking time.
6 Remove the pan from the heat. Keep the rice covered and leave it undisturbed for 10 minutes more.

Pasta with courgettes, tomatoes and pancetta

A simple summer pasta dish that looks beautifully fresh and appetising.

SERVES 6

300g cherry tomatoes
2 tbsp olive oil
15g butter
300g courgettes, sliced into 1cm discs
100g pancetta, chopped
50ml white wine
2 tbsp roughly chopped fresh basil
600g pasta, such as tagliatelle
grated Parmesan cheese, to serve
sea salt
freshly ground black pepper

1 Preheat the oven to 150°C/Gas 2. Place the tomatoes in a small roasting tin, drizzle them with the olive oil and sprinkle with salt and pepper. Place the tomatoes in the oven to roast for 20 minutes.

2 In the meantime, heat the butter in a sauté pan. When it's sizzling, add the courgettes and pancetta and cook for 5 minutes over a medium heat. Reduce the heat and continue to cook for a further 5 minutes on a low heat. Add the wine and simmer for 1 minute, then add the cooked tomatoes. Scatter on the basil and season with plenty of salt and pepper. Remove from the heat.

3 Cook the pasta according to the packet instructions. Drain the pasta, then toss it with the sauce and serve with some grated Parmesan.

Pork escalopes with sage and pancetta sauce

I don't cook pork chops or pork steaks very often. Pork chops always seem rather large for children and I'm sometimes disappointed by the flavour of the pork available in supermarkets. Tasty pork is available in the UK, though, particularly in good butchers' shops, but you do need to look around. These pork escalopes make an appetising meal.

SERVES 6

6-8 pork escalopes, depending on their size
olive oil, for frying

Sage and pancetta sauce
10 sage leaves, finely chopped
70g pancetta, finely chopped
2 shallots, finely chopped
150ml Marsala wine
1 tbsp plain flour
400ml beef stock
2 tbsp crème fraiche
sea salt
freshly ground black pepper

Mashed potatoes
1kg potatoes, peeled and cut into quarters
200ml warm milk
40g butter
sea salt
freshly ground black pepper

1 Pat the escalopes with kitchen paper to make sure they are dry. Heat some olive oil in a large sauté pan and when it's hot, fry the escalopes, 2 at a time, for a few minutes on each side until nicely browned. Lay them in a ovenproof dish once they are browned.
2 Preheat the oven to 180°C/Gas 4. Return the pan to the heat and add a little more olive oil if needed. Add the sage leaves, pancetta and shallots and cook for 2 minutes until the pancetta is golden brown. Pour on the wine and let it simmer for 40 seconds or so. Sprinkle on the flour and stir until combined. Add the stock and simmer gently on a low heat for 10 minutes, then stir in the crème fraiche and check seasoning.
3 Pour the sauce over the escalopes and place the dish in the oven for 5 minutes. Serve with mashed potatoes.

To prepare the mashed potatoes
4 Boil the potatoes in salted water until tender. Pass the potatoes through a potato ricer or use your preferred method to mash them. Return them to the pan and place over a low heat. Add the butter and milk and gently combine. Check the seasoning and adjust as necessary.

Fried gurnard with green sauce and sautéed potatoes

A good green sauce can liven up most fish, chicken or red meat. Make up your own recipe if you are feeling adventurous, changing the spinach for rocket and adding more of one herb or another to produce a strong-flavoured sauce of the right consistency.

SERVES 6

6-8 gurnard fillets
olive oil, for frying
sea salt
freshly ground black pepper
wedges of lemon, for serving

Green sauce
100g spinach leaves
a small knob of butter
25g basil leaves
25g coriander leaves
25g flat-leaf parsley
2 tbsp capers, rinsed and drained
3 garlic cloves
40g white breadcrumbs
20g Parmesan cheese, finely grated
200ml olive oil
sea salt
freshly ground black pepper

Sautéed potatoes
1kg potatoes, peeled and cut into quarters
1 tbsp duck/goose fat
sea salt

1 If the fillets have skin on them, slash the skin 3 or 4 times with a sharp knife. This prevents the fillets from curling too much when you fry them.
2 Heat a little olive oil in a frying pan and fry a couple of fillets for 2 minutes on each side. Season them with salt and pepper, then place to one side while you cook the rest. Serve with wedges of fresh lemon, green sauce and sautéed potatoes.

To prepare the green sauce
3 First sauté the spinach leaves in the butter for a few minutes, until all the leaves have wilted completely.
4 Place the spinach leaves in a food processor with the herbs, capers, garlic, breadcrumbs and Parmesan cheese. Pulse for a few seconds and then add half the olive oil. Pulse again and add the rest of the oil. Keep pulsing until the ingredients are completely and finely blended. Loosen with a little more oil if necessary, then season with salt and pepper.

To prepare the sautéed potatoes
5 Cook the potatoes in salted water until tender. Drain, then once the potatoes are cool enough to handle, cut them into 1cm slices.
6 Heat the duck or goose fat in a large sauté pan and add the potatoes. Move them around gently as they cook so that they brown evenly. Sprinkle with salt.

Lamb and summer vegetables

A one-pot meal, which is quick and easy to prepare. If you can't get fresh peas, frozen ones will do just as well.

SERVES 6

1kg boned lamb shoulder, cut into cubes
2 tbsp seasoned flour
2-3 tbsp olive oil
1 onion, finely diced
100g carrots, peeled and diced
3 courgettes, sliced into 1cm discs
200ml dry sherry
200ml chicken stock
1 tbsp dark soy sauce
1 tbsp tomato purée
400g fresh peas (podded weight)
sea salt
freshly ground black pepper

Boiled rice
500g basmati rice
½ tsp salt
750ml water

1 Toss the cubed lamb in the seasoned flour. Heat 2 tablespoons of olive oil in a large saucepan and brown the lamb in small batches, placing each batch to one side in a bowl while you brown the rest.
2 Keep the pan on the heat and add a little more oil if needed. Fry the onion, carrots and courgettes for 5 minutes, until the onion has softened. Place the vegetables to one side with the lamb. Add the sherry to the saucepan and simmer for 1 minute, stirring to scrape up all the sticky bits stuck to the bottom of the pan.
3 Return the meat and vegetables to the saucepan. Pour on the stock and soy sauce, then add the tomato purée and the peas. Season the stew and leave it to simmer very gently, uncovered, for 1 hour. Serve with boiled rice.

To prepare the boiled rice
4 Place the rice, salt and water in a large saucepan and bring to a lively boil. Reduce the heat to very low, cover the pan and cook the rice for 15 minutes. Stir once during the cooking time.
5 Remove the pan from the heat. Keep the rice covered and leave it undisturbed for 10 minutes more.

Chicken, turkey and tarragon pie

There are often some grey, drizzly days in July when you feel like something comforting to eat. This pie is just the thing.

SERVES 6

2 tbsp olive oil
1 onion, finely chopped
400g chicken breast fillets, chopped into small chunks
500g turkey breast fillets, chopped into small chunks
350g pork sausages, roughly chopped
2 tbsp plain flour
350ml chicken stock
100ml double cream
1 tsp finely chopped fresh tarragon
1 x 230g sheet of ready-rolled puff pastry
sea salt
freshly ground black pepper

Peas and broad beans
200g broad beans, podded weight
200g garden peas, podded weight
sea salt
freshly ground black pepper

1 Preheat the oven to 200°C/Gas 6. Heat the olive oil in a saucepan or sauté pan, add the onion and fry over a gentle heat for 5 minutes.
2 Throw in the chicken, turkey and sausages and cook for 5 minutes, stirring constantly.
3 Sprinkle on the flour and stir it in, then add the chicken stock, cream and tarragon and stir. Season with salt and pepper to taste, then spoon the chicken mixture into a pie or gratin dish.
4 Lay the pastry over the filling and bake in the oven for 20 minutes. Serve with the peas and broad beans.

To prepare the peas and broad beans
5 Cut a slash in the outer skin along the top or bottom of each broad bean before boiling them and they will pop out of the skins easily.
6 Place the beans and peas in a saucepan of boiling water and simmer for 4 minutes. Skin the broad beans, then season with salt and pepper.

Peaches and cream cheesecake

Peaches and cream are a classic combination and just saying the words makes me eager to get stuck into this dessert. When I was growing up, only tinned peaches were available and we would often have them with 'dream topping', rather than fresh cream, which was considered a real luxury.

SERVES 6–8

300g digestive biscuits
120g melted butter
700g mascarpone cheese
3 egg yolks
3 eggs
1 teaspoon vanilla extract
150g caster sugar

Peach topping
4 peaches, cut into quarters
100ml elderflower cordial
400ml double cream

1 Place the biscuits in a food processor and blitz them to fine crumbs. Add the melted butter and give the biscuit crumbs another brief whizz.
2 Turn the buttery crumbs into the bottom of a 24cm spring-clip cake tin and press them down well over the base. Place the tin in the fridge for 20 minutes to chill and firm the biscuit base.
3 Spoon the mascarpone cheese into a mixing bowl and gently mix it with a wooden spoon until smooth. Gradually add the egg yolks and eggs, stirring gently until you have a creamy, smooth mixture. Add the vanilla extract and sugar and mix again. Pour the mixture on to the chilled biscuit base. Preheat the oven to 150°C/Gas 2.
4 Place the cake tin in a nest of aluminium foil – 2 sheets should be enough – and then place the tin and nest in a roasting tin. Pour 2cm of boiling water into the tray and place in the oven to bake for 1 hour. There should still be a wobble to the centre of the cheesecake when it is ready. Leave the oven on.
5 To prepare the topping, put the peach quarters in an ovenproof dish with the cordial. Bake for 20 minutes at 150°C/Gas 2, until the peaches are soft but not mushy.
6 When the cheesecake has cooled completely, whip the cream and spoon it on to the cheesecake. When the peaches are cool, arrange them on top.

Blueberry tart

A mass of blueberries is piled high in a pastry case, making this tart totally seductive. Once the tart is cut, the berries ooze their juice temptingly.

MAKES 1 X 24CM TART

600g blueberries
150g caster sugar
juice of 1 lemon
2 tbsp cornflour

Pastry
300g plain flour, plus extra for dusting the work surface
60g caster sugar
½ tsp baking powder
grated zest of 1 lemon
160g cold butter, cut into cubes, plus extra for greasing the tin
1 egg
1 egg yolk
50ml double cream
½ tsp vanilla extract

1 Grease a 24cm tart tin. To make the pastry, place the flour, sugar, baking powder and lemon zest in a food processor and whizz briefly to combine. Add the butter and process until the mixture resembles breadcrumbs.
2 Add the egg, egg yolk and cream and process just until the mixture starts to bind together. Turn the dough out on to a floured work surface and bring together to form a ball. Wrap in clingfilm and chill for 30 minutes.
3 Place the blueberries, sugar, lemon juice and cornflour in a large bowl and mix together with a metal spoon. Be quite heavy-handed, as you want some of the blueberries to split slightly. Leave for 20 minutes. Preheat the oven to 200°C/Gas 6.
4 Roll out the chilled pastry on a floured work surface and use it to line the tart tin. Place a sheet of baking parchment over the pastry and pile in some baking beans. Bake the tart case in the oven for 10 minutes, then remove the beans and paper and return to the oven for 5 minutes more.
5 Pile the blueberries into the baked pastry case and put it back in the oven for 30 minutes.

Courgette and tomato soup

If you grow your own vegetables you will be inundated with courgettes at this time of year. I use turnip in this soup as well, since we have such a lot in the garden, but you could use potato instead.

SERVES 6

600g courgettes, roughly chopped
500g fresh tomatoes, roughly chopped
400g turnip, peeled and chopped
2 tbsp olive oil
1.5 litres vegetable stock (a stock cube is fine)
sea salt
freshly ground black pepper

1 Put the courgettes, tomatoes and turnip in a large saucepan with the olive oil. As soon as the vegetables start to fry, cover the saucepan with a lid and reduce the heat. Cook for 10 minutes, then pour on the stock. Bring to a simmer, cover the pan and cook gently for 30 minutes.

2 Blend the soup in a food processor or liquidiser, then for super smoothness pass it through a sieve. Return the soup to the pan and season well with salt and pepper. Warm the soup through and serve with lots of bread.

Salmon, chard and potato gratin

Swiss chard, a member of the beet family, is a versatile vegetable. In thick soups and stews it retains its shape and flavour well, but it can also be mixed with meat and fish, adding an extra dimension to gratins, meatballs and pie fillings.

SERVES 6

700g potatoes, peeled and cut into quarters
500g salmon fillet, skinned
300g chard leaves
25g butter
1 onion, finely chopped
25g flour
250ml milk
2 tbsp crème fraiche
50g Parmesan cheese, grated
sea salt
freshly ground black pepper

1 Cook the potatoes in salted water until tender, then cut them into 2cm chunks. Cut the salmon flesh into 2cm chunks.
2 Bring a large pan of water to the boil. Add the chard leaves and cook them for 1 minute. Drain, and when the chard is cool enough to handle, press out any excess water.
3 Return the empty pan to the stove, add the butter and melt on a medium heat. Add the onion and fry gently for 10 minutes until completely soft and transparent. Add the flour and stir. Take the pan off the heat and add the milk, pouring it in gradually and stirring constantly.
4 Return the pan to the heat and continue to stir. Once the sauce has come to a simmer and thickened, stir in the crème fraiche. Reduce the heat to very low and cook the sauce for 5 minutes, stirring occasionally. Season with salt and pepper.
5 Preheat the grill. Chop the chard roughly with a sharp knife and stir it into the white sauce. Add the raw salmon and potato chunks to the sauce, then spoon the mixture into a gratin dish. Sprinkle with the Parmesan cheese and place under a grill for 10 minutes, so that the salmon cooks through and the cheese browns.

Deli-style supper

An Italian meal of antipasti, or a deli-style supper as it is sometimes called, is perfect for a summer evening, especially if you use good quality ingredients. I've suggested home-made bread rolls, roasted courgettes and tomatoes, and some salad leaves dressed lightly with olive oil and balsamic vinegar. The goat's cheese, Pecorino and mozzarella go beautifully with the bread. Include anything else that tickles your tastebuds.

SERVES 6

3 courgettes, sliced thinly lengthways
1 tbsp olive oil
fresh basil leaves
extra virgin olive oil
15 cherry tomatoes, left whole
1 tsp balsamic vinegar
sea salt
freshly ground black pepper

Rosemary and raisin bread rolls
500g strong white bread flour
1½ tsp salt
1 tbsp finely chopped rosemary
250g raisins
100ml warm water
1 x 7g sachet of dried yeast
3 eggs
2 tbsp natural yoghurt
3 tbsp olive oil

Other antipasti
2 tbsp olives
125g buffalo mozzarella
200g goat's cheese
12 thin slices Pecorino cheese
2 handfuls salad leaves

To prepare the courgettes

1 Preheat the oven to 200°C/Gas 6. Place the courgettes and tomatoes on a baking tray, drizzle them with olive oil and season with salt and pepper. Place them in the oven for 20 minutes.

2 Transfer the courgettes and tomatoes to a plate and dress them with a little balsamic vinegar and a scattering of basil leaves. Serve with the bread rolls and other deli items.

To make the rosemary and raisin bread rolls

3 Place the flour, salt, rosemary and raisins in a mixing bowl. Put the warm water in a small bowl, sprinkle in the yeast and leave for 5 minutes.

4 Pour the yeast mixture on to the flour, add the eggs, yoghurt and olive oil and mix to make a dough. Turn the dough out on to a floured surface and knead for 5 minutes. If the dough is too sticky, add a little more flour. Put the dough back in the bowl, cover and leave in a draught-free place for 1 hour.

5 Divide the dough into 6 pieces and knead into smooth rolls. Place them on a baking sheet, cover and leave to rise for 20 minutes. Preheat the oven to 200°C/Gas 6.

6 Using a sharp knife, cut a slash in the top of each roll and then bake in the oven for 30 minutes.

Broken meringues with berry sauce and cream

Meringues were one of my favourite treats when I was a child and they still are. I love the way they tempt the eye, then delight the taste buds.

SERVES 6

3 egg whites
175g caster sugar
a drop of pink food colouring

Berry sauce
300g strawberries
200g blueberries
225g raspberries
2 tbsp caster sugar

Cream
200ml double cream
2 tbsp Greek yoghurt

1 Preheat the oven to 120°C/Gas ½ and line a baking sheet with baking parchment.
2 Put the egg whites in a mixing bowl and whisk until they form stiff peaks. I find it is almost impossible to do this successfully by hand so I use an electric hand-whisk or a food mixer.
3 Add the sugar, a tablespoon at a time, whisking in each addition until all the sugar has been incorporated. Add the food colouring and mix it in gently.
4 Spoon separate tablespoons of the meringue on to the baking parchment and bake for 50 minutes.

To make the berry sauce
5 Place the fruit and sugar in a saucepan. Put a lid on the pan, place over a low heat and simmer gently for 10 minutes.

To finish the dish
6 Whisk the cream until it forms soft billowing peaks, then fold in the yoghurt.
7 Place the meringues in a bowl with the cream and berry sauce, gently break them up and stir before serving in small bowls.

Strawberry sponge pudding

This dessert makes the perfect pudding for a lazy July Sunday lunch.

SERVES 6

- 300g self-raising flour, plus extra for flouring the bowl and dusting the work surface
- a pinch of salt
- 3 level tsp baking powder
- 150g cold butter, cut into cubes, plus extra for greasing the bowl
- 75g caster sugar
- grated zest of 1 lemon
- 100ml water
- 300g strawberries
- cream, for serving

1 Butter and flour the inside of a 500ml pudding basin. Place the flour, salt and baking powder in a food processor. Add the butter to the dry ingredients and whizz until the mixture resembles breadcrumbs.

2 Stir in the sugar and lemon zest, then start to add the water a little at a time until the dough starts to come together. You may need to add a little more water. Turn the dough out on to a floured surface and form it into a ball, then divide into two-thirds and one-third.

3 Roll out the larger piece of dough with a rolling pin and use it to line the pudding basin. Pile the fruit into the basin. Roll out the remaining piece of the dough into a circle large enough to place over the fruit like a lid. Seal this in place with your finger and thumb. Cover the top of the basin with a circle of baking parchment, then cover the whole basin with foil and tie it in place with string.

4 You need a large saucepan with a lid. Put the basin into the saucepan and pour in just-boiled water around the basin to a depth of about 3cm. Put the lid on the pan and simmer the pudding for 1 hour, pouring more hot water into the pan when necessary.

5 At the end of the cooking time, carefully remove the basin from the saucepan and take off the foil and baking parchment. Invert the basin on to a serving plate and the pudding should come out easily. It will probably collapse but the beautiful taste more than makes up for any aesthetic shortcomings. Serve with cream.

Raspberry and gooseberry cream tart

The light green of the gooseberries and the pink of the raspberries make this tart look so pleasing to the eye that everyone will want to tuck in.

MAKES 1 X 23CM TART

Cream filling
250g milk
½ tsp vanilla bean paste
3 egg yolks
25g cornflour
60g caster sugar
25g butter, cut into cubes

Fruit topping
15g butter
1 tbsp soft brown sugar
350g fresh gooseberries, topped and tailed
340g fresh raspberries
icing sugar, for dusting

Pastry
125g butter, room temperature
90g caster sugar
½ tsp vanilla bean paste
1 large egg
250g plain flour, plus extra for dusting the work surface

To make the pastry

1 Cream the butter and sugar in a food processor until light and fluffy. Add the vanilla bean paste and egg and mix briefly. Gradually add the flour and mix, as briefly as possible, until combined. Turn the pastry out on to a floured surface and form it into a ball. Wrap it in clingfilm and chill in the fridge for 30 minutes.

2 Preheat the oven to 200°C/Gas 6. Roll out the pastry on a floured surface and use it to line a 23cm tart tin. Cover the pastry with a sheet of baking parchment and pour on some baking beans. Place the tart tin on a baking sheet and bake for 15 minutes. Remove the parchment and beans and return the tart case to the oven for 5 minutes. Leave to one side to cool completely.

To prepare the cream filling

3 Heat the milk in a saucepan with the vanilla bean paste until almost boiling. Beat the egg yolks, cornflour and sugar in a bowl until well combined, then pour the hot milk on to the eggs, beating as you go.

4 Return the mixture to the saucepan. Add the butter and stir constantly over a low heat until the liquid has thickened. I tend to use a whisk at this point to avoid lumps forming. Leave to one side to cool.

To prepare the fruit topping

5 Heat the butter and sugar in a sauté pan. When the butter is foaming, add the gooseberries and cook on a low heat until they start to burst and feel soft to the back of a metal spoon. Cool completely and then carefully stir in the raspberries.

To assemble the tart

6 Spoon the filling into the tart case and then top with the fruit just before serving. Dust with icing sugar.

In August gardeners can start to relax a little and sit back to enjoy the fruits of their labours. If we're lucky, the evenings continue to be long and balmy and we can spend a lot of time out of doors. Many of us will still be looking for new ways to cook courgettes, which continue to crop plentifully. Make the most of nectarines and peaches coming from the continent, as they are almost always a delight. And the British herbs available this month are wonderful with barbecued meat and fish, or chopped finely in an omelette or tart. The variety of local produce on offer is mouth-wateringly brilliant at this time of year and good food can be prepared with little effort. Fruit trees all over the country are heavy with good things, the plums and greengages are ripening, and will be followed closely by pears and apples. The game season starts on August 12th and then we can begin to enjoy this truly organic meat.

August

Beef patties with spicy salsa

These are spicy, Indian-style burgers.

SERVES 6

2 tsp coriander seeds
2 tsp cumin seeds
1 tsp fennel seeds
1 tsp fenugreek seeds
1kg minced beef
1 onion, very finely chopped
2 garlic cloves, crushed
1½ tsp salt
2 tbsp olive oil, for frying
freshly ground black pepper

Spicy salsa
2 tbsp olive oil
2 shallots, finely chopped
400g tomatoes, roughly chopped
½ red chilli, seeded and finely chopped
1 tbsp finely chopped fresh coriander
sea salt

1 Place the spices in a frying pan and toast over a medium heat, shaking them to ensure they toast evenly. As soon as they start to darken and you can smell their aroma, remove the spices from the pan and grind to a fine powder in a pestle and mortar or a coffee grinder.
2 Tip the spice powder into a mixing bowl and add the beef, onion, garlic, salt and a grinding of black pepper. Mix all the ingredients evenly and shape into 12 small patties. Leave these in the fridge to chill until you are ready to cook them.
3 Heat the oil in a frying pan. Add 4 patties and brown on one side, then turn them over to brown on the other side. Set these aside while you cook the rest of the patties in the same way.
4 Return all the patties to the pan on a very low heat to finish cooking through and then serve with a dollop of salsa and some naan bread (see page 685). A salad on the side would be good.

To prepare the spicy salsa
5 Heat the olive oil in a frying pan, then add the shallots and cook over a medium heat for 1 minute. Add the tomatoes and cook for about 5 minutes, mashing them with a wooden spoon. Add the chilli and coriander and season with salt. Spoon the salsa into a serving bowl.

Avocado, tomato and mozzarella salad with Parmesan toast

A classic caprese salad is made with mozzarella and tomato, but I like to add avocado. This is a light and refreshing supper, just right for this time of year.

SERVES 6

700g cherry tomatoes, cut in half
2-3 tbsp olive oil
1 tbsp finely chopped fresh oregano leaves
1 tbsp soft brown sugar
4 avocados
250g mozzarella cheese, sliced
½ tbsp balsamic vinegar

Dressing
2 good handfuls of fresh basil leaves, finely chopped
2 tbsp olive oil
1 shallot, finely diced
sea salt
freshly ground black pepper

Parmesan toast
6–8 slices of sourdough bread
2 garlic cloves, cut in half
50g Parmesan cheese, finely grated

1 Set your oven at the lowest temperature – 100°C/Gas ¼. Place the halved cherry tomatoes in a roasting tray and spoon 2–3 tablespoons of olive oil over them. Sprinkle on the oregano and sugar, then season with salt and pepper. Place the tomatoes in the oven for 15 minutes to warm through.
2 Cut the avocados in half, remove the stones and slice the flesh. Lay the slices of avocado and mozzarella on a serving plate. Remember that the avocado will go brown if you leave it too long before serving. Spoon the tomatoes on to the serving dish as well and drizzle with the balsamic vinegar.

To make the dressing
3 Place the chopped basil in a mortar with the olive oil, shallot and some salt and black pepper and mash with a pestle to make a green sauce. Drizzle this over the cheese and avocado and serve with Parmesan toast.

To make the Parmesan toast
4 Toast the slices of sourdough on one side. When done, drizzle the other side with olive oil and rub with some garlic. Sprinkle on the Parmesan cheese and place under the grill again until brown.

Green tomato and garlic sauce with pasta

This is a great way of using up all those green tomatoes left at the end of the summer in Britain. Be brave with the garlic and trust me that you really do need this quantity to offset the sharpness of the tomatoes. This is a quick dish to make and very satisfying.

SERVES 6

3 tbsp olive oil
1kg green tomatoes, cored and roughly chopped
6 garlic cloves, finely chopped
2 tbsp roughly chopped basil
500g penne pasta
grated Parmesan cheese, for serving
sea salt
freshly ground black pepper

1 Heat the olive oil in a sauté pan. When it's hot, add the green tomatoes and cook on a medium heat for 45 minutes, stirring occasionally. Add the garlic and cook for 5 minutes.
2 Cook the pasta according to the instructions on the packet and drain.
3 Season the sauce with the basil and salt and pepper and serve with the pasta and grated Parmesan.

Kedgeree

This is just one of many variations to the traditional kedgeree recipe. It can be eaten hot or cold and is definitely worth adding to your repertoire.

SERVES 6

4 eggs
olive oil
400g smoked pollack, cod or haddock
750ml vegetable stock
1 onion, finely chopped
1 tbsp curry powder
2cm piece of cinnamon stick
4 cardamom pods
¼ tsp ground turmeric
400g frozen petit pois
500g basmati rice
160ml canned coconut cream
2 tbsp finely chopped fresh coriander
mango chutney, for serving
sea salt

1 Beat the eggs briefly in a glass bowl. Heat a little olive oil in a frying pan and pour in the eggs. Make an omelette, chop it up roughly and place to one side.
2 Place the fish in a roasting tin and pour in the vegetable stock. Put the tin on top of the stove and simmer the fish for 4 minutes. Drain off the stock and place to one side. Make sure that the volume of the stock is still 750ml – if not add a little water. Place the fish to one side.
3 Heat 2 tablespoons of olive oil in a large saucepan, add the onion and cook it gently over a low heat for 5 minutes. Sprinkle on the curry powder, add the cinnamon stick, cardamom and turmeric and stir.
4 Add the peas and rice, then stir and pour on the reserved stock. Season with a little salt and bring to a good simmer. Cover the pan, reduce the heat and cook very gently for 15 minutes.
5 Remove the pan from the heat and leave covered for a further 10 minutes. Stir in the fish, omelette, coconut cream and coriander and serve with some mango chutney on the side.

Lamb and puy lentils

Cooking is about making things look good, as well as taste delicious – food that is pleasing to the eye adds to the whole experience of eating. What I love about this dish are its subdued colours – the browns of the lentils and lamb and the rich purple of the aubergine.

SERVES 6

1kg leg of lamb, boned
olive oil
1 aubergine, cut into 2cm cubes
2 shallots, finely chopped
½ celeriac, peeled and cut into 1cm cubes
200g puy lentils
400ml vegetable stock
100ml red wine
2 sprigs of rosemary
sea salt
freshly ground black pepper

1 Trim the papery fat from the lamb. Slice the meat into pieces about 2cm thick and cut these in half to make quite big chunks of meat.
2 Heat 2 tablespoons of oil in a large pan and brown the lamb chunks in small batches, placing each batch to one side while you brown the rest.
3 Meanwhile, place the aubergine cubes in a colander, add a good sprinkling of salt and leave for 30 minutes. Pat the cubes dry with kitchen paper. This helps to reduce any bitter flavour and also means they absorb less oil when cooked.
4 Once the lamb is browned, pour a little more olive oil into the empty pan and add the shallots, aubergine and celeriac. Brown them for 5 minutes on a medium heat, then add the lentils, stock and wine and stir.
5 Return the lamb to the pan. Add the rosemary and season with salt and pepper. Cover the pan and cook at a slow simmer for 30 minutes, stirring once or twice. Serve with a green leaf salad.

Stuffed chicken breasts with roast potatoes

These chicken breasts are stuffed with the good flavours of the Mediterranean. If you are careful when frying the breasts you should not lose too much of the stuffing in the pan. You'll need six cocktail sticks for securing the stuffed breasts.

SERVES 6

6 chicken breasts
2–3 tbsp olive oil
1 shallot, finely chopped
1 garlic clove, finely chopped
1 medium courgette, trimmed and diced
1 tbsp capers, rinsed and finely chopped
3 salted anchovies, finely chopped
20g fresh basil, finely chopped
1 tbsp pitted green olives, finely chopped
200ml Marsala wine
20g butter
freshly ground black pepper

Roast potatoes
1kg potatoes, peeled, rinsed and cut in quarters
2 tbsp olive oil
sea salt

1 To prepare the chicken breasts, lay each breast between 2 sheets of foil and give it a good bash with a rolling pin until it is about 7mm thick. Trim the breasts of any flappy bits at the sides – you can use these later.
2 Heat 2 tablespoons of oil in a sauté pan. Add the shallot, garlic and courgette and cook for 5 minutes, stirring occasionally so that the garlic does not burn and everything cooks evenly. Tip everything into a small bowl and keep the pan and oil to use again. Add the capers, anchovies, basil and olives to the bowl. You won't need any salt but a good grinding of pepper won't go amiss.
3 Lay a chicken breast on a board and spoon a tablespoonful of the mixture on to one end. Roll up the breast and secure it with a cocktail stick. Repeat with the remaining breasts and mixture.
4 Return the sauté pan to the heat and add more oil if necessary. Brown the breasts, 3 at a time, turning them carefully so that the stuffing remains inside. Transfer the browned breasts to a casserole dish. Preheat the oven to 200°C/Gas 6.
5 Keep the sauté pan on the heat and add the wine, butter and the bits of chicken that you trimmed off earlier. Simmer for 2 minutes, then season with pepper and pour over the chicken breasts. Cover the casserole dish with a lid or some foil and pop it in the oven for 40 minutes. Serve with roast potatoes and a green salad.

To prepare the roast potatoes
6 Preheat the oven to 220°C/Gas 6. Boil the potatoes in salted water for 5 minutes. Drain and place them in a roasting tin and toss them with the olive oil. Roast for 45–50 minutes until golden.

Grilled salmon with celeriac coleslaw and roasted new potatoes

In the quest for new ways to cook food and create the wow factor at the table it's easy to forget that simple preparation and cooking can produce the best results. Grilled salmon with fresh coleslaw makes a lovely meal.

SERVES 6

6 salmon fillets
olive oil
a squeeze of fresh lemon juice
balsamic vinegar, for serving
sea salt
freshly ground black pepper

Celeriac coleslaw
½ celeriac, peeled
1 apple
1 pear
1 celery stalk
2 tbsp roughly chopped coriander
1 x 240g jar of rapeseed mayonnaise
1 tsp Dijon mustard
1 tsp creamed horseradish
2 tbsp roughly chopped walnuts
sea salt
freshly ground black pepper

Roasted new potatoes
750g baby new potatoes, cut in half
1 tbsp olive oil
sea salt

1 Drizzle the salmon fillets with a little olive oil. Place the fillets under a hot grill, skin-side up, for 4 minutes, then turn them over and grill for another 4 minutes. Season with salt and pepper and a squeeze of lemon juice.
2 Serve the salmon fillets on top of a couple of spoonfuls of coleslaw, with the potatoes on the side. Drizzle each serving with a little balsamic vinegar.

To prepare the celeriac coleslaw
3 Cut the celeriac into matchstick thin pieces. You can grate it, but I think this makes it look a bit mushy. Cut the apple, pear and celery into matchsticks too and place them all in a serving bowl with the coriander.
4 Mix the mayonnaise, mustard and horseradish in a small bowl and season with salt and pepper. Stir this into the celeriac and fruit, then scatter the walnuts on top.

To cook the new potatoes
5 Preheat the oven to 220°C/Gas 7. Place the potatoes in a roasting tin with the olive oil. Season the potatoes with salt and roast in the oven for 45–50 minutes, turning them occasionally.

Black and blueberry pie

Just the title of this recipe makes my mouth water. Before you have cooked it you can imagine the dark juices oozing up over the pastry in that tantalising way. Blackberries have a unique flavour that intensifies when cooked.

SERVES 6

450g blueberries
450g blackberries
50g cornflour
3 tbsp white sugar
grated zest of 1 lemon
1 tbsp water

Pastry
280g plain flour
140g cold butter, cut into cubes
1 tbsp caster sugar
1 egg yolk, beaten with 1 tbsp cold water

1 To make the pastry, place the flour and butter in a food processor and whizz until the mixture resembles breadcrumbs. Add the sugar and mix again briefly, then add the egg yolk and water and mix to combine. Turn out the mixture on to a floured surface and form into a ball of dough. Wrap the dough in clingfilm and chill for at least 30 minutes.
2 Put the fruit, cornflour, sugar, lemon zest and water in a small saucepan and warm through on a low heat for 5 minutes. Set aside.
3 Preheat the oven to 200°C/Gas 6. Grease a 24–25cm pie tin. Divide your pastry into 2 pieces, 1 slightly larger than the other. Roll out the larger piece and use it to line the tin.
4 Spoon the filling into the pie tin and roll out the remaining pieces of pastry to lay on top. Trim the edges and seal with a fork. Place the pie dish on a baking sheet and bake for 35 minutes.

White chocolate, rhubarb and strawberry trifle

Rhubarb and strawberries go beautifully together.

SERVES 6

Trifle sponge
3 eggs
80g caster sugar
70g plain flour
a pinch of salt

Rhubarb and strawberry
200g rhubarb, trimmed and cut into 1cm chunks
2 tbsp brown sugar
grated zest of 1 orange
200g strawberries

Custard
4 egg yolks
1 egg
1 tsp vanilla extract
75g caster sugar
300ml double cream
250ml whole milk

White chocolate topping
200g white chocolate, broken into chunks
250ml double cream

To make the trifle sponge
1 Grease and line a 23cm cake tin. Preheat the oven to 180°C/Gas 4. Whisk the eggs and sugar in a bowl with an electric hand-whisk until thick and mousse-like. This takes about 4 minutes. Using a metal spoon, fold in the flour and salt, then spoon the mixture into the tin. Bake for 20 minutes. Place the cake on a wire rack to cool.

To prepare the rhubarb and strawberries
2 Place the rhubarb, sugar and zest in a saucepan over a high heat. As soon as the rhubarb starts to cook, reduce the heat to low, cover the pan and cook for 5 minutes, stirring occasionally. Add the strawberries and cook for a minute longer. Place to one side to cool a little.

To make the custard
3 Beat the egg yolks and egg in a heatproof bowl with the vanilla and sugar. Mix the cream and milk and heat in a microwave or on the stove until almost boiling.
4 Whisk the cream and milk into the egg and sugar mixture in the glass bowl and place it over a saucepan of water on a medium heat. Stir until the custard starts to thicken and coats the back of the spoon.

To make the white chocolate topping
5 Place the chocolate in a glass bowl. Place the bowl over a saucepan of simmering water, making sure the water does not touch the bottom. Leave until the chocolate starts to melt and then stir gently.
6 Pour the double cream into a mixing bowl and beat it with a whisk until it has a thick, smooth, billowy consistency. Don't over beat as it will turn to butter. Fold the cooled white chocolate into the cream.

To assemble the trifle
7 Cut the cake into chunks and place these in the bottom of a glass serving bowl. Spoon in the cooked fruit, then pour on the custard and spoon on the chocolate topping. Chill until ready to serve.

Mediterranean rabbit stew

Many people aren't keen on the idea of eating rabbit, but please try it – you'll be converted.

SERVES 6

- 1 small aubergine, cut into 3cm chunks
- 2 medium courgettes, cut into 3cm chunks
- a large knob of butter
- 2 tbsp olive oil
- 2 rabbits, each jointed into 8 pieces
- 1 onion, finely chopped
- 2 garlic cloves, finely chopped
- 2 celery stalks, finely chopped
- 70g pancetta, chopped
- 200ml Marsala wine
- 2 medium tomatoes, roughly chopped
- 2 or 3 sprigs of fresh oregano
- sea salt

1 Put the chunks of aubergine and courgette in a colander and sprinkle them with a good teaspoon of salt. Leave them for at least 30 minutes, then pat dry with kitchen paper.
2 Heat the butter and oil in a large saucepan and brown the rabbit joints, a few at a time. Put each batch in a bowl while you brown the rest.
3 When all the rabbit is browned, keep the pan on the heat and add the onion, garlic, celery and pancetta. Cook for 10 minutes, stirring occasionally.
4 Put the rabbit back in the pan and add the Marsala wine. Cook for 3 minutes, then add the tomatoes, aubergine, courgette and oregano. Bring to a simmer and cook gently for 1 ½ hours until the rabbit is tender. Check the seasoning and serve with a rocket salad and crusty bread.

Roasted vegetable salad

It has been a challenge to devise plenty of recipes that don't include meat for this book, but well worth while. I do think we should try to eat meat less often and this is easier during the summer. When I do prepare a vegetarian meal, I'm surprised at how much I enjoy eating it.

1 Preheat the oven to 200°C/Gas 6. Place the beetroots on a large piece of foil and add 2 tablespoons of olive oil, a good pinch of salt and a grinding of pepper. Wrap the beetroots in the foil and place the parcel in a roasting tin. Bake for 40 minutes.
2 Remove the beetroots from the foil, tip them into the tin and add the peppers, courgettes and onion. Pour on another tablespoon of olive oil and season with salt and pepper, then return the tin to the oven for 30 minutes.
3 Trim, peel and quarter the beetroots and place them in a serving dish with the other roasted vegetables. Add the tomatoes, cucumber, herbs, feta cheese, olives and lettuce.
4 Heat a tablespoon of olive oil in a frying pan and fry the haloumi pieces until golden brown, then add them to the salad.
5 Mix the dressing ingredients and dress the salad before serving.

SERVES 6

3 beetroots, scrubbed clean
olive oil
2 red peppers, cored and sliced into 2cm long pieces
3 courgettes, sliced into 1cm thick discs
1 red onion, peeled and cut into quarters
6 tomatoes, cut into quarters
1 cucumber, cut into 2cm chunks
1 tbsp finely chopped flat-leaf parsley
1 tbsp finely chopped fresh mint leaves
200g feta cheese, cut into 1.5cm pieces
2 tbsp Kalamata olives
1 cos lettuce or similar, roughly chopped
225g haloumi cheese, sliced into 3cm pieces
sea salt
freshly ground black pepper

Dressing
3 tbsp olive oil
½ tbsp balsamic vinegar
sea salt
freshly ground black pepper

Pasta al forno

This is one of those useful meals you can prepare in advance and then pop into the oven when you're ready. Great served with garlic bread and a fresh green salad.

SERVES 6

- 100g Swiss chard leaves, roughly chopped
- 2 tbsp olive oil
- 200g green courgettes, trimmed and diced
- 1 garlic clove, finely chopped
- 25g fresh basil leaves
- 2 tbsp water
- 25g butter
- 25g flour
- 500ml milk
- 2 tbsp mascarpone cheese
- 100g Parmesan cheese, finely grated
- 500g penne pasta
- 4 plum tomatoes, sliced
- extra virgin olive oil
- sea salt
- freshly ground black pepper

1 Place the chard leaves in a small saucepan with the olive oil and gently sauté them for 5 minutes over a medium heat. Add the courgettes, garlic and most of the basil. Season with salt and pepper, cover the pan and continue to cook for 10 minutes on a low heat.
2 Transfer the vegetables to a liquidiser or food processor, add the water and blitz until smooth. Place to one side.
3 Put the empty saucepan back on a low heat – you don't need to clean it – and melt the butter. Stir in the flour and cook for 1 minute. Remove the pan from the heat and gradually stir in the milk, mixing constantly with a wooden spoon. Season with salt and pepper and cook the sauce on a low heat for 5 minutes.
4 Add the liquidised vegetables to the sauce, then stir in the mascarpone cheese and half the Parmesan cheese. Preheat the oven to 200°C/Gas 6.
5 Cook the pasta according to the packet instructions. Drain the pasta, tip it back into the pan, add the sauce and mix well.
6 Spoon half the pasta into a lasagne or gratin dish. Place a layer of sliced tomatoes on top, then add a drizzle of olive oil and a sprinkling of Parmesan cheese. Add the rest of the pasta, then another layer of tomatoes, the rest of the basil and Parmesan cheese and finally a good drizzle of olive oil. Bake in the oven for 20 minutes until heated through and bubbling.

Pork with summer vegetables

This one-pot meal is quick to prepare. Pork is often overlooked as the basis for a stew, but it works just as well as beef or lamb.

SERVES 6

1 tbsp olive oil
1kg pork loin, cut into cubes
1 onion, finely chopped
2 celery stalks, chopped
100ml Marsala wine
250ml vegetable stock
(a stock cube will do)
1 tbsp soy sauce
1 tbsp tomato purée
500g new potatoes,
cut in half
200g baby broad beans
200g garden peas
(frozen are fine)
2 courgettes, sliced
200g cherry tomatoes
2 tbsp finely chopped
flat-leaf parsley
sea salt
freshly ground black pepper

1 Heat the olive oil in a large saucepan. Brown the pork cubes in small batches, putting each batch aside in a bowl while you do the next.
2 Keep the pan on the heat and in the oil that's left, fry the onion and celery for 3 minutes until soft. Add these to the meat in the bowl.
3 Return the pan to the heat and add the Marsala wine. Simmer for a few seconds, stirring and scraping up any bits from the bottom of the pan. Return the meat, onions and celery to the pan.
4 Add the stock, soy sauce, tomato purée and potatoes, cover the pan and simmer gently for 20 minutes. Then add the beans, peas, courgettes and tomatoes and simmer for another 20 minutes. Season well with salt and pepper and add the parsley.

Fried fish and crudités platter

There is a long list of ingredients for this recipe, but don't be put off, as most of them just need chopping rather than cooking. This is a great meal for a summer evening. Put everything on big serving plates so everyone can help themselves and tuck in.

SERVES 6

100g raw baby carrots, cleaned, trimmed and cut in half
6 or 7 radishes, cut into quarters
1 red pepper, cored and finely sliced
2 handfuls of olives
3 eggs, hard-boiled and cut into quarters
3 firm tomatoes, cut into quarters
6–12 asparagus stems, trimmed
250g sea bass fillets
220g tilapia fillets
150g raw king prawns (shelled weight)
flour, for dusting
juice of ½ lemon
a handful of torn basil leaves
1 tbsp olive oil
a knob of butter
sea salt
freshly ground black pepper

Garlic mayonnaise
2 egg yolks
3 garlic cloves, crushed
squeeze of fresh lemon juice
1 tsp Dijon mustard
150ml groundnut oil
100ml light olive oil
1 tbsp cold water
sea salt
freshly ground black pepper

1 Arrange the carrots on a large serving platter with the radishes, pepper, olives, eggs and tomatoes. Cook the asparagus stems in boiling water for 3 minutes and add them to the platter.
2 Dust the fish fillets and prawns in flour. Heat the olive oil and butter in a frying pan and as soon as the butter is foaming, add the sea bass fillets, skin-side down. Fry the fillets for 1 minute on each side and then lay them on the serving dish. Do the same with the tilapia fillets, but fry these for a little longer as they will be a bit thicker. Lastly, fry the prawns until they turn pink.
3 Lay all the fish on a separate serving plate and squeeze over some fresh lemon juice. Scatter on the basil leaves and a good grinding of salt and pepper. Drizzle the vegetables with some olive oil and season with salt and pepper. Serve with the fried fish, some bread and the mayonnaise.

To make the garlic mayonnaise
4 Place the egg yolks in a mixing bowl with the garlic, fresh lemon juice, mustard, a good grinding of pepper and a large pinch of salt.
5 Measure the oils into a jug, then start to add them a drop at a time to the egg mixture, whisking constantly. Continue until you have added at least 50ml of the oil then you can start adding it in a steady trickle, still whisking. When all the oil has been added, pour in the water and stir to combine. Check the seasoning.

Roast duck and green lentils

I love cooking with green lentils. They add flavour to a dish but also absorb other flavours successfully and are a perfect foil for rich-tasting foods such as salmon and duck. Green lentils are also highly nutritious, help to reduce cholesterol and contain essential vitamins; star performers indeed.

SERVES 6

2 whole ducks
3 sprigs of rosemary, leaves removed and finely chopped
3 sprigs fresh thyme, finely chopped
3 sprigs fresh oregano, finely chopped
a few basil leaves, finely chopped
3 tbsp olive oil
1 tbsp sea salt
grated zest and juice of 1 lemon
4 garlic cloves, finely chopped

Green lentils
2 tbsp olive oil
2 fennel bulbs, trimmed and thinly sliced
70g pancetta, chopped
4 shallots, peeled and cut into quarters
100ml Marsala wine
400g puy or castelluccio lentils
1 litre chicken stock
2 tbsp chopped flat-leaf parsley
2 tomatoes, diced
sea salt
freshly ground black pepper

1 Preheat the oven to 220°C/Gas 7. Place the ducks in a roasting tin and pierce their skins all over with the tip of a sharp knife.
2 In a small bowl, mix the herbs with the olive oil, salt, lemon zest and juice and garlic. Spread the resulting paste over the ducks, massaging it in with your fingers. Then put the ducks in the oven to roast.
3 After 30 minutes, remove the ducks from the oven and drain off the excess fat. Do this periodically during the total cooking time of 2 hours.
4 Remove the ducks from the oven and set them aside in a warm place to rest for 20 minutes. Serve with the green lentils.

To prepare the green lentils
5 Heat the olive oil in a sauté pan until hot. Add the fennel, pancetta and shallots and cook on a low heat for 20 minutes, stirring occasionally. Pour in the Marsala and cook for another 3 minutes.
6 Meanwhile, boil the lentils in the chicken stock for 20–25 minutes until tender. Season with salt and pepper, then spoon them on to the fennel and pancetta mixture. Warm through and scatter on the parsley and chopped tomatoes.

Sirloin steak medallions with creamy vegetable sauce

Sirloin steak medallions are small, trimmed cuts of sirloin. The cooking times I have suggested here are based on steaks about 2.5cm thick.

SERVES 6

2 tbsp olive oil
6 medallions of sirloin steak
freshly ground black pepper

Creamy vegetable sauce
1 tbsp olive oil, for frying
a small knob of butter
2 shallots, finely sliced
100g chestnut mushrooms, roughly chopped
½ beef stock cube
100ml Marsala wine
100g baby spinach leaves
150g fresh peas (frozen will do), cooked until tender
100ml double cream

1 Start by making the sauce. Heat the olive oil and butter in a sauté pan. Add the shallots and mushrooms and fry them for 5 minutes until the shallots are soft and the mushrooms golden brown.
2 Crumble in the stock cube and stir, then pour on the wine and let it simmer for 30 seconds. Add the spinach leaves and stir until the leaves are wilted and soft. Add the peas and cream and simmer for 5 minutes, then check the seasoning. Set the sauce aside while you cook the steaks.
3 Heat the olive oil in a frying pan. Add 2 steaks and fry them for 1 minute on each side over a high heat. Place them to one side while you cook the rest of the steaks.
4 Return all the steaks to the pan and cook for 4 minutes on a low heat, by which time they should be medium rare. Pour the sauce over them to serve.

Summer fruit tart

Arrowroot is a useful thickening agent and, unlike cornflour, does not add cloudiness or floury flavour. Don't be tempted to thicken the fruit too much, though – it's fine to have some juice flowing out as you cut into the tart. I find that using vanilla bean paste instead of vanilla pods saves time and does not compromise on flavour. It's available in many supermarkets now, but if you can't find it, split a vanilla pod, scrape out the vanilla seeds inside and add them to the pastry in the same way as the paste.

MAKES 1 X 23CM TART

300g blackcurrants
200g strawberries
100g raspberries
3 tbsp sugar
3 tsp arrowroot

Pastry
125g butter, at room temperature
90g caster sugar
½ tsp vanilla bean paste
1 large egg
250g plain flour, plus extra for dusting the work surface

To make the pastry

1 Cream the butter and sugar in a food processor until light and smooth. Add the vanilla bean paste and egg and mix again briefly. Gradually add the flour and mix, as briefly as possible, until combined. Turn the dough out on to a floured surface and form into a ball. Wrap it in clingfilm and chill in the fridge for 30 minutes.

To prepare the filling

2 Place all the fruit in a saucepan and gently bring it to a simmer. Add the sugar, bring the fruit back to the boil, then let it simmer gently, uncovered, for 40 minutes. Stir in the arrowroot, bring back to the boil and then remove from the heat. Let the fruit cool completely.

To assemble the tart

3 Preheat the oven to 200°C/Gas 6. Roll the pastry out on a floured surface and use it to line a 23cm tart tin. Cover the pastry with a sheet of baking parchment and pour on some baking beans. Place the tart tin on a baking sheet and bake in the preheated oven for 15 minutes. Remove the parchment and beans and return the tart case to the oven for a further 5 minutes. Leave to one side to cool completely.

4 Spoon the fruit into the tart and serve in slices with plenty of cream.

Risotto rice pudding with stewed apricots

I think apricots taste much better when they are cooked. Perhaps in a hot country, where you can pick them ripe from the tree, they taste better raw, but the ones we get in the UK have usually been picked too early and then ripened in the shop or not at all. Only cooking releases their full flavour.

SERVES 6

25g butter
3 tbsp caster sugar
300g Arborio risotto rice
1 litre warm milk
100ml double cream

Stewed apricots
8 fresh apricots
2 tbsp soft brown sugar
2 tbsp water

1 Heat the butter and sugar in a medium-sized saucepan until the butter has melted. Add the rice and stir it for 1 minute. Start to add the milk to the rice a ladleful at a time, keeping the heat low. Continue simmering the rice and adding more milk when the previous ladleful has been absorbed until the rice is soft and all the milk has been added. This will take about 40 minutes.
2 Stir in the cream and serve with the stewed apricots.

To cook the stewed apricots
3 Cut the apricots in half and remove the stones. Place the apricots in a pan with the sugar and water. Bring to a simmer and cook, stirring occasionally, for 20 minutes until the apricots have lost any hardness.

Turkey steaks with lemon and rosemary and sweet potato mash

Turkey is an underused meat in Britain and usually eaten only at Christmas and sometimes Easter. The Italians embrace turkey much more enthusiastically and you see it in supermarkets all year round. It's a good meat, as it is white and lean.

SERVES 6

20g butter
1 onion, finely chopped
½ tbsp finely chopped rosemary leaves
2 tbsp olive oil
6 x 100g turkey steaks, each about 1cm thick
200ml white wine
1 chicken stock cube
200ml water
grated zest and juice of ½ lemon
sea salt
freshly ground black pepper

Sweet potato mash
1kg sweet potatoes, peeled and cut into 2cm chunks
1 tbsp olive oil
1 tsp balsamic vinegar
sea salt
freshly ground black pepper

1 Heat the butter in a large sauté pan. Add the onion and rosemary and fry gently for 4 minutes. Remove the onion and rosemary and place to one side.
2 Return the pan to the heat and add the olive oil. Brown the turkey steaks, a couple at a time, for a few seconds on each side. Put each batch to one side as they brown.
3 Leave the pan on the heat and add the wine. Let it simmer for 30 seconds, then crumble in the stock cube and stir. Pour in the water and simmer for 4 minutes. Check that the turkey is cooked through.
4 Return the onion, rosemary and turkey to the pan and add the lemon zest and juice. Season with salt and pepper and simmer for 5 minutes.

To make the sweet potato mash
5 Boil the potatoes in salted water until tender. Drain and return them to the saucepan, then mash roughly over a gentle heat. Stir in the olive oil and balsamic vinegar and season with salt and pepper.

Grilled butterflied sardines on toast with summer salsa

Sardines are a bargain at this time of year and their only drawback is their boniness. My children struggle with them, but I persevere nonetheless. If you can butterfly the sardines they are much easier to grill, and if you also fastidiously remove any stray bones you will be rewarded with a delicious meal.

SERVES 6

12 sardines
olive oil
1 lemon
12 slices of sourdough bread
sea salt
freshly ground black pepper

Summer salsa
3 courgettes, trimmed and very finely diced
1 red pepper, cored and very finely sliced
12 cherry tomatoes, finely diced
6 spring onions, very finely chopped
3 tbsp extra virgin olive oil
2 tbsp finely chopped basil leaves
sea salt
freshly ground black pepper

1 Ask your fishmonger to fillet and butterfly the sardines or do it yourself as follows. Cut the head, tail and fins off the sardine. Take a sharp knife and cut a slit along the bottom of each fish, then pull out the guts. Press the fish down with the palm of your hand slightly and then carefully and slowly pull out the backbone. If you do this slowly, you should get as many bones as possible coming away with the backbone. Run the sharp knife along the edges of the fish, scraping off as many of the remaining bones as you can. Prepare the rest of the sardines in the same way.
2 Place the sardines, skin side up, on a sheet of foil on a grill rack. Drizzle with olive oil and place under a hot grill until the skin starts to brown. Season well with salt and pepper and a good squeeze of lemon.
3 Meanwhile, toast the bread and serve the sardines on warm toast, drizzled with a little more olive oil, with the salsa on the side.

To prepare the salsa
4 Place the courgettes, pepper, tomatoes and spring onions in a serving bowl and pour on the olive oil. Add the basil leaves and mix them in, then season to taste.

Italian country soup

This is my version of ribollita, a classic Tuscan soup. If you use dried cannellini beans you'll get a perfect result, but if you're anything like me, you'll forget to soak them the night before and have to use canned beans. This is no great tragedy and should certainly not put you off making this soup.

SERVES 6

3 tbsp olive oil
1 onion, finely chopped
1 celery stalk, finely chopped
1 garlic clove, finely chopped
400g dried cannellini beans, soaked overnight and boiled until tender or 1 x 400g can of cannellini beans, drained and rinsed
100g green beans, topped, tailed and cut into 2cm lengths
200g potatoes, peeled and cut into chunks
300g Swiss chard leaves, roughly chopped
1 x 400g can of chopped tomatoes
200g courgettes, cut into 2cm chunks
8 sage leaves
1.5 litres chicken stock
300g stale white country-style bread
sea salt
freshly ground black pepper

1 Heat the olive oil in a large saucepan. Add the onion, celery and garlic and cook for 5 minutes, stirring occasionally. Add the cooked or canned cannellini beans and cook for 3 minutes, mashing them slightly as you stir them.
2 Add the green beans, potatoes, chard, tomatoes, courgettes and sage leaves and stir. Pour on the stock and simmer for 40 minutes, covered. You want all the vegetables to cook until they are breaking down, as this adds to the velvety thickness of the soup.
3 Add the bread in torn pieces and simmer the soup for another 10 minutes until the bread has softened and thickens the soup. Check the seasoning before serving.

Red pepper and tomato risotto

This is a simple risotto, but full of flavour.

SERVES 6

1.75 litres chicken stock
1 tbsp olive oil
25g butter, plus an extra knob to add at the end
1 celery stalk, finely chopped
1 onion, finely chopped
1 red pepper, cored and finely chopped
500g Arborio rice
3 plum tomatoes, roughly chopped
2 tbsp finely grated Parmesan cheese
2 tbsp finely chopped flat-leaf parsley
sea salt
freshly ground black pepper

1 Heat the stock in a saucepan and keep it at a gentle simmer. Heat the olive oil and butter in another large saucepan, then throw in the celery, onion and red pepper and cook for 3 minutes.
2 Add the rice and stir, coating it in the oil and butter, for 1 minute.
3 Start to add the hot stock, a ladleful at a time. Once this stock has nearly all been absorbed by the rice, add another ladleful. To cook a risotto well, you mustn't let the rice get so dry it sticks to the pan but always make sure it is still slightly wet when you add the next ladle of stock. Add another couple of ladlefuls of stock and then stir in the tomatoes.
4 Keep adding the stock a ladleful at a time and after about 20 minutes taste the rice to check the texture. It should not be too soft and should still have a slight bite to it.
5 Remove the pan from the heat when you think the rice is ready and stir in the cheese, parsley and a knob of butter. Taste for seasoning and serve.

Ham and mushroom lasagne

This is a superb lasagne and an alternative to the more common version based on beef sauce.

SERVES 6

150g fresh spinach leaves
2 tbsp olive oil
1 onion, finely chopped
20g dried porcini mushrooms, soaked in 3 tbsp warm water
200g canned chopped tomatoes
2 tbsp finely chopped flat-leaf parsley
350g fresh chestnut mushrooms, thinly sliced
50g butter (for the sauce)
50g flour
500ml milk
1 x 375g packet of dried lasagne
350g cooked ham, cut into 5mm dice
150g Parmesan cheese, grated
25g butter, cut into cubes
sea salt
freshly ground black pepper

1 Bring a pan of salted water to the boil, add the spinach and bring back to the boil. Drain the spinach, then squeeze out as much water as you can with the back of a spoon. Roughly chop the spinach and set it aside.
2 Heat the olive oil in a large sauté pan and cook the onion gently for 5 minutes, stirring frequently. Add the porcini mushrooms with their water, the canned tomatoes and the parsley, then simmer on a gentle heat for 5 minutes. Add the fresh mushrooms and the chopped spinach and cook for 10 minutes, stirring frequently, until the mixture is thick and any moisture from the mushrooms has gone. Season with salt and pepper, then set aside.
3 To make the béchamel sauce, melt the butter in a small saucepan. Add the flour and cook on a very low heat for 2 minutes. Remove the pan from the heat and gradually stir in the milk. Return the pan to the heat and bring to a gentle simmer, stirring constantly. Simmer over a very low heat for 5 minutes until the sauce thickens, stirring almost constantly to avoid lumps forming. Season with salt and pepper. Add 5 tablespoons of this sauce to the mushroom mixture. Preheat the oven to 200°C/Gas 6.
4 Spoon a little of the béchamel over the bottom of an ovenproof dish, spreading it out thinly. Place a single layer of lasagne sheets on top, cutting or breaking the lasagne to fit in one single layer. Spoon a thin layer of the mushroom mixture on top, then add a scattering of ham and sprinkling of Parmesan. Cover with another layer of pasta, another thin layer of mushrooms, ham and grated Parmesan. You should have 3 layers of the mushroom and ham mix.
5 Finish off with a layer of pasta, the remaining béchamel sauce and a good sprinkling of Parmesan cheese, then dot with the cubed butter. Bake for about 30 minutes, then serve with a green salad.

Pork steaks with Tuscan beans

I've eaten this many times in Italy, but it tastes just as fine at home in England.

SERVES 6

6 pork steaks
olive oil
juice of 1 or 2 lemons
sea salt
freshly ground black pepper

Tuscan beans
1 tbsp olive oil
1 onion, finely chopped
2 x 400g cans of cannellini beans, drained and rinsed
6 sage leaves, roughly chopped
1 x 400g can of chopped tomatoes
sea salt
freshly ground black pepper

1 First prepare the beans. Heat the olive oil in a small saucepan and add the onion. Cook over a low heat, stirring occasionally, for 10 minutes. Add the beans, sage and tomatoes. Bring to a gentle simmer and cook over a low heat for 15 minutes. Season with salt and pepper.

2 Preheat the grill. Season the pork steaks with pepper and brush them with a little olive oil. Place the steaks under the grill and cook for 5 minutes on each side. Sprinkle with lemon juice and salt and serve.

Chicken pie

I defy anyone not to salivate at the thought of a chicken pie. There are so many different versions and this is just one of them, with some chard or spinach luxuriating in a thick white sauce.

SERVES 6

200g Swiss chard leaves or spinach, stalks removed
1 tbsp olive oil
1 onion, finely chopped
25g butter
25g flour
300ml milk
1 tsp Dijon mustard
600g cooked chicken, roughly chopped
2 tbsp finely chopped flat-leaf parsley
200ml chicken stock
1 x 230g sheet of ready-rolled puff pastry
1 egg, beaten with 1 tbsp milk, to glaze
sea salt
freshly ground black pepper

1 Preheat the oven to 220°C/Gas 7. Bring a large saucepan of water to the boil. Add the chard or spinach leaves and cook for 1 minute, then drain. When the leaves are cool enough to handle, squeeze out as much water as you can. Roughly chop the leaves and place them to one side.
2 In the same saucepan, heat the olive oil and cook the onion for about 5 minutes, until soft. Place to one side with the chard or spinach leaves.
3 Return the pan to the heat and add the butter. Once it has melted, add the flour and stir over a low heat for 30 seconds. Remove the pan from the heat and gradually stir in the milk. Return the pan to the heat and simmer, stirring constantly, until the sauce has thickened. Leave the sauce to simmer over a low heat for 5 minutes, then season with salt, pepper and mustard.
4 Add the chicken pieces and stir in the parsley and stock. Simmer for a couple of minutes, then check the seasoning again. Pile the filling into a 23–24cm pie dish and cover with the sheet of puff pastry. Trim the pastry neatly and brush it with the egg and milk glaze. Bake the pie for 20 minutes until the pastry has risen and is a lovely golden brown.

Saffron cake with summer fruit compote and vanilla cream

Saffron is more often used for savoury dishes but it does very well in a sweet cake, adding a depth of flavour that goes well with fruit compote. Summer fruits are abundant during August so make the most of them while you can. Blink and the apple and pear season will be here once again!

MAKES 1 X 20CM CAKE

180g caster sugar
180g butter, at room temperature
3 eggs
180g self-raising flour
1 tbsp natural yoghurt
1 large of pinch saffron threads, soaked in 1 tbsp warm water
½ tsp ground cinnamon

Summer fruit compote
600g mixed berries, such as blackcurrants, raspberries and strawberries
2 tbsp caster sugar
3 tbsp arrowroot

Vanilla cream
400ml double cream
1 tsp vanilla bean paste
3 tbsp mascarpone cheese

1 Grease a 20cm cake tin and line the base with baking parchment. Preheat oven to 180°C/Gas 4.
2 Beat the sugar and butter together in a bowl with an electric hand-whisk until the mixture is pale and fluffy. Mix in 1 egg, followed by a tablespoon of flour, then add the other 2 eggs in the same way. Fold in the remaining flour, the yoghurt, saffron, water and cinnamon.
3 Spoon the mixture into the cake tin and bake for 35 minutes. Leave to cool for 10 minutes before turning out on to a wire rack to cool completely. Serve with the fruit compote and vanilla cream.

To make the summer fruit compote
4 Place the fruit and sugar in a saucepan and gently bring to a simmer. Continue to simmer, uncovered, for 30 minutes, then stir in the arrowroot. As soon as the compote comes back to a simmer, remove the pan from the heat and set aside to cool.

To make the vanilla cream
5 Lightly whip the cream in a bowl, then fold in the vanilla bean paste and mascarpone cheese.

Chocolate nut rolls

Almonds are one of my favourite ingredients and these circles of nuts and chocolate look very impressive when they come out of the oven. They are not too sweet and better than any processed biscuit or cake you can buy from the supermarket.

MAKES 6–8

150g dark chocolate, broken into pieces
50g butter, cut into cubes
100g mixed walnuts and almonds, chopped
50g ground almonds
50g sultanas
icing sugar, for dusting

Pastry
200g plain flour, plus extra for dusting the work surface
pinch of salt
75g cold butter, cut into cubes
100g caster sugar
1 egg, beaten

To make the pastry

1 Place the flour and salt in a food processor. Add the butter and whizz until the mixture resembles breadcrumbs. Stir in the sugar, then add the egg. Process briefly and then turn the dough out on to a floured surface and bring it together with your hands. Wrap the dough in clingfilm and chill in the fridge for at least 30 minutes.

To assemble the roll

2 Preheat the oven to 190°C/Gas 5. Put the chocolate and butter in a glass bowl and place over a pan of simmering water – take care that the bottom of the bowl does not touch the water. When the chocolate and butter are melted, stir in the mixed nuts, ground almonds and sultanas and set to one side to cool completely.

3 Roll out the pastry on a floured surface to make a rectangle of 30 x 20cm. Spread the chocolate mixture on the pastry and then roll the pastry up like a swiss roll.

4 Cut the roll into 1.5cm slices, place these on a baking sheet and bake in the preheated oven for 15 minutes. Using a palette knife, carefully lift the slices on to a wire rack and leave to cool. Dust with icing sugar before serving.

French bean and shallot tart

French beans are one of those vegetables that are best eaten when in season. When they are young and reasonably fresh, they are good just boiled and tossed with butter, parsley and seasoning. In this recipe, French beans play a starring role in a tart with some shallots and ricotta cheese.

SERVES 6

200g green beans
1 tbsp olive oil
a knob of butter
100g shallots, peeled and sliced
1 tbsp soft brown sugar
3 eggs
300ml double cream
80g Parmesan, grated
4 tbsp ricotta cheese
2 tbsp finely chopped flat-leaf parsley and basil, mixed
sea salt
freshly ground black pepper

Pastry
225g plain flour
a pinch of salt
150g cold butter, cut into cubes
1 egg yolk, beaten with 2 tbsp cold water

To make the pastry

1 Place the flour, salt and butter in a food processor and whizz until it resembles breadcrumbs. Add the egg yolk and water and mix again briefly. Turn the mixture out on to a floured surface and bring together into a ball of dough with your hands. Wrap the dough in clingfilm and chill in the fridge for 30 minutes. Preheat the oven to 200°C/Gas 6.

2 Roll out the pastry on a lightly floured surface and use it to line a 24cm flan tin. Place a sheet of baking parchment over the pastry and then pour some baking beans on top. Place the flan on a baking sheet and pop into the oven for 15 minutes. Remove the baking parchment and beans and return the flan case to the oven for another 5 minutes. Turn the oven down to 180°C/Gas 4.

To make the filling

3 Cook the green beans in boiling salted water until tender. This should take 5–7 minutes, depending on the thickness and freshness of the beans. Drain the beans and chop them into 5cm lengths. Set aside.

4 Heat the oil and butter in a frying pan. Add the shallots and the sugar and cook on a low heat for 15 minutes until the shallots are soft and golden. Set aside.

5 Put the eggs, cream, Parmesan cheese and ricotta in a mixing bowl and season well with plenty of salt and pepper. Mix everything together and stir in the herbs.

6 Lay the shallots in the base of the tart case, arrange the beans attractively on top, then pour on the egg and cream mixture. Put the tart tin on a baking tray and bake for 40 minutes. Serve with a green salad.

Pepper and tomato macaroni

This is a change from the usual macaroni cheese with the addition of some summer flavours.

SERVES 6

1 red pepper
1 green pepper
1 yellow pepper
2 tbsp olive oil
1 onion, finely chopped
1 tbsp finely chopped oregano
1 tbsp finely chopped basil
200ml tomato passata
50g butter
50g flour
500ml milk
140g Gruyère cheese, grated
2 tbsp finely grated Parmesan cheese
2 tbsp crème fraiche
500g macaroni
sea salt
freshly ground black pepper

1 Peel the peppers with a potato peeler, then cut them in half, remove the cores and seeds and dice the flesh.
2 Heat the olive oil in a sauté pan. Add the onion and diced peppers and cook over a low heat for 10 minutes. Increase the heat and cook so that the water from the peppers disappears and they start to become tinged with brown. Add the herbs and passata and cook for 2 minutes, then season with salt and pepper and place to one side.
3 Melt the butter in a small pan, then stir in the flour. Cook over a low heat for 1 minute, taking care not to let the mixture burn. Remove the pan from the heat and gradually stir in the milk. Return the pan to the heat and bring to a gentle simmer, stirring constantly. Continue to simmer over a very low heat for 5 minutes, then season with salt and pepper. Remove from the heat and stir in the Gruyère cheese.
4 Meanwhile, cook the macaroni in boiling salted water according to the packet instructions, then drain.
5 Mix the drained macaroni with the cheese sauce, tomato and pepper mixture and the macaroni, then stir in the crème fraiche. You can serve the dish straight from the pan to save some washing up, and hand the Parmesan round separately.
6 Alternatively, spoon everything into a serving dish, sprinkle the top with Parmesan cheese and place under a hot grill for a few minutes. Either way serve with a mixed salad.

Grilled lamb cutlets with braised white cabbage and baby carrots

The marinated meat makes a change from plain grilled lamb cutlets, nice as they are.

SERVES 6

1 tbsp chopped fresh mint
1 tbsp chopped fresh oregano
3 garlic cloves, crushed
1 tsp salt
4 anchovy fillets
juice of ½ lemon
5 tbsp olive oil
12-15 lamb cutlets
freshly ground black pepper

Braised white cabbage
1 white cabbage, cored and shredded finely
a small knob of butter
squeeze of fresh lemon juice
sea salt
freshly ground black pepper

Baby carrots
300g baby carrots, peeled and scrubbed and cut into 2cm chunks
a knob of butter
1 tbsp finely chopped flat-leaf parsley
sea salt

1 Put the mint, oregano, garlic, salt, black pepper, anchovies, lemon juice and olive oil in a blender and blend briefly, just to combine. Alternatively, use a pestle and mortar to grind the mixture to a paste.
2 Pour the mixture into a mixing bowl with the lamb cutlets and massage it into the meat with your hands. Leave the cutlets to marinate for an hour or so.
3 Heat the grill. Place the cutlets on the rack of the grill and cook them for 7 minutes on each side.

To cook the braised white cabbage
4 Put the cabbage in a saucepan with 2 tablespoons of water and place on a low heat. Bring the water to a simmer, then turn the heat very low. Cover the pan and cook the cabbage for 5 minutes, stirring once or twice. Add the butter and stir, then season with salt and pepper and a squeeze of fresh lemon juice.

To cook the baby carrots
5 Place the carrots in a small pan with the butter and place on a medium heat until the butter starts to foam. Stir and then lower the heat. Cover the pan and cook for 5–7 minutes, stirring occasionally, until the carrots are tender. Season with salt and pepper and the parsley.

Ratatouille

Ratatouille has gained a bad reputation over the years. It's often thought of as a 'throw it all in and stew in olive oil' sort of dish, but it benefits from a little more care and attention. Properly prepared, it is a relatively quick and easy meal to prepare, and one that is very healthy. You need to sweat the aubergines in salt for 20 minutes or so to extract any bitterness from their flavour. It is only then that you can appreciate their unique and interesting taste.

SERVES 6

450g aubergines
300g courgettes
plenty of olive oil
1 onion, finely chopped
2 garlic cloves, finely chopped
14 cherry tomatoes, cut in half
1 x 400g can of chopped tomatoes
1 tbsp soft brown sugar
30g fresh basil, finely chopped
sea salt
freshly ground black pepper

1 Slice the aubergine into 5mm slices. Cut each slice into quarters and place them in a colander with a good sprinkling of salt. Leave for 20–30 minutes and then pat the slices dry with kitchen paper.
2 Cut the courgettes into 5mm discs. You can put these in with the aubergine as well, as they benefit from losing a little of their moisture.
3 Heat a couple of tablespoons of olive oil in a sauté pan. When it's hot, place a layer of aubergine slices in the pan. Once they are golden brown on one side, turn them over and brown them on the other side. Place them in a bowl while you cook the rest. You will need to add more oil as you go.
4 Next put all the courgette discs in the pan and cook on a low heat for 5 minutes, then add these to the bowl with the aubergines. Add more olive oil to the sauté pan, if needed, and fry the onion and garlic on a low heat for 10 minutes until soft.
5 Put all the aubergine and courgette slices back in the pan. Add the cherry tomatoes, canned tomatoes and the sugar and stir gently. Season well with salt and pepper and then sprinkle on the chopped basil. Reheat when ready to serve. This is best served in bowls with some good rustic bread on the side.

Herb and cheese frittata with smoked trout salad

A frittata, the Italian version of an omelette, is actually much easier to make than the French one. For one thing, you don't have to turn a frittata and it is cooked to a firmer consistency than its French counterpart. It can also be eaten warm or cold, although I prefer to tuck in when it is warm.

SERVES 6

2 tbsp olive oil
1 onion, finely chopped
12 eggs
2 tbsp finely chopped mixed herbs (oregano, parsley, winter savory, thyme)
100g Parmesan cheese, grated

Flageolet and trout salad
250g smoked trout
1 red onion, finely diced
2 x 400g cans of flageolet beans, drained and rinsed
2 tbsp finely chopped flat-leaf parsley
3 tbsp olive oil
juice of ½ a lemon
sea salt
freshly ground black pepper

1 Preheat the grill. Heat the olive oil in a medium frying pan, then add the onion and fry for about 5 minutes until soft.
2 Beat the eggs in a bowl, add the herbs and cheese and season well with salt and pepper. Turn the egg mixture into the frying pan and cook on a low heat. Run a spatula around the edge of the pan to free the eggs and continue to cook over a low heat until you can see that the base is done. The edges will cook first, and when you can lift the frittata up at the side with a spatula it is time to finish it off under the grill.
3 Place the pan under the preheated grill and cook until the top is golden brown. Turn the frittata out on a plate and serve with the salad or serve it straight from the pan.

To prepare the flageolet and trout salad
4 Flake the trout into a serving bowl, discarding any skin and bones. Add the onion, beans and parsley, then dress with the oil and lemon and season with salt and pepper.

Beef and onions in red wine sauce

Sirloin steak is delicious but an expensive cut of meat. One way of making it more affordable is to use smaller amounts in dishes with other ingredients.

SERVES 6

1 tbsp olive oil
20g butter
600g sirloin steak, cut into strips about 3cm wide
250g chestnut mushrooms
70g pancetta, chopped
1 onion, finely chopped
1 tbsp flour
200ml red wine
500ml beef stock
sea salt
freshly ground black pepper

1 Heat the olive oil and butter in a sauté pan. Start to brown the strips of steak, a few at a time, until they are a rich brown – about 30 seconds or so on each side. Remove and place to one side while you cook the rest.
2 When all the strips of steaks are browned, pour a little more olive oil into the empty pan if necessary, then add the mushrooms, pancetta and onion. Fry until the mushrooms have turned golden and are not releasing any more water – about 10 minutes.
3 Sprinkle on the flour and then add the wine, stirring as you do so. Let it simmer for 5 minutes, then pour on the stock and simmer gently for 15 minutes. Season with salt and pepper.
4 Just before serving, return the steaks to the pan and warm them through. Serve with some braised carrots and new potatoes.

Fried loin of lamb with summer vegetables

This is a summer vegetable stew, accompanied by lamb, which is beautifully simple to prepare. Cut the vegetables carefully and don't stir them too much once they are in the saucepan. That way they will keep their fresh appearance when served.

SERVES 6

olive oil
1 onion, finely chopped
150g carrots, sliced into 1cm discs
1 red pepper, cored and chopped into 2cm chunks
300g new potatoes, cut in half
200g chard leaves and stalks
1 litre chicken stock
1 x 400g can of chopped tomatoes
150g broad beans, cooked until tender and peeled if you like
a couple of handfuls of finely chopped fresh mint leaves
3 lamb loin fillets (700g in all)
flour, for dusting
sea salt
freshly ground black pepper

1 Heat 2 tablespoons of olive oil in a saucepan. Add the onion and cook for 5 minutes. Add the carrots, pepper and potatoes and cook for 2 minutes, stirring occasionally.
2 Shred the chard leaves and chop the stalks into 1–2cm pieces. Add these to the pan and then pour on the stock. Add the tomatoes and simmer gently, uncovered, for 40 minutes. Stir in the broad beans and mint leaves, then season with salt and pepper.
3 Heat a tablespoon of oil in a frying pan. Dust the skin of the lamb loins with some flour and when the oil is hot, place the loins in the pan, skin side down, and fry them for 1 minute. Turn and cook for 1 minute on the other side. Reduce the heat and continue to fry the loins gently for 5 minutes. Season with salt and pepper.
4 Slice the loins into 2cm thick pieces and serve on top of the soupy vegetables.

Raspberry and chocolate custard pots

These are really simple to make. You can use strawberries instead of raspberries if you prefer, but cut them into raspberry-sized pieces. Use six standard ramekins (8cm wide x 5cm deep) or dariole moulds.

SERVES 6

- 600ml milk
- 125g plain chocolate, broken into pieces
- 2 eggs
- 2 egg yolks
- 2 tbsp caster sugar
- 100g raspberries

1 Preheat the oven to 180°C/Gas 4. Heat the milk in a saucepan. When it comes to the boil, remove the pan from the heat and stir in the chocolate pieces, which will melt in the heat of the milk.
2 Whisk the eggs, egg yolks and sugar together in a mixing bowl and then pour in the chocolate milk, whisking as you do so.
3 Take the 6 ramekins and sprinkle some fresh raspberries into each one. Pour the chocolate liquid on top, dividing it evenly between the dishes.
4 Place the ramekins in a roasting tin and pour water into the tin to a depth of about 2.5cm. Bake for 30–35 minutes until the custard is just set. Cool and chill before serving with extra cream if you wish.

Macerated peaches with vanilla mascarpone and cinnamon shortbread

In culinary terms, to macerate something means to soften it by placing it in a liquid. This dish contains some heavenly Italian flavours.

SERVES 6

6 peaches
200g fresh raspberries
200ml Marsala wine
2 tbsp white sugar

Vanilla mascarpone
2 tsp vanilla extract
200ml double cream
250g mascarpone cheese

Cinnamon shortbread
50g ground almonds
100g plain flour, plus extra for dusting the work surface
100g wholemeal flour
75g caster sugar
½ teaspoon ground cinnamon
225g cold butter, cut into cubes

1 Cut the peaches in half and remove the stones. Place the peaches and raspberries in a serving bowl. Pour on the wine, sprinkle on the sugar and leave to macerate for a least 1 hour. Serve with the vanilla mascarpone and some shortbread on the side.

To make the vanilla mascarpone
2 Gently mix the vanilla extract and cream with the mascarpone and place in a serving bowl.

To make the cinnamon shortbread
3 Preheat the oven to 180°C/Gas 4. Place the almonds, flours, sugar and cinnamon in a food processor. Add the butter and mix until the mixture resembles breadcrumbs. Turn the mixture out on to a floured work surface and bring together into a ball of dough with your hands.
4 Place the dough on a sheet of baking parchment and roll it out into a rough circle, about 5mm thick. Place the baking parchment, with the shortbread, on a baking sheet and bake in the oven for 30 minutes, until the shortbread is just starting to turn golden, but is still pale in colour.
5 As soon as the shortbread comes out of the oven, cut it into neat rectangular pieces, but don't attempt to move it until it has cooled.

Tandoori-style chicken

This is nothing like authentic tandoor-cooked chicken, but it is tandoori in style because of the marinade and the high cooking temperature.

SERVES 6

8–10 chicken thighs on the bone, skin removed
8 tbsp natural yoghurt
3cm piece of fresh root ginger, grated
2 tbsp olive oil
2 tbsp curry powder
4 garlic cloves, crushed
1 tsp sea salt
juice of 1 lemon

Tomato, red onion and mint salad
5 tomatoes, roughly chopped
1 red onion, finely diced
small bunch fresh mint, roughly chopped
4 tbsp natural yoghurt
sea salt
freshly ground black pepper

Boiled rice
500g basmati rice
½ tsp salt
750ml water

1 Place the chicken thighs in a bowl, with the yoghurt, ginger, olive oil, curry powder, garlic, salt and lemon juice. Mix with your hands or a wooden spoon and set aside in the fridge for 1 hour or so.
2 Preheat the oven to 230°C/Gas 8. Place the chicken pieces on a rack over a roasting tin and put them under the grill for 5–10 minutes. Turn the pieces over and grill for another 5–10 minutes. Keep the chicken on the rack over the roasting tin and put them in the oven for 20 minutes. Serve with the salad and some boiled rice.

To make the tomato, red onion and mint salad
3 Place the tomatoes, onion and mint in a serving dish. Spoon in the yoghurt and season with salt and pepper.

To prepare the boiled rice
4 Place the rice, salt and water in a large saucepan and bring to a lively boil. Reduce the heat to very low, cover the pan and cook the rice for 15 minutes. Stir once during the cooking time.
5 Remove the pan from the heat. Keep the rice covered and leave it undisturbed for 10 minutes more.

Pasta with bacon, peas and cream

Pasta with a sauce is always a quick meal to make and much more delicous than pasta ready-meals, which are overpriced and never taste as good as a freshly prepared dish of pasta.

SERVES 6

2 tbsp olive oil
1 shallot, finely chopped
70g sliced pancetta, finely chopped
2 garlic cloves, finely chopped
200g frozen petit pois
4 spring onions, sliced
200ml double cream
30g Parmesan cheese, finely grated
2 tbsp roughly chopped fresh basil
600g macaroni
sea salt
freshly ground black pepper

1 Heat the olive oil in a large sauté pan. Add the shallot, pancetta and garlic and sauté for 1 minute. Add the peas and lower the heat, then cook gently for 3 minutes, stirring frequently. Add the spring onions and cook for another minute.
2 Pour on the cream and let it simmer for a couple of minutes. Sprinkle on the cheese and basil and season with salt and pepper.
3 Bring a pan of salted water to the boil and cook the macaroni according to the packet instructions. Drain the pasta, toss with the sauce and serve.

Eggs with tuna and basil mayonnaise and tomato salad

This is a quick, light, summer meal.

SERVES 6

9 eggs, hard-boiled and cut in half lengthways
6–12 pieces of bread for toasting

Mayonnaise
2 egg yolks
2 tsp white wine vinegar
200ml light olive oil
2 tbsp tinned tuna fish
a handful of fresh basil, finely chopped
sea salt
freshly ground black pepper

Tomato salad
8 medium tomatoes, thinly sliced
1 tbsp olive oil
fresh oregano or marjoram, finely chopped
sea salt
freshly ground black pepper

To make the mayonnaise

1 Put the egg yolks in a small bowl with the white wine vinegar and a good grinding of salt and pepper, then mix until amalgamated.

2 Start to add the olive oil a little at a time, whisking all the time. Don't add the oil too quickly or it will curdle. Keep adding oil and whisking until all the oil has been incorporated and you have a nice thick gloopy mayonnaise. Stir in the tuna fish and basil and check the seasoning. You may need some more salt and pepper.

To prepare the tomato salad

3 Lay the tomatoes on a serving plate. Drizzle with the olive oil and sprinkle with the herbs and some salt and pepper. Serve with the eggs.

To serve

4 Toast the bread and serve with 2 or 3 egg halves on top and a spoonful of mayonnaise.

Gooseberry upside-down cake

Many soft fruits can be used to make an upside-down cake and these cakes are a good way of sparking children's inerest in baking. The way the fruit scattered on the bottom of the cake tin appears in the same place when the baked cake is turned out is a bit of kitchen magic. This sort of wizardry gets people hooked on cooking and turns them into lifelong enthusiasts.

SERVES 6

500g fresh gooseberries, topped and tailed
15g butter
2 tbsp soft brown sugar

Cake
200g butter, at room temperature
200g caster sugar
4 eggs
200g self-raising flour
1 tsp ground cinnamon

1 Preheat the oven to 180°C/Gas 4. Grease a 24cm spring-clip cake tin and line the base with baking parchment.
2 Place the gooseberries in a saucepan with the butter and sugar and simmer gently for 5 minutes, until the gooseberries just begin to lose their shape. Place to one side to cool.

To prepare the cake
3 Using an electric hand-whisk, beat the butter with the sugar for 4 minutes, until the mixture is light and fluffy. Add 1 egg and a tablespoon of flour and beat until incorporated. Do the same with the rest of the eggs, adding a spoonful of flour each time. When all the eggs have been added, fold in the rest of the flour and the cinnamon with a metal spoon.
4 Spread the gooseberries over the bottom of the cake tin. Leave most of the juice behind – you can use it for serving later. Place the cake tin on a baking sheet, as some juice will leak out during the cooking. Spoon the cake mixture over the gooseberries and bake the cake for 45 minutes until the sponge is firm to the touch. Remove from the oven and leave to cool for 10 minutes.
5 Once the cake is cool, invert it on to a plate and serve with some crème fraiche and the gooseberry juices.

Raspberry crème brûlées

I use shallow brûlée dishes for these, but you could use ramekins instead.

SERVES 6

200ml whipping cream
200ml double cream
1 vanilla pod, split lengthways
7 egg yolks
75g caster sugar, plus 6 tsp of caster sugar for the topping
225g fresh raspberries
mint leaves and extra raspberries for decoration (optional)

1 Preheat the oven to 150°C/Gas 2. Combine both creams in a saucepan and scrape the seeds from the vanilla pod into them. Bring to the boil and then set the pan aside.
2 Using an electric hand-whisk, beat the yolks and sugar together in a glass bowl until thick and mousse-like. Pour the warm cream and vanilla seeds on to the eggs and sugar, whisking as you do so. Place the glass bowl over a saucepan of simmering water, taking care that the bottom of the bowl doesn't touch the water. Stir until the custard thickens slightly and coats the back of a wooden spoon, then set to one side.
3 Divide the raspberries evenly between the dishes. Pour the custard into each ramekin over the raspberries. Place the ramekins in a deep ovenproof dish and pour in enough boiling water from a kettle to come halfway up the sides of the ramekin dishes. Place in the oven and cook for 30 minutes. Leave the brûlées to cool, then put them in the fridge until you need them.
4 Before serving, preheat your grill. Sprinkle a teaspoon of sugar over each ramekin and place under the grill until the sugar starts to go dark brown and caramelise. Alternatively, use a kitchen blowtorch to produce the same result. Serve immediately, decorated with a few more raspberries and some mint leaves if you like.

Summer is coming to an end, but the weather can often be good this month and we can still spend time outside, although the nights draw in more quickly and temperatures fall in the evenings. In the kitchen, cooks will find many uses for apples and pears – baking cakes, filling pies and crumbles, roasting and poaching. Quinces are becoming popular in Britain again; the hard, shell-like exterior hiding the beautiful yielding fruit that it can become, with a little help from the oven and some brown sugar and spices. You can also enjoy runner and green beans and lovely flavourful tomatoes. Your menus will probably be a mixture of light and heavier food and you may start to serve Sunday roasts again, if you ever gave them up! I welcome these changes, as I always welcome the ever-changing seasons which lie behind the richness and variety of our lives on this enchanting planet.

September

Ham with spinach and parsley sauce

Ham goes particularly well with creamy parsley sauce. I have added some spinach to the sauce to make it a little more substantial and nourishing.

SERVES 6

1kg unsmoked gammon joint
2 tbsp chutney (any kind will do)
1 tbsp maple syrup

Spinach and parsley sauce
300g spinach leaves, stalks removed
100g flat-leaf parsley, stalks removed
25g butter
25g plain flour
300ml milk
250ml double cream
2 tbsp grated Parmesan cheese
sea salt
freshly ground black pepper

1 Unwrap the gammon, place it in a large saucepan and pour in enough water to cover the meat. Bring to the boil on the stove, then reduce to a gentle simmer, cover and cook for 1 hour.
2 Preheat the oven to 200°C/Gas 6. Remove the ham from the water and place it on a board. With a sharp knife, remove the thick rind. Mix the chutney and syrup and spread the mixture over the gammon.
3 Place the ham in a roasting tin and bake in the oven for 30 minutes. The syrup and chutney will burn on the tin, but the ham will be fine. Remove from the oven and set aside to rest for 15 minutes. Slice as thickly or thinly as you like and serve with the sauce and some baked potatoes.

To make the spinach and parsley sauce
4 Bring a large saucepan of water to the boil. Place the spinach and parsley leaves in the water, pressing them down to cover them with water. As soon as the water starts to simmer again, drain the parsley and spinach into a colander, pressing out any excess water with the back of a wooden spoon. Remove as much water as you can. Place the spinach and parsley on a chopping board and chop finely with a sharp knife.
5 In the meantime, melt the butter in a medium saucepan. Add the flour and remove from the heat. Mix until the flour has combined with the butter, then start to add the milk a little at a time, stirring constantly to avoid lumps. If any lumps do appear, a small whisk should get rid of them.
6 Return the pan to the heat and bring the sauce to a simmer. Cook on a very low heat for 10 minutes, stirring occasionally, then stir in the spinach and parsley. Add the cream and cheese, check the seasoning and simmer gently for 5 minutes.

Cream of carrot soup with mini potato puffs

I have often found carrot soup rather disappointing, but I love this version. It is velvety smooth and the rosemary goes so well with carrots – a welcome change from the coriander often used in carrot soups. The puffs are great fun and go well with the soup.

SERVES 6

4 leeks, trimmed
50g butter
650g carrots, peeled and sliced
3 sprigs of rosemary
1.5 litres chicken stock
150ml single cream
sea salt
freshly ground black pepper

Mini potato puffs
1 tbsp olive oil
1 small onion, finely chopped
250g potatoes, peeled, quartered and cooked until tender
1 tbsp finely chopped flat-leaf parsley
1 tsp curry powder
40g Cheddar cheese, grated
2 tbsp crème fraiche
flour, for dusting the work surface
1 x 230g pack of ready-rolled all-butter puff pastry
1 egg yolk, for glazing
sea salt
freshly ground black pepper

1 Cut the leeks lengthways through the middle to just before the root end and fan out under a running tap. Rinse out any grit that may be sitting between the layers, then shred the leeks finely widthways.
2 Melt the butter in a saucepan and add the leeks, carrots and rosemary sprigs. Sauté for 5 minutes, stirring occasionally.
3 Add the stock and bring to a simmer, then cover and cook gently for 50 minutes. Remove the rosemary sprigs and purée the soup in a blender. Tip the soup back into the pan, reheat and season. Stir in the cream just before serving.

To make the mini potato puffs
4 Preheat the oven to 200°C/Gas 6. Heat the olive oil in a small frying pan, add the onion and cook for 5 minutes until soft and translucent. Remove from the heat.
5 Add the potatoes, breaking them up into bite-sized pieces as you do so. Add the parsley, curry powder, cheese and crème fraiche, taste and check the seasoning.
6 Take a 12-hole fairy cake tin. You won't need to grease it as the pastry is buttery enough not to stick. Dust your work surface with flour, lay out the ready-rolled puffed pastry and use pastry cutters to cut out 12 x 7cm circles and 12 x 6cm circles. Lay the larger circles in the cake tins. Divide the potato filling between them and then cover with the 6cm circles. Seal the edges by pressing around the pies with the end of a teaspoon or your fingertips. Brush each little pie with the egg yolk glaze and then bake in the oven for 10 minutes.

Pork and black beans with courgette and tomato salad

This stew is South American in style, like something you might be served in a Brazilian home. The chorizo provides a smoky depth of flavour that helps to bring character to the stew.

SERVES 6

100g chorizo
2 tbsp olive oil
1 fennel bulb, trimmed and thinly sliced
1 onion, finely chopped
1kg diced pork leg
2 x 400g cans of black beans, drained and rinsed
1 x 400g can of chopped tomatoes
100ml Marsala wine
6 sage leaves, finely chopped
2 tsp paprika
2 tsp soft brown sugar
sea salt
freshly ground black pepper

Courgette and tomato salad
2 tbsp olive oil
400g courgettes, sliced into 1 cm thick rounds
1 garlic clove, bashed
2 tbsp roughly torn basil leaves
100g cherry tomatoes, quartered
2 tsp balsamic vinegar
sea salt
freshly ground black pepper

1 Cut the chorizo into 1cm slices and cut the slices in half. Heat the olive oil in a large saucepan, then add the fennel, onion and chorizo and cook for 10 minutes, stirring occasionally. Add the pork and stir.
2 Add the beans, tomatoes, Marsala, sage, paprika, sugar, season well and cook at a gentle simmer for 1 hour.
3 Check seasoning again and serve with the courgette and tomato salad and some boiled rice.

To make the courgette and tomato salad
4 Heat the oil in a frying pan. Add the courgettes and fry them for 10 minutes on a medium heat until golden brown. Add the garlic and stir for a few seconds.
5 Turn the courgettes out into a serving bowl, add the tomatoes and scatter on the basil leaves. Dress with the balsamic vinegar and season with salt and pepper.

Smoked haddock with spinach and baked eggs

Another of my favourite one-pot suppers, which can be served straight from the dish to the plate, making minimal washing up.

SERVES 6

500g undyed smoked haddock
300ml milk
300g spinach
a knob of butter
1 x 400g can of butter beans, drained and rinsed
grated zest of 1 lemon
6–8 eggs
250ml double cream
bread for toasting
sea salt
freshly ground black pepper

1 Preheat the oven to 200°C/Gas 6. Pop the haddock into a gratin dish, pour on the milk and bake in the oven for 10 minutes. Discard the milk and remove any skin and stray bones from the fish. Flake the fish and scatter it into the gratin dish.
2 Rinse the spinach leaves and place them in a saucepan with the butter and a good grinding of salt and pepper. Cover and cook for 3 minutes until the spinach has wilted and is completely soft. Place it in a colander and press out any excess water with the back of a wooden spoon. Put the spinach on a board and chop it roughly, then spread it over the fish in the gratin dish.
3 Spoon the beans into the dish and sprinkle on the lemon zest.
4 Break the eggs into the dish, spacing them out so that you can serve them easily, and pour on the cream. Season with salt and pepper and bake in the oven for 15–17 minutes until the whites of the egg are set, but the yolks are still soft. Serve with hot buttered toast.

Margherita pizza

I've suggested a meat-free pizza here to make the week's menu more balanced, but you can vary the toppings, adding ingredients such as pancetta or salami.

SERVES 6

Dough
525ml warm water
1 x 7g sachet of dried yeast
2 tsp sugar
750g strong white flour, plus extra for dusting the work surface
2 tsp salt

Topping
2 x 400g cans of chopped tomatoes
4 tbsp olive oil
1 tsp sugar
400g buffalo mozzarella
a few torn basil leaves
sea salt
freshly ground black pepper

To make the dough

1 Pour a little of the warm water into a small bowl and sprinkle on the yeast and sugar. Leave for 2 minutes.
2 Place the flour and salt in a large mixing bowl. Make a well in the centre and add the rest of the water and the yeasted water, then mix with a wooden spoon.
3 Turn the dough out on to a floured surface and knead for 5 minutes. Put the dough back into the bowl, cover and leave to rise for 1 hour or until it has doubled in size.

To make the topping

4 Preheat the oven to 220°C/Gas 7. Gently heat the tomatoes and 2 tablespoons of olive oil in a small saucepan, then add the sugar and seasoning and cook, uncovered, for 45 minutes. Pull the mozzarella apart and put it in a bowl with the rest of the olive oil. Pop a baking sheet in the oven to heat up.

To assemble the pizzas

5 Cut the pizza dough into 6 pieces and form them into balls. Cover with a tea towel and leave for 5 minutes. Roll one of the balls into a circle or a rough rectangular shape, whichever you find easiest.
6 Make sure the work surface is well floured so that the dough doesn't stick to it. Roll 2 pieces of dough at a time as you will probably be able to fit 2 pizzas on the baking sheet.
7 Spread the pizzas with a spoonful or 2 of the tomato sauce. Place some mozzarella on each one and scatter with a few torn basil leaves.
8 Put the pizzas on the hot baking sheet and bake in the oven for 10 minutes until golden and bubbly.
9 Assemble the rest of the pizzas in the same way, returning the baking sheet to the oven to heat through while you prepare the next couple. Serve with a salad.

Curried fish pie

Curry powder can liven up a lot of dishes and it does just that here.

SERVES 6

- 25g butter
- 25g flour
- 1 ½ tsp mild curry powder
- 600ml milk
- 200ml cream
- 150g spinach leaves
- 200g salmon fillets
- 500g pollack fillets
- 300g undyed smoked haddock
- 400ml milk, for cooking the fish
- 4 eggs, hard-boiled and halved
- 1kg potatoes, peeled and cut into quarters
- 200ml milk, for the potatoes
- 20g butter
- 2 tbsp grated Parmesan cheese
- sea salt
- freshly ground black pepper

1 Melt the butter in a small saucepan and stir in the flour and curry powder. Remove the pan from the heat and add the 600ml of milk, a little at a time, stirring constantly. Return the pan to the heat, then add the cream and simmer on a very low heat for 5 minutes. Place to one side.

2 Bring a medium saucepan of water to the boil, then add the spinach leaves and bring the pan back to the boil. Immediately drain the spinach, pressing out as much water as you can with the back of a spoon.

3 Place the drained spinach on a chopping board and chop it finely with a knife. Add the spinach to the white sauce, stirring it in gently, then season to taste.

4 Place the fish in a gratin dish and cover it with the 400ml of milk. Place the dish on the stove, bring the milk to a simmer and cook the fish for 2 minutes. Turn the pieces of fish over and cook for another 2 minutes.

5 Drain the fish and discard the milk. Put the fish back in the gratin dish and season with a little salt and pepper. Add the egg halves, pour on the sauce and gently mix it into the fish.

6 Boil the potatoes in salted water until tender. Mash them in the saucepan and put the pan back on the heat. Add the 200ml of milk and the butter and stir well, then season with salt and pepper.

7 Spoon the potatoes over the fish, sprinkle with grated Parmesan and pop the dish under a hot grill for 5 minutes until the top is nicely browned.

Stuffed shoulder of lamb with kohlrabi salad

Once you have prepared a stuffed meat dish, the cooking process does the rest of the work for you. The heat allows the flavours of the stuffing ingredients to penetrate the meat and you are rewarded with a wonderfully succulent dish.

SERVES 6

1.7kg rolled, boned lamb shoulder
50g soft prunes, stoned and finely chopped
25g flat-leaf parsley, finely chopped
1 shallot, finely chopped
1 egg
1 tbsp olive oil, plus extra for drizzling
2 tbsp pistachio nuts, roughly chopped
2 tbsp white breadcrumbs
1 tbsp flour
150ml white wine
200ml water
sea salt
freshly ground black pepper

Kohlrabi salad
2 kohlrabi, peeled and grated
2 carrots, peeled and grated
1 dessert apple, peeled, cored and grated
6 radishes, finely sliced

Dressing
2 tbsp crème fraiche
1 tsp Dijon mustard
3 tbsp olive oil
sea salt
freshly ground black pepper

1 Preheat the oven to 220°C/Gas 7. Unroll the lamb shoulder and lay it on a large chopping board or clean work surface.
2 In a bowl, mix together the prunes, parsley, shallot, egg, olive oil, pistachios and breadcrumbs. Season with salt and pepper.
3 Spoon the paste onto the unrolled lamb and then roll it up and tie it around the middle. Tie in 4 more places at equal intervals, then tie it lengthways so that the stuffing is nice and secure.
4 Place the joint in a roasting tin, drizzle a little oil over the skin and cook in the preheated oven for 20 minutes. Reduce the oven temperature to 190°C/Gas 5 and cook for another 40 minutes. Remove the meat from the oven, place it on a board and leave to rest for 20 minutes.
5 Place the roasting tin on the stove and mix the flour into the meat juices with a wooden spoon. Pour on the white wine and water and simmer for 20 minutes while the meat rests. Serve with roast potatoes and the kohlrabi salad.

To make the kohlrabi salad
6 Place the salad ingredients in a serving bowl. Mix the crème fraiche and mustard in a small bowl, then slowly add the olive oil, stirring constantly or the crème fraiche will curdle. Season the dressing with salt and pepper and then pour it over the kohlrabi salad and toss.

Vanilla sponge with whipped cream and redcurrants

Redcurrants are not always easy to find in supermarkets, despite the fact that they grow well in Britain. Use another soft fruit if need be, but the redcurrants do add a nice tartness to an otherwise sweet cake, so search them out if you can.

MAKES 1 X 20CM CAKE

3 eggs
180g caster sugar
180g self-raising flour
1 tsp vanilla extract

Filling and topping
150g redcurrants
3 tbsp caster sugar
1 tsp arrowroot
300ml double cream
icing sugar, for dusting

1 Preheat the oven to 180°C/Gas 4. Grease 2 x 20cm sandwich tins and line them with baking parchment.
2 Using an electric beater, cream the butter and sugar for 3 minutes until light and fluffy. Add 1 egg, followed by a tablespoon of flour and mix. Do the same with the other eggs, then fold in the remaining flour and the vanilla.
3 Divide the mixture between the tins and bake in the oven for 20–25 minutes until firm to the touch of your fingertips. Turn the cakes out on to a wire rack to cool.

To make the filling and finish the cake
4 Place the redcurrants in a saucepan and bring to the boil, then add the sugar and simmer for 20 minutes. Add the arrowroot and bring back to a simmer and then remove the pan from the heat and place to one side to cool completely.
5 Whip the cream lightly and spoon it on top one of the cooled cakes. Spread the other cake with the redcurrant mixture and sandwich them together. Dust the top of the cake with icing sugar.

Grandmother's pound cake

Pound cake is an old English recipe and it can be made with fruit or without. With fruit, it is still a beautifully light cake, much more so than your usual fruit cake.

MAKES 1 X 20CM CAKE

- 225g butter, at room temperature, plus extra for greasing
- 225g caster sugar
- 4 egg whites
- 4 egg yolks
- 2 tbsp brandy
- 225g plain flour
- a pinch of salt
- 2 tbsp milk
- ½ tsp mixed spice
- ½ tsp grated nutmeg
- 225g currants
- 225g raisins
- 225g sultanas

1 Preheat the oven to 160°C/Gas 3. Grease a deep 20cm cake tin and line the base and sides with baking parchment.
2 Cream the butter in a food mixer for 5 minutes until it is pale in colour. Add the sugar and mix for a further 3 minutes.
3 Whisk the egg whites until they form stiff peaks and set them to one side.
4 Add the yolks, brandy, flour, salt, milk, spices and dried fruit to the sugar and butter and fold them in gently until well combined. Lastly, fold in the egg whites.
5 Spoon the mixture into the cake tin and bake in the oven for 2 hours. Check that the cake is cooked through by piercing the middle with a skewer – it should come away cleanly. If it doesn't, cook the cake for a little longer.

Pear and almond tart

I am drowning in pears at the moment and this is a good way of using them. It's an easy dessert to make and tastes sublime. Serve it hot for supper; any leftovers are just as good cold the next day with a cup of coffee.

SERVES 6

1 x 250g pack of all-butter puff pastry
flour, for dusting the work surface
175g ground almonds
125g caster sugar
60g butter, melted
2 egg yolks
2 tbsp double cream
1 tbsp brandy
4 ripe pears, cored and thinly sliced

1 Preheat the oven to 200°C/Gas 6. Roll out the pastry on a floured work surface until it is big enough to line the base of a Swiss roll tin measuring 23 x 31cm.
2 Put the ground almonds, caster sugar, melted butter, egg yolks, cream and brandy in a small mixing bowl. Mix everything together with a wooden spoon until you have a thick almond paste.
3 Spread this on the pastry base, leaving a 1cm margin all around the edge of the pastry. Lay the sliced pears in attractive lines on the paste, then bake the tart in the oven for 40 minutes.

Ham and eggs on potato cakes

Gammon is an easy joint to prepare and hard to overcook if you cook it for about 30 minutes per 500g. I usually boil gammon for part of the cooking time and then roast it for the rest, but if you prefer, boil it on top of the stove for the whole time, remove the fatty rind at the end of cooking and dispense with the honey and soy sauce. It's up to you; either way you will enjoy a great meal.

SERVES 6

800g unsmoked gammon joint
2 tbsp runny honey
1 tbsp soy sauce
olive oil
6 eggs

Potato cakes
600g potatoes, peeled, cut in quarters and cooked until tender
200g grated kohlrabi
4 tbsp grated Gruyère cheese
1 egg
6 spring onions, finely chopped
2 tbsp olive oil, plus extra for greasing
sea salt
freshly ground black pepper

1 Place the gammon joint in a saucepan and pour in enough water to cover. Bring to a simmer and spoon off any scum, then partly cover the pan and continue to simmer for 50 minutes.
2 Mix the honey and soy sauce together in a small bowl.
3 Preheat the oven to 180°C/Gas 4. Carefully take the ham out of the water. Cut away the thick fatty rind and then coat the joint in the honey and soy sauce mixture. Place the joint in a roasting tin and bake in the oven for 30 minutes. Remove, leave to rest for 10 minutes and then carve into slices to serve.
4 Heat a little olive oil in a frying pan and fry an egg for each person. Serve the eggs on a slice of ham on top of the potato cakes.

To make the potato cakes
5 Preheat the oven to 200°C/Gas 6. Mash the potatoes, using a potato ricer. Place the mash in a bowl with the kohlrabi, cheese, egg, spring onions and olive oil, then season with salt and pepper and mix well.
6 I make my potato cakes in 6 small tart tins, but you can make 1 big potato cake in a large tart tin. Whichever you use, grease the tin or tins, then spoon in the potato mixture and bake until golden brown. Small cakes will take 20 minutes and a large one about 25 minutes.
7 Remove the potato cakes from the tins when cool enough to handle. If you have made 1 large potato cake, serve it in slices with the ham and eggs.

Seafood lasagne

I like the combination of seafood and pasta and this is a lovely creamy lasagne.

SERVES 6

600ml milk
100g pollack fillet
200g salmon fillet, skinned
50g butter
2 tbsp flour
2 tbsp finely chopped flat-leaf parsley
50g Parmesan cheese, grated, plus extra for the topping
1 tsp dark soy sauce
200g cooked prawns
1 x 375g pack of dried lasagne sheets
sea salt
freshly ground black pepper

1 Preheat the oven to 200°C/Gas 6. Pour the milk into a wide pan, add the pollack and salmon and bring to a simmer. Cook for 2 minutes – you don't need to cook the fish through completely, as it will finish cooking once the lasagne is in the oven. Take the fish out of the milk and put it in a mixing bowl, then pour the milk into a measuring jug.
2 Melt the butter in a small saucepan, then stir in the flour. Remove the pan from the heat and add the fish milk a little at a time, stirring constantly to avoid lumps.
3 Once all the milk has been added, put the pan back on the heat and bring the sauce to a simmer. Cook on a low heat for 10 minutes, stirring occasionally to ensure that the sauce is not sticking to the pan. Season with salt and pepper and then add the parsley, cheese and soy sauce.
4 Remove 4 tablespoons of the sauce from the pan and place to one side. Pour the rest of the sauce over the fish, breaking up the fish as you stir in the sauce and add the cooked prawns. This is the filling for the lasagne.
5 Spoon half the fish mixture on to the bottom of a gratin dish. On top, lay a couple of sheets of lasagne to cover the fish mixture. Spoon the rest of the fish mixture over the lasagne, then place another layer of lasagne on top. Spread the 4 tablespoons of sauce that you set aside over the top and grate over a good sprinkling of Parmesan cheese. Bake in the oven for 45 minutes. Serve with a green salad.

Cheesy leeks on toast

Leeks are just coming into season this month and it's nice to have them back in the kitchen. They have been prized by cooks since Roman times and are now considered 'super' vegetables, as they are helpful in reducing bad cholesterol and linked to the lowering of the risk of heart disease. I think they are super because they taste fantastic and are so easy to cook.

SERVES 6

400g leeks, trimmed
100g grated Gruyère cheese
3 tbsp crème fraiche
1 tsp Worcestershire sauce
1 tsp Dijon mustard
1 tbsp plain flour
2 tbsp white breadcrumbs
7 eggs
6 slices of bread
2 tbsp olive oil
freshly ground black pepper

1 Preheat the grill. Slice each leek through the middle lengthways, almost to the end. Rinse the leeks under the tap by fanning them out under the water.
2 Thinly slice the leeks widthways and place them in a sauté pan on a medium heat. You won't need to add any fat as they will cook in the residual water they were rinsed in. Stir and cook them for 5 minutes until soft.
3 Remove the pan from the heat and add the cheese, crème fraiche, Worcestershire sauce, mustard, flour and breadcrumbs. Stir gently until everything is combined. Then mix in just 1 of the eggs and season with pepper.
4 Grill the bread and then place the pieces of toast in the bottom of a gratin dish. Drizzle them with olive oil and pile the leeks on top. Pop the dish under the grill for 5 minutes until brown and bubbling.
5 Use the same frying pan to fry the remaining 6 eggs and pop 1 on top of each serving of leeks on toast.

One-dish chicken dinner

This is the easiest meal to prepare, but tastes great. My husband loves one-dish dinners because he usually does the washing up!

SERVES 6

2 tbsp olive oil
8 chicken thighs on the bone, skin removed
70g chopped pancetta
2 courgettes, trimmed and cut into 1cm discs
3 carrots, trimmed and cut into 2cm chunks
800g potatoes, peeled and cut into 2cm cubes
2 fennel bulbs, trimmed and sliced
400ml chicken stock
4 sprigs of thyme
1 bay leaf
6 garlic cloves, whole and unpeeled
sea salt
freshly ground black pepper

1 Preheat the oven to 220°C/Gas 7. Heat the olive oil in a large saucepan and brown the chicken thighs. Remove them from the pan and place to one side. Brown the pancetta in the same pan.
2 Place all the vegetables in an ovenproof dish or a medium-sized roasting tin. Put the chicken and pancetta on top of the vegetables and pour on the stock, then tuck the thyme, bay leaf and garlic cloves in among the chicken and vegetables.
3 Season with salt and pepper and cook in the oven for 1 hour. Stir the vegetables around once during this cooking time to ensure that everything cooks through evenly.

Beef and kidney stew with buttered macaroni

When preparing stews, simmering is all important. To bring a stew to a simmer means that you are bringing it the point immediately preceding boiling and you want to keep it like this throughout the cooking time. I hate to see a stew boiling – it's rushing something that is only really created over time.

SERVES 6

- 1kg shin of beef, trimmed of excess fat and cut into 2cm chunks
- 6 tbsp plain flour, seasoned with salt and pepper
- 2–3 tbsp olive oil
- 400g beef kidneys, trimmed, cored and cut into bite-sized pieces
- 250g chestnut mushrooms, thickly sliced
- 1 onion, finely chopped
- 100ml red wine
- 1 tbsp tomato purée
- 1 bay leaf
- 500ml beef stock
- sea salt
- freshly ground black pepper

Buttered macaroni

- 500g macaroni
- 3 tbsp finely chopped flat-leaf parsley
- 20g butter
- freshly ground black pepper

1 Toss the chunks of beef in the flour, shaking off any excess. Heat 2 tablespoons of olive oil in a large saucepan and brown the meat in batches, putting each browned batch to one side while you do the next. You may need to add more oil to the pan as you go.
2 In the same pan, brown the kidneys and set them aside, then cook the mushrooms until nicely golden. Place these to one side with the meat.
3 Keep the pan on the heat. Add a little more olive oil if necessary and fry the onion for 5 minutes on a medium heat. Remove the onion from the pan and set it aside with the meat.
4 With the pan on the heat, pour in the wine and let it bubble away for 1 minute, scraping off any bits stuck to the sides and bottom of the pan. Return the meat, kidneys, onion and mushrooms to the pan.
5 Add the tomato purée, bay leaf and stock, then season with salt and pepper. Bring to a simmer. Cover the pan and cook at a very gentle simmer for 1 ½ hours. Check the seasoning and serve with the macaroni.

To prepare the buttered macaroni
6 Cook the macaroni according to the packet instructions. While the macaroni is still warm, toss it with the parsley and butter and season with black pepper.

Ratatouille and feta tart

Serve this colourful tart with a fresh green salad.

SERVES 6

250g aubergine, cut into ½ cm slices and then into quarters
olive oil
200g courgettes, cut into ½ cm rounds
1 red pepper, cored, seeded and chopped quite finely
1 onion, finely chopped
2 garlic cloves, finely chopped
300ml double cream
2 eggs, beaten
10 cherry tomatoes, cut in half
200g feta cheese, cut into 1cm cubes
a few roughly torn basil leaves
sea salt
freshly ground black pepper

Pastry
225g plain flour, plus extra for dusting the work surface
a pinch of salt
150g butter, chilled and cubed
1 egg yolk, beaten with 2 tbsp cold water

1 Place the aubergine slices in a colander and sprinkle them with salt. Leave for 20 minutes and then pat the slices dry with kitchen paper.
2 In the meantime, make the pastry. Place the flour, salt and butter in a food processor and whizz until the mixture resembles breadcrumbs. Add the egg yolk and water mixture and mix again briefly. Bring the mixture together into a ball of dough, wrap it in clingfilm and chill for 30 minutes.
3 Heat 2 tablespoons of olive oil in a frying pan and fry the aubergine slices, turning regularly to make sure that they brown evenly. You may need to fry the slices in a couple of batches. As the slices are browned, set them aside in a bowl.
4 Return the frying pan to the heat. Add a little more oil and fry the courgette slices for 4 minutes, until softened slightly and brown. Remove the courgettes from the pan and put them with the aubergine.
5 Return the pan to the heat, add a little more olive oil and fry the red pepper, onion and garlic for 5 minutes, stirring as you go. Tip it all into the bowl with the aubergines and courgettes.
6 Pour on the cream and add the eggs, tomato halves and feta cheese, then stir gently to combine. Season well with salt and pepper and scatter on the basil leaves. Preheat the oven to 180°C/Gas 4.
7 Roll out the pastry on a floured surface and use it to line a 24cm tart tin. Prick the pastry all over with a fork. Lay a large piece of baking parchment in the pastry case and scatter some baking beans on top. Place the tin on a baking sheet and put it in the oven for 10 minutes, then remove the baking parchment and baking beans.
8 Spoon the filling into the pastry case. Place the tart tin on the baking sheet and bake in the oven for 30 minutes.

Lamb curry with cabbage mallum

A 'mallum' is a Sri Lankan vegetable side dish. Here it accompanies a lamb curry, which is also Sri Lankan in style, mainly due to the coconut milk. Most children and fussy eaters will enjoy this meal, even the cabbage, which is in season this month.

SERVES 6

1 tbsp vegetable oil
1 onion, finely chopped
1 garlic clove, finely chopped
2cm piece of fresh root ginger, finely grated
2 tbsp curry powder
a large pinch of chilli powder
½ tsp mustard seeds
¼ tsp turmeric
½ tsp cumin seeds
¼ tsp fenugreek seeds
4 cardamom pods
5 curry leaves
2cm piece of cinnamon stick
1 tsp sea salt
1kg diced leg of lamb
300g new potatoes, halved and cut in quarters
200ml coconut milk
100ml water
sea salt
freshly ground black pepper

Cabbage mallum
1 tbsp vegetable oil
1 onion, finely chopped
1 garlic clove, finely chopped
½ tsp cumin seeds
2 tbsp desiccated coconut
2 tbsp water
¼ tsp mustard seeds
¼ tsp turmeric
5 curry leaves
500g shredded white cabbage
sea salt
freshly ground black pepper

1 Heat the oil in a saucepan. Add the onion, garlic and ginger and cook for 10 minutes on a low heat, stirring frequently.
2 Add all the spices and the salt and stir over the heat for 30 seconds. Throw in the lamb and stir well so that all the chunks are coated in the spices.
3 Add the potatoes, coconut milk and water and bring to a simmer. Cover and cook for 45 minutes, then check the seasoning before serving with the cabbage and some boiled rice.

To make the cabbage mallum
4 Heat the oil in a large sauté pan or frying pan. Add the onion and garlic and cook on a gentle heat for 5 minutes.
5 Add the rest of the ingredients, then cook and stir until you hear the cabbage sizzling and the water evaporates – this should take about 3 minutes. Check the seasoning and add more salt if necessary.

Apple and prune crumble tart

This pudding can take a while to put together but it's much quicker if you use a food processor for the pastry and the crumble. Apples are plentiful at this time of year and we cooks need a variety of recipes to keep everyone interested in eating them.

SERVES 6

Filling
400g dessert apples, peeled, cut into quarters and cored
150g soft pitted prunes, cut in half
1 tbsp soft brown sugar
50ml apple juice

Pastry
180g cold butter, cut into cubes
75g icing sugar
2 egg yolks
225g plain flour, plus extra for dusting the work surface

Crumble topping
150g plain flour
75g cold butter, cut into cubes
50g caster sugar

1 Place the apples and prunes in a saucepan with the sugar and apple juice. Cover the pan and simmer for 20 minutes, then set aside.

To make the pastry

2 Place all the ingredients in a food processor and whizz for a few seconds until the mixture resembles breadcrumbs. Turn the mixture out on to a work surface and bring the crumbs together into a ball of pastry dough with your hands. Wrap the dough in clingfilm and chill in the fridge for 30 minutes.

To make the crumble topping

3 Place the flour and butter in the food processor – you don't need to wash the bowl – and whizz until the mixture resembles breadcrumbs. Add the sugar and whizz again for a few seconds, then place to one side.

To assemble and cook the tart

4 Grease a 24cm tart tin and preheat the oven to 200°C/Gas 6.

5 Roll out the pastry on a floured work surface and use it to line the tart tin. Cover the pastry base completely with a sheet of baking parchment and place some baking beans on top. Put the tart tin on a baking sheet and place it in the oven for 10 minutes. Remove the baking beans and parchment and pop the tart case back in the oven for 5 minutes.

6 Spoon the apples and prunes into the pastry case and sprinkle the crumble mixture over the top. Place the tart in the oven on the baking tray and bake for 25 minutes. Serve with cream.

Brown sugar pear cake

This is such an easy pudding to make. Make sure you use ripe pears – it won't work with hard ones. This is good served hot or cold.

SERVES 6

200g ripe pears, peeled, cored and cut into quarters
50g raisins
¼ tsp grated nutmeg
2 tbsp brown sugar
2 tbsp water
250g butter, at room temperature
200g soft brown sugar
4 eggs
250g self-raising flour
2 tbsp honey

1 Preheat the oven to 180°C/Gas 4. Place the pears, raisins, nutmeg, sugar and water in an ovenproof pie dish. Cover the dish with a sheet of foil and bake in the oven for 20 minutes.
2 Meanwhile, cream the butter and sugar together for 5 minutes, using an electric whisk. Add an egg and a tablespoon of flour and mix in, then add the remaining eggs in the same way, with a tablespoon of flour each time. Add the rest of the flour and the honey and fold in with a metal spoon.
3 Spoon the mixture over the cooked pears and bake in the oven for 40 minutes until the sponge is firm to the light touch of your fingertips.

Spinach and sausage tart

Spinach and sausages go well together, as the spinach seems to counteract the richness of the sausages and the pastry. Serve with a green salad and baked potatoes.

SERVES 6

Filling
200g spinach leaves, rinsed and stalks removed
a knob of butter
4 pork sausages
1 shallot, finely chopped
300ml double cream
2 eggs
1 tsp Dijon mustard
50g Cheddar cheese, grated
sea salt
freshly ground black pepper

Pastry
225g plain flour, plus extra for dusting the work surface
a pinch of salt
120g cold butter, cut into cubes
1 egg yolk, beaten with 2 tbsp of cold water

To make the pastry

1 Place the flour, salt and butter in a food processor and whizz until you have a breadcrumb-like mixture. Add the egg yolk and water and whizz again briefly.

2 Turn the mixture out on to a floured surface and bring the pastry together in a ball. Wrap it in clingfilm and chill for 30 minutes. Preheat the oven to 200°C/Gas 6.

To prepare the filling and assemble the tart

3 Place the spinach leaves in a sauté pan with a little salt. Cook the spinach for 5 minutes on a low heat until the leaves are limp and soft. Tip the spinach into a colander to drain and press out any water with the back of a wooden spoon. Chop the spinach. Place the butter in the saucepan in which the spinach was cooked and warm over a medium heat. As soon as the butter starts to foam, add the chopped spinach and cook for 30 seconds, stirring as the spinach absorbs the butter. Remove from the heat and place to one side.

4 Fry the sausages in the same sauté pan until cooked and then cut them into slices about 1cm thick. Set them to one side. If a lot of fat comes out of the sausages, drain some away, then add the shallot and fry for 2 minutes.

5 Roll out the pastry on a floured surface and use it to line a 26cm tart tin. Lay a sheet of baking parchment on top of the pastry and cover it with baking beans. Place the tart on a baking sheet and pop it in the oven for 10 minutes. Remove the baking beans and parchment and bake the pastry case for another 5 minutes.

6 Pour the double cream into a mixing bowl and beat in the eggs, then season with salt and pepper and the Dijon mustard. Mix gently, then stir in the cheese, shallots and spinach until evenly combined.

7 Pour the mixture into the tart base and arrange the sausage pieces on top. Put the tart back in the oven on the baking sheet and bake for 30 minutes.

Salmon and cream cheese omelette

This isn't a true omelette as it is cooked in a gratin dish, but it's the only way I can cook an omelette for six people in one go. If you are reducing the quantities for fewer people, then you could use a frying pan.

SERVES 6

- 1 tbsp olive oil
- 500g salmon fillet, skinned
- 400g potatoes, peeled and cut into quarters (or eighths if large), cooked until tender
- 12 eggs
- 1 tsp finely chopped fresh dill
- 8 tsp cream cheese
- 2 tbsp finely grated Parmesan cheese
- sea salt
- freshly ground black pepper

1 Preheat the grill. Place the gratin dish or frying pan on the stove over a high heat and add the olive oil. When it's hot, add the salmon and fry for 2 minutes on each side. Transfer the salmon to a plate and cut it into chunks.
2 Return the gratin dish to the heat and fry the cooked potatoes until they are golden brown.
3 Crack the eggs into a bowl, whisk them gently and season with salt and pepper. With the gratin dish on the heat, pour the eggs over the top of the potatoes, tilting the dish so that the uncooked egg seeps under the cooked egg.
4 Keeping the pan on the heat, place the salmon pieces on top of the egg. Sprinkle on the dill and dot with the cream cheese. Sprinkle on the Parmesan cheese and season with salt and pepper.
5 Place the dish under the grill for 2 minutes. You want the egg to be a little runny on the top – don't let it dry out or the dish loses its enchantment. Serve in large slices with a green salad and some warm buttered toast.

Penne with courgette sauce

Autumn is here, but there are still plenty of courgettes around, despite the cooler weather. A mixture of yellow and green courgettes looks wonderful in this dish.

SERVES 6

2 tbsp olive oil, plus extra for drizzling
2 garlic cloves, peeled and finely chopped
400g courgettes, sliced into 1cm discs
75g butter
1 mild red chilli, seeded and finely chopped
500g penne pasta
2 tbsp chopped flat-leaf parsley
50g Parmesan cheese, grated
sea salt
freshly ground black pepper

1 Heat the olive oil in a large saucepan. Add the garlic and cook over a low heat for 30 seconds – don't let it burn.
2 Add the courgettes and stir them into the oil and garlic. Keep gently stirring and turning the discs until they are lovely and golden on both sides.
3 Add the butter and continue to cook the courgettes over a very low heat for 15 minutes. Then add the chopped chilli and cook for another 2 minutes.
4 Meanwhile, cook the pasta according to the packet instructions and drain.
5 Add the courgettes to the pasta, then the chopped parsley and sprinkle on the grated Parmesan. Season with plenty of pepper, a little salt and a drizzle of extra virgin olive oil.

Lamb stew with beans

Now the children are back at school, I like to give them good hearty meals in the evening, with lots of vegetables and pulses to build up their immune systems. A good tip for this recipe is to chop the courgettes finely so that they won't feel soggy when you eat the stew.

SERVES 6

3 tbsp olive oil
1.5kg lamb neck fillet, cut into cubes
1 onion, finely chopped
2 celery stalks, finely chopped
1 garlic clove, finely chopped
200g carrots, cut into chunks
2 courgettes, finely chopped
1 tsp ground coriander
1 x 400g can of tomatoes
1 x 400g can of cannellini beans
1 x 400g can of butter beans
1 tbsp tomato purée
1 sprig of thyme
500ml lamb or chicken stock
sea salt
freshly ground black pepper

Mini baked potatoes
1kg new potatoes, unpeeled and whole
1 tbs olive oil
1 tsp sea salt

1 Warm the olive oil in a large saucepan, then brown the lamb chunks in batches and place them to one side.
2 Keep the saucepan on the heat and fry the onion, celery and garlic for 10 minutes until soft.
3 Add the carrots, courgettes and ground coriander and stir, then add the canned tomatoes, beans, tomato purée, lamb, thyme and stock and mix everything together. Cover the pan and simmer over a gentle heat for 1 hour. Serve with the mini baked potatoes if your family have big appetites.

To prepare the mini baked potatoes
4 Preheat the oven to 200°C/Gas 6. Lay the potatoes on a baking sheet, pour the oil over them, then sprinkle with salt and pepper. Bake for 1 hour.

Grilled sea bass on minestrone vegetables

If you are nervous about cooking fish, sea bass fillets are a great place to start. The skin turns a lovely golden colour really easily and the flesh of the fish does not fall apart when you touch it.

SERVES 6

200g green beans
200g courgettes
250g new potatoes
200g carrots
2 tbsp olive oil
2 shallots, finely sliced,
1 garlic clove, finely chopped
1 x 400g can of cannellini beans
500ml chicken stock
1 tbsp soy sauce
a good handful of flat-leaf parsley, chopped
6 sea bass fillets
sea salt
freshly ground black pepper

1 Start by trimming and cleaning all the vegetables, then cut them into 1cm pieces.
2 Heat the olive oil in a saucepan. Add the shallots and garlic and cook for 3 minutes. Add the other vegetables and the canned beans, then pour on the stock and the soy sauce. Season with salt and pepper, but watch the salt as soy sauce is quite salty. Simmer gently, uncovered, for 15 minutes until all the vegetables are tender. Scatter in the parsley.
3 In the meantime, heat the grill. Place the sea bass fillets on the grill pan and season with salt and pepper. Cook under the grill for 1 minute on each side.
4 Serve the vegetables on large plates with the sea bass fillets on top.

Beef fillet salad

This recipe has a long list of ingredients but is very easy to prepare.

SERVES 6

- 6 medium potatoes, peeled and cut into quarters
- 1 kohlrabi, peeled, trimmed and cut into thin matchsticks
- 4 spring onions, sliced
- ½ cucumber, cut into matchsticks
- 6 cherry tomatoes, cut in half
- a handful of basil leaves, roughly torn
- 6 radishes, thinly sliced
- 1 tbsp crème fraiche
- 1 tsp Dijon mustard
- 5–6 tbsp olive oil
- 1 tsp sesame oil
- 400g beef fillet, cut into 2cm thick slices
- 2 Little Gem lettuces
- 2 shallots, thinly sliced
- 1 tsp dark soy sauce
- 1 tbsp cashew nuts, unsalted
- sea salt
- freshly ground black pepper

1 First boil the potatoes in salted water until tender, then drain and place them to one side.
2 Prepare the salad by placing the kohlrabi, spring onions, cucumber, tomatoes, basil and radishes in a bowl. Place to one side.
3 Spoon the crème fraiche and mustard into a small bowl. Slowly add 3 tablespoons of the olive oil, a tablespoon at a time, mixing it in as you add it, then add the sesame oil. Season with salt and pepper. Spoon the dressing over the kohlrabi salad and mix so that it coats all the ingredients.
4 Heat 2 tablespoons of olive oil in a frying pan and fry the potatoes until they are golden brown. Remove them from the pan and place to one side.
5 In the same pan, fry the beef fillet slices for 2 minutes on each side for medium – or longer if you like well-done meat. Place the sautéed potatoes back in the pan with the beef just as you're finishing cooking to warm them through.

To assemble the dish

6 Place some lettuce leaves on each plate, then spoon some of the kohlrabi salad on top. Add some slices of beef and sautéed potatoes.
7 Quickly fry the shallots in a little olive oil for 1 minute, then sprinkle on the soy sauce. Garnish the salad with shallots and cashew nuts.

Roast chicken with herb remoulade

There are few meals as universally appreciated as roast chicken. I have varied it slightly with a herb remoulade, which is a mayonnaise-based sauce. The vegetables ensure that this is still a light, summery meal.

SERVES 6–8

2 x 1.5kg whole chickens
2 tbsp olive oil
sea salt
freshly ground black pepper

Herb remoulade
2 egg yolks
1 dsrtsp white wine vinegar
1 tbsp Dijon mustard
a pinch of salt
200ml light olive oil
2 tbsp chopped fresh basil, parsley and tarragon, mixed together

Courgettes and carrots
15g butter
12–14 baby carrots, sliced into 1cm discs
6 small courgettes, trimmed and sliced into 1cm discs
1 tsp finely chopped rosemary leaves
100ml dry white wine
sea salt
freshly ground black pepper

1 Preheat the oven to 200°C/Gas 6. Place the chickens in a roasting tin and rub them with the olive oil. Season with plenty of salt and pepper. Roast the chickens for 1½ hours or until the juices run clear when you pierce the thickest part of the leg with a sharp knife. Leave the chickens to rest for 30 minutes before carving and serving with the remoulade and the carrots and courgettes.

To make the herb remoulade
2 Mix the egg yolks, vinegar, mustard and salt in a small mixing bowl. Start adding the olive oil in a steady trickle, whisking constantly. When you have added all the olive oil, stir in the herbs, then check the seasoning and set to one side.

To cook the courgettes and carrots
3 Heat the butter in a sauté pan. Add the carrots, courgettes and rosemary and cook for 5 minutes, stirring occasionally. Add the wine and cook for 2 minutes more over a gentle heat, by which time the vegetables should be soft.
4 Cover the pan with a lid if you have one, or a sheet of baking parchment, and cook for 5 minutes more. Season the vegetables well before serving.

Berry milkshake

This milkshake is extremely healthy, despite the tub of ice cream. Milk is a great source of calcium for children; girls especially need to be encouraged to continue to drink milk during their growing years and this is a very enjoyable way of doing it. The fruit is full of vitamin C and if you don't have any fresh fruit, frozen berries will do just as well.

SERVES 6

- 200g blackberries
- 300g raspberries
- 200g strawberries
- 3 tbsp elderflower cordial
- 3 tbsp water
- 2 tbsp caster sugar
- 1 x 500ml tub of vanilla ice cream
- 300ml milk

1 Place the fruit in a saucepan with the cordial, water and sugar. Bring to a slow simmer, partially cover the pan and cook for 10 minutes. Set aside to cool.
2 Place the cooled fruit in a food processor or liquidiser and purée for 1 minute.
3 Pour the pureé through a sieve and then return it to the food processor or liquidiser. Add the ice cream and milk, then whizz again and serve in glasses.

Mixed fruit crumble

There isn't a more perfect time of year for a fruit crumble than autumn, when apples, pears and plums are all at their best.

SERVES 6

200g apples, peeled, cored and cut into quarters
100g plums, halved and de-stoned
100g pears, peeled cored and cut into quarters
a knob of butter
2 tbsp soft brown sugar
50ml apple juice
1 banana, sliced into 1cm chunks

Crumble topping
120g plain flour
100g cold butter, cut into cubes
2 tbsp soft brown sugar
2 tbsp caster sugar
½ tsp ground ginger

1 Preheat the oven to 180°C/Gas 4. Place the apples, plums and pears in a saucepan and add the sugar, butter and apple juice. Cover the pan and cook for 10 minutes, on a low heat until everything is soft.
2 In the meantime, prepare the topping. Put the flour and butter in a food processor and process until the mixture resembles breadcrumbs. Add the sugars and ginger and mix again briefly.
3 Spoon the fruit into a pie dish. Add the banana slices, and sprinkle the crumble mixture on top. Bake for about 35 minutes.

Madeleines

My children fell in love with these when we were in France. The shop-bought ones have too many additives for my liking, so I promised the children that I would try and recreate the little cakes when we got home. You do need to buy a madeleine tray, but the cakes are so quick and easy to make and so very pretty that I think the tray is a worthwhile piece of kitchen equipment.

MAKES 12

50g melted butter, plus extra for greasing
50g plain flour, plus extra for sprinkling
2 eggs
50g caster sugar
25g ground almonds
¼ tsp almond extract

1 Preheat the oven to 180°C/Gas 4. Grease a madeleine tray with butter and sprinkle the insides of the cups with flour.
2 Place the eggs and sugar in a mixing bowl and, using an electric whisk, whisk them together until you have a thick, mousse-like mixture. Fold in the flour, ground almonds, melted butter and almond extract.
3 Divide the mixture between the cups on the madeleine tray and bake in the oven for 10 minutes. Let the madeleines cool for a few minutes and then ease them from the tin and leave to cool on a wire rack.

Twice-baked cheese and spinach soufflés

These soufflés look impressive but they are actually a doddle to make. Serve with a salad and bread.

SERVES 6

50g butter, plus extra for greasing
300ml milk
½ onion
2 cloves
1 bay leaf
50g plain flour
200g spinach leaves
150g Gruyère cheese, grated
1 tsp Dijon mustard
a pinch of grated nutmeg
3 egg yolks
3 egg whites
150ml double cream
sea salt
freshly ground black pepper

1 Preheat the oven to 200°C/Gas 6. Generously butter 6 ramekins, paying particular attention to the bases.
2 Pour the milk into a saucepan. Stud the onion with the cloves and add it to the milk. Add the bay leaf, bring the milk to the boil, then remove the pan from the heat, cover and leave for 5 minutes.
3 Melt the butter in a separate medium saucepan, then stir in the flour. Remove the pan from the heat and very slowly add the warm milk, stirring constantly. Place the pan back on the heat and simmer gently for 5 minutes.
4 Bring a large saucepan of salted water to the boil. Add the spinach leaves, bring the water back to a simmer and then immediately tip the spinach into a colander to drain. Press out as much water as you can, then place the spinach on a chopping board and chop it as finely as you can with a large knife.
5 Stir the chopped spinach into the white sauce along with 100g of the grated Gruyère and the mustard, nutmeg and 3 egg yolks. Stir well to combine, off the heat. Leave to one side.
6 Whisk the egg whites in a clean bowl until they almost form soft peaks. Fold the egg whites into the spinach and cheese sauce, making sure that the egg whites get completely absorbed without over mixing.
7 Divide the mixture evenly between the 6 ramekins. Stand the ramekins in a high-sided roasting tin, then pour 2–3cm of boiling water into the tin. Put the tin into the oven and bake the soufflés for 20 minutes.
8 Remove from the oven and carefully take the ramekins out of the roasting tin. When the soufflés are cool enough, run a knife around the edge of each one and turn them out into an ovenproof dish. Increase the oven heat to 220°C/Gas 7.
9 Pour the cream into the dish around the soufflés and sprinkle them with the remaining cheese. Put them back in the oven for 15 minutes by which time the soufflés will be golden brown and will have risen a little more.

Meat loaf with tomato sauce

This is an excellent supper dish and any leftover meat loaf makes a great filling for sandwiches.

SERVES 6

2 tbsp olive oil
1 onion, finely chopped
2 garlic cloves, finely chopped
70g sliced pancetta, finely chopped
2 tbsp finely chopped basil and parsley
2 eggs
1 tbsp dark soy sauce
500g minced pork
450g sausage meat
200g chicken livers, trimmed and finely chopped
a good grating of nutmeg
sea salt
freshly ground black pepper

Tomato sauce
2 tbsp olive oil
1 onion, finely chopped
1 clove garlic, finely chopped
400g cherry tomatoes, halved
1 tbsp tomato purée
1 x 400g can of chopped tomatoes
200ml vegetable stock (a stock cube will do)
1 tsp sugar
2 tbsp roughly chopped basil leaves
sea salt
freshly ground black pepper

1 Preheat oven to 200°C/Gas 6. Heat the olive oil in a sauté pan. Add the onion, garlic and pancetta and cook for 5 minutes, until the onion is soft. Tip everything into a mixing bowl.
2 Add the herbs, eggs, soy sauce, pork mince, sausage meat and chicken livers, then season well with salt, pepper and nutmeg. Mix until everything is well combined.
3 Spoon the mixture into a 1-litre loaf tin and then knock the bottom of the tin on a hard surface to ensure that there are no gaps or holes in the mixture. Place the loaf tin on a small baking sheet and bake in the oven for 1 ½ hours. You will get a little spillage over the loaf tin so do use the baking sheet.
4 Turn the meat loaf out on to a plate and serve in slices with the tomato sauce and some mashed potatoes (see page 542).

To make the tomato sauce
5 Heat the olive oil in a saucepan, add the onion and garlic and cook for 10 minutes, until soft. Add the cherry tomatoes, purée, canned tomatoes, stock and sugar, then simmer gently, uncovered, for 45 minutes. Check the seasoning and adjust if necessary, then sprinkle on the basil leaves before serving.

Courgette and blue cheese risotto

Despite the onset of autumn the courgettes continue to come. I always have a pile of them in my kitchen and in my desperation to avoid waste, I try to come up with ways of eating them that everyone will enjoy.

SERVES 6

1.5 litres chicken stock
2 tbsp olive oil
2 garlic cloves, finely chopped
400g courgettes, sliced into 1cm discs
25g butter
1 onion, finely chopped
1 celery stalk, finely chopped
500g Arborio rice
200g blue cheese, such as Gorgonzola or Cashel Blue, crumbled into small pieces
2 tbsp finely chopped flat-leaf parsley
sea salt
freshly ground black pepper

1 Pour the chicken stock into a saucepan and bring it to a simmer. Keep it simmering gently while you prepare the vegetables.
2 Heat the olive oil in a large pan, add the garlic and stir to flavour the oil. Take care that the garlic doesn't burn. Add the courgettes, in a single layer, if possible, and fry them for 5 minutes on each side. Add the butter, reduce the heat to low and cook the courgettes for 15 minutes, turning them occasionally until they are a beautiful golden colour. Remove them from the pan and place to one side.
3 Add the onion and celery to the same pan and fry gently for 10 minutes, stirring occasionally. Add the risotto rice and fry gently for 2 minutes, stirring constantly.
4 Start adding the hot stock to the rice, 2 ladlefuls at a time. Stir the rice until the stock is almost absorbed and then add more stock. Keep adding the stock like this for about 20–25 minutes until it has all been absorbed and the rice is cooked to your liking.
5 Add the courgettes and the blue cheese to the rice, gently folding them in. Scatter over the parsley, season with salt and pepper and eat immediately.

Moussaka

If moussaka is cooked with care, it is a most worthwhile dish. It doesn't have to be heavy and oily. Give it a go and I think you'll be pleasantly surprised. The tzatziki is a perfect partner.

SERVES 6

3 aubergines, sliced into 5mm discs
3 tbsp olive oil
grated zest of 1 lemon
1 onion, finely chopped
2 garlic cloves, finely chopped
1 celery stalk, finely chopped
1kg minced lamb
150ml dry white wine
1 tbsp tomato purée
200g canned chopped tomatoes
2 tsp finely chopped fresh oregano
1 tbsp finely chopped flat-leaf parsley
¼ tsp ground allspice
20g Parmesan cheese, grated
sea salt
freshly ground black pepper

Béchamel sauce
600ml milk
1 onion, peeled and studded with 2 cloves
1 bay leaf
50g butter
1 tbsp flour
a grating of nutmeg
sea salt
freshly ground black pepper

Tzatiki
300g Greek yoghurt
2 tbsp olive oil
1 cucumber, diced
2 garlic cloves, finely crushed
1 tbsp finely chopped fresh mint
sea salt
freshly ground black pepper

1 Preheat the oven to 200°C/Gas 6. Place the sliced aubergines in a colander, sprinkling them with salt as you do so. Leave them for 20 minutes and then pat them dry with some kitchen paper or a clean tea towel.
2 Place a heavy-based frying pan on the stove. Don't add any oil, just dry fry as many aubergine slices as you can in a single layer on the bottom of the pan, turning them as they brown – they will only brown slightly. Tip each batch into a bowl while you brown the rest.
3 When all the slices are browned, drizzle them with a tablespoon of olive oil, sprinkle over the lemon zest and season with salt and pepper. Mix the slices with your hands to ensure that they are all nicely coated with the olive oil and seasoning. Place to one side.
4 Next heat 2 tablespoons of olive oil in a large saucepan and fry the onion, garlic and celery on a low heat for 10 minutes, stirring occasionally. Add the lamb and stir until it has all browned.
5 Pour on the wine and let it bubble away for 3 minutes. Add the tomato purée, canned tomatoes, oregano, parsley and allspice, then season with salt and pepper. Stir, then simmer for 10 minutes. Leave to one side.

To make the béchamel sauce
6 Heat the milk in a saucepan with the onion and bay leaf. Bring to boiling point, then remove from the heat, cover the pan with a lid and let the milk sit for about 10 minutes so that the flavours can infuse.

7 Melt the butter in another small saucepan, then stir in the flour. Remove the pan from the heat. Take the onion and bay leaf out of the milk, then slowly add it to the butter and flour mix, stirring constantly to avoid lumps. Season with the nutmeg, salt and pepper.
8 Return the pan to the hob and simmer on a very low heat for at least 10 minutes.

To assemble the moussaka
9 Place a layer of aubergine slices on the bottom of an ovenproof gratin dish. Add a layer of mince, then more aubergine slices and another layer of mince. Finish with a layer of aubergine and then pour the sauce over the top. Sprinkle on the cheese and bake in the oven for 40 minutes. Serve with the tzatziki and a green salad.

To make the tzatiki
10 Spoon the Greek yoghurt into a small serving dish. Slowly add the olive oil, stirring as you do so – if you add it too quickly the yoghurt may curdle. Stir in the cucumber, garlic and mint leaves and season with salt and pepper.

Fish soup with Gruyère croutons

Fish soups are often rather fiddly, but this one can be prepared and cooked in about 25 minutes.

SERVES 6

2 tbsp olive oil
1 shallot, finely chopped
3 garlic cloves, finely chopped
200g cherry tomatoes, cut in half
15g butter
150ml white wine
1 tbsp finely chopped fresh oregano
300g penne pasta
1 litre vegetable stock
200g monkfish fillet, chopped into 2cm chunks
50g pollack fillets, chopped into 2cm chunks
250g cooked prawns
sea salt
freshly ground black pepper

Gruyère croutons
1 small stick of French bread
olive oil
2 garlic cloves, cut in half
100g Gruyère cheese, grated

1 Heat the olive oil in a large saucepan and add the shallot, garlic, tomatoes and butter. Cook on a gentle heat for 10 minutes, stirring occasionally and mashing the tomatoes with the back of a wooden spoon as they soften.
2 Pour on the wine and add the oregano, then simmer for 5 minutes. Add the pasta and vegetable stock and cook the penne at a gentle simmer according to the packet instructions.
3 Two minutes before the end of the cooking time for the pasta, add the fish and prawns and simmer gently for 2 minutes. Check the seasoning, then serve with the cheese croutons.

To make the Gruyère croutons
4 Cut the French bread into 1cm slices. Drizzle the slices with olive oil, then rub them with the cut side of a piece of garlic.
5 Sprinkle the slices with the grated Gruyère and toast under the grill.

Sirloin steak with butternut purée and sautéed mushrooms

When I devised this meal I had in mind the colours as well as the produce of autumn. There is the rich orange of the butternut squash, the deep dark brown of the steak, oozing a little dark red, and then the lush, velvety browns of the mushrooms.

SERVES 6

6 sirloin steaks
olive oil

Butternut purée
1 butternut squash, peeled, cored and chopped into 2cm chunks
a sprig of rosemary
50ml white wine
1 tbsp olive oil
2 tbsp crème fraiche
sea salt
freshly ground black pepper

Sautéed mushrooms
2 tbsp olive oil
25g butter
500g mixed mushrooms, sliced into 5mm pieces
1 tbsp dark soy sauce
sea salt
freshly ground black pepper

To make the butternut purée

1 Preheat the oven to 200°C/Gas 6. Place the squash and rosemary sprig in the middle of a large sheet of foil on a baking sheet. Turn up the sides of the foil slightly, then pour on the wine and olive oil and season with salt and pepper. Bake the squash in the oven for 45 minutes.

2 Remove the rosemary and place the squash, with any juices, in a food processor or a blender. Add the crème fraiche and whizz until you have a smooth purée. If it seems too thick, loosen it with a little water. Check the seasoning and set aside, ready to reheat before serving.

To sauté the mushrooms

3 Heat the olive oil and butter in a sauté pan. Add the mushrooms and sauté for 20 minutes on a medium heat until they are golden brown. Pour on the soy sauce and check the seasoning before tipping them on to a plate.

To cook the steaks

4 To avoid too much washing up, use the pan that you cooked the mushrooms in. Place the pan on the heat. Brush the steaks with a little olive oil and when the pan is hot, fry 2 or 3 steaks for 2 minutes on each side for medium-cooked meat. Remove them from the pan and set aside while you cook the rest.

5 Put the mushrooms back in the pan to warm through and place the steaks on top so everything comes to the table warm. Reheat the butternut purée and serve with the steaks.

STAINLESS
STEEL

Osso buco

This classic Italian dish is simple and quick to make, like so many of that nation's favourites. I guess it isn't more widely made because people assume veal is difficult to get hold of. Veal is now becoming more widely available, and most butchers will be able to get hold of some for you. Make sure you ask for rose veal, which is from humanely reared animals.

SERVES 6

3 tbsp olive oil
6 x 5cm thick pieces of veal shank
150ml dry white wine
200ml beef stock (a stock cube will do)
1 x 400g can of chopped tomatoes
1 x 400g can of cannellini beans, drained and rinsed
sea salt
freshly ground black pepper

Mashed potatoes
1kg potatoes, peeled and cut into quarters
40g butter
200ml warm milk
sea salt
freshly ground black pepper

1 You will need a large wide pan so that you can fit all the veal pieces flat on the bottom of the pan. A heatproof casserole dish is fine. Heat the olive oil in the pan and lay all the veal pieces in the hot oil. Brown them for 2 minutes and then turn them over and brown for a further 2 minutes.
2 Pour the wine over the meat and cook at a gentle simmer for 10 minutes.
3 Pour on the stock, tomatoes and beans. Season well with salt and pepper, cover the pan and cook at a slow simmer for 1 ½ hours. Serve with mashed potatoes and a green vegetable.

To make the mashed potatoes
4 Boil the potatoes in salted water until tender.
5 Pass the potatoes through a potato ricer or use your preferred method to mash them. Return them to the pan and place over a low heat. Mix in the butter and milk and season to taste.

White chocolate and raisin biscuits

The smell of home-made biscuits baking in the oven is hard to beat.

MAKES ABOUT 16

50g butter, at room temperature, plus extra for greasing
80g soft brown sugar
1 egg
a few drops of vanilla extract
70g raisins
50g white chocolate chips
120g plain flour
1 tsp baking powder

1 Preheat the oven to 180°C/Gas 4 and grease a large baking sheet.
2 Place the butter and sugar in a mixing bowl and, using an electric hand-whisk, cream them together for 2 minutes. Stir in the egg and vanilla.
3 Add the raisins, chocolate chips, flour and baking powder and stir in with a wooden spoon until you have a soft dough.
4 Pull off pieces of the dough and roll them into balls with a diameter of about 3cm. Place the balls on a greased baking sheet and flatten them slightly with a fork.
5 Bake in the preheated oven for 15 minutes. Remove, leave the biscuits on the baking sheet to cool slightly and then transfer them to a wire rack to cool completely.

Apple purée with cinnamon toast

This was a firm family favourite when I was growing up.

SERVES 6

800g dessert apples, peeled, cored and cut into quarters
100g soft brown sugar
100ml apple juice
1 x 4cm piece of cinnamon stick

Cinnamon toast
3 tsp ground cinnamon
7 tbsp caster sugar
6–8 slices of white bread
butter, for spreading

1 Place all the ingredients for the apple purée in a covered saucepan over a low heat and bring to a gentle simmer. Cook for 30 minutes until all the apples are tender, stirring occasionally.
2 Remove the cinnamon stick. Spoon the mixture into a food processor and blend until smooth. Serve with the cinnamon toast.

To make the cinnamon toast
3 Mix the cinnamon and sugar together in a small dish.
4 Toast the bread on 1 side only. Spread the untoasted side with butter and sprinkle with sugar and cinnamon. Place the slices under the grill until bubbling and golden. A word of warning: don't wander off when the toast is under the grill as the sugar can burn very quickly.
5 Cut into fingers or triangles to serve.

Celery and potato soup with chickpea fritters

Celery and potato soup is a great favourite of mine, as I love the flavour of celery and this is a good way of making the most of it. The chickpea fritters make this into a nourishing supper.

SERVES 6

25g butter
400g celery, roughly chopped
2 leeks, trimmed and roughly chopped
400g potatoes, peeled and roughly chopped
1.2 litres chicken stock
150ml single cream
2 tbsp finely chopped flat-leaf parsley
sea salt
freshly ground black pepper

Chickpea fritters
1 x 400g can of chickpeas, drained and rinsed
2 garlic cloves
4 spring onions, finely chopped
1 tbsp olive oil
1 tbsp soy sauce
1 tsp ground cumin
1 tsp ground coriander
2 tbsp finely chopped flat-leaf parsley
1 tbsp plain flour
olive oil, for frying
sea salt
freshly ground black pepper

1 Heat the butter in a large saucepan. Add the celery, cover the pan and cook over a low heat for 5 minutes.
2 Add the leeks and potatoes, cover the pan again and cook over a low heat for 5 minutes. Pour on the stock and cook for 45 minutes.
3 When the vegetables have cooled slightly, pour them into a blender and process until smooth. Return the soup to the pan and warm it through. Stir in the cream and parsley and check the seasoning, adjusting as necessary. Serve with the fritters in the soup or on the side, as you prefer.

To make the chickpea fritters
4 Place the chickpeas, garlic, spring onions, olive oil, soy sauce, cumin, coriander and parsley in a food processor and blend until you have a fairly smooth paste. Stir in the flour, then season well. Place the mixture in the fridge to chill for 20 minutes or so.
5 Form the mixture into balls about the size of golf balls and flatten them slightly. Heat the olive oil in a frying pan and brown the fritters for 1 minute on each side until golden brown.

Oven-baked chicken with sausages and beans

You will need a large casserole dish for cooking this recipe. Serve with mashed potatoes (see page 542) on the side if you have hearty appetites to satisfy.

SERVES 6

2 tbsp olive oil
1 x 1.5kg chicken
2 red onions, peeled and quartered
8 pork sausages, sliced into 2cm pieces
3 garlic cloves, peeled and left whole
2 x 400g cans of flageolet beans, drained and rinsed
2 tbsp finely chopped flat-leaf parsley
200ml chicken stock
sea salt
freshly ground black pepper

1 Preheat the oven to 200°C/Gas 6. Heat the olive oil in a casserole dish, then add the chicken, breast side down. Leave it for 2 minutes until the breast is nicely browned, then turn the bird on to its side and brown the leg and do the same with the other side. Remove the chicken and place it to one side.

2 Keep the casserole dish on the heat, add the onion, sausage pieces and garlic, then fry them for 2 minutes on a high heat. Add the beans, parsley and stock, then return the chicken to the casserole dish. Season with salt and pepper, cover the dish and bake in the oven for 1 hour and 20 minutes.

3 Carve the chicken and serve it with the beans, sausages and juices from the pan.

Peach and rosemary cake

Peaches and rosemary might seem an odd combination, but they work very well together. Herbs can add an interesting flavour to a sweet dish.

MAKES 1 X 24CM CAKE

- 3 peaches
- 2 tbsp soft brown sugar
- 2 tsp finely chopped rosemary
- 200g butter, at room temperature, plus extra for greasing

- 200g caster sugar
- 4 eggs
- 200g self-raising flour
- crème fraiche or whipped cream, for serving

1 Preheat the oven to 180°C/Gas 4. Grease a 24cm spring-clip cake tin and line the base with baking parchment.
2 Cut the peaches in half around the middle and remove the stones, then cut them again so that each peach is in 4 pieces. Put them in a mixing bowl with the soft brown sugar and rosemary and toss everything together. Spoon the peaches, sugar and rosemary into the bottom of the cake tin.
3 Place the butter and caster sugar in the bowl and, using an electric hand-whisk, cream them together for 5 minutes until light and fluffy. Add 1 egg and a tablespoon of flour and mix again. Add the rest of the eggs in the same way, with a spoonful of flour each time, then fold in the rest of the flour with a wooden spoon.
4 Spoon the cake mixture into the tin, on top of the peaches. Bake in the oven for 40 minutes, until the sponge is firm to the touch of your fingertips.
5 Remove from the oven and when the cake is cool enough to handle, turn it out on to to a plate. Serve with crème fraiche or whipped cream.

Warm parkin with butterscotch sauce

Parkin isn't like a sticky toffee pudding, despite the treacle and syrup. It is a solid biscuit cake and is delicious simply sliced and buttered or served as a pudding with the butterscotch sauce.

SERVES 6

butter, for greasing
100g plain flour
100g wholemeal flour
1 tsp ground ginger
¼ tsp ground cinnamon
¼ tsp bicarbonate of soda
¼ tsp baking powder
75g soft brown sugar
80g unsalted butter
80g black treacle
80g golden syrup
3 eggs

Butterscotch sauce
225g brown sugar
100ml water
300ml double cream
125g butter, cut into cubes

1 Preheat the oven to 180°C/Gas 4. Grease a 20 x 20cm brownie tin and line it with baking parchment. Put the flours, spices, bicarbonate of soda and baking powder in a mixing bowl.
2 Place the sugar, butter, treacle and syrup in a saucepan and heat gently until the butter has melted, then leave to cool slightly. Add the eggs, beating them well into the mixture.
3 Slowly pour this mixture on to the dry ingredients in the mixing bowl, beating as you go to make a smooth batter.
4 Pour the mixture into the cake tin and bake in the oven for 45 minutes until the middle of the cake is firm to the light touch of your fingertips. Leave the parkin to cool in the tin for 10 minutes before cutting in slices. Serve drizzled with the butterscotch sauce.

To make the butterscotch sauce
5 Put the sugar in a small saucepan with the water and bring it to the boil. Reduce the heat and simmer until the sugar and water start to turn a darker brown.
6 Remove the pan from the heat and gradually stir in the cream, then whisk in the butter. Return the pan to the heat and bring to a simmer, then remove from the heat again. The sauce will thicken when cold, but you can reheat it as long as you do this slowly.

Summer may be well and truly over, but we can have some of the most glorious days of the year this month. Mornings and evenings may be chilly but there is often plenty of golden sunshine, which makes tidying the garden and walks in the country a great pleasure. There are still plenty of fruits to enjoy, particularly apples, pears and quinces. This is a good time to make jams and chutneys from frozen summer fruit and autumn windfalls, and these will serve you well over the coming months. British leeks and sprouts are just becoming available, as are cauliflowers, pumpkins and squash. As the nights draw in, we are inevitably drawn to more warming meals and for cooks this is the start of the season for comfort food. Enjoy eating stews and roasts, apple cakes and fruit pies and luxuriate in the sense of wellbeing that a varied diet brings.

October

Deluxe Bolognese sauce

I call this deluxe bolognese because the chicken livers and pancetta make this version of the classic meat sauce more luxurious than the recipe I included in my last book. I knew I couldn't write a cookbook with recipes for a whole year without including one for bolognese, which is now one of the nation's most popular dishes.

SERVES 6

1 tbsp olive oil
1 onion, finely chopped
1 celery stalk, finely chopped
1 carrot, finely chopped
1 garlic clove, finely chopped
70g pancetta, chopped
500g minced pork
500g minced beef
250ml red wine
200g chicken livers, trimmed and chopped into small pieces
1 sprig of fresh thyme
1 tbsp tomato purée
2 x 400g cans of chopped tomatoes
600g spaghetti
freshly grated Parmesan cheese, for serving
sea salt
freshly ground black pepper

1 Heat the olive oil in a large saucepan. Add the onion, celery, carrot and garlic and cook over a low heat, stirring occasionally, for 10 minutes.
2 Add the pancetta and continue to cook for another 5 minutes.
3 Now add the pork and beef and increase the heat. Cook, stirring continuously, until the meat has lost its pinkness. Add the wine and let it bubble away for 5 minutes.
4 Add the chicken livers, thyme, tomato purée and chopped tomatoes and bring everything to a simmer. Season, cover the pan and leave the sauce to simmer gently for 1 hour.
5 Remove the lid and cook over the lowest heat, keeping a tremble in the sauce, for 40 minutes more. Check the seasoning and adjust as necessary.
6 Cook the spaghetti according to the packet instructions and serve with plenty of grated Parmesan cheese.

Chicken pilaf

I love dishes in which all the ingredients go into one pot to cook together, and are then taken to the table and served straight from the pot.

SERVES 6

25g butter
2 tbsp olive oil
8 chicken thighs
6 cardamom pods, squashed
2 cloves
6 curry leaves
2cm piece of cinnamon stick
1 handful of blanched almonds
1 onion, finely chopped
1 tbsp curry powder (see page 559)
1 handful of sultanas
500g basmati rice
3 hard-boiled eggs, chopped into quarters
600ml water
1 tsp salt

Yoghurt, mint and cucumber
250g natural yoghurt
½ cucumber, diced
1 sprig of mint, finely chopped
sea salt
freshly ground black pepper

1 You need a large saucepan with a tight-fitting lid. Heat the butter and olive oil in the pan and then brown the chicken thighs on both sides until they are a deep golden brown. Fry 4 thighs at a time and spend 10 minutes cooking each batch. Remove the chicken pieces and place to one side.
2 Keep the pan on the heat and add the cardamom pods, cloves, curry leaves, cinnamon stick and almonds and cook briefly until the almonds turn golden brown. A couple of minutes should be enough. Now add the onion and cook, stirring occasionally for 10 minutes, until nice and soft.
3 Sprinkle on the curry powder, then add the sultanas and the rice and stir well. Place the chicken back in the pan, pour on the water and add the salt.
4 Bring to a simmer. Cover the rice and chicken with a circle of baking parchment and put the lid on the pan. Turn the heat down to very, very low and leave undisturbed for 10 minutes.
5 Remove the coverings and give everything a stir, then put the parchment and lid back in place and cook for another 15 minutes.
6 Remove the saucepan from the heat and leave undisturbed and covered for 15 minutes, by which time the rice and chicken should be perfectly cooked. Scatter on the hard-boiled eggs and serve with the yoghurt, mint and cucumber.

To make the yoghurt, mint and cucumber
7 Put all the ingredients in a bowl and mix well. Season with the salt and pepper.

Smoked haddock soup

Summer is well and truly over and something warming but still relatively light is needed for supper. Serve this soup with hunks of crusty bread and you will have a good meal.

SERVES 6

25g butter
500g new potatoes, cut into 2cm pieces
1 celery stalk, finely chopped
1 leek, finely sliced
1 onion, finely chopped
70g chopped pancetta
1 tbsp plain flour
500ml fish stock
1kg smoked haddock, skinned, boned and cut into 2cm pieces
300ml milk
1 tbsp chervil, finely chopped
¼ tsp cayenne pepper
50g young spinach leaves, roughly shredded (optional)
freshly ground black pepper

1 Melt the butter in a large saucepan. Add the potatoes, celery, leek, onion and pancetta and stir briefly.
2 Reduce the heat, then cover the saucepan and cook the vegetables and pancetta gently for 5 minutes. Sprinkle on the flour and stir.
3 Pour on the stock, cover the pan and leave to simmer gently for 10 minutes.
4 Add the fish, milk, chervil, cayenne and spinach, if using, and cook for 3 minutes more. Season with black pepper to taste and serve with crusty bread.

Chive gnocchi with vegetable sauce

Gnocchi do not deserve their reputation for being rather bland and heavy. Made like this, they are light and the perfect accompaniment to a flavoursome sauce.

SERVES 6

900g potatoes, cooked until tender and mashed using a potato ricer
225g '00' Italian flour, plus extra for dusting the work surface
2 small eggs
a small bunch of chives, finely snipped with scissors
a pinch of salt
25g butter, at room temperature
freshly grated Parmesan cheese, for serving

Vegetable sauce
2 tbsp olive oil
1 onion, finely diced
1 garlic clove, finely chopped
2 carrots, peeled and diced
¼ savoy cabbage, finely shredded
1 leek, rinsed and thinly sliced
½ butternut squash, cored and chopped into bite-sized chunks
1 litre vegetable stock
1 x 400g can of chopped tomatoes
1 x 400g can of borlotti beans, drained and rinsed
1 tsp sugar
sea salt
freshly ground black pepper

1 Mix the potatoes, flour, eggs, chives and a good pinch of salt together in a bowl until combined.
2 Sprinkle a clean work surface with flour. Break off lumps of the gnocchi dough and roll these into long snakes, about 1.5cm thick.
3 Cut the lengths of gnocchi dough into 2cm pieces and then press your fingertip into the top of each piece so you have a slight indentation. Place all the gnocchi pieces to one side while you prepare them.
4 Bring a large pan of salted water to the boil. Drop in half the gnocchi pieces and cook them for 2 minutes. Remove them with a slotted spoon and place them in a serving bowl. Cook the remaining half of the gnocchi in the same way and toss them in the butter.

To make the vegetable sauce
5 Heat the olive oil in a large saucepan. Add all the fresh vegetables and cook for 10 minutes, stirring regularly. Next add the stock, canned tomatoes, beans and sugar.
6 Bring to a simmer and season with salt and pepper. Cover and simmer very gently for 45 minutes.

To serve
7 Add the cooked gnocchi to the sauce and warm through. Serve in bowls with plenty of freshly grated Parmesan cheese.

Prawn and mango curry with rice

I am not usually a fan of fruit in curry, but this does work well. I have included a recipe for curry powder here, but use a ready-made curry powder if you prefer.

SERVES 6

1 onion, roughly chopped
2 garlic cloves, peeled
2cm piece of fresh root ginger, peeled
1 small bunch of fresh coriander
2 tbsp water
1 tbsp olive oil
3 tsp curry powder (see below)
1 x 400g can of chopped tomatoes
1 x 400ml can of coconut milk
1 mango, peeled, stoned and cut into chunks
500g raw tiger prawns (shelled weight)
300g potatoes, peeled, cut into quarters and cooked until tender

Boiled rice
500g basmati rice
750ml water
½ tsp salt

Curry powder
1 tbsp coriander seeds
1 dsrtsp cumin seeds
1 tsp fennel seeds
½ tsp fenugreek seeds

1 Place the onion, garlic, ginger, coriander and water in a liquidiser or food processor and blend to a paste. Place to one side.
2 Heat the olive oil in a medium-sized pan and add the onion paste, stirring for 3 minutes. Sprinkle on the curry powder and stir for a few seconds.
3 Add the chopped tomatoes, coconut milk and mango and simmer gently for 20 minutes. Next, add the prawns and potatoes and cook for a few seconds until the prawns turn pink. Serve with boiled rice.

To prepare the boiled rice
4 Place the rice, water and salt in a large saucepan and bring to a good boil. Reduce the heat to very low, cover and cook for 15 minutes. Stir once during this cooking time.
5 Remove the pan from the heat. Keep the rice covered and leave undisturbed for 10 minutes more.

Curry powder
6 Place the coriander seeds in a small, heavy-bottomed pan and heat through for 30 seconds. Add the other spices and toast them until they start to smoke and you can smell their aroma. Transfer to a coffee grinder or pestle and mortar and grind to a fine powder. Store any leftover curry powder in a sealed jar.

Rib-eye steak with sautéed potatoes and runner beans

Good quality rib-eye steaks are a real treat. They are much meatier than fillet and don't suffer so much if they end up slightly less rare than you had intended – something that can easily happen in a hectic family kitchen. Serve with plenty of Dijon mustard for the perfect French supper.

SERVES 6

1kg potatoes, peeled and cut into quarters
2 tbsp duck or goose fat
2 onions, thinly sliced
3 garlic cloves, crushed
4 sprigs of thyme
500g runner beans
6 rib-eye steaks, off the bone
butter
1 bunch of spring onions, chopped
sea salt
freshly ground black pepper

1 Boil the potatoes in salted water until tender. Drain them and place to one side.
2 Heat a tablespoon of the duck or goose fat in a frying pan that has a lid. Add the onions and fry for 10 minutes.
3 Add the garlic and thyme, reduce the heat to very low and put the lid on the pan. Cook the onions and garlic for 30 minutes until meltingly soft and golden.
4 Heat the rest of the fat in another frying pan. Slice the cooked potatoes into chunks about 1.5cm thick and lay them in the fat. Once they are golden, turn them over and continue to fry until they are golden brown all over.
5 Top and tail the runner beans and string the sides if necessary. Slice them horizontally and cook in a saucepan of boiling, salted water for 5 minutes until tender. Drain and place to one side.
6 Fry the steaks in a little butter for about 3 minutes on each side for medium-rare meat, depending on their thickness, of course.
7 Add the beans to the potatoes and sprinkle on the spring onions. Pile the steaks on top, season with salt and pepper and take the pan to the table to serve.

Stuffed chicken thighs with split yellow peas and mash

Split yellow peas are used to make dhal in lots of parts of India. We use them less in Europe, but they are still cherished in the north of England for making pease pudding. I love split peas and think they add a lovely starchiness to soups and stews, essential in the cold winter months. They are also a great source of fibre.

SERVES 6

200g sausage meat
50g pistachio nuts, roughly chopped
50g raisins
2 tbsp white breadcrumbs
2 tbsp flat-leaf parsley, finely chopped
1 tbsp olive oil
6 chicken thigh fillets, skinned
6 slices of pancetta
1 tbsp olive oil
100ml dry white wine
sea salt
freshly ground black pepper

Split peas and mash
2 tbsp olive oil
1 onion, finely chopped
1 celery stalk, finely chopped
1 garlic clove, finely chopped
200g split yellow peas
1 sprig of thyme
1 bay leaf
600ml vegetable stock (a stock cube will do)
200g sweet potatoes, peeled and cut into 2cm chunks
1 large potato, peeled and cut into 2cm chunks
2 carrots, peeled and sliced into 1cm discs
20g butter

1 Preheat the oven to 180°C/Gas 4. Place the sausage meat, pistachio nuts, raisins, breadcrumbs, parsley and olive oil in a mixing bowl and combine with a wooden spoon.
2 Lay the chicken thigh fillets out flat on a wooden board and place a spoonful of the stuffing on each fillet, roll up the fillets and wrap with a slice of pancetta. The thighs won't be completely secure, but should be tight enough not to lose any stuffing when you brown them.
3 Heat 1 tablespoon of olive oil in a frying pan. Brown 3 thigh fillets at a time, taking care when turning them so that no stuffing falls out.
4 Once the thighs are browned, place them in an ovenproof dish and return the frying pan to the heat. Pour on the wine and stir, letting the wine sizzle for 30 seconds and then pour it over the chicken. Season.
5 Cover the dish with a sheet of foil and bake in the oven for 40 minutes.

To cook the split peas and mash
6 Heat the olive oil in a large saucepan. Add the onion, celery and garlic and cook over a medium heat for about 10 minutes, stirring intermittently.
7 Add the split peas and the thyme and bay leaf. Pour on the stock, cover and simmer for 20 minutes.
8 Add the other vegetables, cover the pan again and continue to simmer gently for 25 minutes. Using a fork, mash the butter into the split peas and vegetables and serve with the chicken.

Autumn fruit crumble

Quinces, apple and pears are classic autumnal fare. They combine to make a luxurious, rich crumble that's full of flavour.

1 Preheat the oven to 200°C/Gas 6. Place the quinces, apples, pears and juice in a small saucepan and bring to a simmer. Cover and simmer gently for 5 minutes.
2 Remove from the heat and leave the saucepan covered for 5 minutes until the quinces are soft to the tip of a knife. Stir in the cream and brown sugar.
3 Prepare the crumble by placing the flour and butter in a food processor. Whiz until the mixture resembles breadcrumbs, then add the oats and sugar and mix again briefly.
4 Spoon the fruit filling into a pie dish. Then sprinkle the crumble mixture over the top. Bake in the oven for 20 minutes.

SERVES 6

2 quinces, peeled, cored and chopped into 2cm pieces
3 apples, peeled, cored and cut into quarters
3 pears, peeled, cored and cut into quarters
200ml apple juice
200ml double cream
1 tbsp soft brown sugar

Crumble topping
175g plain flour
100g cold butter, cut into cubes
2 tbsp rolled oats
3 tbsp demerara sugar

Lemon cupcakes

I've had some disasters with cupcake recipes and wasted precious time and ingredients. This is my tried and trusted recipe and I can promise you it works.

MAKES 8

125g very soft butter
125g caster sugar
2 eggs
grated zest of 1 lemon
150g plain flour
2 tsp baking powder
2 tbsp double cream

Icing
75g butter, softened
250g icing sugar, sifted
75ml double cream
grated zest of 1 lemon

1 Preheat the oven to 180°C/Gas 4. Place 8 paper muffin cases in a muffin tray.
2 Place the butter, sugar, eggs and lemon zest in a mixing bowl and beat for 3 minutes with an electric hand-whisk. The cake mixture may curdle but don't worry.
3 Sift the flour and baking powder into the mix and beat for a few seconds. Add the cream and mix again until combined.
4 Spoon the mixture into the muffin cases and bake for 30 minutes. Place on a cooling rack when they are cool enough to handle.

To make the icing
5 Place all the ingredients in a small bowl and beat using an electric hand-whisk, until thoroughly combined.
6 When the cakes have cooled completely, ice them using a knife or a piping bag and decorate with a little extra lemon zest if you like.

Cheese, onion and sausage pie

Once you have made the pastry, which doesn't take very long, this is 'as easy as pie' to make.

SERVES 6

- 1 onion, finely chopped
- 25g butter
- 2 pork sausages, skins removed and discarded and the sausage meat roughly chopped
- 200g potatoes, peeled, cut into quarters and cooked until tender
- 2 eggs
- 4 tbsp double cream
- 1 x 400g can of butter beans, drained and rinsed
- 1 tbsp chopped basil
- sea salt
- freshly ground black pepper

Pastry

- 340g plain flour, plus extra for dusting the work surface
- a pinch of salt
- 170g butter
- 1 egg yolk
- 2 tbsp cold water
- 1 egg, beaten, to glaze

To make the pastry

1 Place the flour, salt and butter in a food processor and whizz until the mixture resembles breadcrumbs. You can blend with your fingertips in a bowl if you don't have a food processor.

2 Add the egg yolk and water and mix again to combine. Turn out on to a floured surface and form into a ball of dough. Wrap in clingfilm and chill in the fridge for 30 minutes.

To make the filling

3 Fry the onion in the butter with the sausage meat for 10 minutes. Place these and all the other filling ingredients in a bowl and mix gently to combine. Season to taste.

To assemble the pie

4 Preheat the oven to 200°C/Gas 6 and grease a 23cm tart tin. Divide your pastry into 2 pieces, then roll out 1 piece and use it to line the tart tin.

5 Spoon in the filling. Roll out the other piece of pastry, place it over the filling and crimp the edges to seal them. Brush the pie with beaten egg to glaze, then pop the pie on a baking sheet and place it in the oven to bake for 40 minutes. Serve with salad.

Lamb and squash curry

This recipe has a long list of ingredients, but it is quick and easy to prepare.

1 Heat the vegetable oil in a large saucepan. Add the onion, garlic, curry leaves, desiccated coconut, cumin, coriander, turmeric and cinnamon stick. Stir and then reduce the heat and cook for 10 minutes, until the onion is soft.
2 Add the lamb cubes and stir, coating the lamb with the onion and spice mix. As soon as the lamb loses its raw look, add the tomato purée, squash, sugar, curry powder and coconut milk. Season, cover the pan and simmer for 45 minutes. Serve with rice.

SERVES 6

2 tbsp vegetable oil
1 onion, diced
1 garlic clove, sliced
6 curry leaves
1 tbsp desiccated coconut
1 tsp ground cumin
1 tsp ground coriander
¼ tsp turmeric
2cm piece of cinnamon stick
700g lamb, cut into cubes
1 tbsp tomato purée
500g butternut squash, peeled and cut into 1cm chunks
1 tsp sugar
1 tbsp curry powder
1 x 400ml can of coconut milk
sea salt
freshly ground black pepper

Butternut and tomato soup with chicken and sweetcorn patties

This soup, served with the patties, makes a delicious meal.

SERVES 6

2 tbsp olive oil
1 butternut squash, peeled and cored and chopped into 3cm chunks
1 onion, peeled and roughly chopped
1.5kg fresh tomatoes, quartered
2 litres chicken or vegetable stock, preferably fresh but a stock cube will do
sea salt
freshly ground black pepper

Chicken and sweetcorn patties
25g butter
1 onion, finely chopped
25g flour, plus extra for dusting the work surface
200ml chicken stock (a stock cube will do)
1 tbsp soy sauce
200g crème fraiche
300g cooked chicken, chopped into bite-sized pieces
3 sausages, skins removed and discarded and the sausage meat chopped into pieces
1 tsp finely chopped tarragon
260g canned sweetcorn, drained
2 x 230g packs of ready-rolled puff pastry
2 eggs, beaten, to seal and glaze
sea salt
freshly ground black pepper

1 Heat the olive oil in a large saucepan. Add the squash, onion and tomatoes, cover and cook over a gentle heat for 5 minutes.
2 Add the chicken stock and simmer for 50 minutes, partly covered. Liquidise the soup and pass it through a sieve. Check the seasoning and serve with the patties.

To make the chicken and sweetcorn patties
3 Heat the butter in a large pan. Add the onion and cook for 10 minutes until soft. Sprinkle on the flour and stir to combine.
4 Add the stock, stirring as you do so. Add the soy sauce and leave to simmer gently for 10 minutes. Add the crème fraiche, chicken, sausage meat, tarragon and sweetcorn and simmer for 5 minutes. Check the seasoning, adding a little salt and pepper if necessary. Set aside to cool.
5 Preheat the oven to 200°C/Gas 6. Roll out the pastry a little more thinly, but not too thin, on a floured surface. Cut pastry circles of 15cm in diameter.
6 Pile a heaped tablespoon of the pie filling on 1 side of a pastry circle. Brush the rim of the circle with some beaten egg and then fold over the circle to seal it into the shape of a semi-circle. Place on a baking sheet and prepare the others.
7 Brush the little patties with some more beaten egg and then bake in the oven for 20 minutes.

Salmon with pancetta, peas and mash

This is a variation on fish and mushy peas.

SERVES 6

2 tbsp olive oil
6 x 150g salmon fillets, with skin
12 slices of pancetta
50ml sherry vinegar
100ml Madeira wine
sea salt
freshly ground black pepper

Peas and mash
1kg potatoes, peeled and quartered
40g butter
300g peas (frozen petit pois will do)
300ml chicken stock
a small sprig of mint, leaves finely chopped
sea salt
freshly ground black pepper

1 Heat the olive oil in a frying pan. When the oil is hot, cook the salmon fillets, 3 at a time for 2 minutes on each side. Place to one side under a sheet of foil to keep warm.
2 Return the pan to the heat and fry the pancetta slices until crispy and brown. Pour away any fat. Place the pancetta with the salmon.
3 Return the pan to the heat and pour on the sherry vinegar. Simmer for 1 minute. Add the Madeira wine and simmer for 1 minute longer.
4 Serve the salmon fillets on top of the pea and potato mash, placing a couple of pancetta slices on top of each salmon fillet. Pour the sauce over and serve with the peas and mash.

To prepare the peas and mash
5 First boil the potatoes in salted water until tender enough to mash.
6 Drain the potatoes and put them through a potato ricer, back into the saucepan. Place the pan over a low heat and stir in the butter, then season to taste with salt and pepper. Remove from the heat as soon as the butter is incorporated.
7 Boil the peas in 300ml of chicken stock for 5 minutes. Pour the cooked peas and stock into a blender and liquidise until smooth.
8 Fold this mixture into the mashed potato, along with the mint. Taste and season with more salt and pepper if necessary.

Macaroni meat sauce bake

A thick meat sauce with macaroni is sure to bring the family to the table eager for supper.

SERVES 6

2 tbsp olive oil
1 onion, finely diced
1 fennel bulb, finely chopped
1 carrot, finely chopped
250g minced beef
500g minced pork
150ml white wine
1 x 400g can of chopped tomatoes
400g macaroni
2 tsp tomato purée
sea salt
freshly ground black pepper

Cheese sauce
25g butter
25g flour
300ml milk
200ml double cream
50g Parmesan cheese, grated
sea salt
freshly ground black pepper

1 Heat the olive oil in a large saucepan. Add the onion, fennel and carrot and cook over a medium heat for 10 minutes, stirring frequently.
2 Add the meat and stir, breaking up the meat until it is all brown. Add the wine and simmer for 2 minutes.
3 Pour on the chopped tomatoes, then add the tomato purée and season with salt and black pepper. Cover the pan with a lid and simmer for 1 hour. Check the seasoning again, then leave to one side.
4 Cook the macaroni according to the packet instructions. Drain and stir into the meat sauce.

To make the cheese sauce
5 Melt the butter in a small saucepan. Add the flour and stir in. Remove from the heat and stir in the milk. Return to the heat. Bring to a simmer and leave to simmer gently for 10 minutes. Season with salt and pepper. Stir in the cream and half the cheese. Leave to one side.

Finishing the dish
6 Preheat the grill. Spoon the macaroni and meat sauce into a gratin dish. Pour the cheese sauce over the top and sprinkle on the remaining cheese.
7 Place under the hot grill for 5 minutes until bubbling and golden. Serve with a green salad.

Grilled gurnard with beetroot and goat's cheese salad and sautéed potatoes

We all know that it's important to eat fish at least once a week for a healthy balanced diet. But stocks of some popular fish are low, so I try to choose varieties that are still plentiful, and avoid buying fish such as cod and haddock too often. There might seem to be many stages to this meal but it is all very easy to do.

SERVES 6

2 garlic cloves, mashed
juice of 1 lemon, plus extra lemon wedges for serving
2 tbsp olive oil
1 tsp salt
6 gurnard fillets

Goat's cheese salad
4 medium beetroots
1 tbsp olive oil
2 tsp balsamic vinegar
100g soft sliceable goat's cheese
1 tsp pumpkin seeds
200g salad leaves
sea salt
freshly ground black pepper

Dressing
3 tbsp olive oil
1 tbsp balsamic vinegar
1 tsp tarragon, finely chopped
sea salt
freshly ground black pepper

Sautéed potatoes
1kg potatoes, peeled and quartered
1 tbsp duck or goose fat
sea salt
freshly ground black pepper

Mayonnaise
2 egg yolks
1 tsp Dijon mustard
1 garlic clove, finely chopped
1 tsp lemon juice
150ml groundnut oil and 150ml light olive oil, combined
sea salt
freshly ground black pepper

1 In a small bowl, mix the garlic, lemon juice, olive oil and salt together. Place the fish fillets in the bowl and rub the mixture over them, then leave to one side until you are ready to grill the fish.

To make the goat's cheese salad
2 Preheat the oven to 200°C/Gas 6. Trim and clean the beetroots, taking care not to cut into the flesh.
3 Place the beetroots on a sheet of foil large enough to wrap them up like a parcel. Drizzle on the olive oil and balsamic vinegar and season with salt and pepper. Wrap the beetroots up, place the parcel a small baking tray and bake in the oven for 45 minutes.
4 Once the beetroots are cooked, peel them and cut off any stalks. Cut into 5mm slices and place them in a serving bowl. Slice the goat's cheese and place this in the bowl with the pumpkin seeds and salad leaves.

To make the dressing
5 Prepare the dressing by mixing all the ingredients together in a small bowl. When you are ready to eat, spoon the dressing over the salad.

To cook the sautéed potatoes
6 Cook the potatoes in salted water until tender, then drain them and leave to cool. When the potatoes are cool enough to handle, slice them into 1cm pieces.
7 Heat the duck or goose fat in a large sauté pan. Once the fat is hot, add the potatoes. Stir the potatoes around gently so that they all get chance to brown. Sprinkle with salt.

To make the mayonnaise

8 Mix the egg yolks in a bowl with the mustard, garlic, lemon juice and salt and pepper.

9 Using a whisk, start to add the oil a few drops at a time, whisking constantly. Keep drizzling in the oil, whisking constantly, until you have added it all. Loosen the mayonnaise with a tablespoon of cold water if it is too thick.

To cook the fish and serve

10 When the salad, potatoes and mayonnaise are ready, preheat the grill and grill the fish for 3 minutes on each side. Season with some more lemon and salt and pepper. Serve some salad on to each plate. Place the fish on top with the potatoes and a spoonful of mayonnaise.

Roast duck with cabbage and roast potatoes

Roast duck has a meltingly rich flavour and is a very rewarding dish to cook – and to eat. It is not a meat you should eat everyday, as it is rather fatty, but once in a while it makes a fine treat.

SERVES 6

2 ducks
1 crisp winter cabbage
1 onion, sliced
1 tsp caraway seeds
1 x 400g can of cannellini beans, drained
1 x 400g can of flageolet beans, drained and rinsed
1 glass of white wine
sea salt
freshly ground black pepper

Roast potatoes
1kg potatoes (Desiree or Maris Piper)
2–3 tbsp duck fat

1 Preheat the oven to 230°C/Gas 8. Place the ducks on racks (if you have them) in a large roasting tin and roast them in the oven for 30 minutes. Drain off any fat in the bottom of the tin and keep it for roasting the potatoes.
2 Reduce the oven temperature to 200°C/Gas 6 and cook the ducks for another 30 minutes. Remove them from the roasting tin and drain off the fat once more.
3 Scatter the cabbage into the roasting tin, along with the onion, caraway seeds, canned beans and the wine. Season with salt and pepper and mix everything together well, then place the ducks on top. Cover the roasting tin with foil and put it back in the oven for another hour.
4 Remove the roasting tin from the oven. Place the ducks on a carving board to rest and spoon the cabbage into a serving bowl. Carve the ducks and serve with the cabbage and the roast potatoes.

To make the roast potatoes
5 Place the potatoes in a saucepan of salted water. Bring them to the boil and then simmer for 5 minutes.
6 Drain the potatoes and place them in a roasting tin with the duck fat. Roast the potatoes in the oven for 1 hour, turning them occasionally.

Baked trifle cake

This dessert is a lovely mixture of different tastes and textures and is well worth making.

MAKES 1 X 23CM CAKE

Sponge
3 eggs
80g caster sugar
70g plain flour
a pinch of salt

Fruit
200g blackberries
200g raspberries
2 tbsp sugar
1 tbsp water

Custard
2 whole eggs
2 egg yolks
2 tbsp caster sugar
1 tbsp cornflour
300ml milk
300ml double cream

Meringue
3 egg whites
175g caster sugar

To make the sponge

1 Grease and line a 23cm round cake tin. Preheat the oven to 180°C/Gas 4. Whisk the eggs and sugar together in a bowl for 4 minutes, until thick and mousse-like.

2 Using a metal spoon, fold in the flour and salt and then spoon the mixture into the cake tin. Bake in the oven for 20 minutes, using a skewer to check whether the cake is done. Remove and leave to cool on a wire rack.

To prepare the fruit

3 Place everything in a saucepan and bring to the boil. Cook at a steady simmer, uncovered, for 30 minutes. Leave to one side to cool.

To prepare the custard

4 Whisk the eggs, sugar and cornflour together in a glass bowl for 2 minutes. Combine the milk and cream in a measuring jug and heat in a saucepan until just before boiling point. Pour the milk and cream on to the eggs and sugar mixture, whisking as you do so.

5 Place the bowl over a pan of simmering water, making sure the bottom of the bowl doesn't touch the water. Stir the mixture until it starts to thicken. Set to one side.

To make the meringue

6 Put the egg whites into a clean bowl. Using an electric hand-whisk, beat the whites for 5 minutes, then add the sugar a tablespoon at a time, whisking as you go, until you have a glossy white meringue.

To assemble the cake

7 Preheat the oven to 150°C/Gas 2. Cut the sponge cake into pieces so that it fits snugly into a pie dish.

8 Pile on the fruit, followed by the custard. Spoon the meringue over the top and bake in the oven for 15 minutes until the merginue is set and just starting to turn a little brown. Spoon into dishes and serve.

Almond apple tart

Almonds are one of my favourite ingredients, whether straight from the shell, roasted, sweetened, spiced or ground. If you could associate foods with emotions I would link almonds with love and romance: they conjure up warm nights, long dinners outside and glowing full moons.

SERVES 6

- 200g ground almonds
- 100g caster sugar
- 1 egg
- 2 egg yolks
- 3 tbsp double cream
- 1 tbsp brandy
- 60g melted butter
- 4 dessert apples, peeled, cut into quarters and thinly sliced

Pastry

- 180g cold butter, cut into cubes
- 75g icing sugar
- 2 egg yolks
- 225g plain flour, plus extra for dusting the work surface

To make the pastry

1 Place the butter, icing sugar, egg yolks and flour in a food processor. Whizz briefly until the mixture resembles breadcrumbs, then turn out on to a floured surface and form into a ball. Wrap in clingfilm and chill in the fridge for 30 minutes.

2 Preheat the oven to 200°C/Gas 6 and place a baking tray in the oven. Grease a 24cm tart tin.

3 Roll out the pastry on a floured surface and use it to line the tart tin. Prick the base of the pastry with a fork. Cover the pastry with a sheet of baking parchment and then pour some baking beans on top.

4 Place the tart tin on the tray in the oven and bake for 15 minutes. Remove from the oven, discard the beans and the baking parchment and return the tart case to the oven for 5 minutes. Remove from the oven and leave to cool for 10 minutes before filling.

To assemble the tart

5 Mix all the filling ingredients, except the apples, in a bowl until smooth. Spoon this almond paste over the bottom of the tart case and spread it out evenly with a palette knife.

6 Arrange the apple slices in a pleasing pattern on the almond paste and then bake in the oven for 40 minutes until golden brown. Serve with cream.

Leek, sweetcorn and fish chowder

Sweetcorn seems to be a universal favourite with children and does have some nutritional benefits. This is a good hearty soup.

SERVES 6

4 corn cobs
25g butter
100g pancetta, chopped
3 leeks, trimmed, washed and chopped into 1cm pieces
1 tbsp flour
600ml vegetable stock (a stock cube will do)
200g ling, cod or pollack fillet, skinned and cut into 2cm chunks
200g salmon fillet, skinned and cut into 2cm chunks
400g potatoes, peeled, quartered and cooked in salted boiling water until tender
200ml double cream
100ml milk
1 tsp Dijon mustard
1 tbsp finely chopped flat-leaf parsley
sea salt
freshly ground black pepper

1 First, stand a corn cob on its end and, using a sharp knife, strip it of its kernels. Prepare the other corn cobs in the same way. Cook the kernels in boiling water for 4–5 minutes until they are tender but still have a slight crunch.
2 Heat the butter in a large saucepan. Add the pancetta and leeks and cook for 5 minutes, stirring occasionally. Sprinkle on the flour and add the vegetable stock. Bring to a simmer.
3 Add the fish and cook for 3 minutes. Add the potatoes, corn, cream, milk, mustard and parsley and simmer for 2 minutes. Check the seasoning, before serving with lots of crusty bread.

Baked potatoes, beans and soured cream

This is a good midweek meal – nourishing, quick and full of flavour.

SERVES 6

6 baking potatoes
2 tbsp olive oil
1 onion, finely chopped
2 garlic cloves, peeled and crushed
2 x 400g cans of cannellini beans, drained and rinsed
2 x 400g cans of borlotti beans, drained and rinsed
1 x 400g can of chopped tomatoes
2 tbsp dark soy sauce
1 tsp sugar
1 tbsp roughly torn fresh basil leaves
butter, for serving
1 x 170ml tub of soured cream, for serving
sea salt
freshly ground black pepper

1 Preheat the oven to 200°C/Gas 6. Pierce the potatoes with a sharp knife, then put them in the oven to bake for 1 ½ hours.

2 Heat the olive oil in a medium-sized saucepan. Add the onion and garlic and fry gently for 5 minutes, then add the beans, chopped tomatoes, soy sauce and sugar. Season with a little salt and pepper and then simmer, gently, uncovered for 45 minutes. Check the seasoning and add more if necessary, then sprinkle on the basil and stir.

3 Split the potatoes, butter them and serve the beans on top with a dollop of soured cream.

Thai fried pork with cabbage

Although there are quite a few ingredients, this dish is very quick to put together. If you haven't got any cooked pork, use cooked chicken breast instead.

SERVES 6

- 1 tbsp vegetable oil
- 1 shallot, finely chopped
- 2 garlic cloves, peeled and finely chopped
- 300g cooked pork or cooked chicken breast, cut into bite-sized pieces
- 2 tbsp fish sauce
- 3 tbsp dark soy sauce
- 1 tsp sugar
- 300g finely shredded savoy cabbage
- 10g dried porcini mushrooms, soaked in 50ml water
- 100ml vegetable stock (a stock cube will do)
- 125g fine egg noodles
- 6 spring onions, finely sliced
- 4 radishes, thinly sliced

1 Heat the vegetable oil in a large sauté pan or wok. Add the shallot and garlic, stir and cook for 30 seconds, then add the pork or chicken and cook for another 30 seconds, stirring constantly.
2 Pour on the fish sauce, soy sauce and sugar and stir fry for 30 seconds more.
3 Add the cabbage, drained mushrooms and stock and cook for 2 minutes until the cabbage is soft.
4 Cook the noodles according to the packet instructions. Just before serving sprinkle the spring onions and radishes into the cabbage and pork and stir in the cooked noodles.

Fried chicken and guacamole wraps

My children always choose wraps when I ask them what they would like for dinner. I am not a great fan, as they are processed and I'm suspicious of any flour-based product that can sit in the cupboard for a month without going off. Nevertheless, I do make wraps once in a while as they are convenient and you can stuff them with good things.

SERVES 6

6 boneless chicken breasts, skinned
2 tbsp egg whites
2 tsp cornflour
1 tsp paprika
1 tsp ground cumin
1 tsp sea salt
2 tbsp olive oil
1–2 packs of tortilla wraps
200g feta cheese, cut into cubes

Guacamole
4 spring onions, finely sliced
2 avocados, peeled and mashed
2 tbsp finely chopped fresh coriander
1 mild chilli, finely chopped
2 tomatoes, finely chopped
juice of 1 lemon
1 tbsp extra virgin olive oil
sea salt

1 Slice the chicken breasts into thin strips. Place these in a bowl and add the egg whites, cornflour, paprika, cumin and salt. Leave to one side for at least 20 minutes before cooking.
2 Combine the guacamole ingredients in a small bowl. Check the seasoning and add some salt if necessary.
3 Heat the olive oil in a frying pan, then start adding the chicken strips in manageable batches. Don't put more than a couple of spoonfuls in the pan at a time or the chicken won't brown. Keep each batch warm while you cook the rest.
4 Cook the tortilla wraps according to the packet instructions.
5 Assemble the wraps by spooning on some chicken, guacamole and feta cheese.

Seafood risotto

This is a lovely full-flavoured risotto and a relatively cheap meal, as mussels are in season at this time of year.

SERVES 6

- 1.5 litres fish stock, seasoned to taste with salt and pepper
- 2 glasses of white wine
- 1kg mussels, scrubbed and de-bearded
- 2 tbsp olive oil
- 300g raw prawns (shelled weight)
- 25g butter
- 1 small onion, finely chopped
- 1 mild red chilli, seeded and finely chopped
- 2 garlic cloves, finely chopped
- 500g Arborio risotto rice
- 200ml canned chopped tomatoes
- 1 tsp tomato purée
- 1 tbsp mascarpone cheese
- 1 small bunch of flat-leaf parsley, finely chopped
- sea salt
- freshly ground black pepper

1 Pour the fish stock into a saucepan and bring it to a gentle simmer.
2 Meanwhile, pour 1 glass of the wine into another saucepan, bring to a simmer and add the mussels. Cover and cook the mussels for 3–4 minutes, until all the shells have opened. Remove the mussels from the saucepan and place to one side, discarding any that have not opened.
3 Keep the saucepan on the heat and add a tablespoon of the olive oil. Fry the prawns in the hot oil until they have turned pink, then add the other glass of wine. Stir for 30 seconds, then remove the prawns and set aside.
4 Return the saucepan to the heat and add another tablespoon of olive oil and the butter. When sizzling, add the onion, chilli and garlic and fry for 5 minutes over a gentle heat, taking care not to burn the garlic.
5 Add the rice to the pan and stir it into the oil and butter for 2 minutes. Add the chopped tomatoes and the tomato purée and stir to combine.
6 You can now start to add the hot stock to the rice, a ladleful at a time, stirring between each addition. As the stock becomes absorbed, add another ladleful and continue like this for 20–25 minutes until the rice is cooked the way you like it. Try not to let the rice get stuck to the bottom of the pan between each addition of stock, as this spoils the texture of the risotto.
7 When the rice is cooked, remove the pan from the heat, stir in the mascarpone, cooked prawns and the parsley. Place the mussels, in their shells, on top of each serving.

Lebanese meze meal

Pitta bread is easy to make at home and is very different from the processed pitta sold in shops. This meal has lots of components, but each step is easy to follow and not at all time consuming.

SERVES 6

Pitta bread
1 sachet of dried yeast
325ml warm water
450g strong white bread flour
2 tsp salt

Fried halloumi
2 tbsp olive oil
1 garlic clove, peeled and smashed
250g halloumi cheese, sliced into 5mm pieces
1 tbsp extra virgin olive oil for the dressing
1 tbsp chopped fresh mint
1 mild red chilli, seeded and chopped

Cucumber and yoghurt salad
1 clove garlic, crushed
a pinch of salt
500ml natural yoghurt
1 cucumber, finely chopped
1 tbsp chopped dill

Houmous
2 x 400g can of chickpeas, drained and rinsed
1 garlic clove
20ml olive oil
juice of ½ lemon
1 tsp salt
1 tsp ground cumin
1 dsrtsp tahini paste

To make the pitta bread
1 Mix the yeast in a little of the water. Place the flour and salt in a mixing bowl and warm the flour in the microwave oven for 30 seconds. Alternatively, place it in a warm oven for 4 minutes.
2 Add the yeasted water, plus the rest of the water to the flour mixture and stir. Turn out and knead for 5 minutes until smooth, then place the dough back in the bowl, cover and leave to rise for 1 hour, until doubled in volume. Knead the dough again and divide it into 8 pieces. Roll out each piece into a ball and then leave covered for 30 minutes to rise again. Preheat the oven to 220°C/Gas 7.
3 Heat two baking trays in the oven. Roll out the balls into 15cm circles, place them on the baking trays and bake for 4 minutes until browned slightly and puffed up.

To make the fried halloumi
4 Place the olive oil and garlic in a frying pan and warm through. Add the halloumi slices and fry until deep golden brown. Remove and place them in a serving dish.
5 Mix the extra virgin olive oil, mint and chilli in a small jug or bowl and pour this dressing over the cheese to serve.

To make the cucumber and yoghurt salad
6 Mix the garlic with a pinch of salt in a small bowl, then add the yoghurt and stir. Add the cucumber and dill and adjust the seasoning to taste.

To make the houmous

7 Put everything into a food processor and pulse until reasonably smooth. Add more olive oil if necessary.

To make the prawns

8 Put the prawns in a bowl, then add the salt, egg white and cornflour. Heat the olive oil in a frying pan, add the garlic and stir.

9 Throw in the prawns and cook them until they turn pink, then remove from the heat. Squeeze over the lemon juice and grind on some pepper.

To make the shredded lettuce

10 Place the ingredients in a serving dish. Sprinkle with olive oil and balsamic vinegar. Season well with salt and black pepper.

To make the butter beans in tomato sauce

11 Warm the olive oil in a saucepan. Add the onion and garlic and cook for 5 minutes.

12 Add the tomato, beans, purée and water and bring to a simmer. Simmer gently for 30 minutes. Season and sprinkle on the cinnamon and coriander and serve.

Prawns

18 large raw prawns, shelled
1 tsp salt
1 tbsp egg white
1 tsp cornflour
2 tbsp olive oil
1 garlic clove, crushed
juice of ½ lemon
black pepper

Shredded lettuce

1 cos lettuce, finely shredded
1 tbsp pine nuts
4 spring onions, finely chopped
2 tbsp olive oil
½ tbsp balsamic vinegar
sea salt
freshly ground black pepper

Butter beans in tomato sauce

1 tbsp olive oil
1 onion, finely chopped
2 garlic cloves, crushed
1 tomato, finely chopped
1 x 400g can of butter beans, drained and rinsed
1 tbsp tomato purée
250ml water
a pinch of cinnamon
1 tbsp chopped fresh coriander
sea salt
freshly ground black pepper

Slow-roasted rolled pork shoulder

I love the wonderful aroma of pork roasting in the oven on a Sunday morning and I hope that the smell of Sunday lunches cooking in the kitchen will be an enduring memory for my children. Serve this with baked butternut squash and apple, and braised fennel and savoy cabbage.

SERVES 6

1 x 2.5kg joint of boned rolled pork shoulder
olive oil
salt
1 tbsp flour
500ml chicken or beef stock (a stock cube will do)

Baked butternut squash and apple
1 butternut squash, peeled, cored and cut into 2cm chunks
1 sprig of fresh thyme
2 Cox apples, peeled, cored and cut into quarters
2 tbsp olive oil
balsamic vinegar
sea salt
freshly ground black pepper

Braised fennel and savoy cabbage
1 tbsp olive oil
70g pancetta, chopped
1 fennel bulb, trimmed and thinly sliced
1 savoy cabbage, cored and thinly shredded
2 tbsp water
a large knob of butter
sea salt
freshly ground black pepper

1 Preheat the oven to 220°C/Gas 7. Place the meat joint in a roasting tin, massage the rind with some olive oil and sprinkle liberally with salt.
2 Roast in the oven for 30 minutes. Reduce the temperature to 160°C/Gas 3 and roast for a further 2 hours. If by this time your crackling isn't sufficiently crispy, increase the heat again to finish it off. Place the meat on a warm dish and leave to rest for 20 minutes.
3 Meanwhile, make the gravy. Place the roasting tin on the stove over a medium heat. Stir in the flour with a wooden spoon, scraping up all the sticky bits from the bottom of the tin. Next add the stock and let it simmer for 20 minutes or so while the pork rests. Carve the meat into thick slices and serve with a jug of hot gravy.

To make the baked butternut squash and apple
3 Preheat the oven to 200°C/Gas 6. Place all the ingredients on a large square of foil, drizzle with the olive oil and season with salt and pepper. Wrap up the ingredients to make a leak-free parcel.
4 Place the parcel on a small baking tray and bake in the oven for 45 minutes. Open up the foil and drizzle the vegetables with the balsamic vinegar and a little more olive oil before serving.

To make the braised fennel and savoy cabbage
5 Heat the olive oil in a large saucepan. Cook the pancetta until it begins to turn golden. Add the fennel and cabbage and stir for 30 seconds, then add the water, cover and simmer very gently for 15 minutes. Stir in the butter and season with salt and pepper.

Spiced apple cake with custard

Apples are at their best – and most plentiful – at this time of year and I'm always pleased when I manage to reduce the pile of fruit in the kitchen before it starts to decay. This is a wonderful cake.

1 Grease an 18cm square cake tin and line the base with baking parchment. Preheat the oven to 180°C/Gas 4. Place the apple slices in a bowl with the lemon juice and brown sugar, then mix so that the apples become nicely coated.
2 Place the flour and caster sugar in a mixing bowl. Add the butter and rub it in with your fingertips until the mixture resembles breadcrumbs. You can do this in a food processor if you prefer.
3 Next, using a wooden spoon, add the milk, eggs, vanilla and spices. Mix so that all the ingredients are evenly combined into a thin batter. Add the apples to the batter.
4 Spoon the mixture into the cake tin and bake in the oven for 35 minutes. Serve in thick slices with custard.

To make the custard
5 Whisk the eggs and sugar together in a glass bowl for 2 minutes.
6 Mix the milk and cream in a measuring jug and heat in the microwave or in a saucepan until just before boiling point. Pour the milk and cream on to the eggs and sugar mixture, whisking as you do so.
7 Place the glass bowl over a saucepan of simmering water, making sure the bottom of the bowl doesn't touch the water. Stir the custard until it starts to thicken and coats the back of a wooden spoon. This custard will not be as thick as bought custard but it will taste great.

MAKES 1 X 18CM CAKE

2 large Cox apples (4 if they are small) peeled cored, cut into quarters and thinly sliced
juice of 1 lemon
2 tbsp soft brown sugar
120g self-raising flour
100g caster sugar
120g cold butter, cut into cubes
100ml milk
2 eggs
1 tsp vanilla extract
½ tsp ground cinnamon
½ tsp ground ginger

Custard
2 eggs
2 egg yolks
2 tbsp caster sugar
300ml milk
300ml double cream

Winter fruit and almond tart

This appetising tart has a shiny, jewel-like look, making me think of Christmas to come and the winter ahead.

SERVES 6

Fruit filling
- 1 apple, peeled, cored and cut into 2cm pieces
- 1 pear, peeled, cored and cut into 2cm pieces
- 100g pitted soft prunes, roughly chopped
- 100g dried apricots, roughly chopped
- 100g sultanas
- 1 tbsp apple juice
- 50g soft brown sugar
- 1 vanilla pod, split down the middle
- 5cm piece of cinnamon stick

Almond paste
- 200g ground almonds
- 100g caster sugar
- 60g melted butter
- 2 egg yolks
- 1 egg
- 3 tbsp double cream
- 1 tbsp brandy

Pastry
- 180g cold butter, cut into cubes
- 75g icing sugar
- 2 egg yolks
- 225g plain flour, plus extra for dusting the work surface

To make the pastry

1 Place the butter, icing sugar, egg yolks and flour in a food processor. Whiz briefly until the mixture resembles breadcrumbs. Turn out on to a floured surface and form into a ball. Wrap the dough in clingfilm and chill in the fridge for 30 minutes.

To make the fruit filling

2 Place all the fruit filling ingredients in a small saucepan, put a lid on the pan and simmer gently for 30 minutes. Remove the vanilla pod and cinnamon stick and place the fruit to one side.

To make the almond paste

3 Mix all the ingredients together in a bowl and place to one side.

To assemble the tart

4 Preheat the oven to 200°C/Gas 6. Grease a 25cm tart tin.

5 Roll out the pastry on a floured surface and use it to line the tart tin. Prick the base of the pastry with a fork. Cover the pastry with a sheet of baking parchment and then pour some baking beans on top of the paper. Place the pastry case in the oven and bake for 15 minutes.

6 Remove from the oven, discard the beans and the baking parchment and return the pastry case to the oven for 5 minutes. Remove from the oven.

7 Add the almond paste to the pastry case and smooth over with a palette knife or spatula. Spoon the fruit filling over the top evenly and bake in the oven for 40 minutes until the almond paste starts to turn golden brown and is slightly firm to the touch.

Chewy pistachio bars

These are a substitute for the processed cereal and biscuit bars that you see in supermarkets. If you make your own, you know what's in them and they are straightforward enough for children to make. If you prefer a crunch to a chew, then cook them for a minute or two longer.

MAKES 9 LARGE SQUARES

100g butter, plus extra for greasing
100g soft brown sugar
1 egg
50g desiccated coconut
50g rolled porridge oats
50g pistachio nuts, roughly chopped
50g plain chocolate, roughly chopped

1 Grease a biscuit tin measuring 30 x 18cm. Preheat the oven to 190°C/Gas 5.
2 Melt the butter in a medium saucepan. Remove the pan from the heat and mix in the other ingredients.
3 Spoon the mixture into the biscuit tin, spreading it right to the edges, then bake for 30 minutes. Remove from the oven, cool and cut into squares.

Meat stew with mustard mash

Although in culinary terms this is definitely a stew, the term doesn't really do it justice. The word 'stew' sounds rather dull and this dish is certainly not that. It's bursting with rich flavours and seems just right for an autumn day. I serve it with mashed potato, but macaroni would do just as well.

SERVES 6

2 tbsp olive oil
25g butter
1 leek, cut into 2cm thick slices
1 large onion, finely chopped
2 carrots, chopped into 2cm chunks
1 celery stalk, finely chopped
2 tbsp finely chopped flat-leaf parsley
400g boneless beef sirloin, cut into 2cm chunks
400g boneless pork shoulder, cut into 2cm chunks
200g pork sausages, skins removed and discarded and the sausage meat cut into 2cm chunks
200ml red wine
200ml beef stock (a stock cube will do)
1 tbsp tomato purée
sea salt
freshly ground black pepper

Mustard mash
1kg potatoes, peeled and cut into quarters
200ml warmed milk
40g butter
1 tbsp wholegrain mustard
sea salt
freshly ground black pepper

1 Heat the olive oil and butter in a large saucepan. Add the vegetables and parsley and cook over a low heat for 2 minutes, stirring occasionally.
2 Add the beef, pork and sausage meat and turn up the heat. Stir and cook the meat until it has lost its outer pinkness, which should take about 10 minutes. Season with salt and pepper.
3 Add the wine and cook at a rapid simmer for about 10 minutes, then add the stock and tomato purée. Bring back to a simmer, cover and cook gently for 2 hours. Check the seasoning and serve with the mustard mash.

To make the mustard mash
4 Place the potatoes in cold, salted water and bring to the boil. Turn the heat down to low and simmer for approximately 10 minutes or until the potatoes are soft.
5 Drain the potatoes and put them through a potato ricer, or mash them in the way you prefer. Return them to the saucepan.
6 Place the pan over a low heat, add the milk, butter and mustard and stir gently. Check the flavour and season to taste with salt and pepper.

Masala potato naans with chestnut and cabbage soup

I suppose that naan stuffed with masala potatoes is the Indian equivalent of a 'chip butty', but who hasn't secretly enjoyed one of those?

SERVES 6

Naan bread
500g strong white bread flour, plus extra for dusting the work surface
2 tsp sugar
½ tsp salt
1 tsp baking powder
150ml warm milk
1 sachet of dried yeast
2 tbsp vegetable oil
50ml plain yoghurt
1 egg

Masala potatoes
2 tbsp olive oil
1 tsp black mustard seeds
1 onion, finely chopped
2cm piece of fresh root ginger, peeled and grated
10 curry leaves
½ tsp turmeric
800g potatoes (not new), cut into 2cm chunks
200ml water
4 spring onions, trimmed and sliced
sea salt
freshly ground black pepper

Chestnut and cabbage soup
2 tbsp olive oil
1 medium onion, finely chopped
1 savoy cabbage, cored and shredded
a large knob of butter
2 tsp finely chopped rosemary leaves
1 garlic clove, peeled and crushed
200g cooked chestnuts
1 tsp curry powder
1.5 litres chicken stock
1 tbsp soy sauce
sea salt
freshly ground black pepper

To make the naan bread

1 Place all the ingredients in a mixing bowl and stir with a wooden spoon. Turn the dough out on to a floured surface and knead into a smooth ball. This will take 5–10 minutes. Put the dough back in the mixing bowl, cover and leave to rise in a draught-free place for 1 hour.
2 Preheat the oven to 200°C/Gas 6 and place a baking tray in the oven. If you have a separate grill, turn this to high as well. If you don't have a separate grill, bake all the naan in the oven first and grill them afterwards.
3 Punch down the dough and divide it into 8 equal pieces. Roll each piece into a tear shape. Slap as many naan as you can fit on to the hot baking tray and bake in the oven for 3 minutes. Remove and place under the grill for a few seconds until the naans brown. Cook all the naans in the same way.

To make the masala potatoes

4 Heat the oil in a medium-sized pan with a lid and add the mustard seeds. When they start to pop, add the onion, ginger, curry leaves, turmeric and some salt and cook over a gentle heat for 5 minutes.
5 Add the potatoes and the water, cover the pan and cook for 5 minutes. Remove the lid, stir and cook for 10 minutes more, returning the lid for a little of this time if the potatoes become too dry. You want the potatoes to be broken up and partly mashed, but not all mashed.
6 Remove from the heat and season with plenty of pepper and more salt if necessary and stir in the spring onions.

To stuff the breads

7 Cut each naan in half widthways and stuff with the masala potatoes.

To make the chestnut and cabbage soup

8 Heat the olive oil in a large saucepan. Add the onion and cook for 5 minutes, then add the cabbage, butter, rosemary, garlic, chestnuts and curry powder, and mix until combined.

9 Pour on the stock, add the soy sauce and simmer slowly for 1 hour. Allow the soup to cool slightly, then blend it in a food processor until smooth. Check the seasoning and serve.

Garlic and tarragon mushrooms with eggs on toast

I love mushrooms on toast. If you cook the mushrooms well to get rid of all their wetness and fry them until golden brown, they are really enjoyable. It's only when they are wet and slimy that people take against them. Top the mushrooms with a fried egg and you'll have a meal that keeps everyone happy.

SERVES 6

30g butter
olive oil
500g chestnut mushrooms, thinly sliced
3 garlic cloves, crushed
1 tsp finely chopped tarragon
6 eggs (duck eggs would be good)
6 slices of bread, for toasting
sea salt
freshly ground black pepper

1 Heat the butter and 2 tablespoons of olive oil in a frying pan. Add the mushrooms and fry them over a high heat for about 10 minutes, until all their moisture has evaporated and they are turning golden brown.
2 Add the garlic and tarragon and cook for 30 seconds more, then season with salt and pepper.
3 Toast the bread and drizzle each piece with a little olive oil. Pile the mushrooms on top of the toast.
4 Add a little more olive oil to the pan if necessary and fry the eggs, then place them on top of the mushrooms. Good served with some dressed rocket leaves.

Chilli meatballs

I am forever trying to come up with variations on the basic meatball. It's strange how balls of relatively cheap meat simmering in a rich sauce can be so appealing, but they are – and my family love them.

SERVES 6

1 red onion, finely chopped
500g minced beef
500g minced lamb
1 tsp paprika
1 tsp curry powder
1 tsp salt
1 egg, beaten
2 tbsp olive oil
soured cream, for serving

Sauce
1 tbsp olive oil
1 onion, finely chopped
1 tsp sugar
2 tsp curry powder
2 x 400g cans of chopped tomatoes
1 x 400g can of kidney beans, drained and rinsed
½ tsp chilli flakes
1 tsp paprika
1 tbsp tomato purée
500ml beef stock (a stock cube will do)
sea salt
freshly ground black pepper

1 Mix the onion, meat, spices and salt together in a bowl and then add the beaten egg. Form the mixture into balls the size of fresh apricots.
2 Heat the olive oil in a frying pan and brown the meatballs all over. Do this 4 or 5 meatballs at a time in order to keep the oil hot. Don't move the meatballs around too much or they will fall apart. I find the best tools for picking them up gently are a spoon and fork.
3 As each batch of meatballs browns, place them to one side. Once all the meatballs are browned, prepare the sauce.
4 Heat the olive oil in a large saucepan. Add the onion and sugar and cook over a low heat for 10 minutes. Add the curry powder and stir for 30 seconds.
5 Add the tomatoes, kidney beans, chilli flakes, paprika, tomato purée and beef stock and bring to a simmer. Taste for seasoning. Carefully put the meatballs into the sauce, cover the saucepan and simmer gently for 1 hour.
6 Serve with a dollop of soured cream and some boiled rice if you like (see page 559).

Mussels in curry cream sauce

Mussels are plentiful at this time of year, so they're very cheap, and they make great fast food. Don't bother with precooked vacuum-packed ones – buy fresh mussels, as they are cheaper and a cinch to prepare. If your mussels are in a plastic bag when you buy them, remove them from the bag as soon as you get home. Leaving the mussels in the bag will kill them and they will then go off very quickly. I make my own curry powder, as I think it is more subtle than the bought type, which often contains too much turmeric and fenugreek.

SERVES 6

- 2 kg mussels, scrubbed and de-bearded
- 2 tbsp olive oil
- 25g butter
- 3 shallots, finely chopped
- 3 tsp curry powder (see page 559)
- 1 glass of white wine
- 3 tbsp double cream
- 1 tbsp chopped fresh coriander
- sea salt and freshly ground black pepper

1 Rinse the mussels in cold water and tap any open ones on your work surface to check that they close. If there is no movement of the shell when you tap them and the shell remains open, then discard.
2 Warm the olive oil and butter in a large saucepan. If you don't have a pan large enough for all the mussels, cook them in 2 batches.
3 Add the shallots and cook for 3 minutes until soft. Add the curry powder, stir and cook for 1 minute, then add the wine and lastly the mussels.
4 Cover the saucepan and cook for 3–4 minutes, until all the mussels have opened. Spoon them into warm serving bowls.
5 Put the saucepan, with the cooking liquor, back on the heat and add the cream and chopped coriander. Simmer for 2 minutes and season to taste. Pour the sauce over the mussels in the bowls and serve with French bread.

Deep-pan pizza

This is not an authentic Italian pizza, but is no less delicious for that.

SERVES 6

Base
500g strong bread flour
2 tsp salt
2 tsp sugar
1 x 7g sachet of dried yeast
2 eggs
50g butter, softened
200ml warm milk
40g finely grated Parmesan cheese

Tomato sauce
2 tbsp olive oil
1 onion, finely chopped
1 x 400g can of chopped tomatoes
a good pinch of salt
1 tsp sugar

Topping
1 x 125g tub of buffalo mozzarella cheese
50g Gruyère cheese, finely grated
leaves from a few sprigs of fresh thyme
olive oil, for drizzling
sea salt
freshly ground black pepper

To make the base

1 Put all the ingredients in a mixing bowl and combine with a wooden spoon, until you have a smoothish dough. Knead for 2–3 minutes only and then return to the bowl. Cover and leave to rise for 1 hour in a warm place. Preheat the oven to 220°C/Gas 7.

To make the tomato sauce

2 Meanwhile, heat 2 tablespoons of olive oil in a medium-sized saucepan, until hot. Add the onion and cook for 3 minutes, until softened.

3 Add the tomatoes and season with the salt and sugar. Leave to simmer, uncovered, for 40 minutes, while the dough is rising.

Finishing the pizza

4 Grease a large vegetable tray measuring about 20 x 45cm – don't worry too much about the size. Ease the dough into the tray and press it to the edges until the whole tray is evenly covered.

5 Spread the tomato sauce over the dough. Break up the mozzarella cheese and distribute evenly over the sauce. Sprinkle with the Gruyère cheese and thyme leaves.

6 Drizzle with a little olive oil and a sprinkling of salt and black pepper. Leave to sit for 10 minutes and then bake in the oven for 25 minutes until golden and bubbling.

Rib-eye steaks with red wine sauce, pommes purée and braised carrots

There were a few dishes I felt I really had to master in order to be a competent cook. One was a good mayonnaise and another was a red wine sauce.

SERVES 6

6 rib-eye steaks
a dash of olive oil, for frying

Red wine sauce
15g butter
1 shallot, finely chopped
2 garlic cloves, left whole but partly crushed
1 tbsp soft brown sugar
8 juniper berries
2 cloves
1 bay leaf
1 bottle of good red wine
200ml beef stock
a knob of butter
sea salt
freshly ground black pepper

Pommes purée
1kg potatoes, peeled and cut into quarters
2 garlic cloves, crushed
1 litre chicken stock (a stock cube will do)
200ml milk
30g butter
sea salt
freshly ground black pepper

Braised carrots
400g carrots, peeled and thinly sliced
a knob of butter
1 tbsp water
sea salt
freshly ground black pepper

1 Heat the butter in a medium-sized saucepan. Add the shallot, garlic, sugar, juniper berries, cloves and bay leaf and cook for 3 minutes.
2 Add the wine and let this bubble away at a steady simmer until reduced to 200ml. This will take 10–12 minutes. Strain the bits and pieces from the reduced wine, then add the stock and simmer for 5 minutes. Season to taste and stir in the knob of butter.
3 Gently massage some olive oil into the steaks. Heat a frying pan and fry the steaks on both sides until nicely browned and pink inside. With a 10cm-thick steak, this takes about 5 minutes on each side, so adjust the time if your steaks are thinner or thicker. Serve the steaks with the sauce, the potatoes and the carrots.

To make the pommes purée
4 Place the potatoes in the stock with the garlic and bring to the boil. Simmer for 10–15 minutes, until the potatoes are tender.
5 Drain the potatoes and remove the garlic cloves. Mash the potatoes using a potato ricer or a fork.
6 Return the mash to the saucepan over a low heat. Stir in the milk and butter, then season well.

To make the braised carrots
7 Put the carrots in a small saucepan with the butter and place on a low heat. As soon as you hear the butter start to hiss, give the carrots a stir. Add the water, cover the pan and set on a low heat for 10–15 minutes until the carrots are tender. Season with salt and pepper.

Dark gingerbread

I can't resist a cake that you can mix in a bowl using just a wooden spoon – no food mixers and hardly any mess. I have have been making this cake since I was about eight years old.

MAKES 1 LOAF

120g butter
120g caster sugar
250g black treacle
280g plain flour
1 tsp bicarbonate of soda
pinch of salt
a 1 tsp ground ginger
1 tsp ground cinnamon
1 egg
200ml natural yoghurt

1 Preheat the oven to 180°C/Gas 4. Grease a 1kg loaf tin and line the base with baking parchment.
2 Warm the butter, sugar and treacle in a saucepan and when they are melted and combined, set to one side to cool.
3 Add the flour, bicarbonate of soda, salt and spices and mix with a wooden spoon until you have a smooth batter. Add the egg and yoghurt and mix again.
4 Pour the mixture into the prepared tin and bake for 60 minutes, until a skewer inserted into the centre of the cake comes away cleanly. Leave the cake to cool in the tin before turning it out on to a wire rack.

Apple and raspberry cake

There are loads of English apples and autumn raspberries at this time of year. This cake makes the most of both these fruits.

MAKES 1 X 18CM SQUARE CAKE

- 200g cooking apples, peeled and cut into 1.5cm chunks
- 100g raspberries
- 175g demerara sugar
- 150g cold butter, cut into cubes
- 225g plain flour
- 2 tsp baking powder
- 3 tbsp milk
- 1 egg

1 Preheat the oven to 180°C/Gas 4. Grease an 18cm-square cake tin and line the base with some baking parchment.
2 In a large bowl, mix the apples and raspberries with the sugar.
3 In another bowl, or using a food processor, combine the butter, flour and baking powder until the mixture resembles breadcrumbs.
4 Add the apples, raspberries and sugar to the flour mixture and combine gently. Then add the milk and egg and mix. The mixture will look very thick, but don't worry, it is supposed to be thick and as the apples cook they will release their juice.
5 Spoon the mixture into the cake tin and bake for 1 hour 15 minutes. Cool slightly, then turn out on to a wire rack to cool completely before cutting into squares.

E.F
BORDEAUX

Spicy beef and tomato broth with garlic bread

This broth really hits the spot on a cool autumn evening and the rich redness of the ingredients, once cooked, looks so enticing. Leave out the red chilli if you don't like its spicy heat.

SERVES 6

2 tbsp olive oil
1 onion, peeled and finely chopped
1 red pepper, cored and finely diced
1 garlic clove, finely chopped
1 red chilli, finely chopped
1kg minced beef
200g potatoes, peeled and cut into 2cm chunks
1 x 400g can of butter beans, drained and rinsed
1 tsp ground cumin
1 tsp paprika
1 litre beef stock
2 tbsp finely chopped fresh coriander
sea salt
freshly ground black pepper

Garlic bread
2 garlic cloves, crushed
50g butter
1 French baguette

1 Heat the olive oil in a large saucepan. Add the onion, red pepper, garlic and chilli and cook for 10 minutes, stirring occasionally. Add the mince and stir until browned.
2 Next, add the potatoes, beans and spices. Pour on the stock and sprinkle in the coriander. Season with salt and pepper. Bring to a simmer, cover and cook for 1 hour. Serve with the garlic bread.

To make the garlic bread
3 Preheat the oven to 200°C/Gas 6. Mix the garlic into the butter.
4 Slice the bread widthways at 2cm intervals, taking care not to cut completely through to the other side as you want the slices to stay attached.
5 Spread the garlicky butter on to both sides of each slice. Wrap the baguette securely in foil and place in the oven for 30 minutes.

Chicken liver risotto

My mother used to make this for us in the 1970s, before I'd even heard of risotto and before it had become the popular restaurant dish it is today. I remember she used long-grain rice as there was no Arborio rice available in Basingstoke in those days.

1 Heat the stock in a saucepan and keep it at a gentle simmer. Heat 25g of the butter and the oil in a separate large saucepan. Add the pancetta, shallot and red pepper and cook for 10 minutes. Add the rice and continue to cook, stirring for 1 minute.
2 Start to add the hot stock to the rice, a couple of ladlefuls at a time, always keeping the rice quite wet, so that it cooks evenly. The rice will take 20–25 minutes to cook.
3 A few minutes before the rice is cooked, heat the rest of the butter in a small frying pan and, when fizzing, add the mushrooms. Cook for 2 minutes. Add the chicken livers and cook for 30 seconds.
4 Now fold the mushrooms and livers into the rice. When the rice is cooked remove the pan from the heat. Sprinkle with Parmesan and parsley and season with salt and pepper. Serve with more grated Parmesan.

SERVES 6

2 litres chicken stock
45g butter
1 tbsp olive oil
70g chopped pancetta
1 large shallot, finely chopped
1 red pepper, cored and finely chopped
500g Arborio risotto rice
20g butter
100g mushrooms, thinly sliced
250g chicken livers, trimmed and chopped into 1cm pieces
2 tbsp finely grated Parmesan cheese, plus extra for serving
2 tbsp finely chopped flat-leaf parsley
sea salt
freshly ground black pepper

Bubble and squeak cakes with fried eggs

Bubble and squeak was devised as a way of using up leftover potatoes and vegetables, which is a great idea. I think that it is so delicious that it's worth making from scratch, even if you don't have leftovers.

SERVES 6

800g potatoes, peeled and cut into quarters
6 or 7 spring onions, trimmed and finely sliced
a knob of butter
400g savoy cabbage, cored and finely shredded
50ml water
1 tsp caraway seeds
2 tbsp finely chopped fresh basil
olive oil, for frying
6–12 eggs, for frying (depending on your family's appetite)
sea salt
freshly ground black pepper

1 Cook the potatoes in salted water until tender. Pass them through a potato ricer or mash in a bowl with a fork, then add the spring onions.
2 Melt the butter in a saucepan and add the cabbage, water and caraway seeds. Season with salt and pepper, cover the pan and cook over a low heat for 5 minutes.
3 Add the cabbage to the potatoes and spring onions. Mix well, stirring in the basil as you go.
4 Taste and adjust the seasoning as necessary. Once the mixture is cool enough to handle, shape it into 100g cakes and place them in the fridge to chill for at least 30 minutes.
5 When you're ready to eat, heat a couple of tablespoons of olive oil in a frying pan and fry the cakes for a few minutes on each side until golden brown. Cook them in batches so that you don't overcrowd the pan. Set them aside and keep warm.
6 Fry the eggs and serve them on top of the bubble and squeak cakes.

Apple and blackberry pie

When I was a child, my mother would take my brothers and I blackberry picking. I loved going along until I was about 12, but found it excruciatingly embarrassing in my teenage years. Now my mother is no longer alive I would give anything to go blackberry picking with her, but such is life. She made the most beautiful bramble jelly with the spoils of our expeditions so it was always worthwhile in the end. We also made pies and this is still one my favourite desserts.

SERVES 6

4 eating apples
2 quinces
1 tbsp water
1 tbsp brown sugar
1 tbsp cornflour
½ tsp ground cinnamon
450g blackberries
2 tbsp caster sugar

Pastry
280g plain flour, plus extra for dusting the work surface
140g cold butter, cut into cubes
2 egg yolks, beaten with 1 tbsp of cold water
1 egg, beaten with 1 tbsp milk, to glaze

To make the pastry

1 Place the flour and butter in a food processor and whizz until the mixture resembles breadcrumbs. Add the egg yolk mixture and process briefly to combine.
2 Turn the mixture out on to a floured surface and form into a ball of dough. Wrap in clingfilm and chill for at least 30 minutes.

To make the filling

3 Place the apples and quinces in a small saucepan with the water, brown sugar, cornflour and cinnamon. Bring to a gentle simmer, cover the pan and cook for 10 minutes. Stir and set aside.

To assemble the pie

4 Grease a pie dish. Preheat the oven to 200°C/Gas 6.
5 Cut the pastry into 2 equal pieces. Roll out 1 piece and use it to line the base of the pie dish.
6 Pile in the blackberries, followed by the cooked fruit, then sprinkle on the caster sugar. Roll out the other piece of pastry and lay this on top of the pie. Trim any overhanging pastry pieces.
7 Place the dish on a baking sheet and bake in the oven for 40 minutes. Serve with whipped cream.

Fruit loaf

When I devised this cake, I just chucked all the ingredients into a mixing bowl and hoped for the best. I kept my fingers firmly crossed until it came out of the oven and was delighted that the recipe worked. Serve in slices, buttered if you like.

MAKES 1 X 1KG LOAF

100g sultanas
50g raisins
50g dried apricots, chopped
50g currants
50g chopped walnuts
100g mashed banana
120g soft brown sugar
225g self-raising flour
1 egg
300ml ale

1 Preheat the oven to 180°C/Gas 4. Grease a 1kg loaf tin and line the base with baking parchment.
2 Place all the ingredients in a mixing bowl and stir with a wooden spoon until combined.
3 Spoon the mixture into the loaf tin and bake for 1 ½ hours until a skewer comes out cleanly when inserted into the centre. Leave the cake to cool in the tin before turning it out on to a wire rack.

Family life moves indoors this month and the kitchen becomes the heart of the house. I like the dark evenings when the whole family is at home, particularly Saturday nights, which seem extra special somehow. Garden produce is less abundant this month, but there are still Brussels sprouts, parsnips, carrots, cabbage, celeriac and leeks to enjoy. Game abounds, particularly partridge, rabbit and venison. It's time to start thinking about the festive season ahead and making plans for how to spend the holiday. This is also the month to make Christmas pudding and mincemeat. Serious gardeners need to dig over flowerbeds, clear the leaves from the lawn and plant bulbs for the spring. In the kitchen, get stuck into making meat pies, thick vegetable soups and glorious steamed puddings. Mussels are in season and cheap, so make use of them in soups and pasta or simply cook them on their own in a little white wine.

November

Winter vegetable soup

Soups are some of the easiest things to cook and you can make up your own recipes, adding the vegetables and flavours you like. If a soup is too thick, you can thin it with water. If it is too thin, add more vegetables. Soups are always well received by the family and are ideal for both lunches and dinners.

SERVES 6

- 2 tbsp olive oil
- 1 onion, finely chopped
- 100g carrots, peeled and diced
- 100g pumpkin flesh, diced
- 1 x 400g can of cannellini beans, drained and rinsed
- 1 x 400g can of butter beans, drained and rinsed
- ½ tsp ground cumin
- ½ tsp ground coriander
- 50g red lentils
- 1 x 400g can of chopped tomatoes
- 750g vegetable stock (a stock cube will do)
- sea salt
- freshly ground black pepper

1 Heat the olive oil in a large saucepan. Add the onion and cook for 5 minutes. Add the diced carrots and pumpkin and stir, then cook for 2 minutes.
2 Add the beans, spices, lentils, tomatoes and stock. Cover the pan and simmer gently for 15 minutes, then uncover the pan and simmer for 30 minutes more.
3 Season with plenty of salt and black pepper. Serve with toasted cheese sandwiches.

Meatballs in a pot

This recipe uses just a mixing bowl and a saucepan, so it is light on washing up, an important consideration for a midweek meal. Once the meatballs have been browned, everything goes into the same pan to cook.

SERVES 6

500g minced beef
500g minced pork
1 onion, finely chopped
2 tbsp finely chopped flat-leaf parsley, plus extra for serving
a little flour, for dusting
3 tbsp olive oil
2 carrots, peeled and diced
2 celery stalks, finely chopped
500g basmati rice
200g frozen petit pois
800ml beef stock (a stock cube will do)
sea salt
freshly ground black pepper

1 Put the minced meat, onion and parsley in a bowl and season well with salt and pepper. Shape the mixture into 3cm round balls, then dip the meatballs in a little flour.

2 Heat 2 tablespoons of the olive oil in a large saucepan and brown the meatballs in the oil. Do this in 2 batches so you don't overcrowd the pan. Place the browned meatballs to one side while you brown the rest.

3 Return the pan to the heat and add another tablespoon of olive oil. Add the carrots and celery and cook them for 3 minutes, stirring occasionally. Pour the rice, peas and stock into the pan and bring to a simmer. Season with a little salt.

4 Gently place the meatballs on to the rice. Cover the pan and simmer the rice gently for 20 minutes. Leave the lid on the pan for another 5 minutes – the liquid should all but disappear. Serve with a scattering of parsley.

Eggs and creamed spinach

My children eat this with real gusto. They sometimes find spinach a little bitter, but this is beautifully creamy with a gentle flavour.

SERVES 6

- 6–10 eggs (depending on your family's appetite)
- 50g butter
- 2 shallots, finely chopped
- 25g plain flour
- 250ml milk
- a grating of nutmeg
- 500g fresh spinach leaves, rinsed and drained
- 2 tbsp double cream
- 2 tbsp white breadcrumbs
- 2 tbsp grated Parmesan cheese
- 6–10 slices of bread for toast
- sea salt
- freshly ground black pepper

1 Place the eggs in their shells in a pan of simmering water. Bring the water to the boil and cook the eggs for 8 minutes. Drain off the water, give the pan a shake to crack the shells and place the pan under cold running water for a few minutes. Drain the eggs again and set them aside, in their shells, on a plate until needed.
2 Heat the butter in a saucepan until gently bubbling, then add the shallots and cook gently for 5 minutes. Sprinkle on the flour and stir it into the butter and shallots for 1 minute. Remove the pan from the heat. Add the milk gradually and stir constantly until combined. Return the pan to the heat and simmer the sauce gently for 10 minutes. Season with nutmeg, salt and pepper.
3 Bring a large saucepan of salted water to a simmer, then add the spinach. Simmer for 1 minute, then drain. Press as much water as you can out of the spinach and then place it on a board and chop the leaves with a knife.
4 Add the chopped spinach to the white sauce and stir gently. Pour in the double cream, check the seasoning and place the sauce to one side.
5 Preheat the grill. Peel the eggs, cut them in half and place them yolk side up in a heatproof gratin dish. Spoon over the creamed spinach sauce, then sprinkle on the breadcrumbs and cheese. Place the dish under the grill for 5 minutes until bubbling and brown.
6 Toast the bread and serve the eggs, spinach and sauce on top of the toast.

Veal and mushroom stew

Veal is at last becoming more widely available in the UK and you can enjoy it guilt free if you only eat rose veal, which is produced with higher welfare standards. In fact, consuming British veal helps to prevent thousands of unwanted male calves being slaughtered. Veal is full of flavour and low in fat, so give it a try.

SERVES 6

3 tbsp olive oil
1kg veal shoulder, diced
1 tbsp flour
1 onion, finely chopped
1 celery stalk, finely chopped
400ml dry white wine
1 x 400g can of chopped tomatoes
200g button mushrooms, cut in half
1 tbsp roughly chopped fresh basil
2 garlic cloves, lightly crushed with a rolling pin but still whole
sea salt
freshly ground black pepper

1 Preheat the oven to 150°C/Gas 2. Heat 2 tablespoons of the olive oil in a frying pan and brown the veal, a few pieces at a time. Transfer each batch to a casserole dish while you brown the rest. Sprinkle the flour on to the browned veal in the casserole dish and stir.
2 Return the frying pan to the heat, add another tablespoon of olive oil and fry the onion and celery for 5 minutes.
3 Pour the wine into the frying pan with the onion and celery and simmer for 1 minute, scraping up any sticky bits at the bottom of the pan. Pour everything into the casserole dish over the meat.
4 Add the tomatoes, mushrooms, basil and garlic, then season well with salt and pepper. Place the casserole dish in the oven and cook for 1 ½ hours. Check the seasoning and serve.

Fish pie

This is a fish pie with pastry. You can lattice the top of the pie or just roll out one piece of pastry and lay it on top of the filling.

SERVES 6

400ml milk
500g cheap white fish fillets, such as pollack or ling
300g salmon fillet, skinned
200g spinach
3 eggs
25g butter
25g plain flour
2 tbsp crème fraiche
2 tbsp grated Parmesan cheese
½ tbsp soy sauce
200g cooked prawns
sea salt
freshly ground black pepper

Pastry
225g plain flour, plus extra for dusting
100g cold butter, cut into cubes
a pinch of salt
1 egg yolk, mixed with 2 tbsp cold water

To make the pastry

1 Place the flour, butter and a pinch of salt in a food processor and whizz until the mixture resembles breadcrumbs. Add the egg yolk and water mixture and whizz again briefly. Turn the mixture out on to a floured surface and bring the pastry together in a ball. Wrap it in clingfilm and chill for 30 minutes.

To prepare the pie

2 Pour the milk into a roasting tin, then place the tin on the stove and bring the milk to a simmer. Place all the fish in the tin and cook for 2 minutes. Turn the fish and simmer for 2 minutes more. The fish should not be cooked completely at this stage. Take the roasting tin off the heat, remove the fish with a slotted spoon and place to one side. Keep the milk for the sauce.
3 Bring a pan of salted water to the boil, add the spinach and cook for 3 minutes. Drain, then press out as much water as you can from the spinach with the back of a wooden spoon. Chop the spinach and place to one side.
4 In the same pan, bring some water to a simmer, add the eggs and cook for 10 minutes. Cool the eggs under cold running water, then shell them, cut into quarters and place to one side.
5 In the same saucepan, melt the butter over a medium heat. Add the flour, then stir and cook for 1 minute on a low heat. Remove the pan from the heat and add the milk you cooked the fish in, a little at a time, stirring constantly to avoid lumps. Simmer the sauce over a low heat for 10 minutes. Preheat the oven to 200°C/Gas 6.
6 Season the sauce with salt and pepper. Stir in the crème fraiche, spinach, Parmesan and soy sauce, then combine with the fish, eggs and prawns. Spoon the filling into a gratin dish. Roll out the pastry and place it over the filling, then bake the pie for about 40 minutes.

Baked potatoes with sausage meat

I tend to use pork sausages rather than buying packs of sausage meat, as I think you can be more selective about the quality of the meat you use this way.

SERVES 6

6 baking potatoes, cut in half lengthways
400ml light chicken stock (a stock cube will do)
200g butternut squash flesh, cut into cubes
2 tbsp olive oil
1 x 450g pack of pork sausages
1 tbsp finely chopped flat-leaf parsley
2 tbsp crème fraiche
sea salt
freshly ground black pepper

1 Preheat the oven to 200°C/Gas 6. Put the potato halves in a roasting tin, cut side down, and pour the stock over them. Place in the oven and bake for 45 minutes.
2 Toss the cubes of butternut squash in a tablespoon of olive oil, then wrap them in a parcel of foil and bake in the oven with the potatoes for 30 minutes.
3 Split the sausage skins and squeeze out the meat into a bowl. Add the parsley, cooked butternut squash, crème fraiche and the rest of the olive oil. Season with a little salt and pepper and mix everything together.
4 When the potatoes have cooked for 45 minutes, take the roasting tin out of the oven. Turn the potatoes over and spoon some sausage meat mixture on to each half. Don't worry if some of the mixture spills over.
5 Put the potatoes back in the oven for 25 minutes, until the sausage meat mixture is cooked and the potatoes are done. Serve with a green salad.

Stuffed baked chickens

As this dish cooks, wonderful aromas drift from the oven. Serve the carved chicken with some mashed potatoes and a green vegetable.

SERVES 6

a knob of butter
80g button mushrooms, sliced
2 tbsp finely chopped fresh basil
80g Milano salami, finely chopped
80g prosciutto, finely chopped
100g white breadcrumbs
2 shallots, finely chopped
1 garlic clove, finely chopped
2 eggs
100g roasted peppers from a jar, finely chopped
olive oil
2 x 1.5kg chickens
150ml Marsala wine
4 carrots, peeled and diced
½ swede, peeled and diced
a few sprigs of flat-leaf parsley
sea salt
freshly ground black pepper

1 First make the stuffing. Heat the butter in a small frying pan until it starts to bubble, then add the mushrooms and cook for 3 minutes until golden brown. Tip them into a mixing bowl and add the basil, salami, prosciutto, breadcrumbs, shallots, garlic, eggs and peppers and mix until combined. Add 2 tablespoons of olive oil to moisten the mixture and season well with salt and pepper. Preheat the oven to 200°C/Gas 6.
2 Spoon the stuffing into the neck cavities of the chickens. Heat 2 more tablespoons of olive oil in a large casserole dish or roasting tin on top of the stove and brown the chickens all over. I find the easiest way to move the birds around is to pick them up with oven gloves, but this does mean you have to wash the oven gloves afterwards!
3 Keeping the dish or tin on the heat, add the wine, let it simmer for 1 minute, then remove from the heat. Add the carrots and swede and season with salt and pepper. Place the parsley sprigs among the chickens.
4 Put a lid on the casserole dish or, if using a roasting tin, cover it securely with foil so that no steam can escape. Bake in the oven for 2 hours.
5 Remove the chickens from the casserole and place them on a board or large serving dish to rest. Serve the chickens carved and jointed, with the vegetables and the accompanying juices.

Mini almond buns with autumn fruit compote and custard

You'll need two fairy cake tins for this recipe, but if you don't have two or you don't have the oven space, then bake the buns in separate batches as they take only a short time to cook. Don't let the ones waiting to go in the oven get too warm or they won't turn out as well.

MAKES 16–18

Almond buns
200g butter, at room temperature
200g caster sugar
3 eggs
150g self-raising flour
50g ground almonds
¼ tsp almond extract

Autumn fruit compote
100g soft pitted prunes, halved
50g dried apricots, halved
2 quinces, peeled, cored and chopped into 2cm chunks
2 pears, peeled, cored and cut into 2cm chunks
2 tbsp soft brown sugar
100ml water

Custard
200ml milk
300ml double cream
1 tsp vanilla extract
3 eggs
2 egg yolks
2 tbsp caster sugar

To make the almond buns

1 Preheat the oven to 180°C/Gas 4. Line 2 fairy cake tins with paper cake cases.

2 Cream the butter and sugar together in a mixing bowl with an electric beater. Add 1 of the eggs and a tablespoon of the flour and mix with an electric beater, then repeat with the remaining eggs.

3 Add the rest of the flour to the mixture, together with the almonds and almond extract. Fold in with a metal spoon until everything is nicely incorporated.

4 Spoon a dessertspoonful of mixture into each paper case and bake the cakes for 15 minutes. Place the cakes on a wire rack to cool just a little, before serving with the compote and custard.

To make the autumn fruit compote

5 Place all the ingredients in a saucepan and bring to a gentle simmer. Turn the heat down to low, cover the pan and cook for 10 minutes.

To make the custard

6 Pour the milk and cream into a saucepan, add the vanilla and heat to boiling point.

7 Put the eggs and yolks into a glass bowl and whisk them with the sugar. Pour the hot milk and cream on to the eggs and sugar, stirring constantly.

8 Bring a saucepan of water to simmering point and place the bowl of custard over, but not touching, the water. Keep stirring the custard until it thickens slightly and coats the back of a spoon.

Honey nut tart

I am totally smitten with this dessert, which is sweet, sticky and full of the flavours of the nuts.

SERVES 6

- 6 tbsp clear honey
- 100g caster sugar
- 225g butter
- 1 scant tsp salt
- 1 egg
- 1 egg yolk
- 100ml double cream
- 200g walnuts and pecans, roughly chopped

Pastry

- 180g cold butter, cut into cubes, plus extra for greasing
- 75g icing sugar
- 2 egg yolks
- 225g plain flour, plus extra for dusting the work surface

To make the pastry

1 Place the butter, icing sugar, egg yolks and flour in a food processor. Whizz until the mixture resembles breadcrumbs, then turn out on to a floured surface and form into a ball. Wrap the dough in clingfilm and chill in the fridge for 30 minutes.

To make the tart

2 Preheat the oven to 180°C/Gas 4. Grease a 24cm tart tin, then roll out the pastry on to a floured surface and use it to line the tart tin. Trim away any excess pastry and then chill the tart case in the fridge while you prepare the filling.

3 Put the honey, sugar, butter and salt in a saucepan and place over a medium heat. Bring the mixture to the boil, stirring as you go. Remove the pan from the heat and leave to cool for 20 minutes or so.

4 Once the honey mixture is cool, stir in the egg, egg yolk and cream. Scatter the chopped nuts over the bottom of the pastry case and then pour on the honey mixture.

5 Place the tart on a baking sheet and pop it into the oven to bake for 1 hour. It's ready when the pastry is brown and the centre of the tart has only a slight wobble to it.

Upside-down quince cake

At the time of writing, I have such a large number of quinces that I am using them rather frantically to avoid letting any go to waste. If you can't find quinces, use pears. Unripe pears would be perfect for this recipe.

MAKES 1 X 21CM CAKE

- 4 quinces, peeled, cored and cut into eighths
- 25g butter, plus extra for greasing
- 2 tbsp water
- 1 tbsp brown sugar
- 1 tbsp runny honey
- 20g chopped walnuts
- 150g butter, at room temperature
- 150g caster sugar
- 3 eggs
- 150g self-raising flour
- 1 tsp vanilla extract
- 1 tbsp crème fraiche

1 Place the pieces of quince in a saucepan with the 25g of butter, water and the brown sugar, cover the pan and simmer for 10 minutes. Stir in the honey and walnuts and then place to one side.

2 Preheat the oven to 180°C/Gas 4. Grease a 21cm spring-clip tin.

3 Place the 150g of butter and the caster sugar in a mixing bowl and cream with an electric beater for 5 minutes. Add 1 of the eggs with a spoonful of flour and mix thoroughly. Repeat with the remaining eggs. Add the rest of the flour, the crème fraiche and vanilla extract and fold in gently with a wooden spoon.

4 Spoon the quince and walnut mixture on to the bottom of the spring-clip tin and add the cake mixture on top. Place the tin on a baking sheet and bake in the preheated oven for 40 minutes.

5 Leave the cake to cool for 5 minutes before releasing the spring-clip tin and inverting the cake on to a plate. Serve with crème fraiche or whipped cream.

Spicy pumpkin soup with onion and tomato rolls

It's pumpkin time again. How quickly it comes round each year. This soup is super-smooth with a good flavour and will enjoyed by everyone in the family. The rolls make this a more filling meal.

SERVES 6

25g butter
1 onion, finely chopped
1.2kg squash (I used a mixture of pumpkin and kabocha, peeled, cored and roughly chopped
300g sweet potatoes, peeled and roughly chopped
2 tbsp curry powder
2 litres vegetable or chicken stock
160ml coconut cream
sea salt
freshly ground black pepper

Onion and tomato rolls
2 tbsp olive oil
1 large onion, thinly sliced
6 tomatoes, cut into chunks
½ tbsp balsamic vinegar
a handful of torn basil leaves
6 bread rolls, sliced in half
sea salt
freshly ground black pepper

1 Melt the butter in a large saucepan. Throw in the onion and cook it for 10 minutes, stirring occasionally, then add the squash and sweet potatoes. Stir, cover and cook over a low heat for 15 minutes. Add the curry powder, then stir and cook for another 5 minutes.
2 Pour on the stock, cover the pan and simmer for 25 minutes. Allow the soup to cool slightly and then blend it in a liquidiser or food processor. Pour the soup back into the pan and stir in the coconut cream. Bring to a simmer and check the seasoning, adding salt and pepper to taste.

To make the onion and tomato rolls
3 Pour the olive oil into a frying pan and fry the onion for 10 minutes until soft and transparent. Add the tomatoes, stir and remove the pan from the heat.
4 Pour in the balsamic vinegar, scatter on the basil leaves and season with salt and pepper. Fill the rolls with the tomatoes and onions and serve with the soup.

Lamb and pea ragù with pappardelle pasta

Frozen peas are a blessing once the fresh pea season is over for the year, and no freezer should be without them.

SERVES 6

2 tbsp olive oil
1 onion, finely chopped
1 garlic clove, finely chopped
1 celery stalk, finely chopped
2 tsp finely chopped rosemary leaves
1kg lamb mince
2 x 400g cans of chopped tomatoes
2 tsp tomato purée
200g frozen peas
100ml water
600g pappardelle pasta
Parmesan cheese, grated, for serving
sea salt
freshly ground black pepper

1 Heat the olive oil in a large saucepan. Add the onion, garlic, celery and rosemary and cook for 10 minutes over a low heat, stirring occasionally.
2 Add the lamb, then stir and break it up with a wooden spoon until the meat has browned all over. Add the tomatoes, tomato purée, peas and 100ml of water, then season with salt and pepper. Cook, uncovered, at a very gentle simmer for 1 hour.
3 Cook the pappardelle pasta according to the packet instructions and serve with the lamb ragù and grated Parmesan cheese.

Fish cakes with red pepper sauce and soft-boiled eggs

I don't think I have ever met anyone who doesn't like fish cakes – even people who are not that keen on fish itself like them. I have included the humble sardine in this recipe which is underused in this country, perhaps because it is so bony. A good thing about fish cakes is that the preparation can be done early in the day so you just have to fry them when you are ready to eat.

SERVES 6

400g salmon fillet, skinned
400g smoked haddock, skinned
300ml milk
500g potatoes, cooked and mashed
1 x 120g can of sardines in oil, drained
1 tbsp soy sauce
1 tbsp roughly chopped or torn basil leaves
white breadcrumbs, for coating
2 tbsp olive oil
6 eggs
sea salt
freshly ground black pepper

Red pepper sauce
1 tbsp olive oil
1 shallot, finely chopped
1 garlic clove, finely chopped
2 red peppers, cored, seeded and roughly chopped
400ml light chicken stock
3 tbsp crème fraiche
sea salt
freshly ground black pepper

1 Preheat the oven to 200°C/Gas 6. Place the salmon and haddock in a gratin dish and cover with the milk. Cover the dish with a sheet of foil and place it in the oven for 15 minutes. Drain, discard the milk and place the fish in a mixing bowl. Flake the fish with a fork.
2 Add the mashed potato, sardines, soy sauce and basil to the fish and season with salt and pepper. Mix everything together lightly with a spoon, then place in the fridge to chill for 30 minutes.
3 Form the mixture into 200g fish cakes and dip each one in the breadcrumbs to coat them. When you're ready to cook the fish cakes, heat the olive oil in a frying pan and fry each cake until golden brown on both sides.
4 Meanwhile bring a saucepan of water to the boil. Add the eggs in their shells and cook for 6 minutes. Peel the eggs when ready to serve, cut them in half and serve on top of the fish cakes.

To make the red pepper sauce
5 Warm the olive oil in a frying pan. Add the shallot, garlic and red peppers and cook over a low heat for 10 minutes, stirring occasionally. Add the stock, cover the pan and cook for 15 minutes.
6 Blitz the mixture in a blender or food processor until smooth and then pass it through a sieve. Pour the sauce back into the pan and put it back on the heat. Stir in the crème fraiche and season with salt and pepper. Serve with the fish cakes.

Leek and blue cheese risotto

Risotto was one of the first more adventurous dishes that I learnt to cook once I had a kitchen of my own. Recently, when I was cooking a risotto, one of the children said, 'Granny made the best risotto', and a whole conversation started as a result. Needless to say Granny did indeed make a great risotto. One of the magical qualities about preparing meals at home is that people start talking, and thoughts and ideas are expressed. This may not sound momentous, but when your family includes two teenage boys anything that interests them enough to offer a thought or opinion is welcome. I don't believe that the same engagement would be sparked over a ready-made risotto.

SERVES 6

1.5 litres chicken stock
25g butter
1 tbsp olive oil
1 onion, finely chopped
500g Arborio risotto rice
2 leeks, washed and finely sliced
50g mild blue cheese, crumbled (more if you like)
6 slices of pancetta
sea salt
freshly ground black pepper

1 Heat the chicken stock in a large saucepan and check the seasoning. You may need to add some salt. Keep the stock simmering gently.
2 In another saucepan, which you will use to cook the risotto, heat the butter and olive oil until it is just starting to foam. Add the onion and cook for 10 minutes, stirring often to make sure that the onion softens but does not brown.
3 Add the rice, then cook and stir for 1 minute. Add a ladleful of the hot stock to the rice and stir, then continue adding more stock, a ladleful at a time, as it is absorbed by the rice. Keep stirring.
4 After 15 minutes, add the leeks and mix them into the rice while adding more stock. The risotto should be ready in another 5 or 10 minutes. The rice should be tender on the outside but have a slight bite inside.
5 Remove the pan from the heat, stir in the blue cheese and check the seasoning.
6 In a frying pan, fry the pancetta until crispy brown and add a piece of pancetta to each serving of risotto.

Lamb roasted on plums with rice and herb yoghurt

This recipe is included courtesy of my hairdresser, Des, who is married to an Iranian and loves to cook Persian food. The dish was described to me during a haircut so forgive me if I lost some of its authenticity on the way home. I carried out her instructions as well as I could remember and improvised where necessary.

SERVES 6

500g plums, cut in half
1 cinnamon stick, broken into 4 pieces
3 sprigs of rosemary
1 x 2kg leg of lamb
2 tbsp olive oil
2 tsp Chinese 5 spice powder
200ml white wine
sea salt
freshly ground black pepper

Rice
2 tbsp olive oil
2 medium onions, finely chopped
400g basmati rice
1 x 400g can of chickpeas, drained and rinsed
½ tsp salt
¼ tsp allspice
¼ tsp ground cinnamon
½ tsp caraway seeds
600ml water

Herb yoghurt
2 tbsp finely chopped coriander
2 tbsp finely chopped flat-leaf parsley
2 garlic cloves, crushed
300ml natural yoghurt
½ cucumber, cut into cubes
sea salt
freshly ground black pepper

1 Preheat the oven to 230°C/Gas 8. Place the plum halves and cinnamon stick in a roasting tin with the rosemary and put the lamb joint on top. Rub the meat with the olive oil, sprinkle on the 5 spice powder and season with salt and pepper. Place the lamb in the oven for 30 minutes.
2 Remove the tin from the oven and pour in the wine, then cover the whole roasting tin with a large sheet of foil. Lower the oven temperature to 170°C/Gas 3½ and cook the meat for 2 hours.
3 Remove the lamb from the roasting tin and leave it to rest for 20 minutes. Pour the juices into a jug and serve with the lamb, plums, rice and yoghurt.

To prepare the rice
4 Heat the olive oil in a large saucepan. Add the onions and cook over a medium heat, stirring occasionally, for 5 minutes. Add the rice to the pan, together with the chickpeas, salt, spices and caraway seeds. Stir to combine.
5 Pour on the water and bring to the boil, then turn the heat to very low. Cover the pan and cook the rice for 15 minutes. Remove the pan from the heat and leave covered for another 10 minutes.

To prepare the herb yoghurt
6 Place all the ingredients in a dish and gently combine.

Ricotta cheese tarts with watercress salad

Using ricotta instead of a hard cheese adds a lightness and freshness to these tarts. The ricotta also blends very well with the herbs.

MAKES 2 X 20CM TARTS
(you may have some left over for lunch the next day)

Filling
1 tbsp olive oil
1 onion, finely chopped
1kg ricotta cheese
1 tbsp chopped flat-leaf parsley
1 tbsp fresh thyme leaves
1 egg
2 egg yolks
2 tbsp crème fraiche
100g Parmesan cheese, grated
sea salt
freshly ground black pepper

Pastry
300g plain flour, plus extra for dusting the work surface
200g cold butter, cut into cubes
a pinch of salt
about 5 tbsp cold water

Watercress salad
250g watercress
4 spring onions, sliced

Dressing
2 tbsp extra virgin olive oil
1 tsp balsamic vinegar
sea salt
freshly ground black pepper

To make the pastry

1 Place the flour and butter in a food processor and pulse until the mixture resembles breadcrumbs. Add the salt and water and briefly mix again. Turn the mixture out on to a floured surface and form it into a ball with your hands. Cover with clingfilm and chill for 30 minutes.

To make the filling

2 Heat the olive oil in a frying pan and cook the onion for 10 minutes until soft.

3 Place the cooked onion in a mixing bowl and add the ricotta, parsley, thyme, egg and egg yolks, crème fraiche and Parmesan cheese. Season well with salt and pepper and gently mix all the ingredients together with a wooden spoon.

To assemble the tarts

4 Preheat the oven to 180°C/Gas 4. Divide the pastry in half, roll out both pieces on a floured surface and use them to line 2 x 20cm tart tins. Using a fork, lightly prick the bottom of the pastry cases in several places.

5 Lay a sheet of baking parchment in each pastry case and place some baking beans on top of the parchment. Place the tart cases on a baking sheet and bake in the oven for 15 minutes. Remove the parchment and the beans and cook for 5 more minutes.

6 Spoon the filling into the pastry cases and bake the tarts for 40 minutes until golden brown and puffed up. Serve with the salad.

Watercress salad

7 Wash the watercress well and mix with the spring onions. Mix the dressing and dress the salad.

Stuffed roast duck with buttered swede and carrots

In my family one duck will just feed the six of us because my youngest still has quite a small appetite. If you are a family of big eaters, you will probably need to cook two ducks and double the stuffing ingredients. The alternative is to serve one duck and lots of vegetables.

SERVES 6

1 duck
200g pork sausage meat
3 soft pitted prunes, roughly chopped
1 apple, grated
6 sage leaves, finely chopped
800g potatoes, peeled, quartered and parboiled
400g parsnips, peeled and quartered
black pepper

Gravy
1 tbsp flour
500ml chicken or vegetable stock

Buttered swede and carrots
15g butter
1 whole swede, peeled and cubed into 1cm pieces
4 carrots, peeled and cut into 1cm cubes
1 tbsp crème fraiche
1 tsp Dijon mustard
sea salt
freshly ground black pepper

1 Preheat the oven to 230°C/Gas 8. Remove the giblets from the duck, place them in a small saucepan and cover them with water. Simmer them gently for 30 minutes, then drain. Discard the giblets and keep the thin stock.
2 Place the sausage meat in a bowl with the prunes, apple, sage leaves and a good grinding of black pepper. Mix until everything is well combined, then push the stuffing into the neck cavity of the duck.
3 Place the duck in a roasting tin. Put the potatoes and parsnips around the duck and place the tin in the oven. After 30 minutes, turn the heat down to 200°C/Gas 6 and roast for another hour, turning the potatoes and parsnips occasionally and basting the duck.
4 Remove the duck from the roasting tin and place it on a board to rest. Transfer the potatoes and parsnips to another dish and keep them warm in the oven. Drain the duck fat from the roasting tin and place the tin on top of the stove to prepare the gravy.
5 Sprinkle the flour into the tin and stir with a wooden spoon, scraping up any bits stuck to the bottom. Pour on the giblet stock and the chicken or vegetable stock and simmer for 15 minutes while the duck rests.
6 Carve the duck and serve with the gravy and vegetables.

To prepare the buttered swede and carrots
7 Heat the butter in a medium-sized saucepan and once it starts to foam, add the swede and carrots. Stir the vegetables in the butter over a medium heat for 3 minutes, then reduce the heat to low. Cover the saucepan and cook the vegetables for 10 minutes or until tender. Stir in the crème fraiche and mustard and season with salt and pepper.

Fruit buns

These are the perfect baked treat for an autumn afternoon. Serve warm from the oven with butter.

1 Mix the yeast with the sugar and milk and leave for 3 minutes.
2 Place the flour, salt, spice, zest, egg, butter and fruit in a mixing bowl and pour on the yeasted milk. Mix with a wooden spoon until a dough forms. Turn the mixture out on to a floured surface and knead for 5 minutes, then place it back in the bowl. Cover and leave to rise for 1 hour.
3 Divide the dough into 6 equal pieces. Shape each piece into a roll and place on a lightly greased baking sheet. Cover and leave to rise for 30 minutes. Preheat the oven to 200°C/Gas 6.
4 Brush the buns with the egg and milk glaze and bake in the oven for 25 minutes. Remove and place the buns on a wire rack to cool slightly before tucking in.

SERVES 6

1 ½ tsp dried yeast
2 tsp sugar
150ml milk, warmed
350g strong white bread flour, plus extra for dusting the work surface
1 tsp salt
½ tsp mixed spice
grated zest of 1 lemon
1 egg, beaten
50g butter, melted
50g raisins
50g sultanas

Glaze
1 egg, beaten with 2 tbsp milk

Creamy rice pudding with quince and blackberry compote

Quince and blackberry are both autumn fruits and their very different flavours go perfectly together.

SERVES 6

8 heaped tbsp pudding rice
300ml milk (you will need to add a little more milk once the rice is tender)
400ml double cream
1 tsp vanilla extract
4 tbsp caster sugar

Quince and blackberry compote
500g quinces, peeled and cored
250ml water
300g blackberries
300g white sugar

1 Put the rice, milk, cream and vanilla extract in a saucepan and place on a low heat. Simmer very gently for 30 minutes, stirring occasionally to make sure that the rice doesn't stick.
2 When the rice is tender, remove the pan from the heat. You may need to add a little more milk to achieve the consistency you like. Stir in the sugar and serve with the quince and blackberry compote.

To make the quince and blackberry compote
3 Place the quinces in a saucepan with the water and bring to a simmer. Cook for 30 minutes, then add the blackberries and sugar and simmer, uncovered, for 15 minutes more.

Potato hash with eggs

In an effort to eat less meat and trying to think of something for an autumn evening meal, I came up with this. Fry or poach the eggs, whichever you prefer. I'm hopeless at poaching eggs so I always fry them.

SERVES 6

1kg potatoes, peeled and cut into quarters
1 tbsp goose fat
½ tsp paprika
8 spring onions, sliced widthways into 1cm pieces
200g salad leaves, washed
2 tbsp extra virgin olive oil
2 tsp balsamic vinegar
6–10 eggs (depending on your family's appetite)
sea salt
freshly ground black pepper

1 Put the potatoes in a pan of salted water, bring to the boil and cook until tender. When the potatoes are cool enough to handle, cut them into 3cm chunks.
2 Heat the goose fat in a large sauté pan and when it is hot add the potatoes. Sauté the potatoes for 10 minutes or so until they are starting to become golden brown and crispy. Sprinkle on the paprika and move the potatoes gently to coat them with the spice.
3 Add the spring onions and sauté them with the potatoes for 5 minutes. Remove the pan from the heat, then scatter on the salad leaves, drizzle with the olive oil and balsamic vinegar and season well.
4 Tip everything into a serving bowl and keep warm while you quickly fry the eggs in the sauté pan.
5 Serve the hash piled on plates with the eggs on top.

Sausage and cabbage stew

Sausages were originally a way of preserving the smaller parts of the pig for winter eating and would have been smoked. You probably find the best fresh sausages in France, where there are laws that regulate the addition of cereals and preservatives. In the UK, sausages have suffered at the hands of factory producers who charged customers for products containing little meat and a lot of additives. Things have changed, though, and it is now possible to buy good quality sausages in the UK. They are well matched with savoy cabbage which is in season at this time of year.

SERVES 6

- 2 tbsp olive oil
- 70g sliced pancetta
- 2 garlic cloves, peeled and smashed with the blade of a knife
- 6 shallots, finely chopped
- 12 pork sausages, skins removed and discarded and the sausage meat cut in half
- 2 x 400g cans of cannellini beans, drained and rinsed
- 6 medium potatoes, peeled and cut into quarters
- 1 cabbage (savoy or white), cored and shredded
- 100g cooked chestnuts, cut in half
- 800ml chicken stock
- a handful of chopped flat-leaf parsley
- sea salt
- freshly ground black pepper

1 Heat the olive oil in a large saucepan. Add the pancetta, garlic, shallots and pieces of sausage and cook for 5 minutes.

2 Add the beans, potatoes, cabbage, chestnuts and stock. Season well with salt and pepper, then cover and simmer for 30 minutes. Sprinkle on the parsley and serve in bowls with some French bread.

Pork with noodles

This dish includes basil and mint, which are used a lot in Thai cuisine, and the recipe has an Eastern feel to it. I am no expert when it comes to devising East Asian dishes, but I think this works well.

SERVES 6

½ star anise
1 tsp ground cinnamon
1 tsp salt
½ tsp ground black pepper
1 tsp Chinese 5 spice powder
grated zest of 1 lime
1 tsp caster sugar
1 tbsp olive oil
1.5kg boned pork belly, rind scored

Noodles
250g medium egg noodles
1 tbsp finely chopped fresh coriander
1 tbsp finely chopped fresh mint leaves
1 tbsp finely chopped fresh basil leaves
1 cos lettuce heart, finely shredded
6 spring onions, cut into 1cm slices
¼ large cucumber, chopped into matchsticks
300g bean sprouts
1 tbsp soy sauce
2 tsp fish sauce
juice of 1 lime
2 tbsp olive oil

1 Preheat the oven to 200°C/Gas 6. Grind the star anise and mix with the cinnamon, salt, pepper, Chinese 5 spice powder, lime zest, sugar and olive oil. Spread the resulting paste on the rind of the pork and on the meat underneath.
2 Place the pork in a roasting tin and cook it in the oven for 1 hour. Preheat the grill and then place the pork under the grill for 10–15 minutes until the rind is nicely crisp. Watch that it doesn't burn.
3 Carve the pork into 1cm-thick slices and serve with the noodles.

To prepare the noodles
4 Cook the noodles according to the packet instructions. When you have drained the noodles, place them in a serving dish with the herbs, lettuce, spring onions, cucumber and bean sprouts. You can cook the noodles in advance and reheat by pouring boiling water on to them when you are ready to add the other ingredients and serve.
5 In a mixing bowl or small jug, mix the soy sauce, fish sauce, lime juice and olive oil, then pour this dressing over the noodle salad.

Pearl barley soup

If you have any leftover gravy in the fridge stir it into this soup as it cooks. It will add a lovely meatiness that intensifies the flavours.

SERVES 6

150g pearl barley
2 tbsp olive oil
1 onion, finely chopped
1 celery stalk, sliced
2 turnips, peeled and cut into 1cm dice
½ swede, peeled and cut into 1cm dice
2 carrots, peeled and cut into 1cm dice
1 leek, trimmed and sliced into 1cm slices
1 x 400g can of chopped tomatoes
1 tbsp tomato purée
1 litre chicken stock
2 tbsp finely chopped flat-leaf parsley
sea salt
freshly ground black pepper

1 Rinse the pearl barley in cold water and place it in a saucepan. Add cold water to cover, then bring to the boil and simmer for 30 minutes. While the pearl barley is cooking, you can prepare the other vegetables.
2 Heat the olive oil in a large saucepan. Add the onion and celery and cook on a medium heat for 5 minutes. Add the rest of the vegetables and stir well to mix everything together.
3 Pour in the tomatoes, tomato purée and chicken stock, then once the pearl barley is cooked, drain and add it to the soup. Bring the soup to a simmer, partly cover the pan and cook for 30 minutes. Season with salt and pepper and sprinkle with the parsley before serving.

Red gurnard in Thai sauce with cucumber salad

Red gurnard is a beautifully textured fish and it stays nice and firm when fried. It's relatively cheap and plentiful, but can be difficult to find unless you live in Cornwall. If you can't get gurnard, you can use sea bass fillets, although these are more expensive. The sauce is Thai in flavour and simple to make.

SERVES 6

2 tbsp olive oil
2 shallots, finely diced
2cm piece of fresh root ginger, grated
1 tsp lemon grass from a jar
1 tsp galangal from a jar
1 mild red chilli, seeded and finely chopped
grated zest of 1 lime
1 tbsp soft brown sugar
1 tbsp fish sauce
2 garlic cloves, finely chopped
1 tsp ground coriander
1 x 400ml can of coconut milk
1 tbsp chopped or torn basil leaves
10 cherry tomatoes
6–10 pieces of red gurnard or sea bass fillet (about 800g in all)
a little flour, for dusting
1 shallot, thinly sliced for garnish

Cucumber salad
½ cucumber, chopped into matchsticks
1 tbsp roasted peanuts, roughly chopped
1 tomato, chopped into bite-sized pieces
1 garlic clove, finely chopped
1 tbsp lemon juice
2 tbsp light soy sauce
1 tsp caster sugar

1 Heat a tablespoon of the olive oil in a sauté pan. Add the shallots and fry gently for 5 minutes, then add the ginger, lemon grass, galangal, chilli, lime zest, brown sugar, fish sauce and garlic and continue to cook and stir for 3 minutes.
2 Sprinkle on the ground coriander, then cook for another minute. Pour on the coconut milk and sprinkle on the basil leaves. Add the tomatoes, simmer gently for 5 minutes, then remove from the heat.
3 Heat the rest of the olive oil in another frying pan. Dust the fish fillets with a little flour and fry them a few at a time. As each batch of fish is cooked, place it in the coconut milk sauce off the heat.
4 Once all the fish has been fried, fry the sliced shallot until golden brown and sprinkle this over the fish before serving with some boiled rice (see page 559) and the cucumber salad.

To prepare the cucumber salad
5 Place the cucumber, peanuts and tomato in a serving dish. Mix the garlic, lemon juice, soy sauce and sugar in a small bowl, then sprinkle the dressing over the cucumber, tomato and peanuts.

Beef and onions in beer

The beer in this recipe helps to tenderise the beef, rather as red wine would. This thick, luscious stew was popular in the 1970s and deserves the resurgence that it seems to be having.

SERVES 6

1–2 tbsp olive oil
a small knob of butter
12 baby onions, peeled and left whole
1 tsp soft brown sugar
1.5kg shin of beef, trimmed of some of the fat and cut into cubes
2 tbsp plain flour
500ml beer
some beef stock
1 bouquet garni, made from thyme, parsley and rosemary
sea salt
freshly ground black pepper

1 Preheat the oven to 150°C/Gas 2. Heat the butter and a tablespoon of the oil in a large casserole dish with a lid. Add the onions and brown them all over – this will take about 5 minutes. Sprinkle on the brown sugar and continue to cook the onions on a low heat for another 5 minutes.
2 Remove the onions, but keep the casserole dish on the heat and start to brown the meat in batches. You will probably need to add some more olive oil.
3 Once all the meat is browned, put the onions back in the dish with all the meat. Sprinkle on the flour and stir well. Pour on the beer and add enough stock to just cover the meat. Pop the bouquet garni into the pan and season with salt and pepper.
4 Bring everything to a simmer on top of the stove, then cover the casserole dish and place it in the oven for 2 hours. Serve with potatoes and savoy cabbage.

Chicken breasts in mustard cream sauce with puréed swede

When I moved to London and was living with my brother in his flat, I gave my first dinner party. I made a chicken dish similar to this and to my delight it went down quite well.

SERVES 6

1–2 tbsp olive oil
20g butter
6 chicken breasts
800g potatoes, peeled and cut into 1cm cubes
2 shallots, finely chopped
1 sprig of rosemary, leaves removed and finely chopped
200ml dry white wine
150ml double cream
1 tsp English mustard
sea salt
freshly ground black pepper

Puréed swede
15g butter
1 swede, peeled and cut into 1cm cubes
100ml chicken or vegetable stock
sea salt
freshly ground black pepper

1 Preheat the oven to 200°C/Gas 6. Heat the oil and butter in a casserole dish, then brown the chicken breasts, a couple at a time, for 1 minute on each side. Place them to one side once they are browned.
2 Keep the casserole dish on the heat and add the potato cubes, shallots and rosemary. Fry for about 10 minutes, moving them around as they start to become tinged with brown – you may need to add a little more oil. Remove everything with a slotted spoon and place to one side.
3 Add the wine to the casserole dish, which should still be on the heat. Stir to release all the sticky bits at the bottom of the dish and simmer for 1 minute. Put the potatoes, shallots, rosemary and chicken breasts back into the casserole dish and season well with salt and pepper. Place a sheet of baking parchment over the chicken and bake in the oven for 20 minutes.
4 Remove the casserole dish from the oven and place the chicken on a serving plate and the potatoes in a bowl.
5 Put the casserole dish on the stove over a high heat until the juices are simmering, then add the cream and mustard and simmer for 1 minute. Spoon the sauce over the chicken and serve with the potatoes and swede.

To make the puréed swede
6 Heat the butter in a saucepan and once it starts to foam, add the swede. Stir to coat the swede in the butter, then turn down the heat and cover the pan. Cook for 5 minutes.
7 Pour on the stock, cover the pan and simmer for 5–10 minutes or until the swede is tender. Tip everything into a blender and liquidise until smooth. Return the purée to the saucepan, season and serve.

Autumn fruit steamed pudding

This is the perfect pudding for Sunday lunchtime and is quick and easy to put together.

SERVES 6

Filling
- 25g butter
- 400g quinces, apples and pears, peeled cored and cut into quarters (cut the quinces a little smaller and keep them separate)
- 2 tbsp maple syrup
- 2 tbsp soft brown sugar
- 200g raspberries

Sponge case
- 300g self-raising flour, plus extra for dusting the work surface
- a pinch of salt
- 2 tsp baking powder
- 150g butter
- 75g caster sugar
- grated zest of 1 lemon
- ½ tsp ground ginger
- 150ml water

To prepare the filling

1 Prepare the filling first so that it has a little time to cool while you are preparing the sponge case. Heat the butter in a saucepan. When it has melted and is gently bubbling, add the pieces of quince. Cover the pan and cook on a gentle heat for 3 minutes.

2 Add the pears and apples and cook for another 3 minutes. Pour in the syrup and sprinkle on the sugar. Add the raspberries and gently stir to combine. Remove from the heat after a few seconds and leave to cool.

To make the sponge case

3 Grease a 500ml pudding basin. Put the flour, salt and baking powder into a food processor. Add the butter and whizz until the mixture resembles breadcrumbs. Stir in the sugar, zest and ginger.

4 Add the water a little at a time, mixing as you go, until you have a ball of dough. Roll out two-thirds of the dough on a lightly floured surface to a thickness of 1cm. Use this to line the basin, then spoon in the filling.

5 Roll out the remaining dough to make a lid and place it over the filling. Cover the top of the pudding basin with a circle of greaseproof paper. Cover this with a generous sheet of foil and tie in place with some string.

6 Put the basin into a large saucepan and pour some water around the basin – don't add too much. Cover the saucepan, bring the water to a simmer and steam the pudding for 2 hours. Keep checking and topping up with hot water when necessary.

7 Remove the basin from the pan and take off the foil and paper. When ready to serve, run a knife around the edge of the pudding and turn it out on to a plate. Serve with custard (see page 625).

Mince pies

I am not suggesting you bake your mince pies in November, but it is a good idea to make the mincemeat so there is one less thing to do in the frantic run-up to Christmas. You can then look forward to the time when you make the first batch of mince pies and enjoy that heavenly smell from the oven.

MAKES 6 JARS OF MINCEMEAT

MAKES ENOUGH PASTRY FOR ABOUT 18 PIES

Mincemeat

- 225g vegetable suet
- 340g raisins
- 225g sultanas
- 340g grated apple
- 340g soft brown sugar
- 340g currants
- 200g mixed peel
- 120g chopped almonds
- grated rind and juice of 2 lemons
- 1 tsp mixed spice
- 100ml brandy

Pastry

- 250g plain flour, plus extra for dusting the work surface
- 150g cold butter, cut into cubes, plus extra for greasing
- a pinch of salt
- 1 tbsp caster sugar
- 2 egg yolks
- 1 tbsp cold water

To make the mincemeat

1 Place all the ingredients in a large bowl and stir well with a wooden spoon. Cover the bowl with a tea towel and leave to one side for a couple of weeks, giving the mixture a stir every day.

2 Spoon the mixture into 6 clean jars. Cut out circles of greaseproof paper and place them on top of the mincemeat in each jar, then seal the jars with lids. This mincemeat should keep nicely for a year.

To make the pastry and assemble the pies

3 Put the flour and butter in a food processor and whizz until the mixture resembles fine breadcrumbs. Add the salt and sugar, then mix again briefly.

4 Whisk the egg yolks with the water in a small bowl and add them to the mixture. Whizz again briefly, then turn the mixture out on to a floured work surface and combine thoroughly until you have a firm dough. Wrap the dough in clingfilm and chill in the fridge for 30 minutes.

5 Preheat the oven to 200°C/Gas 6. Grease a fairy cake tray. Roll out the pastry and use a pastry cutter to cut out circles to fit your tray. I use a 7.5cm cutter for the bottom of the pies and a 6.5cm cutter for the lids.

6 Fill the cases with the mincemeat and then cover each pie with a pastry lid. Bake in the oven for 15 minutes until the pies are golden brown.

ST.LOUIS.MO.
SEP 4
430PM
1913

Coffee and walnut cake

This isn't as light as some versions, as I don't like using margarine in my cakes. I prefer butter, as it is a natural product.

MAKES 1 X 20CM CAKE

200g butter, at room temperature
200g caster sugar
3 medium eggs
200g self-raising flour
1 tsp baking power
1 tsp ground coffee
3 tbsp normal strength liquid coffee
60g walnuts, roughly chopped

Coffee icing
180g butter
200g icing sugar
1 tbsp strong liquid coffee
whole walnuts, to decorate

1 Preheat the oven to 180°C/Gas 4. Grease and line 2 x 20cm sandwich cake tins.
2 Cream the butter and sugar together for 5 minutes, using an electric hand-whisk. Add 1 egg and 1 tablespoon of flour and mix again. Repeat with the remaining eggs. Add the rest of the flour, the baking powder, coffee and liquid and the walnuts and fold together gently with a wooden spoon.
3 Spoon the mixture into the cake tins and bake in the oven for 20 minutes. Turn the cakes out on to a wire rack and leave to cool completely before icing.

To make the icing and assemble the cake
4 To make the icing, cream the butter and sugar together in a mixing bowl, using an electric mixer. When the mixture is creamy and smooth, stir in the coffee.
5 Spread half the icing on top of one cake. Sandwich the other cake on top and ice the top, then decorate with the whole walnuts.

Leek and mushroom pasta

This pasta sauce was devised for my daughter, as her two favourite vegetables are mushrooms and leeks.

SERVES 6

3 tbsp olive oil
2 garlic cloves, finely chopped
6 leeks, finely sliced
250g chestnut mushrooms, roughly chopped
250g mascarpone cheese
500g linguine
3 tbsp grated Parmesan cheese, for serving
sea salt
freshly ground black pepper

1 Heat the olive oil in a large pan, then add the garlic, leeks and mushrooms. Cook for 15 minutes, until some of the moisture has disappeared and the mushrooms are starting to turn golden brown. Stir in the mascarpone cheese, season with salt and pepper and remove the pan from the heat.

2 Meanwhile, cook the linguine in plenty of salted water according to the packet instructions. Drain and toss the linguine in the sauce before serving with some grated Parmesan.

Thai beef curry and green dhal

Shin of beef makes a very tender curry. The meat also takes on the spice flavours extremely well as it takes so long to cook. The green dhal is a great accompaniment, packed full of goodness.

SERVES 6

2–3 tbsp olive oil
1kg shin of beef, cut into 2cm cubes
1 onion, finely chopped
2 garlic cloves, finely chopped
2cm piece of fresh root ginger, grated
½ tsp ground turmeric
1 tsp ready-chopped galangal from a jar
1 tsp ready-chopped lemon grass from a jar
1 tsp salt
1 x 400ml can of coconut milk

Green dhal
1 tbsp olive oil
1 medium onion, finely chopped
1 garlic clove, crushed
¼ tsp ground turmeric
½ tsp mustard seeds
½ tsp cumin seeds
225g green lentils
600ml water
sea salt

1 Heat the olive oil in a large saucepan. Brown the meat in the oil in 2 batches, putting the first batch to one side while you fry the next. Place all the meat to one side.
2 Keep the pan on the heat and add the onion with a little more oil if needed. Fry the onion for 5 minutes on a lowish heat, until soft, then add the garlic, ginger, turmeric, galangal, lemon grass and salt. Stir to combine, then cook for 1 minute.
3 Return the meat to the pan and stir to coat it in all the spices. Pour on the coconut milk and bring to a simmer, then cover and cook on a low heat for 45 minutes. Remove the lid and simmer for another 45 minutes.

To make the green dhal
4 Heat the olive oil in a medium saucepan. Add the onion, garlic, turmeric, mustard and cumin seeds and fry for 3 minutes on a medium heat, until the onions start to become tinged with brown.
5 Add the lentils and the water and bring to a gentle simmer. Partly cover the saucepan and simmer the lentils for 30 minutes until the liquid has all but disappeared and the lentils are tender. Season with salt.

Spicy sausage rolls and quick tomato soup

Freshly made soup and sausage rolls warm from the oven are hard to beat. If you have the patience to make your own pastry, these sausage rolls will be worthy of any table in the land.

SERVES 6

Sausage rolls
250g plain flour, plus extra for dusting the work surface
¼ tsp ground cumin
¼ tsp ground coriander
1 tsp salt
½ tsp baking powder
225g cold butter, cut into 1cm cubes
175ml cold milk
2 X 450g packs of good-quality pork sausages, skins removed and discarded
1 onion, finely chopped
2 tbsp finely chopped flat-leaf parsley
1 egg, beaten, for glazing

Tomato soup
30g butter
1 tbsp olive oil
1 onion, finely chopped
2 tsp paprika
2 tbsp plain flour
1 tbsp tomato purée
2 x 400g cans of chopped tomatoes
1 litre chicken stock (a stock cube will do)
1 tbsp soy sauce
sea salt
freshly ground black pepper

To make the pastry

1 Mix the flour, cumin, coriander, salt, baking powder and butter in a bowl – don't try to incorporate the butter, just mix it with the other ingredients. Stir in the milk to make a lumpy dough.

2 Sprinkle a work surface with plenty of flour and roll the pastry into a rectangle measuring about 16 x 30cm. Fold the top third in towards you and the lower third away from you, as though you are folding a letter.

3 Rotate the dough through 90 degrees and do the same again, rolling the pastry into a 16 x 30cm rectangle and folding it up like a letter. Wrap the pastry in clingfilm and chill in the fridge for 30 minutes.

4 Roll out the pastry again, twice, as you did before, then pop the pastry back into the fridge for another 30 minutes. Repeat once more and chill.

To prepare the filling

5 Preheat the oven to 200°C/Gas 6. Place the sausage meat in a bowl, add the onion and parsley and mix thoroughly. Divide the meat into 6 portions and then shape each portion into a sausage shape.

6 Roll out the pastry and cut it into 6 rectangles to wrap round the sausage meat. Seal the pastry seams with beaten egg.

7 Place the sausage rolls on a baking sheet and brush them with egg. Bake for 30 minutes until golden brown.

To make the tomato soup

8 Heat the butter and oil in a large saucepan. Add the onion and cook gently for 10 minutes. Sprinkle on the paprika and flour and stir for a few seconds.

9 Add the rest of the ingredients and simmer for 30 minutes. Using a liquidiser or blender purée the soup until smooth. Reheat and check the seasoning.

Cod and leek gratin

Buying fish these days is not as straightforward as it was years ago, as we know that many species have been overfished. I try to vary the fish we eat as much as possible and we don't eat cod and haddock very often.

SERVES 6

4 leeks, trimmed
4 tbsp crème fraiche
100g Cheddar cheese, grated
800g cod fillet, skinned
juice of half a lemon
1 tbsp olive oil
3 sprigs of parsley
sea salt
freshly ground black pepper

1 Preheat the oven to 200°C/Gas 6. Cut each leek lengthways to just above the base and then rinse each one under a cold tap. Thinly slice the leeks and place them in a sauté pan on a medium heat. Cook them for 5 minutes until soft, stirring to ensure that they are evenly cooked.
2 Remove the pan from the heat and stir in the crème fraiche and cheese. Season with plenty of salt and pepper.
3 Spoon the leeks into an ovenproof gratin dish. Lay the cod pieces on top and drizzle the fish with the lemon juice and olive oil. Season with salt and pepper, then scatter the parsley sprigs on top. Bake in the oven for 10 minutes, then serve piping hot with mashed potatoes (see page 16).

Potato and turnip omelette

Winter turnips are in season now, so it's good to make use of them. They are not the most glamorous of vegetables – most people prefer the smaller, early summer varieties – but I think the flavours here go well together.

SERVES 6

500g potatoes, peeled and grated
300g turnips, peeled and grated
1 onion, grated
25g butter
3 tbsp finely chopped flat-leaf parsley
4 tbsp ricotta cheese
12 eggs
sea salt
freshly ground black pepper

1 Mix the potatoes, turnips and onion in a mixing bowl, sprinkle with a little salt and leave to one side for 30 minutes.
2 Squeeze all the liquid you can out of the vegetables. Heat the butter in a large frying pan and gently cook the vegetables for 15 minutes, stirring frequently. Remove the pan from the heat. Add the parsley and stir in the ricotta cheese. Check the seasoning and add a little more salt and pepper if necessary.
3 Preheat the oven to 200°C/Gas 6. Beat the eggs in a bowl. Spoon the vegetable mixture into a small gratin dish. Pour the eggs on top and place the dish in the oven for 10–12 minutes until the eggs are cooked through to a sloppy firmness. Serve with bread and a green salad.

Chicken breasts braised in Marsala on cabbage

Marsala is an Italian fortified wine and it is great to use when cooking chicken or beef. It adds a more gentle flavour than red and white wine and it has a sweetness that goes well with meat. It is also good to use when baking fruit.

SERVES 6

6 boneless chicken breasts, skin removed
25g butter
2 tbsp olive oil
100g pancetta, chopped
1 tbsp Marsala wine
1 savoy cabbage, cored and finely shredded
1 tbsp water
2 tbsp crème fraiche
1 tbsp Dijon mustard
sea salt
freshly ground black pepper

Sautéed potatoes
1kg potatoes, peeled and cut into quarters
2 tbsp olive oil or 1 tbsp goose fat
sea salt
freshly ground black pepper

1 Bash the chicken breasts with a mallet or rolling pin to flatten them to a thickness of about 1cm.
2 Heat the butter and olive oil in a large frying pan. Brown the chicken breasts, a couple at a time, until golden on each side. Season with salt and pepper as you go along and put them to one side.
3 Keep the pan on the heat. Add the pancetta and brown it for 1 minute, then pour in the Marsala wine and let it sizzle for 1 minute.
4 Add the cabbage to the pan along with the water. Cover and simmer for 5 minutes. Stir in the crème fraiche and the mustard and season.
5 Lay the chicken breasts on top of the cabbage, cover the pan and cook on a low heat for 5 minutes, until everything has warmed through. Serve with sautéed potatoes.

To prepare the sautéed potatoes
6 Put the potatoes in a saucepan of salted water, bring to the boil and cook them until tender. Drain the potatoes and when they are cool enough to handle, slice them into 1cm slices.
7 Heat the olive oil or goose fat in a large sauté pan and add the potatoes. Stir the potatoes around as they cook to ensure that they brown evenly. Season with salt and black pepper.

Gammon and cider pie

This is a seriously scrumptious winter warmer.

SERVES 6

1.2 kg unsmoked gammon joint
2 tbsp olive oil
1 onion, finely chopped
2 leeks, rinsed and cut into 1cm slices
2 carrots, finely chopped
2 tbsp plain flour
400ml dry cider
2 tbsp finely chopped flat-leaf parsley
1kg potatoes, peeled and quartered
50g butter
100ml milk
1 tbsp wholegrain mustard
50g Gruyère cheese, grated
sea salt
freshly ground black pepper

1 Place the gammon in a large saucepan, cover it with water and simmer for 1 hour. Remove the joint from the cooking liquid and put it to one side, keeping the liquid to use as stock later. When the gammon is cool enough to handle, remove the rind and discard it. Chop the meat into chunks.
2 Heat the olive oil in a large saucepan. Add the onion, leeks and carrots and cook for 5 minutes. Sprinkle on the flour and stir it into the vegetables. Remove the pan from the heat and gradually add the cider, stirring constantly.
3 Next add the chopped gammon and 200ml of the reserved cooking stock to the pan. Put it back on the heat and simmer for 10 minutes or so until the carrots are tender. Check the seasoning and add the chopped parsley.
4 In the meantime, cook the potatoes in salted water until tender, then mash them with a potato ricer. Add the butter, milk and mustard and stir in gently.
5 Spoon the gammon mixture into a heatproof gratin dish. Spread the mash evenly on top and then sprinkle on the cheese. Place the dish under a hot grill for 5 minutes until the topping is golden brown and the filling is bubbling.

Christmas cake

Once you decide to bake the cake you know that Christmas is just around the corner.

MAKES 1 X 20CM CAKE

225g butter, softened
225g soft brown sugar
4 egg yolks
3 tbsp brandy
2 tbsp milk
a pinch of salt
½ tsp mixed spice
½ tsp grated nutmeg
225g currants
225g raisins
225g sultanas
100g ground almonds
225g plain flour
50g glacé cherries
4 egg whites

Glaze and marzipan
25g caster sugar, plus extra for dusting the work surface
1 tbsp water
2 rounded tbsp apricot jam
500g marzipan

Frosting
2 egg whites
600g white icing sugar

1 Preheat the oven to 150°C/Gas 2. Grease and line a deep 20cm cake tin with a double layer of baking parchment.
2 Place the butter and sugar in a bowl and beat with an electric hand-whisk for 3 minutes, until light and fluffy. Add the egg yolks, brandy and milk, then mix briefly until combined. Add the salt, spices, dried fruit, ground almonds, flour and cherries and mix them as well as you can – the mixture will be quite stiff.
3 Place the egg whites in a clean bowl and whisk until stiff. Fold them into the cake mixture.
4 Spoon the mixture into the cake tin and bake for 2 ½ hours. Remove from the oven and leave the cake to cool in the tin. Once the cake is completely cool, remove it from the tin and wrap it up well in foil to keep it fresh until you are ready to ice it.

To finish the cake with marzipan and frosting
5 Place the 25g of sugar and water in a small saucepan and stir over a low heat until the sugar has dissolved. Stir in the jam and bring to the boil, then reduce the heat and simmer for 2 minutes. Remove the pan from the heat.
6 Using a pastry brush, glaze the top and sides of the cake with the apricot jam mixture. Dust the work surface with caster sugar and roll out the marzipan until it is large enough to cover the top and sides of the cake. Lay the cake upside down on top of the rolled marzipan and bring up the sides, pressing the marzipan into place.
7 To make the frosting, beat the egg whites with a fork for 30 seconds until bubbles start to appear on the surface. Sift 300g of white icing sugar into the egg whites and mix it in with a wooden spoon. Sift in the rest of the icing sugar and mix in the same way. If the frosting becomes too stiff, add a couple of teaspoons of warm water.
8 Spread the frosting over the top and sides of the cake with a round-bladed knife. Leave to set before serving.

Autumn fruit jam

You can make a larger quantity of this jam if you have plenty of quinces and storage space. Otherwise, enjoy this small quantity on toast, scones, rice pudding or between the layers of a sponge with some whipped cream. It's also good with pork or duck. As with all jam preparation, make sure your jars and lids are scrupulously clean. And make sure you only ever put a clean spoon into the jam; no buttery knives!

MAKES 3 OR 4 500ML JARS

- 500g quinces
- 300ml water
- 200g frozen blackcurrants, redcurrants or blackberries or a mix of all 3
- 300g white sugar
- 1 tsp allspice

1 First sterilise the jars. Wash them well, preferably in a dishwasher. Preheat the oven to 120°C/ Gas ½, place the jars on a baking tray and put them in the oven for 20 minutes.

2 First peel and core the quinces and cut them in half. Place the peeled quinces to one side and put the peelings and cores in 300ml of water in a saucepan. Bring to a simmer and cook for 30 minutes. Strain and keep the liquid, then discard the peelings and cores.

3 Place the quinces and frozen fruit in the retained liquid and return the pan to the stove. Bring to a simmer, then add the sugar and spice and simmer gently for 1 hour, uncovered. Stir occasionally, mashing the quinces with the back of a wooden spoon as they soften.

4 Remove from the heat, allow to cool and then pour the jam into the sterilised jars. Lay circles of baking parchment on top and then seal the jars when the jam is still hot. The jam should last for 2–3 months.

Ginger butternut cupcakes

These cakes are made using butternut squash, which is in season in November. The squash creates a soft, moist texture that is often lacking in cupcakes.

MAKES ABOUT 18

225g soft brown sugar
200g butter, at room temperature
3 eggs
220g plain flour
2 tsp baking powder
2 tsp ground ginger
1 tsp ground allspice
½ tsp ground cinnamon
2 tbsp natural yoghurt
250g butternut squash, grated
125g walnuts, chopped into small pieces

Icing
200g icing sugar, sifted
125g mascarpone cheese

1 Preheat the oven to 190°C/Gas 5. Beat the sugar and butter with an electric mixer for 5 minutes. Add the eggs 1 at a time, making sure you incorporate each one before adding the next. Add the flour, baking powder, ground spices, yoghurt, squash and nuts and gently stir the mixture with a metal spoon until combined.
2 Line 1 or 2 muffin trays with paper muffin cases. Spoon some mixture into each case, filling each case to about 1cm below the top.
3 Bake the cupcakes in the oven for 25 minutes until they are firm to the touch. Allow them to cool completely before icing.
4 To make the icing, mix the icing sugar with the mascarpone cheese with a wooden spoon. Spread each cake with a dollop of the icing.

Red lentil and chickpea soup with BLT sandwiches

Lentils and chickpeas are a godsend in the winter months, when there are not many fresh interesting vegetables around. The BLTs make this a really popular meal with my family.

SERVES 6

2 tbsp olive oil
1 onion, finely chopped
1 garlic clove, finely chopped
1 celery stalk, finely chopped
300ml red lentils
1 x 400g can of chickpeas, drained and rinsed
1 x 400g can of chopped tomatoes
1.2 litres vegetable stock
2 tbsp finely chopped coriander
sea salt
freshly ground black pepper

BLT sandwiches
6 ciabatta rolls
extra virgin olive oil
1 avocado, peeled, stoned and thinly sliced
2 tomatoes, thinly sliced
1 crispy lettuce
balsamic vinegar
140g sliced pancetta
freshly ground black pepper

1 Heat the olive oil in a large saucepan. Add the onion, garlic and celery and cook gently for 10 minutes. Add the lentils, chickpeas, tomatoes and stock, cover the pan and simmer gently for 40 minutes. Season and scatter on the chopped coriander.

To make the BLT sandwiches
2 Cut the rolls in half. Drizzle each half with a little olive oil. Layer one side with some avocado, tomato and lettuce and drizzle with balsamic vinegar. Season with a little black pepper.
3 Fry the pancetta slices until crispy and lay them on the other side of the rolls. Sandwich the rolls together and serve with the soup.

Asian rice

This dish was inspired by a trip to the Maldives. For lunch, the children would often eat a spicy rice, similar to this, but with fresh tuna. I prefer to use smoked mackerel, as it is more readily available in the UK and there are fewer ethical considerations.

SERVES 6

500g basmati rice
750ml water
2 tbsp olive oil
3 eggs, beaten
100g white cabbage, finely shredded
1 onion, finely chopped
2 garlic cloves, peeled and finely chopped
1 carrot, peeled and cut into thin matchsticks
100g frozen petit pois
2 tbsp light soy sauce
1 tbsp mirin
2 tsp fish sauce
270g smoked mackerel, skinned and broken up with a fork
200g small, cooked prawns
salt

Garnish
3 tbsp light soy sauce
1 tbsp water
1 green chilli
2 garlic cloves, crushed
2 tbsp finely chopped coriander leaves
2 tbsp unsalted cashew nuts
4 spring onions, finely chopped

1 First cook the rice. Place it in a saucepan with a little salt and the 750ml of water. Bring to the boil. Reduce the heat to low, cover the pan and cook for 15 minutes. Remove the pan from the heat and leave covered for 10 minutes.
2 Heat the olive oil in a large frying or sauté pan. Make an omelette with the 3 eggs, chop it up and place to one side.
3 Return the pan to the heat. Add the cabbage, onion, garlic and carrot and cook on a reasonably high heat for about 10 minutes, stirring almost continuously. Add the peas and stir for 2 minutes more.
4 Spoon the rice into the pan. Pour on the soy sauce, mirin and fish sauce and stir. Add the mackerel, prawns and chopped up omelette and stir again gently. Serve in portions with the garnish below.

To make the garnish
5 Mix the soy sauce and water in a small bowl. Scatter in the green chilli, garlic, coriander leaves, cashews and spring onions.

Chocolate squares

This is a great way of using up any leftover cake, even if it is dry and has been around for a while.

MAKES 1 X 18CM SQUARE CAKE

- 500g leftover cake, broken into small pieces
- 100g jam, any sort will do
- 50g mixed nuts, roughly chopped
- 50g cocoa powder, sifted
- 100ml orange juice
- 225g dark chocolate, broken into pieces
- 25g butter, cut into cubes

1 Grease an 18cm square cake tin. Place the leftover cake, jam, mixed nuts, cocoa powder and orange juice in a mixing bowl. Mix with a wooden spoon to combine all the ingredients.
2 Spoon the mixture into the tin, then press the top down with the back of a spoon.
3 Put the chocolate and butter in a glass bowl and place over a saucepan of simmering water, making sure the bowl doesn't touch the water. When the chocolate and butter have melted, give them a stir to combine and then spread the mixture over the top of the cake.
4 Place the cake in the fridge to chill for 1 hour, then cut it into small squares and enjoy.

December brings the winter solstice – the shortest day and longest night of the year. The weather can be more settled, but colder, and it is definitely a time to enjoy good food and being indoors. Christmas preparations are under way and there is an air of excitement about the house. If you haven't already done so, bottle your mincemeat and make the Christmas cake. The pudding should be sitting in its basin awaiting the big day and you will need to decide on your Christmas bird or joint. Gardens sometimes look rather forlorn during December, but if you grow your own vegetables you'll be enjoying Brussels sprouts, leeks and parsnips. There are not many tasks in the garden at this time of year, particularly if the ground is frozen, which is just as well as most of us are busy with preparations for the festive season. To save money on decorations, don't forget that holly and ivy leaves and the branches of cedar and pine, can look very Christmassy and more attractive than tinsel and paper chains.

December

Tomato and fennel soup with toasted Taleggio sandwiches

Taleggio is an Italian cow's milk cheese. It has a strong smell, but melts easily so is great for cooking. These tasty sandwiches are just right with the soup.

SERVES 6

20g butter
2 tbsp olive oil
2 fennel bulbs, trimmed and roughly chopped
1 onion, roughly chopped
2 tbsp plain flour
1.5 litres chicken or vegetable stock
2 x 400g cans of chopped tomatoes
a handful of torn basil leaves
sea salt
freshly ground black pepper

Toasted Taleggio sandwiches
8–12 slices of white or wholemeal bread
150g Taleggio cheese, sliced
2 tbsp olive oil

1 Heat the butter and olive oil in a large saucepan. Throw in the fennel and onion and cook over a medium heat for 10 minutes, stirring occasionally.
2 Sprinkle on the flour and stir, then add the stock and bring to a simmer. Pour in the tomatoes, cover the pan and cook at a slow simmer for 30 minutes.
3 Blend the soup with a hand-held blender or in a liquidiser, then pass it through a sieve for perfect smoothness. Season with salt and pepper and the torn basil leaves and serve with the sandwiches.

To make the Taleggio sandwiches
4 Make 4–6 sandwiches with the Taleggio slices.
5 Heat the olive oil in a frying pan, place a sandwich in the pan and fry until golden brown on each side. Trim the crusts if you like and cut into quarters. Cook the other sandwiches in the same way.

Lamb's liver with sage and onion gravy and pancetta

Lamb's liver is delicious, nourishing and not expensive. Serve this with lots of mash and some spring greens to mop up the tasty gravy.

SERVES 6

800g lamb's liver, sliced into 3cm-wide strips
flour, for dusting
olive oil, for frying
12 slices of pancetta

Sage and onion gravy
20g butter
1 large onion, finely sliced
½ tsp sugar
1 tsp flour
200ml red wine
500ml beef stock
1 tbsp finely chopped sage leaves
1 tsp balsamic vinegar
freshly ground black pepper

Mashed potatoes
1kg potatoes, peeled and cut into quarters
40g butter
200ml warm milk
sea salt
freshly ground black pepper

To make the sage and onion gravy

1 Heat the butter in a medium pan. When it is foaming, add the onion and cook over a low heat for 30 minutes.
2 Sprinkle in the sugar and cook for 10 minutes more, then sprinkle in the flour and stir in. Pour on the red wine and simmer gently for 5 minutes. Add the stock, the sage leaves and balsamic vinegar, then simmer gently, uncovered, for 10 minutes. Season with black pepper.

To cook the liver

3 Dust the liver pieces in a little flour. Heat the olive oil in a frying pan and fry the liver, a few pieces at a time, for a few seconds on each side until dark brown. Liver cooks very quickly and it is easily spoiled so do just brown it on each side and it will be cooked.
4 Place each batch of cooked liver on a plate to keep warm while you cook the rest, then place them in the sauce to serve. Quickly fry the pancetta slices and add a couple on top of each serving of liver.

To make the mashed potatoes

5 Boil the potatoes in salted water until tender.
6 Pass the potatoes through a potato ricer or use your preferred method to mash them. Return them to the pan and place over a low heat. Mix in the butter and milk and season to taste.

Sausages with celery and white cabbage salad and garlic mash

This is a different way to use the celery and white cabbage that are around at this time of year. The dressing makes a change from mayonnaise and is very easy to prepare.

SERVES 6

12 pork sausages
olive oil

Celery and white cabbage salad
300g white cabbage, finely shredded
1 celery stalk, peeled with a potato peeler and cut into matchstick pieces
150g carrots, peeled and finely shredded or grated
2 medium eating apples, peeled and finely sliced
6 spring onions, finely sliced
a handful of fresh basil leaves, roughly torn
¼ celeriac, peeled and cut into small strips

Dressing
2 tsp red wine vinegar
2 tsp Dijon mustard
100ml olive oil
1 tbsp Greek yoghurt
sea salt
freshly ground black pepper

Garlic mash
1.5kg potatoes, peeled and quartered
300ml milk
2 garlic cloves, finely chopped
20g butter
sea salt
freshly ground black pepper

1 Pour a little olive oil into a frying pan, add the sausages and fry them over a reasonably high heat until they are brown all over. Reduce the heat and cook the sausages, for at least 15 minutes until cooked through, turning them occasionally. Serve with the salad and garlic mash.

To make the celery and white cabbage salad and dressing
2 Place all the salad ingredients in a large serving dish. To make the dressing, pour the vinegar into a small bowl, season with plenty of salt and pepper, then stir in the mustard. Gradually pour on the olive oil, whisking constantly. The dressing should thicken slightly. Fold in the yoghurt and stir until evenly combined. Pour the dressing over the salad and mix in.

To make the garlic mash
3 Boil the potatoes in plenty of salted water for 10–15 minutes until tender. Drain the potatoes and place to one side.
4 Pour the milk into the saucepan in which you cooked the potatoes. Add the garlic and heat gently on the stove.
5 Pass the potatoes through a potato ricer into the milk and garlic. Stir to combine. Add the butter and season with plenty of salt and pepper.

Mushroom and borlotti bean soup

This is thick, creamy soup that's full of flavour. I like to serve it with the kipper pate below.

SERVES 6

2 tbsp olive oil
1 onion, finely chopped
2 garlic cloves, chopped
500g mixed mushrooms, roughly chopped (I used portobellini and chestnut mushrooms)
1 x 400g can of borlotti beans, drained and rinsed
1 litre meat or vegetable stock
2 tbsp finely chopped flat-leaf parsley
150ml single cream
sea salt
freshly ground black pepper

1 Heat the olive oil in a large saucepan. Add the onion and garlic and cook over a low heat for 5 minutes, stirring frequently to ensure that the garlic doesn't burn.
2 Add the mushrooms and beans. Once they have started to cook, put a lid on the saucepan and leave over a low heat for 15 minutes, stirring occasionally.
3 Add the stock, bring to a simmer and stir, then cover the pan again and cook for 20 minutes. Blend the soup in a liquidiser and pass it through a sieve.
4 Return the soup to the pan and place over a low heat. Check the seasoning and adjust accordingly, then stir in the parsley and cream. Serve with the kipper pâté and lots of good bread.

Kipper pâté

I find that grilling kippers is the best way of cooking them. This pâté is scrumptious on warm toast.

SERVES 6

200g whole kippers
a knob of butter
150g crème fraiche
grated zest of ½ lemon
leaves from 1 sprig of thyme
freshly ground black pepper

1 Place the kippers on a grill pan. Smear them with some butter and grill for 1 minute on each side. Remove the kippers and when they are cool enough to handle, take off the heads and remove the skin and bones.
2 Place the kipper flesh in a mixing bowl. Add the crème fraiche, lemon zest and thyme leaves and mix gently until thoroughly combined, then season with pepper. Serve on warm toast.

Beef fillet with potatoes, carrots and leeks

Beef fillet is expensive but I've suggested a small joint for this recipe, which should be enough for a family of six if you serve lots of vegetables.

SERVES 6

700g piece of beef fillet
olive oil
sea salt
freshly ground black pepper

Potatoes, carrots and leeks
1 tbsp olive oil
a knob of butter
3 garlic cloves, finely chopped
1 shallot, finely chopped
4 leeks, trimmed, rinsed and sliced widthways
800g potatoes, peeled and cut into 5mm slices
200g carrots, peeled and sliced widthways into 1cm pieces
100ml dry white wine
400ml chicken stock
2 tbsp crème fraiche
sea salt
freshly ground black pepper

1 Preheat the oven to 220°C/Gas 7. Place the beef joint in a roasting tin, drizzle it with olive oil and season with salt and pepper.
2 Place the meat in the oven and cook for 25 minutes for medium-rare meat. Leave to rest for 10 minutes, before serving in slices on top of the vegetables.

To prepare the potatoes, carrots and leeks
3 Heat the olive oil and butter in a large sauté pan, then add the garlic and shallot and cook for 2 minutes. Add the leeks, potatoes and carrots and stir for a few seconds.
4 Pour on the wine and simmer for 30 seconds, then add the stock and bring to a simmer. Season well with salt and pepper, cover the pan and cook gently for 20 minutes. Stir the vegetables once or twice during this time so that they cook evenly. Stir in the crème fraiche and serve.

Game pie and swede with caramelised onions

Game pie is so comforting and a lovely dish for a cold winter evening in December.

SERVES 6

olive oil
700g venison shoulder, diced
300g wild rabbit meat, diced
1 onion, finely chopped
1 celery stalk, chopped
2 garlic cloves
250ml red wine
2 tbsp plain flour
1 tbsp tomato purée
a sprig of thyme
1 bay leaf
700ml beef stock
15g butter
200g chestnut mushrooms, wiped clean and roughly chopped
1 x 230g sheet of ready-rolled puff pastry
1 egg, beaten, for glazing
sea salt
freshly ground black pepper

Swede with caramelised onions
a knob of butter
1 swede, peeled and cut into 1 cm dice
2 tbsp water
1 onion, finely sliced
1 tbsp olive oil
1 tsp soft brown sugar
sea salt
freshly ground black pepper

1 Heat 2 tablespoons of olive oil in a large saucepan and brown the venison and rabbit in batches, putting each batch to one side while you do the next.
2 Empty the pan and add another tablespoon of olive oil. Fry the onion, celery and garlic for 5 minutes, then place to one side with the venison and rabbit.
3 Return the pan to the heat and add the wine. Let it bubble away for 1 minute, giving it a stir, then return the meat and vegetables to the pan. Sprinkle on the flour and stir. Add the tomato purée, thyme, bay leaf and stock, and season well with salt and pepper. Bring to a gentle simmer, cover the pan and cook for 1 hour.
4 Heat the butter in a frying pan and fry the mushrooms for 5 minutes over a reasonably high heat so that they give off their moisture and turn golden brown. Spoon the mushrooms into the pan with the venison and rabbit and stir. Check the seasoning.
5 Spoon the mixture into a pie dish, removing the thyme and bay leaf. Allow to cool while you preheat the oven to 200°C/Gas 6.
6 Roll out the puff pastry, place it over the meat and brush the top of the pie with some beaten egg. Pop the pie into the oven for 20 minutes until the pastry has risen and is golden brown. Serve with the swede and onions.

To make the swede with caramelised onions
7 Heat the butter in a medium saucepan, add the swede and water, then stir. Cover the pan and cook the swede in the butter and its own steam over a low heat for about 15 minutes. Season with salt and pepper.
8 Meanwhile, fry the onion slices in the olive oil for 5 minutes over a medium heat until they start to brown. Sprinkle on the sugar and stir for a moment while the sugar caramelises around the onions. Tip the swede on top and check the seasoning.

Curried mince with potato, spinach and chickpea curry

Curried mince is not the most glamorous sounding of meals, but it is certainly useful and benefits from long slow cooking as here. I like to serve these two curries together with some naan bread. Use the recipe on page 380 for the curry powder if you like to make your own.

SERVES 6

2 tbsp vegetable oil
1 onion, finely chopped
2cm piece of fresh root ginger, peeled and grated
2 garlic cloves, finely chopped
2 tsp ground cumin
2 tsp ground coriander
1 tbsp curry powder
500g minced lamb
500g minced beef
1 tbsp flour
300ml chicken stock (a stock cube will do)
2 tbsp chopped fresh coriander
1 tbsp chopped fresh mint
sea salt
freshly ground black pepper

Potato, spinach and chickpea curry
500g potatoes, peeled and cut into 4cm chunks
1 x 400g can of chickpeas, drained and rinsed
200g spinach
200ml chicken stock (a stock cube will do)
2cm chunk of creamed coconut
sea salt
freshly ground black pepper

1 Heat the vegetable oil in a saucepan that has a lid and is large enough to hold the mince. Add the onion, ginger and garlic and fry gently for 10 minutes, taking care not to burn the garlic.
2 Sprinkle on the cumin, coriander and curry powder and stir for a few seconds. Add the mince and stir until it has browned, then stir in the flour and season with salt and pepper.
3 Pour on the stock, sprinkle in the fresh herbs and simmer gently, partly covered, for 1 hour.
4 Check the seasoning and serve with the potato, chickpea and spinach curry and naan bread (see opposite).

To make the potato, spinach and chickpea curry
5 Cook the potatoes in boiling salted water until tender. Drain and return them to the saucepan with the chickpeas, spinach and stock. Simmer for 10 minutes.
6 Add the creamed coconut and stir intermittently until the coconut has dissolved.

Naan bread

These Indian flatbreads are easy to make and the perfect accompaniment to curries.

MAKES 6

150ml warm milk
2 tsp sugar
1 x 7g sachet of dried yeast
450g plain flour, plus extra for dusting the work surface
½ tsp salt
1 tsp baking powder
2 tbsp vegetable oil
150ml plain yoghurt
1 large egg

1 Place the milk in a small bowl or jug with the sugar and yeast and leave for 5 minutes.
2 Place the flour, salt and baking powder in a mixing bowl, add the yeast mixture, the oil, yoghurt and egg, then mix everything together. Turn the dough out on to a floured surface and knead for 5 minutes. Return the dough to the bowl, cover and leave to rise for 1 hour.
3 Heat the oven to its highest temperature and preheat the grill. Place a baking sheet in the oven to heat up.
4 Divide the dough into 6 balls and roll each ball into an oval. Place a naan on the baking sheet in the oven for 2–3 minutes, then place it under the grill until golden brown. Wrap it in a clean tea towel to keep warm while you cook the rest of the naan breads in the same way.

Lemon curd butterfly cakes

These look almost as beautiful as butterflies.

MAKES 12 CAKES

Cakes
200g butter, softened
200g caster sugar
3 eggs
200g self-raising flour
2 tsp vanilla extract
2 tbsp milk
icing sugar, sifted, for dusting

Lemon curd
50g butter
110g caster sugar
finely grated zest and juice of 2 lemons
2 eggs
1 egg yolk

Vanilla frosting
75g soft butter
250g icing sugar
75g sweetened condensed milk
75ml double cream

1 Preheat the oven to 180°C/Gas 4. Fill a muffin tray with 12 paper cases.
2 Place the butter and sugar in a mixing bowl and beat with an electric hand-whisk for about 3 minutes until white and fluffy. Add 1 egg, followed by 1 tablespoon of flour, and beat in. Add the rest of the eggs, 1 at a time, in the same way, with a tablespoon of flour each time. Fold in the remaining flour with a large metal spoon, then gently stir in the vanilla extract and milk.
3 Divide the mixture evenly between the 12 paper cases and bake the cakes in the oven for 20–25 minutes until firm to the touch. Remove the cakes from the muffin tin and leave them on a wire rack to cool.

To make the lemon curd and vanilla frosting
4 Melt the butter in a small saucepan on a low heat. Add the caster sugar, lemon zest and juice. Stir in the eggs and egg yolk and heat gently until the curd is thick enough to coat the back of the spoon. It will thicken more as it cools. Place to one side to cool.
5 If the whites of the eggs have cooked separately from the yolks, pass the curd through a sieve before cooling.
6 To make the frosting, beat all the ingredients together in a bowl until smooth.

To assemble the butterfly cakes
7 Cut the top off each cake so that the surface of the cake is level with the top of the paper case. Cut these pieces into halves to make the wings of the butterflies.
8 Spread a spoonful of frosting on top of each cake and add a blob of lemon curd in the middle. Position the cut halves of cake in the frosting so that they stand up like butterfly wings. Dust with some sifted icing sugar for a seriously pretty plate of cakes.

Sliced oranges in syrup with ginger madeleines

Oranges in syrup are a rather old-fashioned pudding, but I think they make a welcome break from the rich foods that appear on the table at this time of year. These are English madeleines and are made in the same way as fairy cakes. They are lovely for pudding and there will be plenty left over for tea the next day.

MAKES 20 CAKES

Sliced oranges in syrup
6 oranges
100g soft brown sugar
juice of 1 orange
25ml water
1 tbsp pistachio nuts, roughly chopped
a few cubes of Turkish delight snipped into little chunks (optional)

Ginger madeleines
180g butter, softened, plus extra for greasing
180g caster sugar
3 eggs
180g self-raising flour
20g stem ginger, finely chopped
1 tbsp stem ginger syrup
½ tsp ground ginger

1 Peel the oranges with a sharp knife, making sure you remove all the white pith. Cut the oranges into thin slices and arrange them attractively on a serving dish.
2 Heat the sugar, juice and water in a small saucepan and simmer gently for 5 minutes. Pour this syrup over the oranges and scatter the pistachio nuts and Turkish delight, if using, on top. Serve with the madeleines and some Greek yoghurt.

To make the ginger madeleines
3 Preheat the oven to 180°C/Gas 4. Grease 2 x 12-hole fairy cake tins.
4 Place the butter and sugar in a mixing bowl and beat with an electric hand-whisk for about 3 minutes, until light and fluffy. Add 1 egg and a tablespoon of flour and mix in, then add the other eggs in the same way.
5 Put the rest of the flour in the bowl and fold in the stem ginger, ginger syrup and ground ginger with a metal spoon until combined. Spoon the mixture into the tins and bake the cakes for 10 minutes, until firm to the touch and golden brown. Remove and allow to cool slightly in the trays.
6 When the cakes are cool enough to handle, place them on a wire rack to finish cooling.

Waffles and chocolate sauce

You will need a waffle iron to make these waffles; this is a useful piece of kitchen equipment, as long as you use it reasonably often. It's not too cumbersome to store and cleans easily.

SERVES 6

225g plain flour
a pinch of salt
3 tbsp baking powder
2 tbsp caster sugar
2 eggs
350ml warm milk
75g melted butter

Chocolate sauce
150g plain chocolate
20g butter
4 tbsp double cream

vanilla ice cream, for serving

1 Place the flour, salt, baking powder and sugar in a mixing bowl and make a well in the centre. Crack the eggs into the well, then pour in the milk and melted butter. Gradually draw the dry ingredients into the wet ones, using a whisk, and then beat until you have a smooth batter.
2 Heat the waffle iron and when it's hot, pour in a spoonful of batter. The waffle iron will let you know when the waffles are ready. Keep the waffle warm while you make the rest. Serve with the chocolate sauce and some ice cream.

To make the chocolate sauce
3 Place the chocolate and butter in a glass bowl over a pan of simmering water, making sure the bottom of the bowl doesn't touch the water. Stir occasionally until the chocolate and butter have melted, then remove from the heat. Stir in the cream.

Sausage and chicken pie with spicy chutney

Food that you can serve cold, such as this pie, is very welcome at this time of year, when everyone is busy and you may have unexpected guests.

SERVES 6

Pie filling
800g sausage meat
2 tbsp finely chopped flat-leaf parsley
6 spring onions, finely sliced
50g pistachio nuts, roughly chopped
¼ tsp grated nutmeg
500g cooked chicken breast, chopped into bite-sized pieces
sea salt
freshly ground black pepper

Pastry
350g plain flour, plus extra for dusting the work surface
a pinch of salt
200g cold butter, cut into cubes
2 eggs
50ml cold water

Chutney (makes 2–3 jars)
4cm piece of cinnamon stick
1 star anise
5 cardamom pods
2cm piece of fresh root ginger
50g walnuts, roughly chopped
100g raisins
300g cooking apples, peeled, cored and roughly chopped
100g pears, peeled, cored and roughly chopped
400g soft brown sugar
250ml red wine
2 tbsp treacle
1 slice of orange peel
juice of 1 orange
2 onions, finely chopped

To make the chutney

1 Place the cinnamon stick, star anise, cardamom and ginger in a small piece of muslin and tie securely. Place the rest of the ingredients in a saucepan. Pop the spice bag in and simmer the chutney for 2 hours, until it has thickened and the liquid has reduced by half. Pour into sterilised jars (see page 666). Keeps for up to a year.

To prepare the pie filling

2 Preheat the oven to 180°C/Gas 4. Place the sausage meat, parsley, spring onions and nuts in a mixing bowl and mix well. Season with nutmeg and salt and pepper.

To make the pastry

3 Place the flour and salt in a food processor, add the butter, and blitz until the mixture resembles breadcrumbs. Add the eggs and the water and process again for a few seconds, then turn out on to a lightly floured surface and bring together to form a ball. Divide the pastry into two-thirds and one-third, wrap in clingfilm and chill in the fridge for 30 minutes.

To assemble the pie

4 Grease a 20–21cm spring-clip cake tin. Roll out the larger piece of pastry dough and use it to line the tin, easing it into the sides with your fingers.

5 Spoon half of the sausage meat mixture into the tin, squashing it down. Scatter half the chicken on top and then spoon the rest of the sausage meat on top. Scatter on the last of the chicken.

6 Roll out the other piece of pastry and place it on top of the pie, pressing it down around the rim so that it seals securely. Place the pie on a baking sheet, as there will be some seepage, and bake in the oven for 1 hour and 20 minutes. Remove and leave to cool, then serve cold with the chutney and a green salad.

Truffade

Truffade is a luxurious potato, cheese and bacon dish from the Auvergne region of France. Traditionally, the potatoes are grated and then cooked in lard, so the dish ends up more like a pancake. I have adapted it slightly and use thinly sliced potatoes which are cooked with cheese and bacon until tender. Serve with a green salad to temper the richness of the dish.

SERVES 6

2 tbsp olive oil
100g pancetta, chopped
1kg potatoes, peeled and thinly sliced
6 spring onions, sliced
250g Gruyère cheese, cut into 1cm cubes
sea salt
freshly ground black pepper

1 Heat the olive oil in a large sauté pan. Add the pancetta and fry for 1 minute until it is translucent. Add the potatoes and spring onions and stir over a medium heat for 1 minute. Season with salt and pepper.
2 Cover the pan and leave to cook over a low heat for 15 minutes, until the potatoes are soft. If you don't have a lid for your pan, cover it with a sheet of foil.
3 Dot the top with the cheese, cover the pan again and cook for another 3 minutes. Serve with a green salad.

Celeriac soup

Celeriac is a surprising vegetable. It looks so unappealing raw, definitely an 'ugly duckling', but it becomes something rather lovely once cooked.

SERVES 6

- 25g butter
- 600g celeriac, peeled and cut into 2cm cubes
- 200g potatoes, peeled and cut into 2cm cubes
- 1 medium onion, diced
- 1.5 litres chicken stock
- 100ml single cream, plus extra for serving
- sea salt
- freshly ground black pepper

1 Heat the butter in a large saucepan. When it's foaming, add the celeriac, potatoes and onion. Turn the heat down low, cover the pan and cook the vegetables for 10 minutes. Pour on the stock and simmer, partly covered, for 40 minutes.
2 Pour the soup into a blender and liquidise, then pass it through a sieve for perfect smoothness. Pour it back into the saucepan, warm it through, then pour on the cream and season with salt and pepper. Serve in bowls with an extra swirl of cream if you like and some sandwiches or crusty bread.

Goulash

Goulash comes from the Hungarian word 'guylas', which means herdsman, so it was probably created by such workers. Originally a robust soup, goulash has changed and developed over the years and is now more of a stew, containing meat and vegetables flavoured with paprika. My recipe is far from authentic, as it includes flour and wine, but it's very tasty.

SERVES 6

- 2 tbsp olive oil
- 1kg shin of beef, cut into 2cm chunks
- 1 large onion, finely chopped
- 200ml red wine
- 2 tsp flour
- 4 tsp paprika
- 1 x 400g can of chopped tomatoes
- 500ml beef stock
- 2 tbsp soured cream
- 2 tbsp chopped flat-leaf parsley
- sea salt
- freshly ground black pepper

1 Heat the olive oil in a large saucepan. Brown the beef in batches, taking care not to overcrowd the pan or the beef will steam rather than brown. Set each batch aside while you brown the next.

2 Once all the meat has been browned, keep the pan on the heat and fry the onion for 3 minutes. Place the onion with the beef.

3 With the pan still on the heat, add the wine and let it simmer for 1 minute. Put the beef and onions back in the pan, sprinkle on the flour and stir it in. Add the paprika, tomatoes and beef stock, then season with salt and pepper. Bring the goulash to a simmer, cover the pan and leave to cook over a gentle heat for 1 hour.

4 Remove the lid and simmer very gently for another hour. Check the seasoning, stir in the soured cream and parsley, then serve with some boiled potatoes.

Lemon sole with garlic breadcrumbs and puréed peas and spinach

One of the most popular fish in restaurants in France and England is lemon sole. It has a lovely delicate flavour and goes beautifully with other ingredients. Once it has been filleted by your fishmonger, it is easy to cook in the oven or under the grill, and even inexperienced cooks can get results as good as the most fêted chefs.

SERVES 6

1 tbsp olive oil
100g white breadcrumbs
1 garlic clove, crushed
2 tbsp finely chopped flat-leaf parsley
6 lemon sole fillets
sea salt
freshly ground black pepper

Puréed peas and spinach
30g butter
1 shallot, finely diced
200g frozen peas
150g potatoes, peeled and cut into 2cm cubes
200ml chicken stock
150g young spinach leaves
2 tbsp single cream
sea salt
freshly ground black pepper

1 Preheat the oven to 180°C/Gas 4. Heat the olive oil in a frying pan. Add the breadcrumbs and garlic and fry for 2 minutes until the breadcrumbs have crispened slightly. Stir in the parsley and season with salt and pepper. Remove from the heat.
2 Lay the sole fillets in a gratin dish. Sprinkle the breadcrumbs over the fish and bake in the oven for 12 minutes. Remove and serve the fillets with the pea and spinach purée.

To prepare the puréed peas and spinach
3 Warm the butter in a sauté pan, add the shallot and sauté for 2 minutes. Add the peas, potatoes and stock, season with salt and pepper and bring to a simmer.
4 Reduce the heat, cover the pan and cook the vegetables gently for 10 minutes. Add the spinach and bring to a simmer again, then cover the pan and cook for 3 minutes.
5 Tip the mixture into a blender and mix until roughly blended – it doesn't need to be too smooth. Return the purée to the pan and heat it through. Stir in the cream and add extra stock or water if the purée seems too heavy. Check the seasoning before serving.

Rabbit stew

Ask your butcher to joint the rabbits into shoulders, legs and saddle. This is great served with watercress and a loaf of crusty French bread.

SERVES 6

25g butter
100g pancetta, chopped
20 baby onions, peeled and left whole
3 jointed rabbits
200ml brandy
1 tbsp flour
700ml chicken stock
700g potatoes, peeled and cut into quarters
250g frozen peas
1 sprig of sage
sea salt
freshly ground black pepper

1 Place a large casserole dish on the hob, add the butter and leave it to melt. Add the pancetta and onions and fry for 5 minutes until golden brown. Remove the pancetta and onions and place them to one side.
2 Keep the saucepan on the heat and start to brown the rabbit joints. Do this in batches so that the pan stays hot and the rabbit joints brown rather than steam. As each batch is browned, place it to one side with the pancetta and onions.
3 When you have browned all the rabbit, put the empty pan back on the heat, pour in the brandy and let it bubble away for 30 seconds. Return the rabbit to the pan with the pancetta and onions, sprinkle on the flour and stir it in.
4 Add the stock, potatoes, peas and sage. Season liberally with salt and pepper, cover the pan and leave the stew to simmer gently on top of the stove for 50 minutes. Serve piping hot.

Roast pheasant with red cabbage and chestnuts and bread sauce

To halve the pheasants you will need a large sharp knife, some jointing shears or good kitchen scissors. Lay the pheasant on its breast and cut along one side of the back bone. Then cut along the other side and remove the bone altogether. Turn the pheasant over and cut through the breast so the pheasant falls into two halves. If you are quartering them, cut across each half as best you can.

SERVES 6

3 hen pheasants, cut in half lengthways (if the pheasants are large, cut them into quarters
100ml olive oil
juice of ½ lemon
grated zest of 1 lemon
100ml white wine
1 shallot, finely sliced
2 or 3 sprigs of fresh thyme
a knob of butter, plus more as needed
sea salt
freshly ground black pepper

Red cabbage and chestnuts
1 red cabbage, cored and thinly sliced
100g chestnuts, roughly chopped
½ tsp mixed spice
30g butter
25g soft brown sugar
1 tsp salt
100ml Marsala wine
50ml red wine vinegar
freshly ground black pepper

Bread sauce
300ml milk
1 onion, peeled, left whole and studded with 3 cloves
1 bay leaf
6 heaped tbsp fresh white breadcrumbs
1 tbsp double cream
20g butter
sea salt
freshly ground black pepper

1 Preheat the oven to 200°C/Gas 6. Place the pheasant halves in a large roasting tin or 2 smaller ones. Mix the olive oil with the lemon juice, zest, wine, shallot, thyme and seasoning. Massage this mixture into the pheasant halves and leave them for 15 minutes.
2 Heat the knob of butter in a frying pan and brown each pheasant half, skin side down, placing them back in the roasting tin with the marinade juices and shallot once golden – don't brown them too long. The butter will tend to burn so it's best to rinse out the pan after you have browned about 3 halves and add fresh butter.
3 When all the pheasants have been browned, deglaze the pan with a little white wine, simmer for 30 seconds, then pour it over the pheasants.
4 Roast the pheasants for 25 minutes. Serve with the cabbage, bread sauce and roast potatoes (see page 725).

To prepare the red cabbage and chestnuts
5 Place all the ingredients in a large saucepan and bring to a simmer. Turn the heat down low, cover the pan and cook for 1 hour. Check the seasoning before serving.

To prepare the bread sauce
6 Put the milk in a saucepan with the onion and bay leaf and bring to the boil. Remove the pan from the heat, cover and leave for 10 minutes so that the flavours can infuse. Remove the onion and bay leaf, then stir in the breadcrumbs. Put the pan back over a low heat and simmer for 3 minutes. Stir in the cream and butter and season well.

Brioche

The best way to make brioche is in a food mixer with a dough hook. To make it by hand requires expertise in the traditional French method of bread making, which most of us don't have. Be careful to give the dough enough time in the mixer at each stage, before and after you add the butter. The dough is ready when it moves away from the side of the bowl as the dough hook goes through it. You need to stop the machine at intervals and scrape down the dough so that it is worked evenly.

MAKES 1 BRIOCHE LOAF

- 1 x 7g sachet of dried yeast
- 2 tbsp lukewarm water
- 375g strong white flour
- ½ tsp salt
- 2 tbsp caster sugar
- 5 eggs, beaten
- 1 tsp vanilla extract
- 175g butter, softened, plus extra for greasing
- 1 egg yolk, mixed with 1 tbsp water, to glaze

1 Mix the yeast with the water in a small bowl and leave for 5 minutes for the yeast to activate.

2 Place the flour, salt, sugar and eggs in a mixing bowl, add the yeasted water and the vanilla extract and mix until you have a smooth wet dough.

3 Knead for 5 minutes as best you can. The mixture should be sticky so use an electric food mixer with a dough hook, if you have one. Don't be tempted to add more flour to the mixture. Cover the bowl with a tea towel and leave the dough to rise for 1½ hours.

4 The next stage is to add the butter to the dough. I also do this with a food mixer, but it is possible to do it with your hands. Once all the butter has been incorporated into the dough, leave it to rest for 5 minutes.

5 Meanwhile, grease a 1-litre loaf tin and preheat the oven to 220°C/Gas 7. Shape the dough into a thick sausage shape and place it in the loaf tin. Cover with a tea towel and leave for 30 minutes.

6 Brush the top of the brioche with the egg glaze, then bake the brioche for 45 minutes. Turn out on to a wire rack to cool, then serve with butter and jam.

Plum whip

If you called this prune mousse you probably wouldn't get a very enthusiastic response, but 'plum whip' sold it to my family. It's a good winter pudding and a welcome change from heavier pies and crumbles.

SERVES 6

225g soft prunes (stones removed)
270ml double cream
2 tbsp runny honey
250g vanilla ice cream
a handful of pistachio nuts, chopped, for serving

1 Place the prunes in a small saucepan and pour in water just to cover. Put a lid on the pan and simmer the prunes for 15 minutes.
2 Whip the cream in a bowl until fluffy and light, then set to one side.
3 Once the prunes are cooked, blend them in a liquidiser with 120ml of the cooking water. Add the honey and ice cream to the liquidiser and blend again.
4 Fold the prune mixture into the whipped cream and chill in the fridge. Serve with a scattering of chopped pistachio nuts.

Steamed pudding with apples and mincemeat

Christmas is coming, so use up any leftover mincemeat from last year in this steamed pudding – or, if you are really organised, take the chance to test this year's batch.

SERVES 6

Pudding
200g butter, softened
200g caster sugar
3 eggs
200g self-raising flour
1 tbsp milk
1 tbsp maple syrup
grated zest of 1 orange

Topping
10g butter
1 quince, peeled, cored and cut into 1cm chunks
3 small apples, peeled, cored and cut into 1cm chunks
1 tbsp orange juice
2 tbsp soft brown sugar
3 tbsp mincemeat
2 tbsp maple syrup

To prepare the topping

1 Melt the butter in a medium saucepan. Add the quince, cover the pan and cook over a low heat for 5 minutes.
2 Add the apples and orange juice and cook for about 3 minutes, covered, also over a low heat. Stir in the sugar, mincemeat and syrup, remove from the heat and set aside.

To make and assemble the pudding

3 Grease a 1-litre pudding basin and spoon the topping into the base.
4 Put the butter and sugar into a mixing bowl and beat with an electric hand-whisk for 3–4 minutes until light and fluffy.
5 Mix in 1 egg and a tablespoon of flour. Mix in the other 2 eggs in the same way, with a tablespoon of flour each time, then fold in the rest of the flour with a metal spoon. Gently mix in the milk, syrup and orange zest.
6 Spoon the pudding batter into the basin on top of the mincemeat mixture. Cover the basin with a small circle of greaseproof paper, then tie a larger sheet of greaseproof or foil over this and tie it in place securely with a piece of string just below the top of the basin.
7 Place the basin in a large saucepan. Pour water to a depth of 2cm into the saucepan and bring to a simmer. Cover the saucepan and simmer for 2 hours, checking the water level from time to time and topping it up with boiling water when necessary.
8 When ready to serve, untie the greaseproof paper. Run a knife around the inside of the basin and invert the pudding on to a plate with a slight lip to hold the juices. It should come out easily and the juicy topping will run down the sides. Serve with plenty of cream.

Cream of cauliflower soup with soft duck eggs on toast

Creamy coloured and delicious, cauliflower is certainly welcome in my kitchen at this time of year.

SERVES 6

1 tbsp olive oil
20g butter
1 onion, finely chopped
2 garlic cloves, finely chopped
1 large cauliflower, trimmed and cut into large chunks (about 800g)
1 large potato, peeled and cut into quarters
1.5 litres chicken or vegetable stock
a sprig of thyme
100ml single cream
sea salt
freshly ground black pepper

Duck eggs on toast
3 duck eggs
2 tbsp olive oil
1 garlic clove, slightly smashed
6 slices of bread

1 First make the soup. Heat the olive oil and butter in a large saucepan. Add the onion and garlic and cook over a low heat for 5 minutes.
2 Add the cauliflower and potato chunks to the pan and stir, then cover the pan and cook the vegetables over a very low heat for 5 minutes. Pour on the stock, add the sprig of thyme and simmer for 35 minutes.
3 Remove the thyme sprig, then liquidise the soup and pour it back into the pan to warm through. Stir in the cream and season with salt and pepper. Serve the soup with the duck eggs on toast.

To prepare the duck eggs on toast
4 Place the duck eggs in boiling water for 6–7 minutes; they should be slightly soft but not too runny.
5 Heat the olive oil in a frying pan, add the garlic clove and fry it gently for 1 minute. Place the slices of bread in the garlicky oil and fry on both sides until golden brown and crispy.
6 Peel the duck eggs very carefully and slice each one in half lengthways. Pour the soup into bowls and put a piece of toast in the centre of each bowl of soup, with an egg half on top of the toast.

Prawns and sea bass in tamarind sauce, with carrot and cashew nut curry

I think fish curry is a real treat and it's quick and easy to prepare. If sea bass is too expensive, choose a firm-fleshed fish that doesn't disintegrate when cooked. Sea bream would work very well.

1 Heat the oil in a large sauté pan. Add the onion, garlic and ginger and fry for 5 minutes, until the onion is soft. Add the tomatoes and cook for 3 minutes longer. Stir in the curry powder and the tamarind paste and cook for 1 minute.
2 Add the sea bass to the pan and cook for 1 minute. Then throw in the prawns to warm through.
3 Add the water and bring to a simmer, then remove the pan from the heat and stir in the yoghurt and coriander. Taste for seasoning, adding salt and pepper to taste. Serve with the carrot and cashew nut curry and some boiled rice.

To make the carrot and cashew nut curry
4 Heat the oil in a small frying pan or saucepan. Add the shallot and cook for 2 minutes until it starts to turn golden brown.
5 Add the garlic and chilli and stir for 30 seconds. Put the mustard seeds into the pan and once they start to pop, add the carrots, nuts and water. Cover the pan and cook the curry over a low heat for 5 minutes. Season with salt and pepper.

To prepare the boiled rice
6 Place the rice, salt and water in a large saucepan and bring to a lively boil. Reduce the heat to very low, cover the pan and cook the rice for 15 minutes. Stir once during the cooking time.
7 Remove the pan from the heat. Keep the rice covered and leave it undisturbed for 10 minutes more.

SERVES 6

2 tbsp olive oil
1 onion, finely chopped
2 garlic cloves, finely chopped
2cm piece of fresh root ginger, peeled and grated
2 medium tomatoes, roughly chopped
1 tbsp curry powder (see page 380 for home-made)
1 tbsp tamarind paste
500g sea bass fillet
200g cooked, peeled prawns
100ml water
2 tbsp natural yoghurt
2 tbsp chopped coriander leaves
sea salt
freshly ground black pepper

Carrot and cashew nut curry
1 tbsp olive oil
1 shallot, finely chopped
1 garlic clove, finely chopped
1 green chilli, seeded and finely chopped
1 tsp mustard seeds
400g carrots, grated
2 tbsp unsalted cashew nuts
50ml water
sea salt
freshly ground black pepper

Boiled rice
500g basmati rice
½ tsp salt
750ml water

Potato pancakes with creamed chicken

The inspiration for this recipe came from an old cookery book called 'Cooking for Two: A Handbook for Young Housekeepers', published in 1926. The foreword states that 'the best things are nearest... do not grasp at the stars, but do life's plain, common work... certain that daily duties and daily bread are the sweetest things of life.' I'm not sure about the daily duties, but I agree with the other sentiments when it comes to cooking.

SERVES 6

Pancakes
- 450g potatoes, peeled and cut into quarters
- 250g plain flour
- a large pinch of salt
- 1 tsp baking powder
- 300ml milk
- 3 eggs
- 6 spring onions, finely chopped
- 1 tbsp soy sauce

Creamed chicken
- 25g butter
- 25g flour
- 500ml milk
- 1 tbsp Dijon mustard
- 50g Gruyère cheese
- 4 cooked chicken breasts, chopped into bite-sized pieces
- 2 tbsp finely chopped flat-leaf parsley
- 200g cooked peas
- 100g sliced pancetta
- sea salt
- freshly ground black pepper

To make the potato pancake batter

1 Put the potatoes in a saucepan of salted water, bring to the boil and cook until the potatoes are tender enough to mash or pass through a ricer. Set aside.

2 Put the flour, salt and baking powder into a mixing bowl, make a well in the middle and pour in the milk and eggs. Mix gently with a wooden spoon, drawing the flour into the liquid gradually so that you don't get any lumps. Add the spring onions, mashed potato and soy sauce, then season and place to one side to rest.

To make the creamed chicken

3 Melt the butter in a small saucepan and add the flour, stirring to combine. Remove the pan from the heat and pour on the milk gradually, stirring constantly. Return the pan to the heat and simmer gently for 10 minutes, stirring occasionally.

4 Stir in the Dijon mustard and cheese, then season with salt and pepper. Remove the sauce from the heat and add the chicken, parsley, and cooked peas.

5 Fry the pancetta until crispy and add before serving.

To assemble the dish

6 Lightly oil a frying pan and place it over a medium heat. Dollop tablespoons of the pancake batter into the pan, leaving space between each one, and turn with a pallet knife after about 30 seconds. Remove and keep warm while you cook the rest of the pancakes.

7 Place 2 or 3 pancakes on each plate and heap some creamed chicken on top.

Smoky Argentinian beef stew

I adapted this recipe from one I found in a little book someone gave me on Argentinian food. There is a very strong cookery tradition in Argentina, which is influenced by the many European immigrants who have settled there over the centuries. Beef tends to dominate the menu in most restaurants and a favourite way of cooking beef is the asado, in which the meat is cooked over hot white ash from a nearby fire. I've tried to get some smoky flavours into this dish.

SERVES 6

- 2 tbsp olive oil
- 1 onion, finely chopped
- 2 garlic cloves, finely chopped
- 1 celery stalk, finely chopped
- 200g chorizo sausage, sliced into 1cm rounds
- 750g minced beef
- 2 tsp ground coriander
- 2 tsp ground cumin
- 1 litre beef stock
- 1 x 400g can of chopped tomatoes
- 3 carrots, peeled and cut into 1cm discs
- 3 potatoes, peeled and cut into chunks
- 2 sweet potatoes, peeled and cut into chunks
- a sprinkle of chilli flakes or powder
- 1 x 400g can of kidney beans, drained and rinsed
- sea salt
- freshly ground black pepper

1 Heat the oil in a large saucepan. Add the onion, garlic and celery and cook over a low heat for 10 minutes, stirring frequently.
2 Add the chorizo and cook, stirring, for 5 minutes.
3 Add the minced beef, increase the heat and cook until the beef has turned brown. Sprinkle on the spices, add the stock, tomatoes, vegetables, chilli flakes and kidney beans. Season with salt and pepper.
4 Bring everything to a simmer, cover the pan and cook the stew gently for 1 hour. Check the seasoning and serve.

Rice with basil

This was something I used to make my mother when she came to stay with me and we wanted something easy to prepare and fresh tasting to eat.

SERVES 6

400g basmati rice
½ tsp salt
600ml water
6 eggs
2 tbsp vegetable oil
25g butter
1 garlic clove, finely chopped
200g button mushrooms, cut into quarters
1 onion, finely chopped
120g French beans, cooked until tender and cut into 2cm pieces
1 tsp sugar
6 tbsp light soy sauce
20 basil leaves, roughly torn

1 Put the rice in a saucepan with half a teaspoon of salt and 600ml water. Bring the water to a rolling boil, cover the pan and reduce the heat to next to nothing. Cook the rice for 15 minutes, then remove the pan from the heat. Leave the rice covered and undisturbed for 10 minutes.
2 Break the eggs into a glass bowl and beat them gently for a few seconds with a fork. Heat a tablespoon of the vegetable oil in a wok, or a large frying pan. Pour in the eggs and make a large firm omelette. Slip the omelette out of the pan and cut it into strips, then place to one side.
3 Return the pan to the heat and add the last tablespoon of vegetable oil and the butter. When the oil and butter are hot, add the garlic and the mushrooms and fry until the mushrooms start to turn golden brown. Add the onion and cook for 5 minutes until soft.
4 Add the cooked rice, beans, sugar, soy sauce and the pieces of omelette, then heat through. Sprinkle on the basil leaves and serve.

Spanish pork stew

This is a good, thick stew which has a glorious impact on the senses: the vibrant colour, the smoky intense smell boosted by the chorizo, and the full flavour that will undoubtedly please your taste buds.

SERVES 6

- 1kg boneless pork shoulder, cut into cubes
- 200g chorizo sausage, sliced into 1cm pieces
- 1 tbsp flour
- 2 tbsp olive oil
- 1 onion, finely chopped
- 100ml red wine
- 15g porcini mushrooms, soaked in warm water
- 1 savoy cabbage, cored and finely shredded
- 100g pitted, soft prunes, roughly chopped
- 1 x 400g can of chopped tomatoes
- 500ml chicken stock
- sea salt
- freshly ground black pepper

1 Preheat the oven to 160°C/Gas 3. Place the pork and chorizo in a bowl, sprinkle with the flour and season with salt and pepper.

2 Heat the oil in a casserole dish. When it's hot, brown the meat, a couple of tablespoons at a time so that it browns quickly. Place each batch of meat to one side while you brown the next.

3 Once all the meat has been browned and put to one side, fry the onion for 5 minutes and add to the meat.

4 Return the casserole dish to the heat and add the wine. Stir for 30 seconds or so, scraping up any sticky bits from the bottom of the dish.

5 Drain the mushrooms and chop them roughly. Add them to the casserole dish, with the meat and onions, cabbage, prunes, tomatoes and stock.

6 Bring everything to a simmer, stir and season. Put a lid on the casserole dish and place it in the oven for 1½ hours, by which time you will have a beautifully smoky tasting stew. Serve with baked potatoes.

Stuffed slow-roasted goose with bread sauce

This is an alternative to turkey for Christmas day.

SERVES 6

4.5kg goose
sea salt
freshly ground black pepper

Stuffing
2 tbsp olive oil
1 onion, finely chopped
6 sage leaves, finely chopped
1 fennel bulb, trimmed and finely chopped
2 apples, peeled, cored and roughly chopped
50g soft pitted prunes, roughly chopped
¼ tsp mixed spice
150g whole cooked chestnuts, roughly chopped
450g sausage meat
6 shallots, peeled and quartered
sea salt
freshly ground black pepper

Gravy
1 tbsp flour
500ml chicken or meat stock

Bread sauce
300ml milk
1 onion, peeled, left whole and studded with 3 cloves
1 bay leaf
4–6 heaped tbsp fresh white breadcrumbs
1 tbsp double cream
20g butter
sea salt
freshly ground black pepper

1 Preheat the oven to 140°C/Gas 1.
2 To make the stuffing, heat the olive oil in a frying pan and gently fry the onion for 5 minutes. Spoon it into a mixing bowl and add the sage, fennel, apples, prunes, spice, chestnuts and sausage meat. Mix thoroughly to combine all the ingredients evenly and season well.
3 Spoon the stuffing into the goose cavity. Scatter the shallots in the bottom of a roasting tin and place the goose on top. Pierce the skin of the goose all over with a sharp knife, and season it with sea salt and pepper, then place in the oven for 3 hours.
4 Drain off the goose fat after 2 hours and save it for roast potatoes. After 3 ½ hours of cooking, increase the oven temperature to 180°C/Gas 4 and cook the goose for another 30 minutes to crispen the skin.
5 Remove the goose from the oven and leave it to rest for 20 minutes on a board before carving. Drain off the fat from the roasting tin, taking care not to drain away any of the goose juice or the shallots.
6 To make the gravy, place the roasting tin on a medium heat on the hob. Sprinkle in the flour and stir it into the juices with a wooden spoon. Pour on the stock and simmer the gravy for 20 minutes while the goose is resting. Check the seasoning and adjust to taste. Serve the goose with the hot gravy and bread sauce.

To prepare the bread sauce
7 Place the milk in a saucepan with the clove-studded onion and the bay leaf. Bring to the boil. Remove from the heat, cover the pan and leave for 10 minutes so the favours can infuse. Remove the onion and bay leaf. Stir in the breadcrumbs and simmer for 3 minutes on a low heat, then stir in the cream and butter and season.

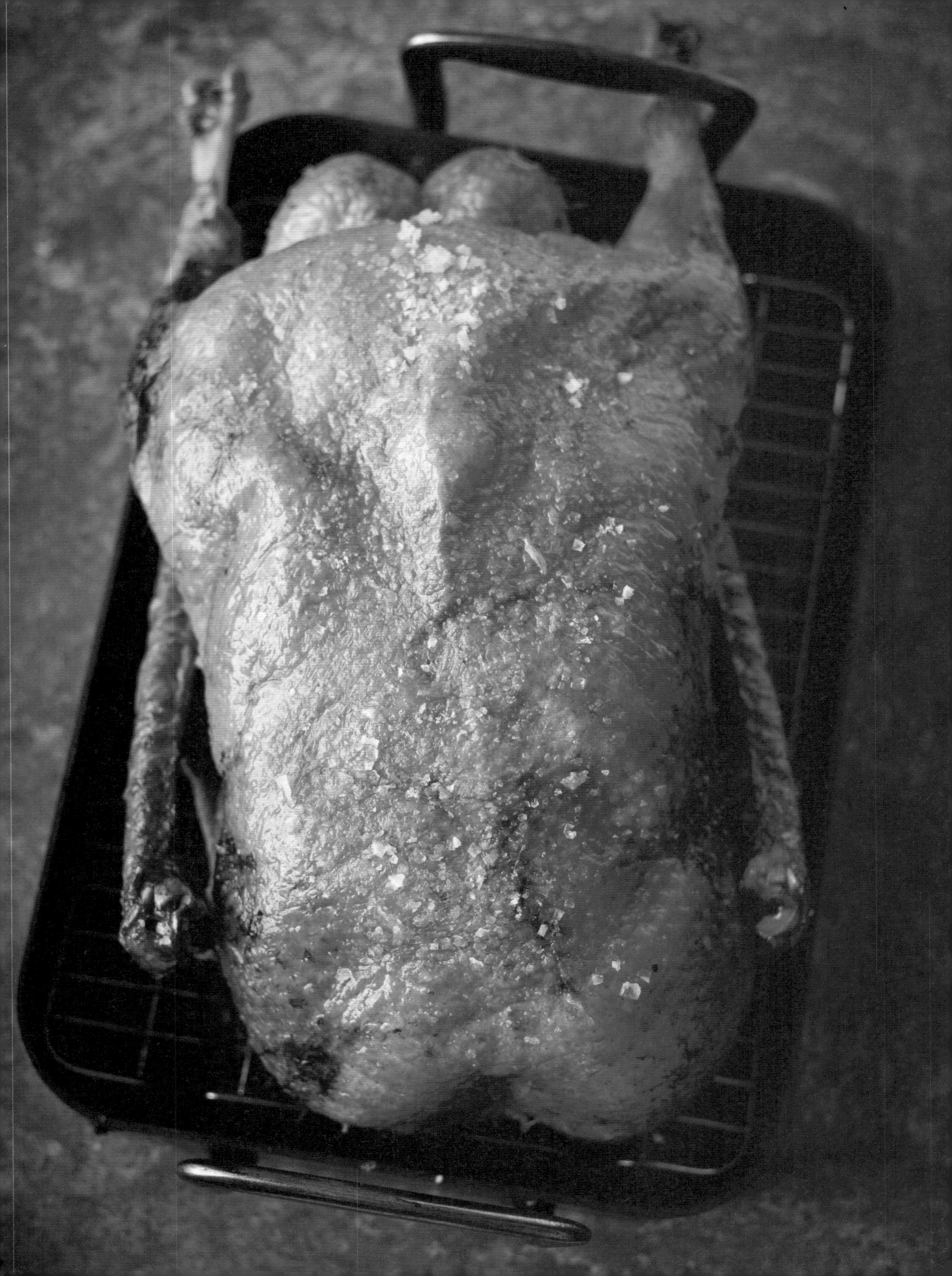

Rich chocolate cake

A successful, everyday chocolate cake has to be easy to prepare and have a lovely moist texture. A cake like this is hard to resist.

MAKES 1 X 23CM CAKE

150g dark chocolate, melted
225g butter, softened, plus extra for greasing
225 soft brown sugar
4 eggs
3 tbsp double cream
1 heaped tsp baking powder
225g self-raising flour

Icing
150g icing sugar
200g dark chocolate
50g butter
1 tbsp golden syrup
125ml double cream
chocolate flakes (optional)

1 Grease and line 2 x 23cm sandwich tins. Preheat the oven to 180°C/Gas 4.
2 Place the melted chocolate, butter, sugar, eggs, cream, baking powder and flour in a mixing bowl. Mix with an electric mixer until smooth and combined. Divide the mixture evenly between the 2 cake tins and bake in the oven for 30 minutes.
3 Test the cakes with a skewer inserted into the centre – it should come out clean. Remove the cakes from the oven and set to one side until cooled slightly, then turn them out on to a wire rack.

To make the icing
4 Sieve the icing sugar into a mixing bowl.
5 Melt the chocolate and butter in a glass bowl over a pan of simmering water, making sure that the bottom of the bowl doesn't touch the water. Remove from the heat and add the golden syrup.
6 Pour this mixture over the icing sugar and beat until you have a smooth and glossy icing. Stir in the cream.
7 Sandwich the cakes together with some of the icing and spread the rest on top of the cake. Decorate with some flaked chocolate if you like.

Christmas pudding with Cumberland butter

I have changed my usual Christmas pudding recipe and now include some grated butternut squash and brandy to make sure that the pudding is beautifully moist. Cumberland butter is traditionally made with rum not brandy, but either is fine.

MAKES 2 X 1 LITRE PUDDINGS

250g vegetable suet
60g plain flour
250g raisins
125g mixed peel
½ nutmeg, grated
½ tbsp mixed spice
½ tbsp ground cinnamon
250g white breadcrumbs
250g sultanas
125g currants
60g almonds, chopped
a pinch of salt
100g butternut squash, grated
150ml milk
50ml brandy
juice and finely grated zest of 1 lemon
4 eggs

Cumberland butter
250g butter, softened
250g soft brown sugar
5 tbsp brandy
a grating of nutmeg
¼ tsp mixed spice

1 Place all the dry ingredients in a mixing bowl. Add the butternut squash, milk, brandy, lemon juice and zest, stirring them in well. Add the eggs, 1 at a time, stirring well between each addition.
2 Grease the pudding basins with butter, then spoon in the pudding mixture, leaving 1cm clear at the top of each basin. Cover the top of each pudding with a round of greaseproof paper and then wrap each basin in a double layer of foil and tie around the top.
3 Pour water to a depth of about 4cm into a large saucepan and pop the pudding in. Put a lid on the saucepan and simmer the pudding for 4 hours. Check the level of the water and top it up regularly with boiling water. You'll probably need to cook the puddings in separate pans or one after the other.
4 Once the puddings are cooked, remove the foil and greaseproof paper and replace with dry greaseproof paper and 2 layers of foil. This will ensure that the puddings stay fresh.
5 On Christmas Day or whenever you want to eat the pudding, simmer the pudding as before, for 2 hours. Serve with the Cumberland butter.

To make the Cumberland butter
6 Cream the butter with an electric hand-whisk, until it turns pale. Add the soft brown sugar gradually, beating as you go. Still beating continuously, add the brandy – just a few drops at a time or it will curdle – and fold in the spices. Pile the butter into a dish to serve.

Parsnip soup with focaccia

A creamy vegetable soup is a welcome change from rich food at this time of year and parsnip has a great flavour.

SERVES 6

20g butter
600g parsnips, peeled and chopped into chunks
1 onion, chopped
1 celery stalk, roughly chopped
1 tbsp curry powder
1.75 litres meat or vegetable stock
200ml single cream
2 tbsp finely chopped fresh coriander
sea salt
freshly ground black pepper

Focaccia
280ml warm water
4 tbsp olive oil
1 x 7g sachet of dried yeast
1 tbsp finely chopped rosemary
500g white bread flour, plus extra for dusting the work surface
2 tsp salt

1 Heat the butter in a large saucepan. Add the parsnips, onion and celery and cook over a low heat for about 10 minutes, stirring occasionally. Sprinkle on the curry powder and stir, then cover the pan and cook over a very low heat for 15 minutes.
2 Add the stock and bring to a simmer, then cover the pan again and cook the soup gently for 30 minutes. Season with salt and pepper.
3 Whizz the soup in a blender, then strain through a sieve for an extra-smooth finish. Pour it back into the pan and reheat gently. Stir in the cream, add the coriander and check the seasoning. Serve with the foccacia.

To make the focaccia
4 Pour the warm water into a mixing bowl and add 3 tablespoons of olive oil. Sprinkle on the yeast, stir briefly and leave for a couple of minutes. Add the chopped rosemary and the flour and mix in with a wooden spoon or your hands. You should end up with a dough that is soft but manageable.
5 Turn the dough out on to a lightly floured surface and knead it for about 7 minutes. Place the dough back in the mixing bowl, cover with a clean tea towel and leave it to rise at room temperature for 1 ½ hours.
6 Gently roll the dough out into a rectangle measuring 20 x 30cm and put it on a baking sheet. Cover and leave to rise for 45 minutes. Gently press your fingertips into the dough, making dimples in it, then leave it to rise for a further hour.
7 Preheat the oven to 200°C/Gas 6. Sprinkle the dough with the remaining tablespoon of olive oil and the salt and bake in the oven for 25–30 minutes. Leave the focaccia to cool in the tin for 5 minutes and then turn out on to a wire rack to cool a little more.

Sausages with chestnuts and baby onions

This dish is full of winter flavours. I love the way cooking and eating has become so much more interesting, as more varied ingredients have become available and we have become more adventurous cooks. When I was growing up, we had a good diet but we would never have dreamed of having a sausage stew made with chestnuts and shallots, served alongside creamy mashed potato.

SERVES 6

2 tbsp olive oil
12 or more pork sausages (depending on how appetites)
70g pancetta, chopped
10 baby onions, peeled and halved
200g cooked chestnuts
2 garlic cloves, finely chopped
1 tbsp flour
100ml red wine
200ml beef stock
1 sprig of sage
freshly ground black pepper

Mashed potatoes
1kg potatoes, peeled and cut into quarters
40g butter
200ml warm milk
sea salt
freshly ground black pepper

1 Heat the olive oil in a large saucepan and brown the sausages, a few at a time, setting each batch aside while you fry the next.
2 When you are browning the last few sausages, throw in the pancetta, onions, chestnuts and garlic and fry for 2 minutes or so.
3 Put the rest of the sausages back in the pan, sprinkle on the flour and stir. Pour in the red wine and simmer for 2 minutes, then add the beef stock and sage.
4 Season with pepper, cover the pan and simmer for 30 minutes over a low heat. By the end of the cooking time you should have a rich and flavoursome mix of sausage, chestnuts and onions in a thickish gravy. Serve with the mashed potatoes.

To make the mashed potatoes
5 Boil the potatoes in salted water until tender.
6 Pass the potatoes through a potato ricer or use your preferred method to mash them. Return them to the pan and place over a low heat. Mix in the butter and milk and season to taste.

Baked hake with saffron mayonnaise

Try to find Cape hake that is farmed in a sustainable way. The supermarkets don't usually stock any other type, as hake is so overfished in Europe. Pollack or sea bass would also work well in this recipe.

SERVES 6

1kg potatoes, peeled and cut into 1cm slices
1 red onion, thinly sliced
2 courgettes, trimmed and sliced into 1cm discs
15 cherry tomatoes, cut in half
finely grated zest of 1 lemon
juice of ½ lemon
2 tbsp olive oil, plus extra for drizzling on the fish
1kg hake fillets
a handful of fresh basil leaves
sea salt
freshly ground black pepper

Saffron mayonnaise
2 egg yolks
½ tsp white wine vinegar
a pinch of saffron threads, soaked in 1 tbsp water
150ml ground nut oil
150ml light olive oil
sea salt
freshly ground black pepper

1 Preheat the oven to 200°C/Gas 6. Place all the vegetables in a roasting tin. Add the lemon zest, juice and oil and mix well so that everything gets coated with oil and lemon. Season well with salt and pepper, then place in the oven for 1 hour.
2 Remove the roasting tin from the oven and give the vegetables a good stir. Place the fish fillets on top and drizzle with a little olive oil. Return the tin to the oven for another 15 minutes. Meanwhile, make the mayonnaise as below.
3 Season the fish with salt and pepper and some torn basil leaves and serve with the vegetables, mayonnaise and a green salad.

To prepare the saffron mayonnaise
4 Place the egg yolks in a mixing bowl. Add a pinch of salt, some pepper and the vinegar and stir, then pour in the saffron liquid and threads and stir.
5 Mix the oils together in a measuring jug. Start adding the oils to the egg yolk mixture, a little at a time, whisking constantly. Once all the oil has been added, check the seasoning and adjust if necessary.

Kidney bean curry with parathas

I first ate this in the Maldives where it was served with meat and fish dishes, but I think it is excellent served on its own as a meat-free meal. It's very economical, too. Make the parathas first and then start the curry.

SERVES 6

Parathas (makes 12)
175g wholemeal flour
190g strong bread flour, plus extra for dusting
½ tsp salt
3 tbsp olive oil
200ml water
olive oil, for frying

Kidney bean curry
2 tbsp olive oil
1 tsp mustard seeds
1 onion, finely chopped
1 tbsp ground coriander
1 tbsp ground cumin
¼ tsp turmeric
2 x 400g cans of kidney beans, drained and rinsed
300g potatoes, peeled and cut into 2cm chunks
1 x 400g can of chopped tomatoes
150ml water
¼ tsp chilli flakes or more if you want your curry really hot
2 tbsp natural yoghurt
2 tbsp chopped coriander
sea salt
freshly ground black pepper

To make the parathas

1 Mix both the flours and the salt together in a bowl. Pour on the olive oil and stir it in with a spoon. Add the water and bring the dough together with your hands, then leave it to rest for 30 minutes.

2 Divide the dough into 12 pieces and shape them into balls. Roll each ball out into a thin round – a little dusting of flour may help. Using a pastry brush, brush the rounds with olive oil, then fold each one in half.

3 Brush the semi-circle with oil and fold in half again to make a triangle. Using a rolling pin, roll this triangle shape into a larger, thinner triangle. Don't worry too much about the shape.

4 Put a little olive oil in a frying pan and fry each paratha for about 1 minute on each side until golden brown.

To make the curry

5 Heat the oil in a saucepan, then add the mustard seeds and onion and cook gently for about 5 minutes. Sprinkle in the spices, stir and cook for 30 seconds.

6 Add the beans, potatoes, tomatoes and water, cover the pan and simmer gently for 20 minutes, until the potatoes are tender. Stir in the chilli flakes and yoghurt, then remove from the heat. Season with salt and pepper and the fresh coriander leaves. Serve with the parathas.

Peppery beef stew

At this time of year, red peppers are a great way of boosting your vitamin C intake. Vitamin C is particularly important as it helps the body absorb iron from other vegetables, and a red pepper has three times as much vitamin C as an orange.

SERVES 6

2 tbsp olive oil
1kg beef skirt, cut into 2cm pieces
1 tbsp flour
2 red peppers, cored and diced
1 onion, finely chopped
1 celery stalk, finely chopped
300ml red wine
1 x 400g can of chopped tomatoes
1 tbsp tomato purée
2 sprigs of thyme
200g crème fraiche
sea salt
freshly ground black pepper

Roast potatoes
1kg potatoes, peeled, cut into quarters and rinsed in cold water
1 tbsp goose fat
sea salt

1 Preheat the oven to 150°C/Gas 2. Heat the olive oil in a saucepan and brown the beef pieces, a handful at a time. Place the browned beef in a bowl and sprinkle with the flour.
2 Keep the pan on the heat and add the peppers, onion and celery, with a little more olive oil if necessary. Sauté the vegetables for 5 minutes over a medium heat, then remove them from the pan and place them with the meat.
3 With the pan still on the stove, increase the heat to high, pour on the wine and let it bubble away for about 3 minutes. Return the meat and vegetables to the pan and add the tomatoes, tomato purée and thyme sprigs. Stir in the crème fraiche and season with salt and pepper.
4 Bring to a simmer, then cover the pan and cook the stew in the oven for 1½ hours, by which time the meat should be tender. Check the seasoning again just before serving. Serve with roast potatoes and spring greens.

To prepare the roast potatoes
5 Preheat the oven to 220°C/Gas 6. Parboil the potatoes in salted water for 6 minutes. Drain them and then bash them around in the pan before you put them in the roasting tin.
6 Add the goose fat and then roast the potatoes in the oven for 50–60 minutes until golden brown, turning them occasionally during this time.

Poached chicken in parsley sauce with spring onion mash

Although this dish takes 2 hours to cook there is nothing stressful about it. You can pop it in the saucepan and forget about it and then do the finishing steps when you are ready to eat.

SERVES 6

1 x 2.4kg whole chicken
500ml dry white wine
1 carrot, peeled
1 onion, peeled
1 sprig of parsley
sea salt
freshly ground black pepper

Parsley sauce
25g butter
2 tbsp flour
cooking stock from the poached chicken
250ml double cream
1 tbsp Dijon mustard
3 tbsp finely chopped flat-leaf parsley
sea salt
freshly ground black pepper

Spring onion mash
1kg potatoes, peeled and cut into quarters
25g butter
6 spring onions, trimmed and thinly sliced
250ml milk
sea salt
freshly ground black pepper

1 Place the chicken in a large saucepan. Add the wine, carrot, onion and parsley, then season well with salt and pepper. Pour in enough water to cover the chicken and place a lid on the saucepan. Bring to a simmer and cook for 2 hours.
2 Remove the chicken from the pan and set to one side to cool. Strain the vegetables from the stock. Return the stock to the pan, bring to the boil and simmer vigorously, uncovered, for 30 minutes.

To make the parsley sauce
3 Melt the butter in a medium saucepan, then stir in the flour. Remove the pan from the heat and gradually stir in 800ml of the chicken stock.
4 Return the pan to the heat and bring the sauce to a simmer. Cook over a low heat for 10 minutes, then stir in the cream, mustard and parsley and remove from the heat.
5 Remove the meat from the chicken, cut it into bite-sized pieces and stir into the sauce. Check for seasoning and heat the chicken and sauce through before serving with the spring onion mash.

To make the spring onion mash
6 Put the potatoes in a saucepan of salted water, bring to the boil and cook until tender. Drain and set to one side. Heat the butter in the same saucepan and fry the spring onions in the butter for 2 minutes.
7 Pass the potatoes through a potato ricer and tip them back into the saucepan with the spring onions. Add the milk and gently stir it in. Season with black pepper and more salt if necessary.

Slow-braised shoulder of lamb with winter vegetables

All you have to do to make this dish is brown the lamb and vegetables, add the stock and cook it in the oven. It is easy to serve and absolutely delicious.

SERVES 6

- 2 tbsp olive oil
- 1 x 1.5kg boned and rolled shoulder of lamb
- 1 large red onion, cut into quarters
- 500g potatoes, peeled and cut in half
- 4 turnips, peeled and cut into 8 pieces
- 3 carrots, peeled and each cut into 4 pieces
- ½ swede, peeled and cut into 4cm chunks
- 3 cloves garlic, peeled and left whole
- 150ml red wine
- 1 large sprig of parsley
- 400ml meat stock
- sea salt
- freshly ground black pepper

1 Preheat the oven to 150°C/Gas 2.

2 Heat the oil in a casserole dish on top of the stove. When it's hot, add the lamb shoulder and brown it all over. Remove the lamb, but keep the pan on the heat.

3 Add the vegetables and stir them in the fat for about 2 minutes, browning them slightly as you do so. Place the vegetables to one side with the meat.

4 Pour the wine into the dish and simmer for 3 minutes, scraping up any sticky bits from the bottom of the dish as you go.

5 Return the joint to the dish with the vegetables and the parsley sprig and pour on the stock. Season with salt and pepper and bring to a simmer on top of the stove, then pop the dish in the oven for 2 ½ hours.

6 Take the casserole dish out of the oven, remove the meat and leave it to rest for 15 minutes. Keep the vegetables warm in a low oven. Serve the vegetables and gravy in large bowls or plates with good thick slices of lamb.

Fresh pineapple with passion fruit and minted Greek yoghurt

Cut the pineapple as thinly as you can when you prepare this dish. The slight sourness of the passion fruit seeds partners the sweetness of the pineapple well. I would serve this dessert any evening of the week but it is particularly good after a rich heavy meal.

SERVES 6

1 sweet pineapple
4 passion fruit, cut in half
1 tbsp finely chopped fresh mint
5 tbsp Greek yoghurt
1 tbsp soft brown sugar

1 Peel the pineapple and cut it in half lengthways. Remove the core and cut the flesh into thin semi-circles. Lay these on a serving dish. Scoop out the seeds from the passion fruit with a teaspoon and sprinkle them over the pineapple slices.
2 Mix the mint leaves into the yoghurt and sprinkle the brown sugar on top. Serve with the fruit.

Apples and pears with cinnamon biscuits and custard

Crisp biscuits, melting fruit and creamy custard – this is a wonderful combination of textures and flavours.

SERVES 6

- 400g apples, peeled, cored and cut into neat bite-sized chunks
- 300g pears, peeled, cored and cut into neat bite-sized chunks
- 1 tbsp soft brown sugar
- 1 tbsp maple syrup
- 2 tsp water
- ½ tsp ground ginger
- 300ml double cream, for serving

Cinnamon biscuits

- 110g plain flour, plus extra for dusting the work surface
- 50g caster sugar
- 25g ground almonds
- ¼ tsp ground cinnamon
- 60g cold butter, cut into cubes
- 1 egg yolk, beaten with 2 tsp milk

Custard

- 4 egg yolks
- 50g caster sugar
- 1 tsp cornflour
- 300ml double cream

1 Place the apples, pears, sugar, syrup, water and ginger in a saucepan. Bring to a simmer, cover the pan and cook gently for 10 minutes until softened – some apples might take a little longer than this. Set aside to cool.

To make the cinnamon biscuits

2 Place the flour, sugar, almonds and cinnamon in a food processor and mix briefly. Add the butter and whizz until the mixture resembles breadcrumbs. Add the egg yolk and milk and mix again briefly.

3 Turn the dough out on to the work surface and work it into a ball, handling it as gently as possible. Wrap the dough in clingfilm and chill it in the fridge for 30 minutes.

4 Preheat the oven to 180°C/Gas 4 and lightly grease a baking sheet. Roll the dough out on a floured surface and cut out 12 circles measuring 7cm across. Place these on the baking sheet and bake for 10 minutes.

To make the custard

5 Mix the yolks with the sugar and cornflour in a glass bowl. Heat the cream until it is just about to boil, then pour the cream on to the eggs, whisking constantly. Place the glass bowl over a saucepan of simmering water, making sure it doesn't touch the water, and stir until the custard has thickened slightly.

To assemble the dish

6 Gently whip the 300ml of double cream until it holds its shape. Spoon some cream on to 6 of the biscuits. Spoon some apples and pears over the cream, then top with the remaining biscuits. Serve with the custard on the side.

Stollen

Stollen is a German Christmas cake and is really a fruit-enriched bread with a glug of brandy and lots of marzipan. I love it! This recipe makes two stollen so you can pop one in the freezer – stollen freezes really well.

MAKES 2 STOLLEN

100g mixed peel
125g sultanas
125g raisins
100ml brandy
1 x 7g sachet of dried yeast
300ml warm milk
500g strong white bread flour, plus extra for dusting the work surface
100g wholemeal flour
1 tsp salt
60g caster sugar
50g butter, melted
1 egg, beaten
500g ready-made marzipan
1 egg beaten, for glazing

1 Soak the mixed peel, sultanas and raisins in the brandy, overnight if possible, or for an hour or so at least. Mix the yeast with a little of the warm milk in a small bowl and leave it for a couple of minutes.
2 Place both flours, the salt and sugar in a mixing bowl. Make a well in the centre and add the melted butter, the rest of the warm milk and the egg, then pour on the yeasted milk and mix in with a wooden spoon.
3 Turn the dough out on to a floured surface and knead for 5 minutes, then return it to the bowl. Cover with a clean tea towel and leave it to rise in a warm place for 1 hour.
4 Drain the soaking fruit (drink the brandy if you want to!) and knead the fruit into the dough as gently as you can. Be patient – it will feel as though the fruit isn't going to become absorbed but it will be eventually. Place the dough back in the bowl, cover with the tea towel again and leave for 30 minutes.
5 Cut the dough into 2 pieces and roll each piece into a rough 23cm square. Cut the marzipan in half and roll each piece out until it is a couple of centimetres smaller than the dough square. Place a square of marzipan on each dough square and roll the square up like a Swiss roll. Place each roll, seam side down, on a baking sheet, cover and leave to prove for 30 minutes.
6 Preheat the oven to 200°C/Gas 6. Brush the stollen with the beaten egg and bake for 10 minutes. Reduce the oven to 190°C/Gas 5 and cook for another 20 minutes. Don't worry if some of the marzipan escapes, this is all part of the 'home baked' look. Cool on a wire rack and serve in slices.

Provençal chicken

Not a typical winter dish but one that will provide some relief from festive indulgence.

SERVES 6

2 tbsp olive oil
10 chicken thighs on the bone, skin removed
1 onion, finely chopped
2 garlic cloves, finely chopped
leaves from 1 sprig of rosemary, finely chopped
1 red, 1 yellow and 1 green pepper, cored and diced
400ml white wine
2 x 400g cans of chopped tomatoes
2 tsp paprika
4 tsp sundried tomato paste
a pinch of saffron threads
100g pitted black olives
2 tbsp finely chopped flat-leaf parsley
sea salt
freshly ground black pepper

Mashed potatoes
1kg potatoes, peeled and cut into quarters
40g butter
200ml warm milk
sea salt
freshly ground black pepper

1 Heat the olive oil in a large saucepan and brown the chicken thighs all over, a few at a time. Place them to one side and season.
2 Add the onion, garlic, rosemary and peppers to the pan and cook over a medium heat for 5 minutes, stirring frequently. Add the wine and cook for 5 minutes more.
3 Add the tomatoes, paprika, tomato paste and saffron threads, then season with salt and pepper.
4 Partly cover the pan and simmer gently for about 40 minutes. Five minutes before the end of the cooking time, throw in the olives and parsley and check the seasoning. Serve with plenty of buttery mashed potatoes.

To make the mashed potatoes
5 Boil the potatoes in salted water until tender.
6 Pass the potatoes through a potato ricer or use your preferred method to mash them. Return them to the pan and place over a low heat. Mix in the butter and milk and season to taste.

Pea and spinach soup with baked goat's cheese toasties

The goat's cheese toasties go perfectly with this soup, but if your children don't like goat's cheese, make some crispy olive oil croutons instead.

SERVES 6

2 litres vegetable stock
(a stock cube will do)
1kg frozen peas
400g spinach leaves, washed
sea salt
freshly ground black pepper

Goat's cheese toasties
3 x 100g round goat's cheeses
(2cm thick)
6 slices of bread
a drizzle of olive oil

1 Pour the stock into a large saucepan and bring it to a simmer. Add the peas and spinach, cover the pan and simmer for 20 minutes. Liquidise the soup in a blender and then pass it through a sieve for super-smoothness.
2 Pour the soup back into the pan, add plenty of salt and pepper, then reheat. Serve the soup in shallow bowls with a goat's cheese toastie in the middle of each bowl.

To make the goat's cheese toasties
3 Preheat the grill. Cut the goat's cheeses in half to make rounds about 1cm thick. Lightly toast the slices of bread and cut them into circles to match the goat's cheese rounds.
4 Place the goat's cheese rounds on top of the rounds of toast and drizzle them with oil. Put them on a baking tray and grill until brown and bubbly.

Lamb chop stew

This stew is quick to prepare, then can be left to cook in a low oven while you get on with other things.

SERVES 6

- 2 tbsp olive oil
- 10–12 lamb chops
- 1 onion, finely chopped
- 2 garlic cloves, peeled and crushed
- 1 celeriac, peeled and cut into 2cm chunks
- 400g potatoes, cut in half
- 1 aubergine, trimmed and cut into 2cm chunks
- 1 tbsp ground coriander
- 300g frozen peas
- 1 sprig of fresh rosemary
- 500ml chicken stock
- sea salt
- freshly ground black pepper

1 Preheat the oven to 150°C/Gas 2. Heat the olive oil in a casserole dish on top of the stove. Brown the chops in the oil, a few at a time. Place the chops to one side, leaving as much of the oil as possible in the dish.
2 Put the onion in the casserole dish and cook gently for 5 minutes until softened. Add the garlic, celeriac, potatoes, aubergine and coriander, then stir and cook for 3 minutes.
3 Return the chops to the pan. Add the peas, rosemary, and stock and season with salt and pepper, then bring to a simmer. Put a lid on the casserole dish and place it in the oven for 1½ hours. Serve the lamb on top of the cooked vegetables.

Dutch apple and pear pudding

This recipe was inspired by one I found in an out-of-print cookbook. The original used just apples, but a combination of apples and pears works well. The pastry is truly heavenly.

SERVES 6

400g eating apples, peeled, cored and cut into thick slices
400g pears, peeled, cored and cut into quarters
finely grated zest and juice of ½ lemon
2 tbsp brown sugar
2 tbsp golden syrup

Suet pastry
110g vegetable suet
225g self-raising flour
1 tbsp caster sugar
a small pinch of salt
125–150ml cold water

1 Lightly grease a 23cm pie dish. Preheat the oven to 200°C/Gas 6.
2 To make the pastry, place the suet in a bowl, add the flour and rub it in gently with your fingertips for 1 minute. Add the sugar and salt and mix briefly to combine. Pour on 125ml of the water and mix, adding a little more if the dough is too dry. Form the pastry dough into a ball and divide it into 2 pieces. Roll out 1 piece of pastry and use it to line the pie dish.
3 Pile the apples and pears into the dish, then pour on the lemon juice and add the lemon zest. Sprinkle on 1 tablespoon of the brown sugar.
4 Roll out the other piece of pastry and place it over the fruit, sealing the edges of the pastry together with your fingertips. Drizzle the golden syrup on top of the pie and use a pastry brush to smooth it over the surface. Sprinkle the other tablespoon of brown sugar over the syrup.
5 Place the pie dish on a baking sheet and bake in the oven for 30 minutes, by which time the pastry will be crisp and golden brown. Best served warm.

Rice pudding trifle

This is a favourite pudding in our house. The combination of custard, creamy rice pudding and raspberries can't fail as a tip-top dessert.

SERVES 6

Sponge
butter, for greasing
3 eggs
80g caster sugar
70g plain flour
a pinch of salt
raspberry jam

Custard
1 egg
2 egg yolks
200ml double cream
200ml milk
2 tbsp caster sugar

Rice pudding
80g Arborio risotto rice
300ml milk
200ml double cream
1 tbsp caster sugar

Topping
200g fresh or frozen raspberries
400ml double cream, whipped

To make the sponge

1 Grease a 23cm cake tin and line the base with baking parchment. Preheat the oven to 180°C/Gas 4.
2 Whisk the eggs and sugar in a bowl with an electric hand-whisk until the eggs are thick and mousse-like. Using a metal spoon, fold in the flour and a pinch of salt, then spoon the mixture into the prepared tin and bake in the oven for 20 minutes.

To make the custard

3 Whisk the egg and yolks in a glass bowl with the sugar. Heat the cream and milk together in a small saucepan until just before boiling point, then whisk the hot cream and milk into the egg yolks and sugar.
4 Place the glass bowl over a pan of simmering water and stir until the custard starts to thicken. This is quite a thin custard, so once it's coating the back of your wooden spoon and you feel it's thickening slightly it should be ready. Remove from the heat and set aside.

To make the rice pudding

5 Place all the ingredients in a saucepan and bring to a gentle simmer. Cook over a gentle heat for 25 minutes until the rice is tender.

To assemble the trifle

6 Slice the sponge cake in half through the middle and spread 1 half with raspberry jam. Sandwich the halves of cake together and cut into chunks. Place these chunks in the bottom of a trifle dish and scatter the raspberries over the top. Pour over the custard, then spoon the rice pudding on top and finish off with the whipped cream.

Mini nut and chocolate tarts

These sweet little tarts are perfect as a pudding or a tea time snack.

MAKES 12

Filling
- 50g walnuts, roughly chopped
- 50g macadamia nuts, roughly chopped
- 25g white chocolate, roughly chopped
- 25g milk chocolate, roughly chopped
- 75g butter
- 30g soft brown sugar
- 2 tbsp golden syrup
- juice of ½ lemon
- 2 eggs, beaten

Pastry
- 150g plain flour, plus extra for dusting the work surface
- 75g cold butter, cut into cubes, plus extra for greasing
- 50g ground almonds
- 25g caster sugar
- 1 egg, beaten with 2 tbsp cold water

To make the pastry

1 Place the flour and butter in a food processor and mix until the mixture resembles breadcrumbs. Add the ground almonds and sugar and mix briefly until combined. Add the egg and water and mix again briefly.

2 Turn the mixture out on to a lightly floured surface and form it into a ball of dough with your hands. Wrap in clingfilm and chill for 30 minutes.

To prepare the tarts

3 Preheat the oven to 180°C/Gas 4. Grease a 12-hole fairy cake tray or 2 x 6-hole trays. Place the nuts and chocolate pieces in a small bowl and put to one side.

4 Place the butter, sugar and golden syrup in a small saucepan and heat gently until the butter has melted. Remove the pan from the heat and stir in the lemon juice and eggs.

5 Roll out the pastry on a floured surface. Using a 7.5cm pastry cutter, cut out circles of pastry to line the fairy cake tray. Sprinkle a teaspoon of the chocolate and nuts into each pastry case and then pour a little of the syrup mixture into each case so that it comes just up to the top of the each tart.

6 Bake the tarts in the oven for 15 minutes until the filling is set and golden brown. Remove the tarts from the tin and place them on a wire rack to cool.

MADE IN ENGLAND
SEAMLESS

WEIGHTS

Metric	Imperial
10g	½oz
20g	¾oz
25g	1oz
50g	2oz
75g	3oz
110g	4oz
150g	5oz
175g	6oz
200g	7oz
225g	8oz
250g	9oz
275g	10oz
350g	12oz
450g	16oz (1 lb)
700g	1lb 8oz
900g	2lb
1.35kg	3lb

LIQUID MEASURES

Metric	Imperial
30ml	1fl oz
55ml	2fl oz
75ml	3fl oz
150ml	5fl oz (¼ pint)
275ml	10fl oz (½ pint)
570ml	1 pint
725ml	1 ¼ pints
1 litre	1 ¾ pints
1.2 litres	2 pints
1.5 litres	2 ½ pints

DIMENSIONS

Metric	Imperial
5mm	¼ inch
1cm	½ inch
2.5cm	1 inch
5cm	2 inches
10cm	4 inches
15cm	6 inches
18cm	7 inches
20cm	8 inches
23cm	9 inches
25cm	10 inches
30cm	12 inches

OVEN TEMPERATURES

Electric oven	Electric fan oven	Gas mark
120°C	100°C	½
140°C	120°C	1
150°C	130°C	2
160°C	140°C	3
170°C	150°C	3½
180°C	160°C	4
190°C	170°C	5
200°C	180°C	6
220°C	200°C	7
230°C	210°C	8

ACKNOWLEDGMENTS

Alex, Emma, Gavin and Rose at Smith & Gilmour for their superb design and art direction, and for their expert advice and assistance.

Dan Jones for his beautiful photographs and his approachable and helpful attitude during the many photo shoots.

Morag Farquhar for the imaginative props she sourced for the photographs.

Jinny Johnson for her excellent editing skills, her enthusiasm and her sense of calm when faced with 521 recipes.

Jill Hamilton for her administrative services and for always encouraging me to devise another 'one pot' recipe, her favourite type!

Li Boatwright for her support and commitment to the book and the Food Education Trust.